"Diaries of a Maverick Professor"

by

Gábor Szikszay-Farkas

authorHOUSE

1663 LIBERTY DRIVE, SUITE 200
BLOOMINGTON, INDIANA 47403
(800) 839-8640
www.authorhouse.com

First published by AuthorHouse 10/14/04

ISBN: 1-4184-6717-0 (e)
ISBN: 1-4184-6718-9 (sc)

Printed in the United States of America
Bloomington, Indiana

This book is printed on acid-free paper.

Acknowledgements.

The author wishes to express his gratitude and dedicate this book to his Muse: Jo L. Drabik, who miraculously popped into his life when he already –half heartedly- began to write this (sort of) memoir. She was such a godsend (literally!) and at such a time when, in defiance of the 'motto' to part one, she was instrumental in renewing the author's life for a **third** term. Without him ever knowing her, this book would certainly not exist.

Naturally, her superior (and teem-mate) Dr. P. Speert carried out the **actual 'renewal':** on the operating table! This operation assured the **quality** for that 'third life'.

Also, it would not only be neglectful but more than that: sinful, not to include Dr. J. Waters who managed to 'fix' (and tune) the author's 'engine' by inserting two stents into the right artery of his heart, to keep it humming for that **third term.**

Recognition is also due to his dear and trusted friend Attorney Henry S. Miller who provided all the initial encouragements, and many more since, to this undertaking. He succeeded in convincing the author that he should go ahead with it because the writing is good (enough). Henry, you know how much I lacked self confidence to write in English. Thanks Henry! This shall be a memento to you.

In spite of the discouraging and totally frustrating endeavor of getting this book published the author wishes to acknowledge the help that Attorney Susan Julian Gates extended to him in this regard. She was instrumental to arrange an American, edited version of this book to be published by 1-st Books. The proverb that: 'it is much easier to write a book than to get it published', is a very true statement. Thus, I acknowledge the help of Mr. Tom Kinley, the Author's Service Representative at 1-st Books who was most helpful in every respect to get from a manuscript to the finished book.

There were quite some – if not really many – other people, friends, acquaintances who did read the manuscript and expressed their liking the entertaining quality of this book, versus the fast paced 'criminal fiction' which seemed to dominate today's market. To them I also owe my gratitude.

G. Sz-F.

Table of Contents

Foreword

The idea to write this book was born on July 23-rd of the year 1993. That was the second, and last day of my trial against the University, for illegal termination of employment of a tenured faculty member, denying lawful benefits, breach of contract, etc. Due to jury manipulation (by the judge!) the confused twelve members could not come up with a needed 10 votes (out of 12) to declare the terms of the termination illegal, null and void. Although they all agreed that there were mistakes made by both parties in the termination settlement agreement, they failed to fallow up with the logical conclusion that therefore a new agreement should have been negociated. In those days, when people out in the workforce, could be terminated, -or even just laid off- at a 24-hour's notice, the idea of a professor having his position (of many years) been "protected by tenure" was something deemed objectionable for the average working class citizen. I still think that the judge was building on this sentiment.

This loss resulted in a devastating trauma of unmatched proportions to anything in my **"second life".** (See the motto for part one!). It profoundly shook my confidence in the United States' Judicial System making me suspicious of anything this system promised or provided for its citizens in terms of justice. **'Justice for all'** became a frivolous expression in my thesaurus. It is little wonder that the judges are losing the respect of the citizenry at an unprecedented (and alarming) rate; a shame on this great, great, great nation. The nation deserves better. Much better.

My disillusionment with the system induced a soothing nostalgia in me for the frontier-justice days of the romantic wild-wild West, which I knew only from the Zane Grey, Max Brand, etc. western fictions, which I grew up on in the prewar years in Hungary. My brother, Laci, (there is mention of him in the following pages) and I, as kids, acted out many of the episodes (quite often on horsebacks) we read about in those (relatively) simplistic novels, in which the 'Good' eventually always triumphed over the 'Bad'. However, the interim differences between the two, were, not infrequently, settled by a .45 caliber Colt. Once-and-for-all.

This volume introduces the "Maverick Professor" to the reader and leads him, or her! (hopefully more of 'her'-since, so far, ladies who read the manuscript – seemed to like the imminent stories much more than men) through a long list of typical immigrant's difficulties of trying to fit into a – somewhat — alien culture and to his state of mind, when he is almost ready to give up his 'dream'. The actual, **legal troubles**, will follow as a sequel to this volume, by which time all the circumstances will, gradually, become familiar to the reader.

This book is not an exciting, high-tension, fast-paced, criminal story for which a great proportion of readers –now-a-days - are looking forward to in a book. Here the emphasis is on the entertainment side. It, honestly, is trying to **'entertain'** rather than **excite.** You, the reader! shall be the judge if it succeeded to do so.
G. Sz. – F.

Brentwood, September, 2003.

Part One

Seeking the Ideal Career

Motto:

"You only live twice
Or so it seems,
One life for yourself
And one for your dreams"...

From the theme-song of "**James Bond
agent 007**" movie of the same title.

The Shaker Heights duplex

Chapter One.
(The Interview)

The telephone kept ringing in my newly arranged office-den in the basement of our Shaker Heights duplex. We really began to love the place. I was in the middle of putting together a proposal for preliminary engineering work to be done for one of the firm's clients for which I was working. It was already well past 5-PM. After a number of rings I realized that it's time to pick it up. A distinguished baritone on the other end said:

-Hallo! This is Allan Gifford speaking from East Machias, Maine. I wish to talk to Mr. Szikszay-Farkas, is this his number?

-Yes, this is he speaking. What may I be helping you with?

-I am the chairman of the Engineering Sciences Division of Lowell Technological Institute in Massachusetts. Actually I should be on vacation but I am still struggling with the faculty hiring for the Fall semester. So, I am calling from our summer place in Maine. I went through on some back issues of the Journal of the A.A.U.P.* where I found your advertisement in "Faculty Positions Wanted". From the mailing code number I was able to track down your name and telephone number. Let me ask you my first and most important question: are you still available for the position"?

-Excuse me? Which position are we talking about? I had put in three different advertisements under different code numbers".

-Well, the one you put in for: Transportation Engineering. I didn't know you also had other ads. That is the one we need to be filled by the Fall. Are you now gainfully employed"?

-Yes, I am.

-Does that mean you're no longer interested in the position? Actually that was the main purpose of my call; to find out whether you still are interested. Your ad appeared in the January '69 issue and today is already middle of July. If, however, you are still interested, we should be talking about it more".

-Yes, I am always interested. Teaching was my primary, chosen profession after realizing that I will never attain a **security clearance** while the cold war will last", I said matter of factly.

-How much time do you need to give notice to your employer'? -Well, I don't think we are there just yet. But anyway, that is hard to guess right now. I have just started at this Architect / Planner firm in March. We are currently expanding to include engineering and surveying into the profile of our services. I am responsible to facilitate this expansion. Actually, I suspect that the boss (the owner) would be profoundly disappointed to hear about my notice. He has pinned very high hopes to succeed to break into and offer these new areas. He gave me full control to oversee every move along this line of expansion. He has taken me everywhere to every conference he attended, he has authorized full mileage reimbursement on the use of my vehicle. And last, but not least, he has just given me a third raise in 4 months".

-Oh, by the way, how much do you make yearly"?

-Currently my base pay is $ 17,000. All expenses, and mileage paid on the use of my car. He pays for medical insurance, and matches half of my contribution to an IRA".

-Gee, I am sorry; you must know that we can not match that. But, we can offer you State benefits that are not exactly negligible. This is a State Institution, you know"?

-No, not really. From its name it hasn't been apparent to me".

-Then, my second point in calling you up was to satisfy my curiosity about your English communication skills. Naturally I noticed your foreign accent immediately. Even when I found out your name through the Journal's advertising division I guessed, merely from your name, that you must originate, someplace from central Europe. But I was mostly interested in your communication skills. And, ... I'm happy to conclude that I have no trouble, whatsoever, understanding you".

-Frankly, I had no trouble along this line any time before, save perhaps the first 2-3 years, after I arrived as an immigrant to Canada. I was fortunate to have people around me who, constantly, lovingly, and very patiently polished my language skills, my pronunciation. The Canadian Pacific Railway's Prairie Division, where I was assistant to the Division Engineer, had an engineering department secretary, who's brother was

English Department Head at the University of Alberta, and she took me under her wing, so to speak, … corrected my sentences, …insisted on me drafting the answers to all the technical inquiries, correspondence, …so, I think I shall be grateful to her for doing so, … I shall never forget her".

-May I propose a meeting here at the School, at your earliest convenience? When could you come down here? At least for a day"?

-I can only do that on a Saturday. I am extremely busy. I've been contacted by some of my former clients, once they found out I am back in the area. I am sure you must've noticed from the ad that I was a professor at Akron U. before going back to graduate school. I was carrying on a consulting practice on the side. I was called on doing evaluations of development plans submitted to the Try- County Regional Planning Commission, among other things. But let's just say that I can get away on most Saturdays" I said a mouthful for an answer.

-Could you come at the end of the week? This Saturday? I send you a ticket to an early flight from Cleveland. That is here by mid morning. I should pick you up at Logan. I will call you Friday evening if everything is arranged or leave you a message to that effect by my secretary", he said.

-All right. I think it's worth pursuing this possibility. Thank you."

-Oh, … I almost forgot to ask; are you a citizen"?

-Not of the US. I am a Canadian citizen. Why? Is that a condition for the position? Because, then we may call the whole thing off".

-No. Not really. But are you intending, … eventually, … to become naturalized? A statement of intent would usually do.

-Okay, then I am looking forward to meet you in Boston this Saturday, the 19-th. Good night.

—-—- *

I went upstairs. Maria, my wife confronted me:

-Who was that again at this late hour? Didn't you promise me that there will be no more evening business calls"?

-Well, I bet you don't even guess what's happened just now".

- Don't tell me the man from the Boston mapping firm called with a fabulous offer, replied Maria, "You said: that must be a very, very good offer, or you won't even consider moving to the East.

-Yes, I did say that. But this is now something I was dreaming about ever since Akron. In fact, I recalled, it was the dean at the University of Alberta, who outlined an ideal engineering career for me, after I passed that state exam. You know how much I liked that set-up in Akron. Now, the chairman of Engineering Sciences Division called from a school some 30 miles north of Boston. He practically offered me a position right over the phone. If I could combine the two jobs, the teaching with that of the consulting, into one, I am practically back to where I was at Akron; Teaching at this school and consult with this mapping firm in Boston. From that, ...who knows? ...it could be a good source of clients, I am sure I could line up some development projects sooner or later... Thus, ... hey, I have to call up this Dorfman guy in Brookline and propose a meeting, preferably at the same day, when I go to the interview with the dean, sometime in the evening, **after** my interview. Oops, I am still not used to this new academic title; I never heard of "Chairman of Engineering Sciences Division".

-Yah, but not now, for goodness sakes! said Maria. You know how people dislike being called-up at supper time.

-I am sure this guy would not mind, I said, "he sounded pretty desperate to find someone with my qualifications when I first answered his ad. I told him then that he better be able to make it worth my while to move away from here. But now, like I said, if a combination can be worked out ...

-You and your eternal combinations! -remarked Maria; Why can't you be happy here? Why chase that dream of teaching? You know you can never really advance in that world without those damned three letters following your name," said Maria.

-Well, honey, please don't forget that I do have a set of three letters behind my name, which are worth more, at least for me, than those other three letters to anyone else. I earned the M. Sc. much harder than many, many Ph.D.-s theirs.

-They will eventually squeeze you out, regardless of how good you are, or even because of it! Just watch, and think again, what happened at Akron; The more you know, and you make them feel it, the more you will be a thorn in their butt! said Maria, sarcastically.

-Well, my pal, my darling pal, this time the Akron fiasco will not repeat itself. I will make sure of that right at the interview.

With that I went downstairs and called Dorfman. In a few sentences I explained this new possibility, the looming position at the Lowell school. Surprisingly, he seemed to know quite a bit about the school, including about some of the professors there. He was getting more and more enthusiastic and proposed a meeting at the airport after the interview. He then asked me to let him know, definitely, what transpired at the interview to see if there were any more plans to make. Or, if this new combination somehow went bump. Dorfman expressed his concern over the job with his Company being contingent upon, quasi subordinated to my appointment to the professorship. I suggested not to put the cart before the horse, thus: wait and see.

*—- *—- *

Friday morning, July 18-th Gifford's secretary, Priscilla, called our phone at the residence at Shaker Heights, a suburb of Cleveland. Maria answered the phone with a minimum of concern. Priscilla wanted to speak with me. After she learned that she may not call me at work, she left a message for me with Maria, that an hour before boarding time I can pick up my tickets at the American Airline's check-in counter. Also, that Mr. Gifford will wait for me at Logan Airport's domestic terminal at the American Airline's arrival gate.

Maria did not call me at the office. She did not want to excite me unnecessarily. When I got home in the afternoon, my first question was: "Well, is it go, or what?"

She gave me the message from Gifford. I turned somber; didn't utter a word for a while. Then, almost at a whisper, I was half telling to myself: "so, looks like it's getting really serious".

After that, everything went like clockwork. Saturday morning there were not many passengers, and as I stepped out of the tube I scanned the entire lobby with a single glance. I walked directly to the distinguished looking, elderly gentleman standing next to the desk at the arrival gate. Just as I began to ask him if he, possibly, was Mr. Gifford, so did he ask if I was I, and we both spoke simultaneously. We, somehow instinctively knew that we met the right person. We just said our full names matter of factly. Gifford then asked if I had any luggage to pick up, but I hadn't any.

After some pleasantries we started walking out of the terminal towards the parking lot, which was inside the building! This arrangement caught my engineering eyes, and I made a favorable comment. I felt that I better put my "Transportation Engineer's hat on and start really wearing it.

-A pretty advanced concept,…this here, eh? I really like it I said, perked up. "What's the daily number of flights this airport is handling" Mr. Gifford? I asked.

-I really haven't got the faintest idea. The airport is practically new, and it is still being added onto, here and there, all the time" said Gifford. Driving out of the airport loop Gifford slowed down pointing to his right.

-By the way, I have made reservations for you here at the Airport Hilton, for tonight. This is it right here. It is not too bad, and has the advantage that you can get to your return flight real easily tomorrow. The hotel's little shuttle bus will take you to your gate in the morning".

-Thanks, sure, I appreciate it. It looks really neat."

Gifford was driving through the Sumner tunnel, then turned toward Causeway Street and over the bridge to Memorial Drive. Driving through Cambridge, he pointed out the old buildings of MIT, his Alma Mater. All the while speaking about himself; his youth at MIT, his years in Germany after graduation, during the Great Depression. Never missed showing off his knowledge of the environment, the main streets of Cambridge, etc. I could sense an aura of nostalgia.

-Mr. Gifford, I asked, -can you spare a map of the area?- so I can follow where we are?

-Sure, there is one at the back seat. Pull that out." The drive to the school took longer than an hour. Several professional questions were thrown into the conversation.

I knew well that these were (or really supposed to be) part of the interview, but did not mind answering them in that spirit. Gifford took a great deal of time to describe his early European professional experience. The Germans put him into construction engineering, where he was working, (mostly observing!) how the new "Autobahn" concept was formulated by the Germans, right after Hitler came to power. By 1934 he was being earmarked to be sent to the States, study the Pennsylvania Turnpike for a few months with a team of German engineers, then return with some practical suggestions. He right then asked me if I was, at all, familiar with the early Autobahn features, and their similarity to the Pennsylvania Turnpike. The question really hit home with me. Immediately, I pointed out the lack of adequate break-down lanes, and some excessive grades which ought to, unduly slow down heavy vehicles, which, in those days, in Europe did not have "power to spare". Of course, Gifford knew about the first part, but lacked detailed know-how about the second.

The parking lots at the school were just about empty. The sun was high. The blacktop pavement almost melted under the sun on the faculty lots. There were only a few stalls in the shade, cast by the three-story old buildings which were mostly accommodating class rooms. Gifford was now really "at home".

-What would you like to see first, Mr. Szikszay-Farkas, he asked; I don't think classrooms are going to show you much. You must have seen too many in your life. But perhaps we could grab a quick lunch in the cafeteria?
-An excellent idea," I offered.
The cafeteria was not only empty, it was actually closed. By this time even the summer session students were no longer around. So, then we turned up-street on Textile Avenue into the sub-shop, run by a young Greek fellow, who had his ways of fixing Greek salad, with anchovies, one of my summer favorites. Gifford was a gracious host and did not stop telling about the history of the old Textile Institute; that was well known not only on the East Coast, but all the way to the Midwest, even beyond.
The textile industry was no longer around, it moved to the South: Georgia and the Carolinas. A goodly part of the machinery was still kept in the basement of Kittson Hall. But, ... who knows how long? The enrollment fell to an all time low, so, the days of the textile engineering curriculum offered here, were numbered.

Instead, the Plastics Department has recently launched its curriculum. I casually asked Gifford if he has seen the movie "The Graduate", then reminded him what was the only word of advice offered to Benjamin, the recent graduate by one of his father's colleagues; "Plastics"! said Gifford, "and that's right, the Department has already brand new laboratories, a growing faculty and student body".

-What shall we see first? asked Gifford after lunch.
-How about some laboratories"? I asked. Drafting/design rooms, drafting table arrangements, computational facilities?
-Oh, we are really not that advanced yet, replied Gifford. But the Wang Co. donated some programmable calculators, which we are

currently using in the Surveying Laboratories for problem solving. The master unit sits in the professor's office who is coordinating the surveying instructions. He teaches that course 'off the top of his head', also an MIT man. You'll like him, I am sure. Your surveying background is a very substantial one, I noticed from your resume", said Gifford; "Herm uses the pocket size book that he edited, for the class, as a textbook".

This was the first unpleasant news I heard at the school. The second one was more deplorable: the ancient instruments lined-up in neat order on custom built cabinets and enclosures for their tripods. It reminded me to a museum exhibit Smithsonian style. .

-We have just acquired an Askania theodolite, so we can show the students some novelties", said Gifford. "Everyone in the class will have a chance to use it in the field. This course is well liked by the sophomore civil engineers. The first part of the Fall Semester and the second half of the Spring Semester is held in the field. Right here on and around the Campus grounds".

It was time to get down to the business part of the interview. In Gifford's large office we sat down, he behind his desk, I in front of it.

-We actually do need a formal application from you for our file Mr. Szikszay-Farkas", he said. "So why don't you take a set home with you, then, when you had a chance to fill them out, you just return them by mail. But let me ask this question first: you **are** interested in the position are you not?

-Yes. I take a set home with me. However, I think we should discuss a few philosophical concepts concerning this position. So, may I suggest that you start enumerating the requirements of the School. What exactly is the Civil Engineering Department looking for; Also, may I have a rundown on the current faculty profile?

-Sure, here is a set", he said handing me a couple of sheets. "It contains the relevant data for each faculty member. You can look it over and ask about anyone of them. There are currently only seven, but we will have nine by September. Two additional faculty is approved by the Division. All good fellows, you will see", he said while I was studying the profiles.

-I see that I am the only alien; would I be the one to balance the demographics'"? I asked somewhat concerned. "Actually, strictly speaking, I do not qualify for minority. Foreign national origin only 'enhances diversity' but it does not help enhance minority statistics" I remarked, just to be on the record.

-Well, do you remember I asked you over the phone whether you intend to become a citizen'"? he started explaining to minimize my concern, "When you're naturalized, you are no longer a foreigner! And this is about the only requirement, and, of course, loyalty to the Commonwealth. This sheet shows your rank, and salary. There is this new idea about requiring a so called: terminal or professional degree. By the way, are you a registered professional engineer, and or surveyor"?

-I have registrations in Canada and Ohio, but that will be my first goal, that is, to transfer my out of state registrations, or just do whatever it takes to become registered. Without that I do not even consider this job. If I don't be registered at the end of the school year, you may start looking for a replacement. But there is something very important I have to discuss with you. I fully intend to carry on a consulting practice as I had in Akron. I was the only faculty member with a professional registration and practicing on the side from my home office, as a base.

-Before you go any further, may I ask what's happened there?" asked Gifford with keen interest. -"You may just summarize it".

Well, it was like this; I was hired by the dean in the summer, under much the same circumstances as we are facing here. After an initial luncheon with another faculty member, who was doing "consulting work" -so called, on his evaluation sheet- that filled an important niche in the local construction industry, namely: breaking concrete cylinders in the structural engineering laboratory and issuing certificates on the University's letterhead as to their ultimate breaking stress. This was an ongoing practice for years, with the full consent of the Dept. Head, who died at the end of the spring semester. He was teaching the surveying and the highway geometric design courses. The dean needed a quick replacement, so, he put an urgent ad on a flyer in the Ohio State University's C.E. Dept. bulletin, which I answered on short order. The dean took us to lunch, but was somewhat tardy, so I had an opportunity to 'talk shop' with the structural professor. He seemed to like me and passed on some information about various consulting opportunities in town. Just a half a year prior to this incident I was transferred to the Akron office by the design firm in Cleveland, where I worked then, so, I also knew my way around Town."

-Are you going to get to the part how it turned sour Mr. Szikszay-Farkas"? he interrupted somewhat impatiently.

-Oh yah, in a jiffy. The dean at the end of the lunch invited me back to his office and instructed the college secretary to take care of the paperwork. I was hired for a two-year temporary term. I started in September. At the same time a new Department Head was hired, who originated from the same country as I did. He had a Ph. D. from WVU in Water Resources, the ink still wet on his diploma. The man was obnoxious, green with envy about my practice. He wanted to work his way into my practice, but I soon found out that I can not use him. He also wanted to 'get in' on the breaking of cylinders business, but could not come on strong because the structural fellow was on tenure long ago, whereas he was still wet behind his ears. To make the long story short: the new Department Head, [my countryman] after two years, persuaded the dean not to extend my contract.

-Yah, sort of a familiar story", said Gifford, looking out on the great double window onto the Merrimack River. "I happened to know a few such stories myself, I can add this to the list".

-So, Professor Gifford, my most important question is: what are the chances for this to repeat itself here"? I asked.

-Well, Mr. Szikszay-Farkas, all I can say, and mark my word, that until I am here, the chances for anything like this to happen are, virtually, nil. But let's get going. I still have to take you to the Airport, and then keep going to our place in Maine, a good 5-6-hour drive.

-Yes, I agree.

—-—-*

The heat began to diminish by 4 PM when Gifford drove back to the airport. Nothing but personal matters were discussed during the drive. Gifford opened-up his life's frustration with the after war obsession with the Ph.D. degree of any administration at virtually any university in the country. He mentioned that, even at his Alma Mater he could not get a meaningful teaching assignment without that degree. Even his experience in Germany was not given the appropriate credit when it came to promotion. The most he ever got was instructorships in various laboratories, specially in soil mechanics, which was then a dynamic, growing field within the civil engineering curricula nationwide.

Broken-hearted he turned his back on MIT,(at the time the most prestigious technical institutions in the country, as well as on a global scale) and was looking around at different opportunities elsewhere. The Federal Department of Energy had announced opportunities in the [new] field of atomic energy, so he applied for a position at one of the Department's opening, which paid over one-and a half times the salaries of the average salaries in the engineering field. Not to mention the average salaries in academe.

So, it looked like he too, as many other dreamers, found his niche in the never ending search for the ideal technical employment. The pay was good, which assured domestic peace (even happiness in 'suburbia', with good, well equipped and staffed schools) not something to be overlooked when it comes to domestic life. But the advancement, like: into policy making positions, were almost nil without significant political connections. These are the elusive things you can not acquire in a short time. And life is short. Too short for that.

From his monologue I learned more than many other previous discussions I ever had with fellow employees at other places of former employment. I simply melted into the philosophical atmosphere of my future boss. And, suddenly, I felt myself very much at the home-like atmosphere of the past decade: in academe.

While he was telling all about his frustrations, and the never ending search for the ideal place in the technical world, I was rewinding my own exposures to just such a search lately. And then I quickly remembered my odyssey; driving around some 10,000 miles east of the Mississippi trying to find employment (actually any kind of employment from advertisements) not just in academe, but in the general engineering field as well. Never could I forget my visit to one of the largest engineering firm in the world(*) with one of their headquarters in New York City- earlier the same year 1969, when one of my professors at Cornell secured for me an interview with the overseas soil study-group's leader. It took me an hour and a half within a 10- block radius around their building in Manhattan, to find a parking place for a Volkswagen and had to walk some six blocks back to the building. I was about ready to forfeit the entire interview. But eventually had it, where my most important concerns were how to live and come to work every day in the Big Apple. It turned out that no one in the group lived in the City; they opted for Westchester County and for Connecticut near the commuter line. They encouraged me, nevertheless, to accept the position, since I will be mostly out of the country anyways, on assignments somewhere in Africa, or the Far East; so why should I care about these sort of things so much.

Fate was actually playing a dirty trick on me with this truly unexpected opportunity. It was only two years ago, in August of 1967 that I had to refute a signed contract with the Saudi Arabian Government's brand new University of Riyad for a 3-year term tenure-track position in the

Transportation Engineering Division. The reversal of the contract came as a result of a two-three day family deliberation that took place in August of the year 1967, when my term at Akron had already expired and I still had not found other possibilities. I was getting ready to leave for the Desert Kingdom by myself, because Maria refused to go with the two children to a totally 'strange land', where women have not even the right to drive a car. She announced that she would rather starve with the two kids right here in America than to move to the desert, regardless of how much money they are ready and willing to pay. All our friends said we went cuckoo. I was adamant in my stand that I was not, I signed that contract, didn't I? Within two days my fellowship at Cornell was approved like a "Deus ex Machina" and we packed to leave Akron, as it turned out later, for good.

Then I continued my story from here. Gifford was listening eagerly. I described the professional ideal lifestyle for my type of individual, that I learned back in Canada from that dean at the University of Alberta, my untold ideal and role model. Gifford then, leaning back in his seat said: "Mr. Szikszay-Farkas I am going to be committed that you achieve those ideals, while you are at our Institution". For a long time this sentence was echoing in my mind which was, by the way, faithfully fulfilled by my future boss.

After Gifford dropped me off at the Airport Hilton Hotel the two of us seemed to know each other more than almost any other two men in such a short time. The chemistry was extraordinary, probably for both of us. I was struggling in later years to find out what was behind it. (I had an idea what could this have been, but what it actually was, that remains one of eternal unknown).

* - * - *

I had not much inclination for any other activity than to call up Dorfman's office from my room, and leave a message to the effect that I am in the Airport Hilton, and ready to meet him at the bar from 6 PM on forward. That I am going to be wearing a light checkered suite and a very light silken tie, and will be sitting at the bar counter, close to the piano.

A lady piano player was almost like rehearsing some pieces from the musical: My Fair Lady; which was not entirely amateurish but not too much more advanced either. She was positioned near the bar, and a small crowd was perched on the few benches around her piano. Some of them were humming the tunes along. I made one half-hearted attempt to suggest to her to play some numbers from older American Musicals: such as from Victor Herbert's operettas, but she did not seem very enthusiastic to comply. Nevertheless she gave it a try and stumbled through the tune "In old New York"… from the "Red Mill", sort of to show her pedigree in the musical world.

___ ___*

Shortly after 7 PM a fellow, about my age, in a dark business suit stepped-up to me at the bar stool. Without hesitation he introduced himself as Geoffry Dorfman, and asked if he has made a mistake by assuming that the gentleman was Mr. Szikszay-Farkas.

-No mistake indeed! I was expecting you," I said.

-Fortunately the crowd is not what it used to be on a Saturday night. But, that, perhaps is due to the heavy rainfall outside," said Dorfman, "As a matter of fact that is the reason for my being this late."

-No harm done, I said; "It is so cozy here; and I actually succeeded to persuade the pianist to play some of my old, nostalgic favorite tunes. Would you like to join me at a drink"? I asked him.

-I was planning to be the host tonight," said Dorfman "so please allow me to take over from here", playing the gracious host, rather successfully. What did you have?" he asked.

-Oh, well, …that's kind of unorthodox, one of my own concoctions, it is called "Rumhatten", but no bartender seems to be familiar with it, as yet, under this name".

-No matter then; why don't I just order the same thing for you, may I"?

-Oh, certainly! Thank you, I acknowledged his courtesy with a flair of a European gentleman.

Dorfman struck me as very much of the successful business man. Even here at the bar he was carrying with him his attaché-case. After some bragging about his familiarity with the New England business environment he abruptly turned and inquired about the out- come of the interview at the school.

As it turned out, he did not know the key person involved, that is: Gifford, at fist hand. But he seemed to know quite a lot about the 'second in command' : Herm Shea. He was known in several of" State people's circuits, and gatherings, thus, all of those events Dorfman was frequenting for precious connections. According to Dorfman, Shea's oldest son was a State Rep. He presented such vivid familiarity with Shea's demeanor, that later, when I became familiar with him myself, it was unmistakable to recognize.

Dorfman was noticeably thrilled to learn that an offer and appointment of me to the faculty of the Civil Engineering Department was imminent by the school's president (Lydon) perhaps before August, pending the submission of a formal application.

Something was subtly suspicious about Dorfman not emphasizing his own job offer, instead just let it be a sort of background decoration to the faculty position, which offer was verbally estimated by Gifford to be in the vicinity of $ 12,000. plus all State Employees' benefits. Somehow Dorfman's $ 18,000.+ job did take a second place to the professorship at the school. Later I quickly began to understand why this was so.

But he did elaborate on the work his firm is involved in, namely: tax-mapping. This was a recently mandated mapping activity by the Commonwealth of Massachusetts. The goal was that eventually all the Cities and Towns must complete a parcel identification plan primarily for taxation purposes. A new system. The maps will not have to be rigorously accurate to surveying standards. But every single parcel of land in separate ownership should have to be identifiable and designated by some numbering system.

Dorfman, describing his background in this field, mentioned survival workshops in the National Guard, where he picked-up quite a bit of experience in dealing with maps. He made no bones about not being either a surveyor or engineer. He described himself as a self-taught "mapping specialist" offering tax mapping services, which did not require any professional registration. He proudly declared that he does possess two very important traits in this endeavor: a strong business background (a degree from the Babson Institute) and even more important: connections.

The drinks were refilled, and emptied again. Dorfman suggested to sit over at the table's section. Without much ado he ordered the "Boston Scrod" (a local specialty, he explained) and suggested me to do the same, in view of my unfamiliarity with this fish. "Try it you'll like it" he jokingly remarked.

After the fish, which was indeed excellently done, and all the trimmings, I had no room left for dessert. Dorfman was very talkative which I liked, because he could present every situation as if he were a participant in it. He was an actor. A good one too.

I was curious about how he did succeed to build his clientele. So he described how he mailed out fliers offering his tax mapping services to every Town's Board of Assessors, attended every meeting municipalities held in connection with mapping, with contracts and bidding procedures, elaborating on his "expertise" in the field, referring to himself as a "mapping consultant".

Perhaps the most enlightening about his character was how he described his previous employment as a "gopher" at an old, well established surveying and mapping firm in Boston. He was not at all surprised, when I did not wink an eye at his expression of gopher. I knew the term well from my current position at the Architect- Planner firm.

I was naive enough at first, when I mentioned my old friend, Feri, (short for Francis, he was the one who found me my current position in Cleveland, when I was one of the 50,000 odd scientists, unemployed, as a result of the space program dieing in January of 1969) that this flamboyant boss of mine just hired a young man with obscure credentials and activity, who is not even a "professional", is hardly visible in the office, and I hear that his salary is one of the highest among us yupies. He, Francis, was who explained me that he is the firm's most important man: he keeps the firm in business. He is the job procurement specialist, he digs-up new projects through his "connections". That is why he is being referred to as the 'gopher'. So don't be suspicious or envious of him" explained my fried Feri.

Dorfman went on describing how he noticed that two foreigners at the office, (East-German immigrants) were slowly, but persistently preparing their departure from the firm. Systematically building close contact with any prospective, future client for the time when they are ready to leave the nest. This was, by the way the time, he became familiar with Herm Shea, who was doing consulting (actually trouble shooting) for the firm. Herm evidently knew the owner from way back before the war through the good ol'boys network, when he was doing this sort of consulting during the Depression as a young instructor at MIT supplementing his rather meager salary.

Dorfman went on telling me more and more about Herm, how he was sporting his pipe, almost wearing it as an accessory, giving emphasis to his academic position. Herm was also well liked and regarded at the firm and seemed to possess quite an arsenal of knowledge in the surveying field. Dorfman admitted his lack of familiarity with Herm's detailed credentials, but did not miss flattering me about my credentials being very solid, very up-to-date and derived from the most prestigious institutions, such as Ohio State, (at the time being the world leader in the field of geodesy and isostasy) the programs of which he seemed to be sufficiently familiar with. He came across to me as a pretty shrewd operator.

Finally he arrived at his offer of a position of a sort. The core of it was a part time (one day a week) "consulting" at anyone of his current tax mapping operations, which regularly took place at the Town Hall of the municipality being mapped, in close proximity and access to the Assessors' existing parcel records and (if any) existing parcel I D sketches and plans.

This position was very similar to the trouble shooting position of Herm, described by Dorfman earlier the evening. Then he came forward with his bigee: He talked about his dream being to do all the necessary professional services namely: the photogrammetric base mapping and the ground control surveys in-house. His present firm: Ariel Airmap was 'contracting out' these services. This meant a goodly portion of the mapping contract being "given away" the profits never actually realized and, what's worse, dished out right at the beginning of the project.

Dorfman then asked me how would I feel about becoming a partner of an affiliate firm, to be established soon. Although the ground control field work would not require -by current standards- professional surveyor's registration, still, sooner or later this service would inevitably run into, or overlap with, the realm of professional engineering or surveying or both. Therefore, it should be desirable for me to become registered either as one or the other, or both.

Obviously I agreed wholeheartedly, and recalled Gifford's like question at the interview. Then he inquired about my instruments and other field equipment. I informed him that I own a small transit, as well as a small builder's level.

Then Geoffry asked me about my plans for the move down to New England. What sort of arrangements, if any, did I make.

-Well, I don't have any position into which I should move down here," I said, "Remember? I just came from the interview that ended this afternoon. And, I certainly are not planning to move away from a fairly well paying job, into a one day per week troubleshooting job. I still haven't got the professorship. Without that I would be in limbo around here. So why don't we play it by ear for the time being. At least until I got the appointment".

-Okay," he said, "fair enough. But make sure you let me know the minute you got it. I have all sorts of connections by which to help you get settled. There is my wife' cousin, he is a Realtor. I am sure he will be able to come up with a house in a decent neighborhood. Alas, do you have school-age kids?

-Sure, a boy and a girl, the newest one is not even a year old. The boy, Andy, is getting into junior high next year. Susie is two years younger.

-Then you even have to watch the community you will locate into, he said. "You can make a right choice, or you can make a big mistake too. There were some very surprising turnabouts within the same community in these crazy 60-s.

Then, very paternally, he assured me that I can count with his help in every way, which did make me feel good. And suddenly the ominous New England began to brighten up.

The storm outside was easing off somewhat. It was also getting very late, considering that this was to be a dinner meeting and the business part was only tentative in nature. Both of us, however, deep down, anticipated the position to materialize, and our move to New England imminent. After he gave me some local telephone numbers -the Realtor's for sure- we said good by.

Upstairs, from my hotel room, I had a beautiful view of the airport, the harbor and its facilities, and beyond; the bright light of the lighthouse beaconing at the far shore. The storm subsided just about completely. The first day and night I ever spent in this city. I was tired to the point of exhaustion. Totally oblivious to what this day brought in the life and of my career and that of other people, I went to bed and fell asleep. It was July the 19-th in the 1969-th year of the Lord.

Next morning on route to the terminal through the shuttle bus' radio news the word Chappaquiddick was popping up repeatedly, in connection with the Kennedy name, that turned the few people in the bus all excited. It did not mean much more to me than the name of a small island someplace off the larger island of Martha's Vineyard. And then I began to realize that the previous day have touched the career -and indeed the life- of other people as well. I was still basically a Midweste'ner, didn't know much about New England and its politics.

The flight home to Cleveland was interrupted by one stop at Providence, Rhode Island. By then almost everyone was talking about the "mysterious" accident at Chappaquiddick.

Chapter Two
(Burning the Bridges)

The Monday, and the following week, was agony at the Architect / Engineer / Planner Firm. On one hand I knew that pretty soon I will have to start composing my letter of resignation; but on the other hand, being burned so many times before, I held off acting out anticipated happenings, which may backfire later on. So, I was ducking out questions about "where was I during the week-end" from one of the young (very experienced) architect kid, who told me weeks ago, that he was being considered at the University of Pennsylvania for a faculty position in architectural engineering, and he put me down as a reference for his qualifications and experience.

A very nice kid, some 10-years to my junior, was working thru the summer under my supervision for the handling of the utilities at a sizeable, new building rehab complex, not far from the downtown of Cleveland. He gave my name as one of the references at the firm's, where he was employed for the better part of the '60-s, as his 'engineering supervisor'. Evidently the Department head called over the weekend, wanted to talk to me about his experiences, as well as his personality, getting along with fellow workers, etc.

I had a somewhat closer relationship with him than with the other employees so I felt somewhat guilty about 'letting him down', although no one was obligated to be at the firm's disposal on week-ends, on the phone or otherwise, unless there was an emergency in connection with a particular job.

I told him that I was called out of town on the weekend; so if he would have told me that he expected an out of town call for the purposes of giving reference, I would have handled it from…where- ever I was at the time… I did not want to tell him that I, myself was at an (or even two) interviews at a New England Technical School and a private 'Consultant'. The Chappaquiddick incident did come up during the conversation, just as a conversation piece. Nothing more, and I, of course neglected to mention, that I was there, in Massachusetts on an interview, about an engineering teaching position at the very date when the discovery of the accident took place.

As it turned out, a couple of weeks later, he was the first one to learn, that I myself got an offer for a faculty position at the Lowell Technological Institute. We became labeled, at the firm, as 'the academics', when it became known that we are leaving the firm in September in favor of an academic position.

But when I thought it was agony waiting for the appointment to come, not being able to mention anything at all to anyone at the firm, when the appointment finally did come, (it was the beginning of August) I found myself in a very difficult position trying to wrap up everything almost in the last minute to enable me to leave at all; It was even more agonizing how to handle matters from here on; I was in a state of bewilderment, puzzled, unable to know how to handle the situation with the boss…I was never in a position ever quite like this before.

It took me the entire weekend to compose a letter of resignation to the boss. I was unable to quote any grievances, any discontent, (I was the 4-th highest paid employee within the organization) what was I supposed to bring-up as a true and valid reason to quit my position?

As always, I resorted to the only humanly acceptable way: I had to tell the truth; however painful it was, I had to tell him somehow, about my dream, the only redemption in this foreign land that seemed my life worth living here. I elaborated on the situation I was at Akron, that situation which collapsed and evaporated my dream due to envy, and greed of others who were placed above me on the employment scale. I also praised the organization I was in, with him at the helm, and, finally the working relationship with my fellow employees, which I assumed was exemplary, given the awful short time within which it was achieved.

I read and reread it so many times, that I had it just about memorized. Then I came to the realization, that there was a philosophical flaw in it:

If everything was as described in this letter of resignation, why on Earth was I resigning in the first place? This was an awesome problem to solve. I was not capable to go at it on my own.

I visited Francis, my good old buddy, with whom we fled our country in 1956, after the Soviet takeover. By the way, he secured this position through his connections and acquaintances for me. He thought that the best thing would be to come up with total honesty. That I shall explain to him, that it now seems to me closer than ever to realize my dream. (It was about this time that the 'Sound of Music' was released and playing everywhere in the cinemas, one of the theme songs being "Climb Every Mountain".) That there is no point in praising the organization that I am planning to leave. But to describe to him how it seems now possible to "find my dream" so close, almost within reach.

I made the suggested revisions and let it fly as such. The following Monday morning I put the letter on the boss's desk. He was away at the time, but…as it turned out to be (of which I was totally unaware of), that his wife too, was part of the organization, and she discovered the letter. Immediately she summoned the 'gopher', who took me out for lunch. This move, by the way, was one of the most mysterious, inexplicable thing that ever happened to me prior to this case. (I mentioned the 'gopher' before already).

First of all, I did not know how on Earth did he find out about the letter in the first place. Second, what gave him the authority to talk to me like he did. Although he did not come on strong scolding me for doing underground work, instead he was becoming philosophical. Somehow it still disturbed me that he knew about the letter before the boss did. Very calmly he announced the staff that "Gabor and I are going out for lunch". I knew he also had an expense account, so this was not going to hurt his own pocket book. Naturally I noticed, that he was not heading towards the small diner just down the street, that most all of us frequented. Instead he walked me down to the classy restaurant that was a couple of blocks away.

He was becoming educational. He began to explain, what I was unfamiliar with: that the 'boss' is a super connected guy; If I had academic aspirations, why on Earth did I not come forward and told him about it. Although he was 'just' an assistant professor at Kent State in the architecture department, … but … but … but "you have no idea what he could do if he wanted to do something for someone, specially someone like me, whom he happened to like immensely. "You don't even know how much" he said, and I thought he was exaggerating already.

He was being greeted by the host, who evidently knew him quite well and asked him about his father, who evidently was even better known in all of Cuyahoga County. We got seated right away and the cocktail waitress asked him about his 'usual', then turned to me: "and how about you sir?" I didn't want to flabbergast her with my concoctions with the rather simple, but totally unknown names I gave my drinks. To avoid repeating the scene at the Airport Hilton's bar, I just ordered a dry Martini.

-So, you want to be a professor? That is not much of an achievement! Do you really think that is 'success'? They are dime a dozen now-a-days. How much does a professor make? For instance, how much did they offer you down in that place in Massachusetts? I wouldn't be surprised to learn that you are even taking a cut. Come on! Give! Start talking".

-Look Jim; You must be familiar with the expression: money isn't everything. Important? Yes, certainly! We all live on money. But this professorship happens to mean an awful lot to me. Specially now; two years after I made the first biggest career mistake of my life. This seems now like a redemption; like a second chance, that not too many people get in life. We were a teaching family; my father was a professor, my mother a high school teacher. You did not see how unreasonably proud they were of me at the time they visited us in Akron. Coming from the Victorian era philosophy: they thought that this is it (for me); this is everything, I am a made man. They had no idea how really volatile my position was in Akron, or, as a matter of fact anywhere else, without a tenure. All they saw was that I was well known; That faculty members-colleagues - greeted me on the street and greeted them too, after they found out that they are my parents and are visiting from "the old country". They were overwhelmed".

-But Gabor, you are in the wrong! I can't understand for the life of me why would you want to have a career that most everybody looks down upon? You know! **"Those who can, do! those who can't, teach."** You are among the ones who can, and do! Forget about the ones who can't. This is America. You must do what you are best at and keep doing it. That leads to success".

He took a minute silence; we were getting our main course. This restaurant was a cut above the others. Stockbrokers, real estate developers, and their brokers and attorneys frequented this place.

Jim now switched to diplomacy.

-So you really want to be a professor? he asked again. "A Herr Professor"? he was poking fun with me. "Is that it? Do you realize that it would take the boss a few words with the dean of the engineering college, either at Kent State, or Cleveland State, as a matter of fact, and you would get may be a visiting professorship for the time being, which would convert to a permanent one when the opportunity arrives. But how do you envision yourself with us? with our organization? Do you want to do it on a part time basis? You know full well that we need a full-time guy."

-Jim, you do sound very convincing, all right. I think that is an essential ingredient of your job. And don't get me wrong, I admire you for it. But you don't know about my other ambitions and, what's probably worse, you are not familiar with: my weaknesses. Sure, you probably know my entire resume inside-out, and ... backwards too, but you don't know the stuff that's not in it".

-What do you mean? he asked, somewhat puzzled. He sensed that perhaps he was being lured into a trap, where he would lose his control over the situation, on which he worked so well. "What do you mean?" he repeated the question, trying to throw the ball back into my court.

-Look Jim, remember the other day you organized that meeting with the guy who passed out the decks of golden gilded cards. And I had no idea for some time, what this gimmick is all about, ...that is, until I looked at the back of the cards and saw the B & O Railway logo on them. Then, instantly it hit me: he was a PR. man".

-Yah, so? what are you getting at? I thought you made a pretty good impression on the guy; He was quite pleased with your experience and knowledge about railways. You hit it off so well with him that I was beginning to get scared that he is going to lure you away from us. And, that put me on the alert", he paused. "Of course I knew your railway engineering background at the CPR. That was the whole point, we couldn't afford to loose you to him, not to him, a prospective partner in a joint venture. I had to show him that we do have the technical expertise right in-house", he said.

-Okay. Now comes the part that I am lacking", I said, "and was trying to avoid being dragged into by the PR man. He, of course, knew the business; I knew the railway technology. But didn't know a fart about solid waste. I knew it stank, ...I also knew that it used to be burned, but that's about it. All this handling, processing, doing weird things with it, ... and the regulations, the environmental wacos were coming up with around the clock? ... you know? that really, really scared me. Does this mean I will have to be back to college every time we have a prospecting engineering endeavor on our hands which we don't even know we have yet, and on top of it, I don't even know much about", I said with a lot of frustration in my voice.

-You shouldn't worry about these minor details, he said looking me strait in the eye. "We can get a guy who does know all about it right from the college where the boss teaches architecture as his hobby", he said with some irony in his voice, reflecting his opinion about the teaching business. "You supposed to look at this whole thing from the top and, mark my word: I am sure you will be familiar with all those details that scares the hell out of you now, in no time. "I am planning to take you to the conference next week where the mayor and the chief engineer of the City will be the speakers on solid waste. The Army Corps of Engineers will be there too; That will be an eye opener for you.

-Jim, you must know I appreciate what you are trying to do. But please try to understand, that I put in a lifetime of studying an area of science and engineering to know everything about, be confident that I know it up to date, or even at the leading edge of it… and I think I did put in a tremendous effort to achieve this and am still not quit sure that I got there. Now you want to put on top of all these things that I never really learned about. This is much like a "perpetual student", like a professional student.

-Well, I don't want to disappoint you, but you know, if you will become a Herr Professor, that's where you will end-up, a perpetual student.

When we left the restaurant, he turned to me:

-Gabor, forget about the pressure talk, it is part of my vocation", and he stopped at the corner halfway back to the office. "But promise me one thing and that is: that you will think about it, Okay? Promise?" With that he extended his hand; "will you think about it? I am not going back to the office just now, I have to take care of some other business", he said.

-I shall do that, I said and shook his hand. "I did just that a lot, an awful lot lately, more than my fair share", I said. Then I turned and went back to the office. I knew I had my mind made up I knew I had to clime this new mountain.

*___*___*

In the office I had to make preparations for the upcoming events. I still did not have even a temporary successor appointed, because the boss still did not know -officially- about my resignation, so, there was no urgent need to start putting together work pieces for turning it over to someone. But I had to start making arrangements for a visit back to Massachusetts to secure a place to stay, rent or buy a house on a rather short notice.

I called Doug Johnson, the Realtor relative of Dorfman, billing the charges to my home phone. He had not as yet set up his own office in Westford; As it turned out he was temporarily operating from one corner of his father's Travel Agency that was located in downtown Chelmsford. I tried to explain who I am and about the situation I am in, but he said he already knows about all that.

-Why don't you just tell me what sort of place you are looking for, the price range, the size of the house, the location, etc." he said in a very, very confident, businesslike voice. "Or perhaps, were you not thinking about first taking an apartment for a while, and when you are here, we will have more time to look for more precisely what you need".

-Mr. Johnson, I want to ask a few questions about"… but here he abruptly interrupted me:

-Please! … please call me Doug! Geoffry must have told you that that is my name and that all my friends call me that. So would you please do likewise?"

-Well, I haven't even got a chance to meet you, … If you would call me Gabor"…

-Don't worry about that now, we shall see you soon. But let me ask you: are you planning to come down for a visit before you take-up your position in the fall? Let me suggest you do so. It would be beneficial, believe me."

-That is exactly the purpose of my call Doug, and I was just trying to ask you about the number one thing in real estate… you know? … location, location"

-and location! sure, sure" he said.

-So, I looked at the map of the area, and saw that the Town of Dracut is really so close to the school"… practically next door"

-Gabor, let's not jump too fast", he said, "for that we have to set some priorities first; so let me ask the questions. Do you have school age children"?

Yes, two of them" I said. "Both in elementary school".

-So, now: Gabor, you want to zero in on a town that has good public schools, then, preferably in good commuting route to and from the Institute; Then, … also, the town should be a good and respectable address"…

-Hey, hey, Doug!…. sorry to interrupt you, but, you have just lost me, …what was this thing about … the town … an address? In every town you have an address… No?"

-Gabor, this call will cost you a fortune," he said somewhat concerned, "we will talk about these sort of things at length, when you will be here. Just tell me now:…apartment or a house?

-We would really like to settle down, you know, … so, it is: house! Moving has become a dirty word in our family lately. I bet you don't realize, don't even guess, how many times we have moved in the last couple of years.

-Okay, what price range should it be"… Let me help you,…Where do you live now? I mean, what kind of living arrangements? You know, … there are some real estate chains that handle complete relocations. They commit to sell your home where you are moving from; We are ill equipped to do that. But maybe your case is not too complicated and a local Realtor will be able to handle the sale at the other end".

-Doug, I guess it is rather complicated, the place is a duplex with an office in the basement for myself. So, let's skip all this now. Just let me know how shall we meet, what's the best way to get to your place, etc? you know what I mean?

-Sure. There is a limo service from the airport, that drops you off directly at the Carriage House Inn; Right here in Chelmsford. The minute you arrive give me a call and I come and pick you up, he said. "It's not the first time I am doing this, you know; A lot of people are moving into town lately, they are coming to Wang. So, once you're here, we'll go and look at places. When are you planning to come?"

-Most likely this Saturday; The plane is here by 10 AM. That's how I came last time, I said.

-Well, Okay. We'll find you something. Don't worry. See you then."

* —-*—-*

Linda Leigh was a very successful Realtor in Shaker Heights. She found us this duplex for a fabulously low price. The house was in super-duper condition, the owner was a fanatic in keeping up the place. This was the first time I saw a lawn-sweeper that was a hand pushed rotary broom with a wide and light bag mounted behind it. Each time, after he cut the grass, he went through the lawn with this sweeper. He showed me how best to do it. The manicured lawn was one of his prides in the neighborhood.

The other one was the automatic/electric garage door opener, which he lubricated once a week, and, of course, he had to show me that too. Everything was meticulous. He then told the story of the basement, which he finished a few years ago for his business to be moved down there. That enabled him to rent the upstairs to a nice young family. Since he paid off the mortgage on the house, that rent became a very handy income. I asked him to tell me something about his business.

For the last 20 years he was doing appraisals for a bank where he said he had good connections, from way back W. W. II. It was a decent endeavor, providing him with a comfortable living; he was able to choose the time when he was going out to appraise and take pictures of properties.

The minute he learned that I am a registered surveyor, he was taking his time to elaborate on his connections. He said that I could be doing the same thing with the 'certified plot plans' for the bank, which the mortgage department also needs. "But, that you should be concentrating on doing when you are getting closer to retirement", he explained, "because you seem to be more ambitious to me than retiring to something like this. This could be something like a hobby later on for you".

He seemed to have his mind firmly set on the $ 40,000.00 which was the asking price. And I could see he really knew his prices. Linda was leaving us alone for all this time, because she knew what was coming when she introduced us to each other, me as the interested buyer. She said she will be back shortly and rather let him show off all his amenities. When she returned we were still in the midst of looking through several of the recent improvement on the house that he did for his tenant. He explained that he got rid of the tenant in the anticipation of a more rapid sale.

Driving back to the real estate office Linda began to prompt me about my intentions with the house. I told her that this price is outside of our reach, and the fellow seem quite firm with his price.

-Mr. Szikszay-Farkas, I still would advise you to make an offer, she said. "There are certain circumstances, that could make you a very, very happy buyer for a price that you could afford".

-Okay, I said, "what puzzled me all along was: why is he -or rather: are they- (since the house was in both of their names) selling it. It is almost unbelievable that they should part with such a lifetime achievement property".

-Well, like all unusual things in life this one too has a story behind it", she began with the story. "You know, it's like this: they are in the middle of divorce proceedings, and there seems to be no other solution, than to sell the house. She is determined to go to Florida to live with or near her folks. The divorce was in a deadlock, in view of the lack of a settlement. But, now at the end of April - early May, the interest about their house is picking up", she said and glanced at me meaningfully. She was an extremely good looking woman, only a few years my junior, and evidently she knew her business. "I have shown this property to at least four prospective buyers lately, and they all thought the price was kind of stiff. So they (the owners) are now kind-of softening up a bit", she said, looking at me again with that incredible smile locked right on me.

-Well, Linda, I am going to call you Ms. Leigh, unless you will begin to call me Gabor ..." I began to state my point.

-Sorry, it is office policy, that the independent sales help should not embark calling the clients by their first names, but ... if you insist ...Gabor, I feel like, that you people should have this house; "it is just so right for you, ...we, in the office maintain a list of prospective tenants, all checked out: their credentials, references, incomes, etc. verified. I am sure we can get you a tenant for the upstairs apartment in no time".

-Linda, be realistic this time, please" I said, "what is the ultimate price that you think we can get the house for?"

-I think, if you make an offer for 35-thousand, they will start dickering, ... then you raise it to 36 thousand and be firm, ... they will let it go. They may want us to ease off on our commission somewhat, which ... if it is presented to the boss the right way, he might agree with it".

-Okay, lets make-up the papers", I said as we arrived back at the office. "I do have a question, though; How come we haven't seen the 'missus' at all"?

-Because she has spent the winter in Florida already with her folks, Linda explained, "she is due to return on May 15-th. This will be a pleasant surprise for her", she added, I mean, ... if it's sold by then.

-You know, I am really surprised to hear people splitting-up in their late 50-s", I said, "this guy must be close to 60 I guess".

-Yah, ... already well over that, and he has a younger woman who stays with him while his wife is away" Linda said, "but don't quote me on that", she said putting on her irresistible smile again.

The offer was accepted, and the passing went like clockwork. and so, we got the house for 36 grand's. Mr. Dennison, the former owner, even took me to the bank he was working for, and helped arrange a mortgage for us. And then, the story turned into a fairy tale…One of the young attorneys at the bank was looking for an apartment in a decent neighborhood. They just had their first child. So we rented the upstairs apartment before we even moved in ourselves.

We had to wait until Mr. Dennison moved his belongings out, which did not take long. He also left most of his garden tools in the back part of the garage, as he promised he would.

We also had to leave our two older kids in the parochial school in Cleveland Heights to finish at the end of May. They have just started in this parochial school in March when we moved from Ithaca, NY. where they attended public school for a year and a half. The constant moving did not take such a toll on them, as it did on us, though we couldn't really tell at the time.

Until July, we never thought that we will spend no more than three months in this really, really nice house. Our Gabor Junior, was just a few months old, and Maria spent a very enjoyable summer in the new house with the kids. There was the swimming club exclusively for residents of the neighborhood some two blocks away; admittance for just a token of a fee, actually it was all included in the membership fee. This is the abbreviated story of how we got hold of the duplex at Shaker Heights from which we now have to move in a very short order. Selling it never occurred to us at this point because there was a number of uncertainties in the venturous move to New England.

What if anything goes bump, plans do not fall in place, my not becoming registered P.E. or Land Surveyor, … no professional practice develops… all and all: just too many contingencies. Selling would mean to burn all bridges behind us. At least there will be something to fall back on, to return to and start over. Selling it, was a no!

*__-*__-*

-Hi Gabor, how was your flight?" asked Doug Johnson, as he came to pick me up at the Carriage House Inn. "Actually, I think I have some good news for you", he said. "Get right in, our office is only a few minutes from here", he said, as we got into his car.

I noticed that the heat was not as unbearable as in July, at the time of the interview. We settled in the corner of his father-s office where he started to show me the pictures of the houses he had selected to show me. I asked for a town street map of Chelmsford so as to help me picture their location relative to the Technological Institute, which was in Lowell and really had no easy access at the time. Doug showed me the various possible routes to the school, but each one ended up having to drive through half the City. The situation with the bridges over the Merrimack River was grossly unsolved; at times, for an out-of-towner, they seemed like part of an unfinished traffic scheme. One of the bridges crossed the River at a high level, right through the center of Campus, but the approaches on both sides were in a total congested state. This phenomenon was not apparent in the middle of July when the streets were empty, hardly a car on the road.

So I asked him again "What about Dracut Doug, wouldn't that be a better location? you don't have to cross the river".

-Gabor", first, you don't want to put your kids into the Dracut school system, second, there is the "address issue" I began to tell you about over the phone. Here, in New England the name of the Town you live in, sort of defines you. A town either has a prestige, or: it doesn't. Chelmsford does, and Westford does, and Groton does, and I could give you a list, he said. "People are looking for these towns to locate in. Their schools are a cut above, because they have more money, better school facilities, better teachers, and so on, because people have the money". He ended his lecture.

-But Doug, aren't the taxes also a lot higher in these towns"? I asked him.

-Well, maybe, but remember, you get what you pay for". "So I have selected for you some places here in Chelmsford".

Then he drove me to a few older houses which were listed with him. As we entered in some of them I was alerted by the decor, and re-decor; styles I was unaccustomed to. One looked like a country "Kuria" in the old days in Hungary, not unlike the one we had on my father's farm, where we grew-up, but without the spaciousness around it. These were also farmhouses left here from the Civil War era, but were already stripped from the land surrounding them, victims of subdivisions. Some were in dire need of repair; in most cases the owner already retired at a milder climate, and the house let to tenants, who, obviously skipped much of the upkeep, or maintenance, never mind spending on improvements.

Then the prices. I was genuinely stunned to learn that they had an asking price I could not go near to. They were costing more than our duplex at Shaker Heights, which was in a superior condition in comparison to these, and had an almost positive cash-flow. I was disappointed and mildly discouraged.

-Is this all there is, Doug" I asked, and I could tell he had sensed the low spirit in my voice.

-No! by no means; there are newer development houses, the sort I am sure you are familiar with" he said encouragingly. "those are more affordable too, but I just wanted you to see these, … some really suggest, you know, … status, … old families, … old money, you know? The trouble with the development houses is that they are… most of them still are, under construction, you know, …it is that season, the summer… and, I can't see how they can be finished by school-start in September".

-All right let's see some of them" I said.

-Good, but I suggest we have a quick lunch first", and he drove down a short stretch on the main drag, Route 110, where he turned into the parking lot of a Howard Johnson's.

"Oh, Gabor, I forgot to ask you, are you flying back tonight or tomorrow"?

-Tomorrow morning, with the 9:45 Allegheny Air.

-Did you make reservation for a room for tonight"? he asked.

-No, why, I thought I will head back to Logan after we finished tonight and stay there at the Hilton like I did last time, you know, at the interview", alas, when I met your cousin there, you know'? I said, showing off my familiarity with this new location in the World.

-But you have no reservation there either, right"? he asked. -True", I admitted.

-Well, let me advise you that after lunch we head right back to the office and arrange something for you before it's too late", he said. We can try the Hilton, as you said, but I am not sure… Everything seems to be so busy nowadays. But staying close to the airport is always a good idea,' if you have a flight to catch".

-Doug, are you suggesting that I am in trouble? Look, here we are, sitting in HOJO's", after we finished lunch we can reserve a room" I said, and in the morning I can get a ride with the limo to the airport"

-Gabor, this is the last place on Earth where I want you to go to sleep", he said laughing, "because you never get any sleep. Do you realize the noise here, just about all night? and, on top of it, it's Saturday night,… look at the highway overpass there, right above us, just forget about it".

We drove back to his office, where he first called the Hilton. No room there of any kind, not for tonight. Then he called The Carridge House, where the limo stops; nothing there either,…he turned to me and said, sort of explaining: "these chinks are taking over everything, ever since Wang started hiring them by the thousands, and, …you know, Saturday = interviews. But don't worry, my father has a friend at the Drum Hill Motel, You remember, we drove by it, he will get you a room there and you can reserve the limo for the morning".

In the afternoon he took me to a few of the "Hicks" developments. All large, one acre lots, 3000 square foot houses, some even more expensive than the ones we saw in the morning. He could not find a single one that could be moved into, come September.

Back to the office again, telephone calls; More calls, to developers. Then finally he turns to me: the guy at "MacBro Construction" says he has one under construction nearing the finishing touches, but,… September first, or actually Labor Day, is kind of close, but if the deal is done, they will see to it that it gets finished.

-Do they have a picture? and where is it? Not out in the boondocks, I hope. Doug, can you show me a floor plan, at least"? I asked him.

He called the same guy back and asked him about which model this is, and whether he, Doug has a copy of that model. Shortly he pulled it out from a pile of architectural renderings, and showed me the plans. I said "let's go".

Taking a turn next to HOJO's (which I already recognized) we took a cutoff under the over-pass and down a narrow, hidden kind of roadway, then came to a stone walled corner of a side street, there he slowed down, and said "this must be it". Then he turned off the road onto an unfinished driveway, stopped, and we got off. The place looked totally abandoned, there were no workers around. It was already past 4 PM. We could look the place over at our will. Everything was taking shape, even the heating system was installed but the decor and finish carpentry was missing. And, of course, the floor, the stairs, etc. Three nice bedrooms, a deck in the back, a full basement with a single car garage at the end of the driveway. There was room for a fireplace, but no chimney, these were all extras. Something to be done later.

-Doug, this is it, no use chasing the goose any further. This has essentially everything we need, at least for a start. Let's get it"! I said. "Now the main thing is to have it ready for September 5-th, or latest the 6-th, Saturday, so that we can move in by then. Monday is Labor Day, and the classes at the University do not start before the 8-th; The 3-rd, 4-th and 5-th being orientation and registrations".

Back to Doug's office. Purchase and sales agreement, deposit check, telephone call to the Construction Co. "Can it be signed by someone?

No? Okay. "I go by the listing broker tonight, put a 'sold' sign on the place and, …and then we will finish the paperwork… Monday morning, Okay". Then he turned to me and said "Gabor, it looks like you got it".

-One more call", he said, "to my father, I want to find out what he had arranged for you for tonight" he said.

When he finished, he turned to me and said: "let's go it's already almost 6 o-clock, they are holding your room until 6 PM. We'll be there in a few minutes, that's one of the beauties of this town. There is a swimming pool out front, you had a long day, eh'? you can cool down before supper", he said smiling. "You'll like it; Honestly, isn't life good'"? he asked then. (I said to myself: hey, sure it is, he must be counting his commission already; one day's work's worth.)

The Motel was just off the Route 3 rotary with easy access to it. He dropped me off in front of the 'Office' and said: "you ask for Brian, he'll take care of you… and …of course, I will be in touch… have a good flight". We shook hands and he drove off.

I called Maria, told her I found a place, that I have the plans, and that I will bring a set with me. She wanted to see them but of course there was no such thing as FAX in those days. So, I tried to describe it as best I could. I assured her that she will like it. I also told her that I am bringing the plans with me home.

The limo picked me up in the morning and we made good time to Logan, it was Sunday, light traffic. The muzak on Allegheny was all to my liking; light classical. In those days there were a number of stations that played music that had melodies, some even half way decent lyrics. Then the stop at Providence, and the whole thing was getting familiar. Only the hoopla about Chappaquiddick was nowhere to be heard; As if it had never happened.

Doug called once more at home on the 26-th and said that the papers were all signed the day before, and that the contractor agreed to the few critical terms I had in the contract. The most important for us was the completion date on September 6-th, to be ready to move-in.

-Gabor, how are you going to finance the sale" he asked. "Do you have financing ready"?

-Depends on what do you call ready, I said; we have some money for down payment, if that's what you mean. I am sure you have some banks up there which would grant us a mortgage loan in short order" I said. "Your cousin was bragging about your banker connections".

35

-Okay, I will have a couple of forms ready for you to fill out when you arrive, he said; we also have some connections to the Lowell 5-cents bank, so I would not worry much about it, if I were you, "by the way, did you sell your place in Cleveland? or made arrangements to do"? he asked with some concern.

-No, not really, Doug, we decided not to sell it", I said, "you know it is a duplex and on top of it: it produces positive cash flow which is kind of cool, under the circumstances. You know, I've got burned too many times before, last time in Akron; just imagine what if I don't make it to tenure here, then we still have something to fall back on. So we rented the place, the present tenant, a young attorney for the bank, which holds the mortgage and lives in the upstairs apartment, will move down into our place on September I-st and brings his colleague, another attorney from the bank, to rent the upstairs. There will be a few hundred dollars left over each month for us. Can you ever think of anything better".

-Gabor, this sounds too good to be true, he said with a trace of envy in his voice; "you know the expression: somebody up there likes you"? he asked again.

-Yes, I do. I now have to pray for him [upstairs] to keep it that way. Now; we are planning to arrive on the 4-th of September, the movers will leave from here on August 30-th on Saturday, and so will we; we will be driving both cars, Maria the wagon, and I my little buggy, the Carman Ghia. We wouldn't push it, rather taking a leisurely drive along Lake Erie to Niagara Falls, then along the NY Throughway, we drop in at a friend of ours in Ithaca, with whom I went to some classes jointly at Cornell in grad-school. We have it pretty well planned", I said with a lot of contentment and really thought, the second time in my life in the US. since Akron, that… "everything's going my way".

* - - - * - - - *

The Labor Day weekend was rapidly approaching. The boss came and went, and he was around, but, somehow he seemed like preoccupied with his tasks. He had not called me and did not come to my cubicle either. It almost seemed like if he was deliberately avoiding me. I thought it was really strange.

I was in the middle of turning over the few unfinished work-pieces to a draftsman, who was mostly working on those projects, and was grossly familiar with them. He was designated by the boss for this task. The atmosphere was somber, to say the least.

On the last day, the 29-th, Friday, as I arrived in the morning, the receptionist stopped me in the front hall and said that the boss wants to see me. Finally, I thought, uncertain of what this will be: a showdown? a lecture, perhaps? some deep moralization? this last one I had to dismiss right away, he wasn't that type. For all possibilities, though, I felt I had to brace myself.

-Gabor, he said as he rose from his chair, and shook my hand, "take a seat", and he pointed to the chair at his side. "You do recall, I am sure, a couple of months ago I had these management consultant guys in here to evaluate our entire operation" I didn't utter a word just nodded my head. "I specifically asked them to give me a profile of each professional on our staff; do you recall speaking with the bearded fellow, Larry"? I nodded again in ascent. I don't, of course, have a full record of the conversation, but it looks to me that they made a mistake in your case; Or you were not fully honest with them; just suffice it to say that I really had no idea that you were not happy, or at least satisfied with your position here", he said and waited for a while it appeared, for my answer.

-Bill, I am in a very, very uncomfortable situation, also I am overwhelmed emotionally, this being the last day and all, and this time I am really not sure if I am going to do the right thing. Let me just say one thing, and I am sure it will say the most important thing I wanted you to know in this regard: had this offer come next year, after spending at least a year with you here, I would, most likely not have considered it".

-Thank you, he said looking down to his desk; After a short silence he continued with his thoughts: "Tell me something about the civil engineering profession of present day, what is this turmoil that spurs them, ... they are in an upheaval, they can not stay within the framework of an organization. You do remember back in February when I first met you, that there was a civil engineer/surveyor here at the same position we hired you for; actually you were replacing him. He was the independent type; he wanted to be in his own business, he offered to stay on with our organization on a consulting basis. Now you are leaving for some other reason. What's going on"? Tell me: am I on the right track? is this a realistic endeavor I am pursuing, trying to hire the engineer/surveyor as an in-house expert, to offer this as an in-house service? why am I not succeeding in this endeavor? The management experts show that we offer the professionals good or slightly better than average compensation. I value your input in this regard. Let's say I want to learn" and he was now staring directly at me.

37

-Bill, it's not the money! I am willing to repeat this as many times needed. I think, but please don't quote me, it is the type of individual. You seemed lately to end up with strong willed individualistic, self assured people; I can really see my predecessor. In a way I belong in the same category myself. I probably have resigned earlier, had you not given me the latitude to handle myself vis-a-view the clients, and the negotiations with them. This meant an awful lot to me; like I said, If this offer had come next year..."

-Tell me one more thing, that intrigued me: had you advertised for this faculty position while you were here, or how did it come about"?

Then I described the telephone call from the chairman, how it came out of the blue, that he was searching to fill this (vacant) position since last fall and found my ad in an old copy of the AAUP Bulletin that I had placed while still at Cornell.

-Thank you, again, it is needless to say how much I, or rather we all, will miss you. And now, I think the office staff is planning to take you out for a farewell lunch... so, check with them".

Chapter Three
(The move)

Our little caravan consisted of merely two vehicles: the Ford Fairlane Station wagon, as the flagship of the endeavor, driven by Maria. This was the logistical center, containing the everyday needs of the members of the venture i.e. several changes of under garments, the laundry collection center, some cleaning supplies, etc. and, of course, the food and drink supplies (in two picnic cooler boxes, filled with goodies purchased at the Hungarian outlets of the Westside Market in Cleveland) for the entire population of 'five'. This still did not include the two cats (a mama and daughter cat duo), the older animal dating all the way back to the good old Akron days of the mid sixties, and the daughter, a beautifully striped tiger-cat, born in Ithaca, NY. during the Cornelian times of the late sixties. If it were slightly larger it could have easily be mistaken to an ocelot, henceforth came its name: "Ocee".

The passenger list also included our newly born, barely half year old Gabor Junior, who was placed under direct supervision of his older sister: Susanna, for the duration of the trip.

The Ford wagon, only 4-years old, but showing all the notorious weaknesses acknowledged by the manufacturer itself, like: the doors and locks of virtually all side doors. The best one to hold up against the wear-and-tear was the rear door, an important functional part of any station wagon. Somehow the designers had the notion that this door will be the most heavily used one, and designed it so much more durable on the expense of the side doors.

But the engine! … In my opinion, it was Ford's ever most successfully designed and built engine, that could perhaps one day move into the

'Pantheon' of best engines built by the automotive industry: 'The Great 289 cu.in. V/8, with its "ample power plant, and remarkable gas economy. (Still a 'carburetor job' at the time.)

The second vessel, a VW Carman Ghia, as most often tenderly referred to as "my little buggy", driven by myself, closely following the flagship, with Andy, our oldest son as the sole passenger and, with a minimum amount of luggage, due to its limited cargo hold.

It may have sounded a bit exaggerating to refer to this ensemble as a 'caravan'. But, considering the reference customarily being made to Christopher Columbus' naval ensemble of three ships as a 'fleet', it is not a long stretch of imagination to refer to this overland expedition of two vehicles as a caravan.

As the result of a short conference at a rest area in the Buffalo region the decision was formulated that the caravan will re-consider the plan to stay at Niagara Falls due first to the heaviest tourist season traffic in the area, and second, that the sun was still high enough for a good two hours of progress to an overnight stop on the old highway. Route 20, which was loaded with Motels, the majority boasting swimming pools in their front yard.

It barely past 5 PM, when the flagship pulled in to the harbor (more commonly called parking area) of an old-fashioned Inn, that boasted in front of the building: 'Country Style Restaurant'. It proved to be a welcome move by the two elder crew members, who in minutes after the docking (now more commonly called: "check-in procedure) were exploring the local waters, (pool) for their cleanliness and temperature. The reports came in shortly as: very satisfactory.

In view of the fact that our family was used to later, versus early dinner, it was close to 7 PM when we were gathering in the restaurant. This proved itself a near disastrous mistake. By ordering the chef's special: 'roast duck family style' was gradually turning into a minor disaster at a quarter of 8 PM when the scouts returned with the somewhat favorable report that the duck will be done "shortly" as they put it in the kitchen.

The crew was nearly revolting by the time the roast duck arrived at the admiral's table. The revolting escalated when the fowl was getting portioned out on the plates, all pinkish, sort of a medium rare consistency, requiring an undue amount of chewing. Chalking down this selection to 'experience' the officers consoled themselves with the New York (local) red cabernet, which was excellent.

After a leisurely breakfast, we set sail to Ithaca, an easy 3- hour cruse, where we visited our friends Mariann and Joe from the college days. I took some environmental systems courses offered in the School of Civil Engineering in one of which I had Joe as my classmate. He, being an architect B.A. in earlier years from Cornell, he returned in '67 to work on his Master's. I started my Ph. D. studies in the fall the same year. This is what, in hindsight, I put down as the greatest blunder of my career, and perhaps, my life.

Mariann, on the other hand, was a freelance housewife, and when finally, in October, Maria started working in the office of the dean of the College of Architecture and City and Regional Planning, we had to advertise for a part time housekeeper/kids' supervisor to perform these duties for about two and a half an hour each afternoon from 2:30 -when the kids came home from school- to about 5 PM when we came home from work. This rapport turned later on into 'a friendship between us, which went much deeper then anticipated at the beginning.

Mariann's family was old Yankee, one of her ancestors came to America on the Mayflower. They were 'well to do', bordering perhaps on wealthy. Joe on the other hand sprung from a very solid, middle class, civil servant family. This, by no means can be equating with being distressed, (he attended and graduated from Cornell, after all) but was possessing 'limited means'. The couple, (considerably younger than us), were in the category of the yuppie/hippie type. Fed up with Vietnam, (where, by the way, Joe was in active service and, even before that, he served in the US Army overseas, in Germany with the occupying forces) they were surely part of the rebellious generation, and to some limited extent, to its life style.

Mariann's parents, among other things, had a sort-of exclusive but modest place on Cape Cod, even before her father retired from the Hospital in Philadelphia where he was chief of staff. The couple, proudly trying to "make it on their own", shunning the substantial assistance her parents could have, and seriously intended to lavish upon them. They rented a very modest place in the college town part of Ithaca, right at the Cayuga Heights line, and from here their only son went to the same public school as did our own two kids.

I was never aware of Joe receiving any fellowship. And we were often wondering with Maria, how was it possible for the couple with one school age child to subsist on Mariann's earnings as household help, more so: at part time, as it was the case. Although Mariann was, by then, an only child (her sister died years before) and as being the only heir apparent, could have drawn a modest monthly 'advance' on her future wealth. All we knew for a fact, that wasn't really hidden from us, that when they really needed a replacement car on an emergency basis, because their old one quit, the parents transferred adequate funds into their joint account, from which then Joe wrote a check to the dealer, for the new car.

Our case was substantially different from theirs. We had to work for any and all assets and income we ever managed to secure. There was never anyone on which we could depend financially. And we didn't mind to work, on the contrary: I always loved working. It would have been inconceivable for me not to work. I didn't always loved what I was doing, but most of the time it was in the general area of my interests and endeavor.

When we came to Cornell all I had was a teaching fellowship on which, it was not meant to raise a family. All this was in lieu of the professorship at the University of Riyadh, for which I had a signed contract for a renewable 3-year term, that was leading to tenure. The remuneration for that position was in excess of ten times this fellowship at Cornell, and over three times my professor's salary at Akron U. But that was the prevailing world economy at the time. As events proved themselves later on, this blunder could never be remedied. For a long, long time after, the failure, namely: to shut the door in the face of opportunity, was hanging over my head as Damocles' sword on the Parkas' thread.

We arrived at around noon. In the meantime they moved from the hill down to the City of Ithaca, where Joe secured a position for himself with the City as "Planner". It was a boring job at the beginning, which most entry level jobs usually are, but at least it was a well paid job counting the excellent municipal benefits. They even bought a small single family home within walking distance to the City Hall. They seemed happy.

Mariann was totally overwhelmed when she learned about my appointment at the Institute. She simply couldn't believe that I could ever obtain such a position "in Massachusetts". "That place is predominantly Irish-Catholic and Yankee", she told me. "How have you thought ever to fit in there with such a faculty? Have you considered all the social circumstances? What are the chances for a Hungarian, with a foreign accent for success"? I reminded her of the missed opportunity at the fall of a mere two years ago, when we first arrived and met at Cornell, as an alternative to the faculty appointment in Saudi Arabia, where **everyone was a foreigner**, and the host country bent over backwards to please them and keep them. In the entire following decades: education was the buzzword in the Kingdom; brand new, modern schools grew right out of the desert sand, that had to be staffed by competent (foreign) teachers. It was a heroic effort, as I found out much later. But that's a different story.

It was Sunday, the middle day of the holiday long weekend. Mariann was adoring the half-year old Gabor Jr. who reciprocated most of the attention and endearments bestowed on him. They invited us to stay for the night. It was no point to arrive at an un- familiar place late at night, with the baby and the household in tow. Andy and Sean were only a couple years apart in age, and they quickly refreshed their interrupted two-year old friendship. They went over to the Cayuga Falls that had all sorts of interesting things in store for them, like trout, salamanders and turtles, fascinating for ten and twelve-year old boys.

And we socialized. I had to tell everything about how I got hold of the position and the appointment. I could sense a mild degree of envy on Mariann's part.

-So, you will be living in Massachusetts; and so close to the Cape and my parents' place. Joe, you should have tried to get a faculty position some place there", she said, turning to Joe.

-Honey, aren't you happy here? I thought it was our dream ever since our undergraduate years to locate here, settle down in this picturesque town and live out the rest of our days here", he said with a trace of admonishment in his voice, "and look, we have it all, right here".

-True. But you know how much I like the Cape. Ever since my youth I was crazy about it. Everything my father taught me about fishing, those unforgettable summers … Oh, I just love it".

-Well, honey don't forget that we will be having our own place pretty soon, just after you get that building lot up on the dunes, deeded to our name by your father's partner, the surveyor: Red. We can be there every summer, … and the holidays too." I promised you a lovely, contemporary-design house", he added.

-Oh, come on", said Mariann, turning to Maria, "he has not designed a single building ever since he graduated from the Architectural college. But, … why not? let him try."

This was the first, but not the last time I heard about that building lot on the dunes. Some years later, when I first met Dr. Brady personally at their place on the Cape I learned more about the details of the Land Court Case that his 'friend: Red', the surveyor filed with the Court for their partnership in that land deal. Dr. Brady dished out the money for the purchase, then, Red surveyed and subdivided it into lots. From that point on the entire affair became nebulous to me. Somehow, I failed to understand how Dr. Brady ended up with one lot for Mariann and Joe, and, as I learned, Red's daughter also got her lot. Even-Steven. This was the lot on which later in the '70-s Joe and Mariann built their summer place.

Gabor Jr. was put to bed early. We were somewhat worried that he does not get enough sleep and will become too exhausted by the trip. We had supper at a local restaurant, which were in abundance in this yuppie college town and retired after that. The two cats were extremely uneasy and were giving us hints that they considered the trip way too long.

Next morning, on Labor Day, we embarked on the last stretch of our journey. Our destination was still quite a ways. The capitol and the other two cities Troy and Schenectady were a good three hours on the way, after which, there came the Mass Pike, and Rt. 495,also about the same length.

The first casualty of the entire venture came suddenly and unexpectedly. After Worcester we left the Mass Pike and turned onto Rt. 291, which had some sections still under construction, where warning of blasting forced us to make lengthy stops. At the last of these stops as Susie got out of the wagon 'Ocee' jumped out, dashed into the bushes at the side of the road and did not let herself be caught any more. The more we went after her, the deeper she penetrated the unfamiliar territory, and, eventually, she got lost and we lost her.

It was late afternoon when we arrived at the Drum Hill Motel. Luck was on our side because the man at the front desk remembered me from a couple of weeks ago and let us have the last 'double room' available. We made ourselves at home as best we could. The contents of the picnic and cooler boxes were dangerously depleted, but we managed to assemble an evening meal. All it was necessary was to find a convenience store and get some milk for Gabor Jr. and some soft drinks for the crew. With this the journey was considered successfully completed. We were all ready for bed.

Next morning I went on my scouting mission. The first stop being Doug's Real Estate office. Our luck proved itself to have run out with our arrival last night.

-Hi Doug, I greeted him as I entered. Before I could even continue, he took over.

-Hi Gabor, I see you made it all right. Unfortunately I don't have very good news for you, he said apologetically.

-Doug, you know my only, most important question: can we move in or what? Is the house finished?

-Well, yes … and …no. Let me give you the story. The house is finished. The floor guy was there Sunday morning and applied the finish coat of iron oil. No one must step on it for at least 48-hours. The subcontractor shuns all responsibility if this rule is not observed. That's one thing. The other is that you have to take care of the financing. I have filled out two applications in your name, one to the Lowell 5-cents Bank, (this is the one where we have connections, as I told you) and the other one is the Middlesex Bank. Both have good rates and both have a good supply of mortgage money. So, here is what you do:

-Doug, please! this time things are not as easy as they look. This time I am here with the whole family. And, on top of that, the movers have indicated that the household stuff will arrive either tonight or tomorrow morning. So we just have to finalize the trans- action today." I said with some desperation.

-Okay, here, take all the papers and see first the 5-cents Bank. If you have any problem, call back here. Where are you staying?

-In the Drum Hill Motel, where you took me last time. But all we have is a double room, they call it, but it is really one room with two double beds.

-Right, these are the facts of life. Anyway get moving, we'll take care of you, he said encouragingly.

I went downtown Lowell with the papers and met the top loan officer. He took my application and asked if I had an attorney. I asked in return: why? I can read the deed. Then I enumerated my credentials: Mr. Kingsly, I am an engineer and a land surveyor. I was appointed assistant professor in the Civil Engineering Department of the Lowell Technological Institute this past August. I am here to start the academic year tomorrow; I have brought with me some of the Convertible Bonds

I own. I am sure we can use them as additional collateral to the house itself, which will be mortgaged. I am sure the bank will look at me as a man of substance, and there is no doubt on my mind that I qualify for the loan," I pleaded. "But time is of the essence. My household furnishing will arrive latest tomorrow, and we just have to move that into the house, or it will be put into storage; Then we have to stay at the Motel until we can close on the sale. Then we have to move the furnishing, and the contents too, over into the house. So what do you say?"

-Well, all I can say is that we have a problem case on our hands," he said with some genuine concern. "But I must say that you have totally convinced me … you see, you walked in here doing all the right things, when someone is in a totally new environment. You introduced yourself, enumerated your credentials, which, by the way are really considerable, I must say; Then 'you offered additional collateral …so, what can I say? I am totally impressed, and …let me assure you that I personally will look after it that this matter will get to a speedy conclusion."

-Actually, Mr. Kingsly, all I need in a great hurry is a letter of commitment, that I can take to the Realtor, and he has arranged with the developer that he will let us move in if he has that", I said trying to diminish the magnitude of the problem at hand.

-Oh, yah, I recall you said that you have no lawyer, … who is the Realtor involved?"

-It is Doug Johnson, from Chelmsford." I said, and it sounded like a magic mantra to Mr. Kingsly because he called in his secretary and told her to type up a letter of commitment to me; then instructed me to follow Mrs. Silva, who will type up the letter and I can take that right with me. I had the feeling that our luck has just turned back in the right direction again.

When I returned to the Realty, Doug was already out and I was told to leave the letter at his desk so he could find it at his return. Then I drove back to the Motel, which was our temporary headquarter. Decision was reached. We went to a Chinese restaurant just around the rotary, for a family lunch. After that I navigated the entire ensemble to the new house. We could not go inside because we still did not have the keys. But we walked all around it, peeked in every conceivable (and reachable) window, and the front door and the rear door from the deck. All we could see was the shiny floors, the freshly painted walls, and some of the cabinets in the kitchen.

The driveway was paved, unlike the last time I saw it. Two large oak trees were right at the corner of the driveway entrance, so close to one another that they looked like twins. I called them 'twin oaks'. The stone wall at the street out front, was kind of beat-up, there, I envisioned already an upcoming project, but that must wait till next year. This fall's schedule was overloaded already, too many things were planned. Also, I had to wait and see how busy my schedule will be at the Institute. My thoughts were way ahead of present matters.

On the way back to the motel we stopped by at the realty and found Doug back at his base. He was introduced to the family members, which calmed the ruffled moods. Then he rapidly filled in the details of the past few hours. Number one: the contractor's attorney would not let him surrender the keys to us, and allow us to move into the house before the passing. The papers could be ready by Thursday, or maybe Friday, to be signed. They also checked with the bank and found out that the mortgage money would be available after the Board's Thursday meeting, thus: we are actually in very good shape by all accounts, you will own the house on Friday, after the passing", he concluded his report. Then I asked him:

-Doug, do you know the joke about the recently widowed Italian guy at his wife's funeral reception"? I asked him.

-No, I really don't specialize in ethnic jokes, I am sorry".

-That's Okay, I said, "anyway, it is not really a dirty joke, but considering all the ladies present let me just concentrate on the punch line: "but what about tonight"?

-Oh, yah, I see what you are getting at. So, for all practical purposes, and, for the next couple of days, you will need something more 'homey' is that it"?

-Yes, that is definitely one part of it. Now, for the second, if our household stuff arrives tomorrow, what are we going to do with it? where is it going to be put? Can't we at least put it in the garage"? I asked him again.

-Well, Gabor, I think you haven't got enough problems right now that is why you are foreshadowing new ones. Let's cross each bridge as we get to it, all right? If the mover is here tomorrow, we will deal with that situation at that time. But let's get you a more spacious accommodation for the next few days", he said very confidently. "Here is what you do: keep driving north on Route 3-A into South Nashua (about 5-miles from your motel at the Rotary) and as you cross the line into New Hampshire proceed about another mile and on your right you will see the Hannah

Dustin Motel's sign. Drive right to the office, and ask for an 'efficiency' unit, and do it on the double. I am going to phone them while you will be on your way. Then, if you got one that's good enough, then you come back and check-out of the Drum Hill, Kapish? Now don't waste more time, good by".

-Thanks Doug! I stepped forward and stretched my hand out towards him; he grabbed it and we both squeezed on it. Then I again had it confirmed, that the real estate man is a slightly different breed of human being. You just about hade to be born for it.

We piled into the wagon and did exactly how Doug was explaining the way. At the 'Hannah Dustin' we were in for our first real pleasant surprise. The place was immaculate compared to some of the ones we saw so far; a roomy little flat all on one floor, a kitchenette, with more cabinet space than we anticipated to use, and a well kept little back yard with our own barbecue set-up at a handy distance from the rear door. The only trouble was, when we learned that these 'efficiencies' are on a weekly rental. It didn't matter, it just simply didn't matter, we took it on the spot, and did it perhaps too grabby, but not if you consider, that you were away from home for the fifth day; it wouldn't matter to you or anyone.

We moved over to the Hannah Dustin the same afternoon. The kids just loved it. They could go out and have fun in the yard; also, they wasted no time to check out the swimming pool. While they did so, I surveyed the possibility to start a fire for our first barbecue in New England. Somehow I felt right 'at home' what ever that meant here under these, knowingly temporary circumstances, and if I, so far, was under the impression, that the Midwest was the region where barbecue was invented, I was in for some surprise as we were resuming our New England stay.

Next morning, Wednesday, 3-rd of September all of a sudden, became busy for all of us. Maria took the two older kids to the Chelmsford Public School to register for the school year. It turned out to be a more complicated procedure than they expected. Susanna had to register at the elementary school in the precinct where our new home belonged territorially. Andy, on the other hand had to register at the McFarland School.

I reported to the Trustees' Room in Comnock Hall where president Lydon introduced the new faculty to the Trustees after which a brief reception followed. Here I met the other addition to the Civil Engineering faculty: a very young, straight out of grad. school man from MIT. Handsome, almost to the point of dashing, nevertheless sort of quiet, kind of on the modest side, which quality made him even more attractive to any stranger.

His area of expertise was structures, at the time this was selected as major study area by most of the civil engineering seniors. Computer applications, the other most fashionable major, was not an offered field for civil engineering students. There were several computer courses offered by the electrical engineering department for those students attracted by computers. Years later a computer science department was started mainly by mathematics faculty members.

Gifford did the introduction of the new faculty members hired for the civil engineers, ex officio, since he was also the civil department head. The other department heads in turn introduced their new members. After each short introduction by the department head, the member was expected to say a few words about himself, and his endeavors, his intra and, occasionally, extra-curricular pursuits. This was my very first public appearance -and speech!- in which I emphasized the practical aspects I was intending to convey to my pupils. My foreign accent did not bring more than the expected –mild shock- to the audience. I was confident though that everyone present in the trustee's room was able to understand me. What I lacked in my linguistic attribute I was trying to make up by my poise. In my own short introduction I put most of the emphasis on my considerable practical experience. And, I proudly announced that I will be opening my private consulting practice just as soon as I obtain my professional registration from the State Board.

After the ceremonies the buffet was opened for a light lunch, Following this the people began to mingle and gradually drift off, although there was a 'short' orientation session scheduled for the afternoon. I didn't feel I would get much out of this program, after all, I had my own private show in the summer with Giff (as I soon learned he was being called; his closer friends, however, had a more endearing version of that). I, myself was only beginning to address him Giff when he started calling me Gabor. He came to me and said he was pleased by both of our performances and asked me if we have managed to move into the house. I said no, we will pass papers on Friday, but we haven't got our furniture yet. The movers promised it for today. He seemed a bit concerned and asked where we are staying, and he took a mental note of that.

I was eager to get away as soon as I could because I had to do some follow-up on our furniture shipment. First I drove to the house in Chelmsford. I found our neighbor at home, so I introduced myself, putting emphasis on my being their 'new neighbor'. Then I asked if they saw a mover, a big Mayflower van snooping, or wondering about earlier today, but she couldn't say. She made some remarks about how she "loved" my accent which she wouldn't dare guessing where it was from. I consoled her that most people had great difficulty placing it, because we kids grew up in a bilingual family thus it is sort of a mixture right there.

-Oh, yah, but where do you come from? she asked curiously.

-From Cleveland, I answered, "we are really Midwesterners".

-Oh, I understand, but that is not what I meant" she began to explain. "You see our name is Barrisano, my husband's family came from Italy, but he attended school here, so he has no foreign accent, ... now, you see what I was trying to find out, was where you came from before that …"?

-Mrs. Barrisano, that is really a long story, because I could tell you simply: from Canada, but that would lead to further confusion, and now I have to hunt down our movers, because they probably got so frustrated, that they may just unload everything onto the driveway.

-Well, if you have other things to do, you can leave a key with me for the garage, or the house, and I let them unload it right into the house" she said encouragingly.

-Mrs. Barrisano, I am really grateful for all you are trying to do for us, but …you see … we don't own the house just yet, therefore I don't have a key" and it appeared to me for an instance that I have lost her. So I went on: "You, see, we'll be passing on the deal on Friday, then we will have the key and, of course, we can move in, but in the meantime, the furniture will have to be put into storage. So, you would do us a great big favor if you would tell the mover, if he gets here, to call the Hannah Dustin Motel, unit 12 where we are staying. Here is the number"…

-Oh, we know the Hannah Dustin, it is in South Nashua …

-So, Mrs. Barrisano, I now have to find out where the mover is and more importantly, when is he going to get here", I said impatiently, then handed her my last business card with the address of the firm in

Cleveland, "and this is the correct spelling of my name and thank you very, very much".

Then I went on my wild goose chase, Fist stop: who else? our friend, Doug, the Realtor. With him we had an abbreviated version of a strategic council meeting. He pointed out that at this point, being already past 4-PM, chances are the movers will not come today any more. Then, for tomorrow, if they will show up, we shall direct them to our large garage in Westford, where we will be moving in October. They are still working on the remodeling, but there is ample room in the garage, and … actually, it would be only for a couple of days … right? I understand that your passing is scheduled for this Friday, so, you can start moving everything over to your house over the weekend.

"So, Gabor, why don't you just go home, relax, and enjoy your pool, maybe with a tall glass of 'Pina Colada' in your hand. Look what a gorgeous weather we are having, just do as I said".

-Doug, you seem like a multi talented guy, don't you, by any chance have a psychiatric nurse's training on top of all other things a real estate man is expected of"? I think your free advice was even medically correct" I said, saluted, made an about face and walked out.

At home, or rather the motel, I started reporting to Maria the entire day's happenings: at the Trustee's room, Giff, and his concerns, etc. including my encounter with our neighbor lady.

-How was she'? was she nice",? was her first question.

-Well, … sure, she was very kind, offered to watch out for the Mayflower van. If and when it arrives she will tell the driver to call here".

-Yah, but, you know I still can't find the place on my own".

-But my pal, I am going to give you a street map of the town, that I'd just picked up for us from Doug", I said. "But first let me obey Doug's instructions. Where will I find my swimming trunk"?

She grabbed it from one of the suitcases and handed it to me, "and now, I said "we have to find some frozen Pina Colada mix. You see, my dear, these were the orders".

-I really don't like the way these movers are handling our shipment", she said. "What if something happened to our stuff on the road? Then we may never get it".

-Oh, darling, you really know how to make everybody worry" I said. "Actually, …well, …look at the bright side. The later they arrive, the closer we get to the passing day, which as it stands at the moment, is going to be on Friday, …I would be tickled to death if they would arrive on Friday; then we could have them move everything right in, everything, right into the appropriate rooms … and we never would have to move twice … you know what I mean"?

We didn't have the Pina Colada mix. But later on in the evening we found the best supermarkets in the area, and began to sample their offerings and prices. The food was not very much more expensive than in the Midwest. Then came a very pleasant surprise: someone told me in the morning that New Hampshire is the Tax Haven which expands onto the liquors as well, which we will find considerably less expensive than elsewhere. And he was right. The liquor store prices were a great surprise.

Andy and Susie had to be driven to school every morning. There was no school bus service from Nashua, being over the state border. Maria already knew the way to the Chelmsford center schools, so she drove them, and also picked them up. It was supposed to be only for two more days, tomorrow and Friday, … or so we thought.

Later in the evening Maria asked me if I was the only foreigner among the new faculty. I told her that it seemed like I was, but I definitely was now the only foreigner in the Civil Engineering Department. "What about colored", she asked, "any of those"?
-Well, I have not seen any today, that's all I can say, but, listen to this: tomorrow will be registration day in the new gymnasium, and Giff told us that we, the new ones will not have to be there, so that will give me the free time trying to track down the movers; then, on Friday the old faculty puts up a big barbecue specifically for the new faculty not too far from here, some place in Tyngsboro, on a golf course/country club sort of a place. And it will start at or after 10 in the morning. Now, this is something I definitely have to attend, but … I am not sure if spouses and kids are also invited, this I could not make out very clearly … but, most likely not, because kids are supposed to be in school or what? anyway, …we'll cross that bridge when we get there as the saying goes. Tomorrow is another day, so let's get some sleep.

Thursday my first stop was at the realty again. Doug's wife came in, evidently after she dropped off their oldest boy at the Westford Elementary. The ladies of Doug's father's Travel Agency introduced me to her and said: "this is Gabor, he seems to be working here lately"…

-Oh, I heard so much about you from Doug, It's so nice to meet you…So you will be working with my cousin Geoffry" she said. "They are all excited to have you on board with his firm".

-Well, it seems that I will have to remind him that my primary obligation is teaching at the 'Tech' but, one of these days I may have some time on my hand to call him up, but not just now; my immediate concern is to find out about the Mayflower movers, and of what happened to our furniture".

-Doug should be in shortly, I am sure" she said, "he will help you with that problem too".

He didn't come in shortly. In the meantime, however, I studied the Yellow Pages and found two Mayflower's warehouses close by, one in Nashua, the other in Billerica. I called the latter, since that is in the State of the shipment's destination. The woman at the other end persuaded me to call the company's 'tracing center' which is located in Minneapolis, they can trace, and hopefully find, any shipment that is on its way to its destination. Also that they will be open for business shortly, at 8-AM 'Central Time', and make sure you have your 'bill of lading' in front of you because they will ask you all sorts of data that is on the bill".

I called a few minutes after 9:00 AM, our time. Sure enough, they wanted to know all sorts of numbers, the point of origin and destination, dates, etc. etc. She needed a local number where she can call back. I gave her the number of the realty, and waited. And waited some more.

I then began to study the various charts, photographs, bulletins on the board where the properties are displayed along with their asking prices. As a result I had to conclude that we really got a good deal on our house. It was in a good location, easy access to major routes, yet, a mere spit from the center of town. I was at a disadvantage, though, when the descriptions named localities totally unknown to me.

Then I studied the map; Memorized a couple of possible routes to Lowell Tech. But I did that from our new place, on Golden Cove Road in anticipation that we will be there latest at the end of the week. This was wishful thinking, as it turned out.

When Doug came in, he was not surprised to see me sitting at a side table, one of his sales associate's, which was unoccupied.

-Hi Gabor, say, you are a surveyor aren't you", he asked, but it sounded more like a statement. "Do you want a job-with our realty"? We have a couple of small developers, who want us to get into promotional stuff, and you know, some of the places they are buying, have only been surveyed in the last century. They need to be surveyed and subdivided", then he was staring at me.

-Come on Doug, you know I am not even registered yet, I can't legally do any of that stuff", I said. "Can't you wait a little"?

-No Gabor, we can't, we are in a mini-boom, you must have noticed some of it's signs when you came down in the summer", he said which reminded me of all those developments we visited. "You know, I was talking with Geoffry the other day" he continued, "and he relayed to me that one of the first order of business should be of your getting registered. Evidently he has lined-up more work then you can handle", he said while he was wagging his head.

-Well, if you ask me, I think that is a mistake, who is going to do them, I mean working on them"? I asked the rhetorical question. "But, don't get me wrong, I think it's absolutely essential and … wonderful to have work lined-up waiting for you, but again … you better be prepared to deliver! Deliver, -that's the key word" I said "if you want to succeed".

-Of course, you got it right", he said, "but don't you want to get to know the status of your loan application? Let me call-up the VP at the bank and ask him".

He called up the bank and talked with the secretary. It took him some time before he was satisfied with the information she gave him. Then he hung-up and turned to me: "Gabor, the board is in meeting right now, and all I could get out of her is that your loan is on the list of those being 'recommended' for approval. So, you see… it is as good as done. I'd say, you and I, better plan on passing tomorrow, so that *you* can move into your house". Then after a short pause he said: "Gabor, your mover is not calling, and … since we were put on the waiting end of the game by them, we will wait, and wait some more, but only until tomorrow. Then we'll swing into action", he said. Again after a short pause: "so when would you like to schedule the passing"?

-Doug, best would be early afternoon, and I tell you why, … there is a great big barbecue scheduled by the old faculty for the new faculty on the grounds of some golf course in Tyngsboro and I surely have to be there. I think I am in no position to decline anything like this, what's more, I think it would be awfully rude".

-Yah, sure, you stuff your face with the burgers, drink the obligatory half dozen cans of Budweiser, shoot the breeze with the guys, chat up

54

their wives, see which one is frustrated enough to start an affair with you ... you know the usual stuff ... new man around the block, you know what I mean"?

-Doug, you can't be serious, is that the 'usual' behavior? but wait just a minute, as far as I know this is not a family event, it supposed to be faculty, and the students doing the cooking for their professors ...this is how I understood", I said with some uncertainty in my voice.

-Of course I am not serious, you shouldn't be either, but you will find out about it tomorrow, don't worry, just don't worry, more yet: never worry, Okay"?

-Okay Doug, if you say so; but one more thing: the VP asked me Tuesday if I have an attorney, then when I said I don't, he asked me who my Realtor was, and I told him it is you; So, are you going to represent me there tomorrow?

-Look Gabor, I know the bank's attorney, and I will represent not really you, but the seller-developer. But I suggest you just represent yourself, why on earth have so many attorneys? remember this: the less attorneys, the better, the smoother things go".

Front &
Side

Side &
Rear

The Chelmsford House

Chapter Four
(Digging in.)

-Can you please tell me how do I get to the Tyngsboro Golf Course",? I asked the man behind the counter in the variety store at the East end of the 'Tyngsboro Bridge', the most conspicuous land- mark in the vicinity. It certainly was, at the time, still is.

-You are practically there", he said, "Follow route 113 for not quite a half a mile and it's on your left, you can't miss it", the fellow said. This phrase: you can't miss it, became a signature New England expression, as I learned later on.

I turned in on a driveway that looked like leading to a great green expanse, and soon enough I saw some benches, a roofed shelter and a bunch of youngsters were busying themselves with starting fires, (some already roaring), students picking up big boxes filled with hamburger patties. Then two big barrels filled halfway with ice was dragged by two kids into the shade of the shelter. Cases of Budweiser's were being packed into it.

I slowed to a virtual stop and looked around, trying to find where we were supposed to park. Then a kid ran to my car and asked:

"Oh, you are from Ohio'? gee, you must have come a long way".

-You're not kidding, I have, …really! and now that I am here I want to find a shady parking place! You think you can help me with that'"?

-What are you, a new professor"? or something"…

-Look, all I can promise you now that I will be a good professor, I said, "I can not promise you that I will be **your** professor, only if, you will promise that you will be a diligent civil engineer. Got it"?

-Oh, …yah, I guess so" he said, scratching his head, "Trouble is,…I am not a C.E., I am an electrical" he said with a cloud over his face.

-Who's trouble you think that is, yours or mine"? I asked him, which seemed further to confuse him … "Okay kid, I am not about to torture you with more questions, why don't you just say: look prof: this is not the time or the place to ask all these questions, save those for the classroom, right "? "Now what about that parking in the shade"? I tried summing it up.

-Actually there is not much shade around here, this is a golf course, ….hey, you must be a picky prof", he concluded, then pointed towards the row of cars at the edge of the grassy field.

I drove to where he was pointing and parked next to the last car in the row. By then a fellow about my age was approaching me.

-I think you are our new transportation man, is that right"? he asked, "my name is Dan Lepine" he said, I teach statics to the sophomores.

-Now, I am going to give you an earful: my name is Gabor Szikszay-Farkas" I said, "you must have heard it already lately, I am indeed the transportation man, as you put it".

-Well, come on, let's meet the other guys", he said and started towards the shelter, the only solid shade around. He was steering me towards Herm Shea, who offered his hand from the comfty seat he was sitting in and immediately asked; "what's your pleasure Gabe? It really doesn't matter here, because all you can have is Bud", he said. I was suddenly taken aback, which I was trying not to show. Then I was searching my memory, like mad, trying to find where he could have gotten this name, which I have not heard once, since I got to New England. I was trying to play it cool, and was trying to hide my slight annoyance, when he simply said:

-Herm, simple enough, eh? Herm Shea in full", he said and all of a sudden a picture that I stored in my mind incarnated in front of me; Did I see him before? Where was it? In a flash it hit me: Sure, Geoffry Dorfman drew that picture for me at the Airport Hilton's bar that night in July. But something was missing, … but what? And then, …oh, yah: Herm didn't sport his pipe. That's it! I would still have put my bet on him if I had been asked to guess which one here was Herm Shea.

-Bill Hapkins! … said the distinguished looking tall, middle aged fellow sitting next to Herm, and offered his hand for a shake. "Is that what you want us to call you, what Herm just called you, Gabe? That is short for Gabor, or Gabriel, isn't it? Herm is good with names, ... anyway welcome aboard".

-Indeed, it is, that's what my colleagues used to call me, ... in Akron, that is" I said still kind of surprised.

It looked like they already had a burger on the bun, just finishing up. Bill then called over one of the seniors, whom he knew by his name, and the kid asked me what I would like to have.

-I think I just have what the rest of the gang had" I told him "but say, can you toast that bun on both sides for me please"?

-Sure, no problem", he said, "we also have some relish or mustard, would you want some? Sullivan, Joe Sullivan is my name, we have two of them in this class, the other one is my brother, Bob", he was finishing his introduction.

-Hold the relish Joe, that is usually on the sweet side, for me it is, ...I can't stand it, but if I could have some onions ... and mustard, since you offered it ... Okay? please", I told him.

-No problem" he repeated it again and rushed over to the grill, where he uttered his instructions to his helper. Another New England signature expression: 'No problem', it is being routinely used instead of a simple 'your welcome'. All this interrupted our introductions, but there was no rush, no hurried atmosphere, so we just went on with it.

-Gampanelli, ... he said, with his smile, while I again mumbled my name, which the young fellow, the youngest in the C.E. faculty acknowledged, "we met already before at the Trustee's introduction", he said, "so if you call me Dario, I shall call you Gabe, is that Okay"?

-Sure thing, oh, here comes my burger, ... thank you", I said to the chef's helper when he handed me my burger on the toasted bun.

-Are you our new structures prof"? he asked me handing me the burger on the paper plate, with some potato chips.

-I am sorry to disappoint you, but I am not much good at structures, but if you happened to need help in just about anything else, I'd be glad to help you out", I said, then pointed to Dario: "he is your new structures prof, straight out of the mint, he will make you suffer not me", and I turned him towards Dario.

-I am glad to see that you are friendly with the kids, Gabe", said Herm, "did they like you at Akron? I would have guessed that they did", he said. While I was staring at him in disbelief he went on: "You perhaps figured, that Giff told me a few things about your difficulties there".

-Herm, I think they all liked me. But there was a strange affinity between us, more pronounced with the foreign students, for some obscure reason; there were quite a few foreign students there, mostly from Southern Europe and the Middle East. A Greek student came for office consultation almost on a daily basis. At the end of the last semester he brought me a Greek artistic plate, the kind you hang on the wall, you know, showing the Acropolis, … He spoke acceptable German, picked it up under the German occupation as a young kid".

-Gabe, this is quite normal, you would expect something like that" he said, "it must be the culture, they were sensing the common cultural background" he said. "With the American kids you may find a stiffness towards your cultural background".

-Do you really think that's behind it Herm? Well, I am not so sure, … There were these two brothers from Saudi Arabia, both civil engineering majors. They were from the Middle East, there was really no common cultural base, and they were crazy about me. They came to help me with my field work on Saturdays, … I wanted to pay them just like any other helpers, … they told me I would offend them if I try to pay them, … I had student field helpers lined up who wanted to do some practical work. I quickly screened out the ones who were useable, some even quite good. And these two kids: when they learned that my contract was not renewed in 1967, for weeks, they were crushed, nearly devastated, … Now, …they were Arabs, Moslems to boot, …no cultural base to speak of, right? they were the ones who arranged a meeting for me with the dean of the engineering college when he came to Washington, to recruit faculty for the new Riyadh University. One of them: 'Taj', flew down to Washington with me to be my interpreter - and reference- in case we needed one, as it turned out. I ask you: what was there in common with these two kids? Certainly not culture" I asked, but Herm didn't answer.

-For one thing", I continued, "we both had foreign accents! Do you think that is enough an explanation for the 'affinity' I was talking about"?

Herm has become known, later on, as the 'philosopher', he certainly was one. After a while, since I was still gazing at him, he said: "Gabe, I think you got me, I don't know! I really don't know!"

I was finishing my second Bud, way short of the obligatory six-pack prescribed by Doug, the Realtor the day before, and it was already half past noon. I realized that I had to leave, if I wanted to get to the Bank by I-PM. There was the passing coming up that I could ill afford to miss or even be late at.

* _ _ _ * _ _ _ *

-Good evening Gabor, said Doug as I walked into the conference room of the Lowell 5-cents Bank. I looked at my watch, it was about 8 minutes after l:00 PM. Then I turned and started out of the room.

-Oh, I am so sorry", I said, "this must be another passing that is scheduled for the evening" I said, "I have to find the one that I was scheduled for one PM…"

-Gabor, you son of a gun, he interrupted me, "I can't even joke with you any more? I bet you did not follow my advice regarding the picnic. How many cans did you pour down? you're still not relaxed, you're up-tight", he said scolding me. "Come on, I want you to meet attorney Halloran, he is the Bank's attorney" he said.

-Professor, I heard about you, …Richard Halloran", … and we shook hands. "As you know I will represent the Lowell 5-cents Bank. Do you have your wife, Maria with you, or is she coming later to sign the mortgage deed"? he asked.

-I was unaware that she must be here to sign it too", I said, turning to Doug: "Why didn't you tell me she will have to come with me? You want me to call her to come down here, now"?

-Well, Professor Szikszay-Farkas" attorney Halloran turned to me sort of 'announcing: "you were so confident that you can 'represent yourself', therefore you didn't bring an attorney with you, did you"?

-Attorney Halloran, I had all my confidence in the Bank's lawyer! I simply knew that there can not be any slip-ups, therefore I am safe to rely on the bank's attorney, in this case: yourself! But, … may I hire you hereby to represent me"?

-Professor! the deed is made out in both your and your wife's name, therefore, …I could be hired only if I will represent the both of you … and in that case …I may be found in conflict of interest"… and he waited for a reply.

-Well, I certainly want no conflicts! But, what I was going to suggest, was, that after we are through with the transfer of the deed, I will take the Mortgage Deed with me home, …or rather to the motel that we still call home, …have Maria sign it next to my signature, and bring it back to your office Monday morning. Then, since you Mr. Halloran, as the bank's attorney, are still holding the 10-K 'Automatic Sprinkler' convertible bonds, that I left with Mr. Kingsley, which as of today are worth at least

16,000 dollars, I would say your client, the 5-cents Bank, is better than adequately protected with collateral,… Am I right"?

-Gabor, get with it! said Doug almost shouting, "there are no enemies here! We certainly are not your enemies. Didn't I tell you before to loosen up, get rid of the tightness, in other words; r-e-1-a-x! Don't you see that Attorney Halloran is playing with you? …So, don't try to be a legal expert, just stay on your half of the playing field: which is surveying and engineering… stick with it! We here will take care of the rest. Okay"?

-Okay, so here I am, humbling myself, and I do whatever is necessary to have this deal go through," …as long as I can pick up the keys tonight for the house" I said and was waiting for their reaction. It was Attorney Halloran who then took over the tenor.

-Professor; … my wife is also a professor at Lowell Tech, she is in the Department of Mathematics. So, … as such, I am now dealing with my wife's colleague! Now, … let's go over these papers, so we could all go home afterwards, Okay"?

With that he started to shove the single most important paper: the mortgage deed in front of me to sign, -in duplicate-, which I did, and gave me the original to take with me. After that, he handed two checks to Doug, and a copy of the deed to me, and said that he will record the "original" with the Registry Monday, when I bring back the mortgage deed signed by Maria. Doug then handed me two sets of keys to the house and with this, it was all over; At least for now. I shook hands with both of them, and … starry eyed, I started to the door. I looked at my watch: it was not quite 1:30 PM.

I drove right to the house from there. Tried all the keys to all the doors; They all worked. The garage door was a little tight, though. The deck at the rear of the house was rather on the small side, but, it was still a deck, after all, to sit and enjoy the outdoors, and … of course, …have barbecues … in good weather that is, … hey, why only in good weather? I asked myself. We could put a corrugated fiberglass roof over it, and …then we can have barbecues even if it rains. Now, there … another project. Stop that! I told myself.

I went over to the Barrisano's. She was in the middle of picking tomatoes, …vine ripened tomatoes. They even looked delicious.

-Good afternoon, Mrs. Barrisano, I said, "aren't they beauties" I asked, "not like the ones you get from the store", I said trying to warm up the atmosphere around us, "I have news for you: now we are really neighbors, … I mean officially".

-I was wondering if you will ever show up … but do you realize that your mover didn't show up either? We were totally puzzled, what happened? We thought you have changed your mind and didn't want to buy the house after all".

-No, I can assure you that we now own the house, since just about 1:30 PM, this afternoon; We have just passed papers".

-Well then, hi neighbor", she said … and, after wiping her hand stretched it towards me. "Your grass is coming pretty well, look, … the man from the developer was here twice to water it", she said and pointed towards the back yard, "that side gets more of the sun"…

-Thank you Mrs. Barrisano, I now really have to go find our shipment. I can't even guess what could have happen to it" I said and with that I got into my buggy and drove out to Nashua, the motel.

As I entered the driveway I noticed the whole family at, and in the pool. So I stepped up to Maria, who was just feeding Jr. and dangled the house keys on my middle finger. "We could move in now, if we had anything to move in" I said, "did they call from the movers"? I asked Maria, while kissing both her and Jr.

-No such luck, she said, "we better renew our stay at the office today, they asked if we are going to stay another week" she said. "Just watch, the minute we renew our lease here, the movers will be coming, may be even tomorrow".

-To me this sounds like wishful thinking, but I have my doubts. Now, I better call their number there at the 'tracing center'. Then I started to our unit.

I again talked to the clerk, giving her the particulars about the shipment. She still did not find it. I told her that Monday morning our attorney will call and then we can no longer settle this matter amicably, we are here in a motel, crammed up with the family for the second week now, and they better find that shipment on the double, or we will sue for everything, all the damages, even the motel rent, and attorney's fees".

Then all of a sudden I recalled Doug's admonition about me being up-tight, no relaxing … so I went to the fridge, got some tea-ice cubes into a glass, and poured an unmeasured amount of the good old Ronrico, topped it off with a generous amount of Stock Sweet Vermouth, took my shirt off, my slacks too, changed into my swimming trunk and headed out to the pool. What a life, … nothing but fights, … always fighting, to stand-up for yourself, never ever give-in, or you're doomed. Took deep slugs from the drink, stepped in the pool, and in no time I began to relax.

------*

The first general faculty meeting took place Monday in one of the smaller auditoriums, capable of seating 250 plus participants. It was a formal event as much as it could be in a rather mixed body representing the four major - or traditional - as well as the more up-to-date engineering fields. These were relative newcomers, such as Plastics and Nuclear engineering. Then, as this was a general faculty meeting, meaning the 'Engineering Sciences Division' it was chaired by the Provost, who always reminded me of Dean Hardy at the University of Alberta, and at the panel was sitting our Division Chairman: Al Gifford.

In view of the fact that he was assuming the responsibilities of civil engineering department head as well, our department was often looked at as 'a headless beast' by the others, which of course, was not the case. In reality Giff (as I will be referring to him most of the time in the future) was running the department affairs with an iron fist, keeping it on its **traditional course**.

His second in command was Herm Shea, who actually was running the department on a day to day basis. Next room to his office was located the department office, which was the 'department's secretary's office' as well.

It was sort of reminiscing for me to observe this meeting with its ceremonial qualities, which I saw in Budapest, at certain occasions, whenever my father took me to the meeting of the faculty of Natural Sciences at that university.

The provost took a roll call of the new additions to each department, and as the new member was called by his/her name, he or she obliged to stand up. Then each department head repeated essentially the same introductory speech he did on the first day in the Trustee's room, but this time for the benefit of the entire faculty. When Giff came to the part where he introduced me, he made it a point to pronounce my name as correctly as possible for the faculty members' benefit. The new members were standing until the last of the introduction was concluded at which time the old faculty was applauding in unison. Then we all became seated.

While the provost conducted his State of the Institute speech whispers began to erupt here and there in the auditorium, that actually served as a reminder to get it over with as soon as practicable. At one point the gentleman behind me was whispering into my ears, asking if I was by any chance a relative of a professor Jozsef Szikszay-Farkas, who is regarded here as the Father of Meteorology, who, to his knowledge, is also a Hungarian. I could hardly believe my ears, and said:

-Yes, indeed, he is also **my** father", I whispered back only slightly turning my head. I then, still not knowing who he was, stopped the unruly conversation. When he saw my determined conformist attitude, all he whispered was asking me if he could see me after the meeting. I again nodded with my head inconspicuously.

As soon as the faculty was dismissed both of us were walking out of the pews so as not to miss each other. Out in the hall he moved his arm towards me: "I am professor Curtis," he said, looking straight in my eyes. As he was sensing my quandary, he quickly added: "I am head of Meteorology, in the Earth Sciences Department". There, I wasn't quite sure if I was sensing an ever so slight English accent. "I am familiar with your father's works" he went on.

-Which ones? I asked, "the ones before the fifties, or the Textbooks, which are the more recent ones"?

-Well, now, you have put me on the spot, Mr. Szikszay-Farkas, oh, I am sorry, Professor Szikszay-Farkas ... a slip of the tong, really".

-Well, I was not intending to do that; but, you know, there is a slight difference between the two categories" I was trying to set the records straight. "You see, in Europe he became known mostly by his global studies, the 'big picture' so to speak. These were the defining works, this put him on the palette of the scientific community". I said, and watched his intense attention. "I myself am not too familiar, in details, with these works, ... The more recent ones, done under this system, you know, the communists ...were mostly text books, some research result spurted stuff, ...like Microclimate, that sort of things, were done while he was already promoted to full professorship, and director of the Meteorological Institute", with this I concluded my clarification, fearful that it went overboard.

-You know, we actually don't know all that much", he said," the ones you mentioned, we have some of his textbooks from the translations clearinghouse, but I think that's about all. We have not heard anything at all from him since the early fifties. Why is that? What happened"?

-Gee, now you have put me on the spot, Professor Curtis" I said, kind of apologetically, "That is rather a long, very long story, and a very gloomy one I am afraid".

-Well, then let me invite you to the cafeteria, where you can take your time telling me all about it".

We walked the short distance to the basement of the dorm next to the library, which at that time was nearing completion. Then as we sat down with our coffee, he sensed that I may be reluctant to talk if we would have unwanted company, he picked a small table, which could accommodate only the two of us.

-Well I don't really know where exactly to begin"… I said trying to put together a comprehensive, yet as brief as possible a report for him; "Actually it began way back after the War. As I am sure you know, in 1945, while Hungary was already occupied by the Soviet forces, the communist underground jumped above-ground at the wink of the eye and took over virtually all internal affairs in the country. It had no opposition of any kind in the wake of the Soviet tanks on the ground. One of the communist provisory government's first order of business was to confiscate all capital, that is to say: income producing investments: land, factories, commercial establishments, banks, etc. etc. which, of course, brought the economy to a screeching halt, over and above what the war did to it already".

-Was your family affected by this move in any way" he asked.

-I am afraid this is getting too long and I am not making much of a progress. I will try to speed it up. My father was a big land owner, we had a mixed farm: dairy-, wool-, orchard and vineyard and timber; 1200 acres in all; Wine being one of the main product line, certainly the most lucrative one.

-Taking all these production entities into state ownership, was however, only the tip of the iceberg; along with this came the actualization of Lenin's dogma: this layer of the people: the bourgeoisie, had to be destroyed. They became enemy number one, unless, they show willingness to change, to adopt to 'democratic' ideas. My father was cleared by the various screening committees, since he had lined-up proof of collaborating with the underground and was instrumental in hiding and arranging to save Jews during the most bloody Nazi period in 1944 till the end of the war. Based on these testimonies one of the committees brought a resolution (in writing) which excluded 50 acres from the confiscation, and entitled him for this much land ownership. But, as it turned out later, this move perpetuated his belonging to the 'enemy' class.

During these times came his promotion too. He organized the 'chair' of Meteorology within the University, and the Institute, of which he became the director. Even after the total communist party takeover of the government, (1949) he was still a high flyer, with research grants, and the use of much of the University's experimental farms. This was the 'real' birth of 'Microclimate'. I was one of his research assistants, did much of the field observations while still in Junior and Senior High. At that time we were still hoping to get our farm back someday, when the regime collapses. He set high hopes to this. I was the 'farm boy designate' in our family. After a sip of coffee I continued:

-It was through his influential connections that we, the three kids, all were admitted to the university.

-Professor Szikszay-Farkas I enjoy immensely your description of 'history' –because, let's face it, this is history- but are we getting to the gruel part"?

-We are almost there; towards the end of 1952, after the textbook era, he was eyed by the 'Party' (him being fiercely independent all along) and was called in to party headquarters. He was put to the final test: The activist painted a picture in no uncertain terms: he is considered being 'the enemy' until death, he was told; but, …but, … there are many in his shoes, who cooperate, and find life better than tolerable, some indeed privileged, as opposed to the majority of the population. So, he is being picked (by the Party) to become the dean of the College of Natural Sciences. He is hereby given 48-hours of deliberation, which must follow by either a yes, or a no answer. (Mandatory Communist Party membership included.)

- Extremely politely, he declined. There began his doom. An agent 'provocateur' was planted on him, who, after much profiling managed to fetch an earlier acquaintance of his, who one afternoon in the restaurant at lunch, sold him four 20-Frank ('Napoleon') gold coins, thereby, 'saving him from starvation', as he told my father. Needless to say, next morning in the wee hours the secret police [AVO] drove out to our villa, grabbed him out of bed, and took him in 'for questioning'. Then they turned to the rest of the family members and were ordered to surrender any and all gold, including any and all jewelry, which will be 'inventoried' and receipted; with this, they were also taken to AVO headquarters. I was the sole exception, because once we were ordered to clad, they realized that I was putting my uniform on, including my sidearm, which under the regulation quoted by me I refused to surrender to the policeman. (He was not my superior). Under special instruction through the phone they ordered me to leave at once and report to my army post. It was Kafkaesque.

-And what happened to him after all this" Professor Curtis asked, totally overwhelmed by this drama.

-We never saw him for 4 months until his 'trial' was arranged. We were allowed to hire an attorney. After we found one in the family circles, he told us that there really is not much he could do, since there were unexpected complications popping up, turning the accusations onto the political crime category, and probably all he could do is to plea for leniency, based on my father's faithful service in the promotion of science. The attorney did that rather eloquently, because my father eventually was sentenced for only 4 and one half years in a gulag.

-Oh, my god" he said, totally crushed, "I am so sorry to have brought this up, …you know we had some tough time in this country too, …you must have read about the senator McCarthy era, but of course that was in the opposite direction, as you well know".

-Well, all I can add to this is that 70% of the people in Hungary would welcome a McCarthy era there, at least until a role reversal to the current government would result", I offered.

-And how is he doing now"? he asked genuinely concerned.

-A meager pension was granted him some years after the 1956 uprising, and its retaliation. My brother and myself are sending him monthly $ 20. each of us. But we are not going through the regular bank exchange, because they would get hardly anything for the $ 40. We do it through third-hand banking, where the hard currency does not enter the country, thus, it is untouchable by the police; we send it to someone in Europe, who needs supplemental income, which their [well to do] relatives in Hungary are buying from us and pay for it in domestic currency to our father, based on a much more advantageous rate.

-This is greatly interesting, thank you for it", he said. "How is he health wise"?

-Not very well, I am afraid, he developed some complications lately in his throat. He was an avid smoker ever since the first World War. Now it seems to backfire on him", I said.

-Professor Szikszay-Farkas, when you see him, or write him next time please relay my very best wishes. Some day you should come and visit our department. We made a lot of progress since then, mostly in technologies".

-I shall do that". With that we parted.

I went to the 'Department Office' to check my mail box. It was amazing: The school year barely started and there was a cornucopia of paper in the space bearing my name under it. "What is all this stuff? I asked myself. Then, gradually, I began to recall my mail-slot in the dean's office at Akron, where we did not have such massive amount of paper, in fact the department office did not have separate mail-slots for the five civil engineering faculty members. That was a cozy little setup, almost family style.

Then I met our department secretary: Joan Fallon. She must have been a good few years to my senior. Always impeccably dressed, with a well adjusted demeanor, a somewhat dry sense of humor, and formal, very formal, both in her speech, and her interaction with the faculty members. She never addressed anyone of us by our first names, whereas, I couldn't miss noticing that, specially the elder members were always calling her: Joan. I was trying to be on the safe side, so for a considerable length of time I always called her Mrs. Fallon specially, since, first of all: this was her married name, and second: I did not know her maiden name.

She was socializing with the other department secretaries, had her coffee breaks with them in our faculty lounge, where I never set foot for years, because I was suspecting that the place was primarily a gossip exchange, mainly among the female staff who seemed to be in an absolute majority at break-time.

After a few pleasantries pertaining to our trip from Ohio, she was asking me about my address and phone number, which she needed for administrative purposes. I confessed that I really haven't got any, so she naturally became intrigued about our predicament, of which I did not make a secret, I was rather talkative about it which she received with a Mona Lisaesque smile, elicited, I felt sure, by my accent she was not yet used to.

-Mrs. Fallon, I am telling these things to you really freely in strict confidence", I said, "because you are our secretary and that means you can and will keep a secret".

-Are you trying to tell me that you are staying in a motel for the second week now"? she asked with some astonishment, which I thought was somewhat theatrical, but as it turned out, was genuine. "After a trip like this", she now again sounded incredulous, "and I heard you have a baby with you, … how is your wife able to manage"?

-Mrs. Fallon,"I took over from here, "She is a very capable woman, and let me tell you, we have been in much more miserable circumstances before in our lives; Anyway, it is not nearly as bad as it sounds, after all, we have a so called: 'efficiency' in that motel.

-But did you find yourselves a 'regular' place already, you know what I mean? an apartment or something more permanent"? she asked.

-Mrs. Fallon, we have a brand new house in Chelmsford, but we can not move in because the movers can not locate our furniture shipment. So, after my 1 PM class, I have to go and find myself an attorney who will teach them the rules of transporting other people's goods. Do you by any chance happened to know a good one"? I asked.

-A good one"…it seemed she was searching her memory.

-Well, you know" I said, "my brother used to refer to lawyers as the 'leeches of society', describing me that the nice person is not a good lawyer, …a good lawyer is a fighter, …a brute, a pest, possessing a vocabulary matching that of sailor's, definitely not a 'nice person' by any means, that is a **good** lawyer" I said.

-Professor Szikszay-Farkas, I am afraid I don't know anyone like you just described, but my husband knows one downtown, he would, I am sure, get results for you", she said, "if you want me to, I can try to call him and make an appointment for you this afternoon".

-Please! Please"! I almost begged her. "I better get to my office upstairs, and get organized for my first lecture, I don't have any of my class notes or even books, those are all packed in boxes" and with that I left her.

Faculty office space was one of the most chronic ill of Ball Hall. The faculty was assigned offices all over the place, in various buildings, that didn't have anything to do with engineering. My first office was on the top floor of Ball Hall: 'The Engineering Building' in a room, within one of the chemistry labs. It had a nice view of the parking lot, but more than that, it had privacy, it had no telephone, it had access only through the laboratory, which, I found out later, was used only twice a week by one morning and one afternoon class. Monday, Wednesday and Friday it was quiet as a tomb. It had some extrinsic advantages: the building was not designed or built with an elevator, so, to ascend to the office meant to climb two stories of 21 stairs each, providing a mandatory exercise which was hard to come by on busy days.

The first lectures are usually short. As a rule. You introduce yourself to the class, which in my case was somewhat cumbersome; I put my name on the board, so that they have the correct spelling, then I explained the intricacies of the pronunciation, which evidently did not cause undue hardship to this class. Then you [usually] hand out a course outline, which I did not have, but I gave the class the reference textbook. Explained about certain policies concerning quizzes, exams and grading.

-Professor, you mean you don't use the bell-curve to adjust the grades of the class"? one smart Alec asked, "does that mean a whole class can fail"?

-Or pass, with a good grade" I said, "the only difference being that of the point of view, yours seemed to be the pessimistic view, but I am an optimist".

-Then, … in the lab everyone has to complete a design assignment which will have to be **individual** work" I said, "don't even think about copying your buddy's work, because everyone will have a slightly different assignment, kapish"? Then another thing: I will take attendance before every lecture. And now I am going to read you your rights: Your presence is required! …to be absent is your unalienable right, …for which you will have to bear the consequences; is this clear"? I asked the class.

-Professor, do you always want us to address you: Professor"? another one asked.

-Well, that's what I am to you, am I not"? I asked him. "What else did you have in mind to call me"? Another thing: every time you ask me, or address me to tell me something, I expect you to tell me your last name, so that I will be getting to know you all! Is that Okay with you"?

The class was quiet, no one uttered a single word.

-Also… and mark me well, … if I ask a question to the class I am expecting an answer, … even a short answer, which in most cases should satisfy my curiosity whether you understood something I said, Okay? This is, kind of important for me."

-Yes! chanted the class.

-Good"! I exclaimed.

-Professor! Holzman!" he said, "Yes Mr. Holzman, you must be a very bright student, you follow instructions extremely well, what is your question"?

-Must we always speak to you in English? or … can we use some other language"? … Perhaps, … Hungarian"?

-Mr. Holzman! the official language of instruction in the classroom or lab is English! so, as common courtesy to others I will expect this language to be used" I said, "and I solemnly promise the entire class that I will attempt to use the same myself, ... to the best of my ability, Okay"?

The ice broke at once. The class was utterly amused. The atmosphere changed considerably. Some of the students could hardly stop laughing. I hoped I made their day, ... and, they surely made mine.

Down at the office Mrs. Fallon gave me the address of attorney O'Hara along with the message that he is expecting me in the afternoon. I was on my way in a heartbeat.

Attorney O'Hara listened carefully as I explained the problem about the Mayflower movers, then gave him the telephone numbers of the tracing center in Minneapolis. He called, introduced himself as Attorney O'Hara and asked the person on the other end if he could speak with someone in their legal department. Then a lengthy discussion ensued, as a result of which he repeated the address of destination and promised that Tuesday morning: either the shipment will arrive at the address and be unloaded without any damage, or: he is going to file a complaint at the Lowell Superior Court and claim a long list of damages and have the papers served at Mayflower's Billerica offices. Then he gave them our telephone number at the motel and left instructions to call us in any case, any time.

Next morning, Tuesday the 9-th, a call came to us in unit 12. The employee explained that they had located the shipment in another company's warehouse in Bridgewater, Massachusetts. Nobody could explain how it ended up there. Now the other company wants $ 180.00 storage fee for the 9 days of storage and then they will release the shipment.

Another call went to attorney O'Hara with this news. He was in his office, and promised to call them up and let us know what happened.

Attorney O'Hara thereby established himself, in my brother's terminology as 'a good lawyer' without showing all the qualities I have enumerated to our secretary about lawyers' qualifications. This somehow opened up another category of attorneys: the quiet, but intimidating and ultimately very effective, result oriented, no nonsense kind of lawyer. I learned a good few years later that Attorney O'Hara was Town Council for the Town of Dracut. But that is a different story which I am going to deal with at that time. I always hoped that by sheer luck

I will befriend an attorney, whom you can genuinely trust, and for the next few years it seemed like Attorney O'Hara will become that 'friend' and attorney.

And so, finally Wednesday the IO-th of September the other company's truck delivered the shipment at 22 Golden Cove Rd. where a small army was receiving the shipment in ovation out on the street. Even Mrs. Barrisano came over with a tray of drinks in her hands. A warm welcome by any standard. As it turned out later, the two of us were the sole occupants of that entire subdivision, at least for that first winter season.

The ordeal was over. I called Attorney O'Hara and thanked him for the results which were obviously to his merit. When I asked him about his fee, he said I should consider it as an introductory offer, and … a "Welcome to New England". This certainly baffled me about lawyers in general.

The remaining item was the Telephone company's giving us a working line with a number, which we received by the end of the week.

Over the weekend I moved the boxes of books and notes to my office in Ball Hall and spent the rest of the time putting the lecture material together for the following week. Finally we made it.

Chapter Five
(Making Professional Headways.)

The weather in the month of September was beautiful. We thought if it is like this in New England we made a wise move. We knew about the 'Indian summer' in this part of the country too, but we never really experienced it, and it was said that it usually came later, like in October, around "foliage" time.

We were pretty well settled in the new house on Golden Cove Rd. The kids liked the school. Andy was riding the bus with the Barrisano kids. On the first PTA meeting we, as new parents were introduced to the old timers. Of course my accent raised some eyebrows but this sort of thing was no longer an event, I got so used to it. Andy's home room teacher elaborated on the depth and the overall goal of the newly introduced French language program, and outlined the limits they will be bound by in conveying the mastery of this 'Romance' language. Because both of our kids were born in Canada somehow she thought that we were French-Canadians, but I informed the class of parents that we were not, and that our accent originates thousands of miles to the east [of Canada].

The classes at Lowell Tech were quite enormous. Unusually so, by any formerly known standards. The sophomore class, a total of 102 had to be broken down to three sub-sections of approximately 30-some students each. The juniors were not nearly as numerous but still forming two sections each, over 30 pupils.

These excessively large enrollment figures were partially a result of low priced, state subsidized education, as well as the baby boomers coming of [college] age. The former lured a high percentage of out of state students to the school, while the latter was

a natural cause of demographics. The impact of the high enrollment was causing the need for additional faculty all across the engineering college.

I myself had to repeat the same lecture I gave in the morning to the other section in the afternoon. Needless to say how boring this was for the professor. As a result sometimes the two sections got not quite identical lectures, not because of me, but mostly because the questions from the audience caused a deviation. Such could not be repeated retroactively to the morning class. I suggested to Gifford that may be it would be beneficial to the entire class to combine the two sections into one for the lectures only and breaking down the class into even smaller lab sections instead. But he quoted the administration's policy of more 'intimate' class sizes, which to some [administrators'] minds induced the concept of 'better learning'.

This was the emerging era of the new Sophism, to promote a liberal education, to eradicate the elitist college student image, which by the way began to erode already. A mere decade ago a college educated person was looked upon as a superior being, offering them unheard-of starting salaries, sometimes double that of non- college graduates. I have seen graduates of Cornell's Engineering schools demanding starting salaries double that of technicians with on-the-job training, with some years of experience. The latter being much more valuable to an engineering office regarding output. But this was another intangible asset to a firm, which could boast a higher number of college graduates on their payroll. The impressing of a prospective client started right in the reception area of a firm where the employee's degrees were proudly displayed. The larger area of the wall was covered by diplomas, the more impressive the firm looked. Also, they increased their possibilities for job procurement, which was nothing to be overlooked, specially in tougher economic times.

The administration's idea was to turn out 'employable' graduates. The ones that could get a job offer upon graduation, or even before. The reality was that only a handful in each class became singled out at recruitment times; mostly the ones with some other, like computer, experience, which, unfortunately was nonexistent in the post WWII vintage curricula. The engineering offerings were reflecting the post war technologies. The most hurtful area was in the computational facilities and their usage by [civil] engineering students.

Those classes which could have benefited the most from an available computer (and program) more individualized to the solution of tedious lab problems, were still using desk calculators, for instance, to compute elevations along the profile of a road. The vintage laboratory problems clearly demonstrate this. The solution for a vertical curve still constituted the tougher lab problems, not because the math was overly difficult but because the chances for committing an error was greater. I still think that my greatest contribution to the practical solutions of lab problems, as parts of overall design exercise, was in the introduction of various shortcuts, graphical [rapid] checks to be performed to detect any [large] errors in the numerical solutions.

Since we were struggling with chronic shortages of computers (as well as access to them wherever available), course content and even curricular revisions would have been necessary in order to preserve at least the 'core' requirement of a particular civil engineering discipline. A best example to this is the geometric solution of two intersecting [straight] lines. There were several suggested solution to this comparatively simple problem which was an integral part of the most elementary math and geometry courses, in which the **conceptual** solution was amply demonstrated, but by the time it boiled down to be applicable in road and intersection design it lost all significance as a **practical** solution. And don't get me wrong, this was not the Mathematics Department's fault. They were teaching **classical concepts: eternal truths**.

So, I tried to introduce the class to the state of the art practice, which at that time was the COGO/ROADS problem-solving oriented computer program language. This was developed by Charles Miller at MIT under heavily subsidized [by industry] research grants to his group of Graduate Students. It was readily suited for 'batch processing' which was ideal for a class environment, where a number of students could submit each one of his own set of computations in a 'batch'. The Computer Department returned each student's print-out along with his 'input deck' in the bins designated for that class. The tedium was finally removed from the problem solving task and replaced by the 'thinking process' involved in the preparation of the input. The GIGO (garbage in/garbage out) had a considerable damping effect on the usage of the system because the students got easily frustrated by it. But this skill, whoever mastered it, did get them job offers.

The numerous philosophical discussions I had with Giff were along these lines. The usual conclusion was: "I agree with you wholeheartedly Gabe, but let's not rock the boat in these 'difficult times'. If I were you I would not antagonize the class which would soon get up in arms if you try to 'deviate' drastically from the course content. Just remember the sixties", he said with a good dose of admonition. I had no choice but to agree with him.

The truth was that the school was struggling with identity. Civil engineering was not even offered four-five years ago. Giff and Herm started the Department practically from scratch.

* --- * --- *

The sophomore surveying class had its regularly scheduled Saturday morning field work exercises. These took place on and around the ball field. Almost every C.E. faculty member was involved in it. We had at least 10-12 teams, performing a particular task, such as measuring distances by a steel tape. The results later had to be handled ('reduced') in the classroom lab sessions, along with some other field tasks, such as leveling.

By the middle of October on one of these Saturdays, on intuition, I drove home to Chelmsford for a quick lunch. As I drove in the driveway Maria was about getting ready to drive Andy to the hospital but she didn't know where the closest one was. So, I hand carried Andy over into my car and drove with him right back to Lowell, where I was already well familiar with the St. Joseph hospital, since I drove by it every morning. At the Emergency Room the nurse unrolled his foot from the towel Maria wrapped him into, and when I glanced down to it I saw his toe dangling from its bone. When the nurse noticed the drained color of my face she knew exactly what to do: she pushed me out the door to the hallway. There, at least I had a chance to call the department office and let them know that I will be absent for the rest of the afternoon due to an emergency.

* --- * --- *

It was high time to establish contact with the Airmap firm and Geoffry Dorfman himself. Although money was still not a burning issue this extra-curricular activity could not be postponed any longer. After all, this was one of the decisive factors in the entire move.

We met the next Saturday at his office in Brookline. I was in no time under the spell of the old buildings which resembled some of the similarly zoned places in old Budapest, and the nostalgic atmosphere renewed itself as I entered the three story office building on Harvard Street.

Upstairs, Geoffry waited for me, cordial as ever I could recall our last personal encounter at the Airport.

-Hi Gabe, we have been anxiously waiting for you to appear as soon as you could, because there are quite a few projects that need your attention" he said for a start. "But let's sit down and discuss the terms under which you will be fitting into this organization.

-Okay, with me", I said, "I do realize that my involvement must be kept to a limited extent, until I will get my professional registration. I know I will have to be patient, and incidentally, that is what I expect from you in return", I said, realizing that I will probably be in the sidelines until then.

-So, let's start", he said. "There is the Tewksbury tax mapping going on at present, where we will need your input. I have alerted the guys to set aside the problem cases, and hand them to you as soon as you could get to that. Tewksbury is practically next door to you, so when will you have your free day in the week"?

-Thursdays I have no classes", I said, "so let's start next Thursday and we'll see how it works out".

-Fine, this is how you do it: you go down the Town Hall and tell the Assessors that you will be working with the mapping guys. They will show you to the room where the work is being done. Tommy, the head guy will introduce you to the others, and will give you the problem parcels. We have a planimetric-photogrrammmetric base map on which we do the assembly. I am sure you will be on top of it right away", he said. "We will then agree some basis on which you will get paid for your time".

-Can't we agree on it right now"? I asked him somewhat perplexed. "At least for the time being, you know? I am sure you have an idea how much my time would be worth", I said tentatively, "for instance, how much are these guys making an hour"?

-You can't compare that, because they are on salary, and get certain benefits packaged into it", he started lecturing again.

-Well Geoffry, I still haven't heard a figure" I said sort of tired getting hung up on a simple thing like this. "You don't pay benefit to me, so why don't we say ten dollars an hour, and, ...of course we will leave it open to see how it works out, ...and, later on we may need to adjust it" I said quasi closing the case.

-I was going to suggest eight bucks an hour, that's sixty four bucks for your one day a week, I don't think that's bad for a start" he said smiling; "and you know, we have some other smaller works for you in the field, that doesn't require stamp, and you can do those on Saturdays, or whenever", he said smiling again as I saw him holding out the carrot in front of me.

-All right" I said, finally closing this deal.

-And Gabe, let me remind you to get in touch with the Registration Board's secretary about transferring your Ohio registration, or ... just re-registering here" he said. "There will be forms to fill out, galore, I am sure, so let's get the ball rolling... and if there are any difficulties arising on the way, ...don't worry about that, ...we know a few people", he said, this time honestly smiling, and we shook hands on it.

I never anticipated such bickering. On the other hand I had to respect his shrewd business sense. I concluded that I have a lot to learn from him in this regard.

Next Monday I called the Board's secretary in Boston. She promised to send the forms immediately. There, another matter was on its way. Progress was in the air. I liked that. I couldn't stand it if things stood still, if nothing happened.

* _ _ _ * _ _ _ *

A letter was forwarded from our Shaker Heights address to our 'new Golden Cove Road place. It came from my special committee chairman: McNair, who was my faculty adviser during my studies for the Ph.D. degree at Cornell University. He had bad and sad news for me in it. One of the members of the three member special committee has died at the end of the summer, in cancer.

He was suggesting for us to get together trying to figure out what to do next, and perhaps come up with a replacement, for which he had an individual tentatively picked. He would like me to meet him. It dawned on me right away, that he didn't even know about my new position, and, naturally, our new address as well.

I called McNair the same evening. We talked for quite awhile. I attempted to describe all that happened to us since we left Ithaca and particularly: I left Cornell, after I passed my candidacy exam. I had the feeling that he felt, … if not exactly guilty, but definitely bitter in January of '69 when most fellowship fundings were abruptly stopped. He was noticeably relieved when I told him about my current position. He inquired about the faculty here and the general philosophy of the school.

I told him about the private consulting possibility here, which he did not receive too enthusiastically. Nevertheless he thought it a good idea, in fact a virtual must, that I will get my registrations not only in surveying but in civil engineering as well. Then I promised him that I will make an attempt to see him on a Saturday quite soon. He, on the other hand, mentioned that the American Congress on Surveying and Mapping will have its annual organizational assembly in November, where a lot of our acquaintances will be present, some on various panels. "Please make sure to come, even if you have to bear all the cost for it. It will not be in the overly expensive downtown Hilton, but this time the directors came up with the idea to get the populi to Gaithersburg, Maryland for the three day event where even parking is a lot simpler than in Washington. "It might be very much worth your while", he said, and with that we parted.

When I told Giff about it and asked if there might be some money in the budget to cover the cost of these sort of participations he immediately ordered me to fill out the request form, and hand it to Priscilla, who will put it through the works. "How many classes will you miss"? he asked.

-Only the Friday classes will be missed, because I will leave right after the Wednesday afternoon class, and drive down someplace as far as the Southern tip of New Jersey. From there the next morning I will get into Gaithersburg, no problem".

-You could give the classes some reading assignment, if you think" said Giff smiling, "but I think they would be happier if you don't do it.

Usually you end up having to explain it again anyway". We both agreed on that note.

*--- *--- *

The conference in Gaithersburg was incredible. I couldn't believe the crowd right from my home state: Massachusetts. McNair was really showing off with me. I must have been looking real well, because Dorothy made a remark that I look like a debonair. McNair introduced me to one of the speakers from the Department of Public Works, (better known at the time as the Mass. Highway Department) a Mr. Clohecy, whom he evidently knew, since he was "Mr. Geodesy" himself, and as such, in charge of geodetic control information in the Commonwealth.

Mr. Clohecy was a self taught man. He rose through the ranks starting with the Department during the Depression as a young college student, working during summers. After the hard times were over, he became party chief, still later he was supervisor of the new 'precise traverse' program. I asked him where he went for his geodetic studies, where was such a program offered in this country.

-Quite simply: there was none", he told me. But he got hold of the Coast and Geodetic Survey's special publications, which served well as textbooks on the subject. He was an autodidact. Later he held seminars for the Department personnel. Quite a career! indeed he was then the number one person in this field in the Commonwealth. He, of course, immediately recognized Herm Shea, whom he also knew more than superficially. He mentioned that there is another man from the Department, who was, at one time a subordinate of his, and his son attends Lowell Tech. He probably is a sophomore in the civil engineering department. Shortly he introduced me to Mr. Swanson who was in his early fifties. I was not at all surprised that I am becoming introduced to all these people, as the young star in geodesy and a faculty member at Lowell Tech. After all, I was the oddity, I was the newcomer, I had the accent, but because of my academic position, I was phenomenally well respected by them. They too, were showing off with me. Mr. Swanson asked me to "please look out for my rambunctious son, because he thinks he is an 'I know it all' kind of guy".

80

Next day came the bigee; Friday morning McNair took me to a table at breakfast and without much preliminaries introduced me to Mr. Schofield, as the secretary of the surveying division of the Registration Board. In this capacity he was also the chairman. He also served on the Civil Engineers' board, which consisted of more than one member. Mr. Schofield invited us to the table to have breakfast with him. McNair let me do the talking which consisted mostly of my schooling. The minute Ohio State came into the discussion Schofield was entirely overwhelmed, but inquired more about my **practical** experiences. McNair took over from here, mentioned something about my handling of the ortho-stereo plotter, that plots in the x-z plane, (a new instrument acquired by the school at Cornell) merely by taking a good look at it. I then began to elaborate on my participation of the adjustment computation workshop, where I was "instrumental" in developing some new coordinate transformation techniques, utilizing the least squares method and blending it into the COGO problem solving language.

Without saying much more, Mr. Schofield asked "Professor Farkas, are you strictly a thinker, or do you consider yourself a 'doer' as well?" I enumerated my background as a registered professional in Ohio, and the various special projects I worked on by invitation of local engineering firms. I quite graphically told the story of my redesigning the Thistledown Racetrack to international standards and while setting the theodolite at one of the symmetry axis point in the center line of the track, a small plane landed some 20-ft from me on the grass, and shortly, a couple of white-shirt, black- tied young gents emerged from the plane and asked me who I was. Instead of answering right away I gave them all a hard time for 'almost knocking over' the instrument, and that they should know better, at least next time. As it turned out they were the representatives of Edward J. DeBartolo, the owner of the Race Track, (infamous for organized crime affiliations.) My apologies were somewhat late, but these people were, after all, much to my junior. They looked like college kids to me. As it turned out later, the year before they actually were. One of them just graduated from accounting, the other one was a junior 'in management'; I was almost nothing to them, … an employee, … a subcontractor".

-Mr. Schofield, I am not the ivory tower kind of a scientist; If a new method, a new instrument, a new approach or a new hardware is being developed, I find it worthless if it has no immediate practical applicability; I do consider myself very much a doer".

All together, I think I made a fairly good impression on Mr. Schofield. Proof for this was that at the gala dinner he was looking for me, handed me his card and 'asked me' to call him at my earliest convenience when 'back at home'. Little did I know that McNair alerted him that I actually have a pending application at the Registration Board in Massachusetts.

* --- * --- *

The following Thursday Dorfman came to visit us at the Tewksbury operation. He knew that I went down to Gaithersburg, because he called the home on Friday and learned from Maria that I went down there for the conference. He called me out for lunch and asked me all about it. I summarized shortly what was going on there, that I met a few real big-wigs, among them Lou Schofield. This was the big bomb. Dorfman immediately said: "Gabe! you are as good as registered in Massachusetts. If I were you I would call Schofield right after lunch right from here, if for no other reason than to find out what he has in his mind".

After lunch I called the Schofield Brothers in Framingham, and asked for Mr. Lou Schofield. When he answered the phone he asked me right away, when could I meet him for lunch in Framingham. I told him that I could do it on Tuesday, but all I have is about a couple of hours between the labs. He said this will not take too long, but in the meantime would I be so kind and call up his old time employee, at Essex Survey Service in Salem and ask for Frank, who will explain the situation to me. He will already know about me, so just tell him I got you for him for 'that' project. He needs to invite me as a consultant to one of his ongoing projects that involves triangulation adjustment. "I am sure you will have no problem handling that. "So, then I will see you soon, on Tuesday".

* --- * --- *

-Good morning, Essex Survey Service, may I help you"? said the receptionist on the other end of the line.
-Yes, my name is Gabor Szikszay-Farkas, I wish to speak with Mr. Hancock, Mr. Frank Hancock" I told her.
-He is busy right now, he is in the computation room where he is not supposed to be bothered, is he expecting your call"?

-Well, I don't know, all I know that I was supposed to call him and, … that he already knows about me" I told her, and waited.

-Oh, good morning professor", said the man on the other end as if he knew me from school, "you were highly recommended to us by Lou Schofield, I am so glad you called" he said with genuine enthusiasm. "We have here something that got us into a cul-de-sac, so to speak, if you know what I mean"?

-Mr. Hancock, I know…

-Professor, would you do me a favor and call me Frank? I'd appreciate it; so you know, what I was trying to say was that we, … sort of, …got hung up on one of our project, … actually, got stuck, if you know what I mean …?" He stumbled, did not quite know how to get to the problem.

-Mr. Hancock, …er, sorry! Frank; Lou was telling me in broad outlines that you will need my help with some control survey adjustment, … but …I am kind of at a loss, …what I am trying to say is, …that I am not sure, where, …my modest capabilities would, … you know? fit in, … I am not fully familiar with the requirements of the Commonwealth of Massachusetts, …I want you to be aware, that I am not as yet registered in Massachusetts, so, how could I…?

-Professor, would you please stop this sort of talk, first: this job is not located in Massachusetts! Second: Massachusetts requirements do not enter into the picture"…

-Frank, is it in Ohio?, because then I would take care"…

-No, professor, it is not in Ohio or even in this country, it is in the Turks and Caicos Islands; you know? in the Caribbean,… it is a bunch of islands and cays under British Protectorate"…

-Frank, I think now we really arrived at the core of the problem, because I don't know anything about their laws, survey regulations, is what I mean" I said, "and Lou made no mention at all that this work is in another country, and I feel kind of uneasy… and you still are addressing me 'professor' …

-Okay! let's simplify this whole matter" he said. "Number one: I wish you would allow me to call you 'professor' because this is how we put you down as our consultant, and it gives us a kind of pride…you know? prestige …number two: we have all the British Overseas Survey Directorate's Manuals of Instructions, etc, …number three: all of those things happen to be in the metric system, which you must understand, we lack the experience with,… we are, after all, practitioners of surveys here in Massachusetts, and, …number four: we simply and basically, need you; More: we now depend on you", he finally finished his plea. "Will you please, help us?" he asked.

-Mr. Hancock, now that you elaborated the various problem areas, I am beginning to see my way through this maze", I said "however, …I am sure you realize that, I am looking forward to quite a lot of unproductive time that I will have to spend studying those regulations, and …frankly, you have to show me and explain me what, if anything you have done so far already, so that I can be instrumental in planning the entire control survey mission for you,"…

-Professor, let me tell you the facts of life: Lou and I were down in the Islands for two weeks before Thanksgiving, and set up our triangulation scheme, we monumented the points with the markers and did all the angle observations, we also measured two base lines with our crew and borrowed the Schofield's Geodimeter, you know the way our Coast Survey instructions describes it, …the entire island is covered with a network of triangles, …we have all this material here, you are welcome to study it, at your leisure, …so, what do you say? When can you come down here to us"? He pleaded with me.

-Well, this is not the very best time right now, you know, … we are getting ready to close the semester, exams, grading, the works, you do remember from your college years, …but if you would meet me on a Saturday, like the end of this week, on December sixth, we could look things over, and then I will have a better picture…" I said.

Then he gave me directions to their office in Salem. I was wondering, if he really knew what we are getting involved in. It sounded like that the Brits were expecting a rigorous adjustment, together with error analysis. As I began to think about it more, I realized that one important thing he never mentioned and I never asked: how the island will be located in the Caribbean See? Was there an already known point? Or more? or on an adjacent island? So there will be a lot to talk about on Saturday.

------*

-Professor, I will be with you in a few minutes, Lou Schofield said to me as I arrived in his office in Framingham, "Please step outside to the rear parking lot, where my car is parked and we'll leave in a minute". He drove to a cozy little place, not far from the office, which looked like [one of] his favorite restaurants. Naturally the hostess greeted him by his last name, and she led us right to our table. She must have sensed that I was Lou's guest, so she asked me if I will have a cocktail. Yes, please, a gin-Martini with a couple of olives. Lou ordered the same perhaps just out of politeness.

-Well, Professor Farkas, I think I have some good news for you" he said looking at me for my expression.

-How so?" I asked somewhat puzzled, "I am always eager to hear those..."

-I think I will get right to the point. The Board discussed your application yesterday, and concluded that your qualifications are superior to what's expected in the profession. I was asked though: about your references by some of the members, you know, ...whether I had them checked out, ... that sort of things". I told them about the conference and McNair, and all the rest, and they had the feeling that you should demonstrate your competency in other than the 'Public Land Survey System', you know, ... because you came from Ohio, and here in New England we don't have that system.

-Gee, I hope this doesn't mean that they don't trust me that I can do 'metes and bounds'", I said, "so, what do they want me to 'demonstrate' to them?

-Well, you know, I thought you must have done surveys other than in the PLS System, remember, the one you mentioned, that Race Track? whatever it's name? something along those lines".

-Oh sure, that's no problem. Like the one in the City of Akron 's control system, which is all tied to Ohio's northern grid. I did bunch of works: a City Park Rehab job, a very comprehensive engineering and surveying job" ...

-Yah, I was sure you'd done something like this", he said, "can you submit that one, for instance, do you have a copy of it? Or can you get one? I am sure that would do. You know these practitioners are convinced that the academics lack the practical sense, the 'doers touch'. This is what I asked you then at the breakfast, remember"? he asked and was eagerly waiting for my answer.

-Mr. Schofield, I think I know exactly what you are referring to, I have seen such lousy work performed by the civil engineering department head in Akron, that I would have been ashamed to show it to anyone. But there was really nothing 'wrong' with it, it ...just had to be turned over to a draftsman so that it should **look professional**, I always did my own graphics, including the lettering".

-Good, I knew it! That would do, for sure. Now, as far as your engineering registration is concerned that'll be flying through, literally, it was approved practically on the spot; You will be receiving your certificate very soon. They could not play around with that, considering that there are a number of members registered, who did not finish even the 4-year degree program. The fact that you have a Master's Degree, …it would have been flying into their face, …if you know what I mean", he said self satisfied. "So; do you think this was good news, Professor"? he asked.

-Actually, I don't know what to say; I am overwhelmed" I said. "Mr. Schofield, in the back of my mind I always held that good old honest, hard work, should get its reward sooner or later, and this seemed to be proven now".

We had a short break in the conversation to finish up our main dishes. The waitress asked us about dessert, but neither of us had room for any. I was waiting to see if he brings up the subject of the Essex Survey Service job, but since he did not, I decided that I will. I just wanted to know more about it from him.

-Mr. Schofield, there is something I was going to ask you a few details about. Remember you asked me to contact Mr. Hancock, …

-Oh yah, how did that go? Frank called me yesterday, I was not in, and this morning I was busy, …so, you two have an understanding? … I, knew it, I just knew it", he said, and I could tell he was glad.

-Actually, I must tell you too, that, as he described the job, it is no picnic; that is a big job; I had asked him some details, which he did not have all the answers for, …and, I didn't even asked all the questions, like what kind of computational facilities does he have, how large of a set of normal equations can it solve, what is the BOSD datum surface, etc. etc." I said, and noticed that perhaps I should not have mentioned even this much. "I am going to meet him this Saturday to talk more about these things, and he also promised to let me have the British Manuals and stuff".

-Yah, you know, I was down with him for over a week, for the observations, and we made a trip to the local BOSD guys in the Town of Cockburn, which is on the main island on Turk, and we did pick up quite a few things". He seemed puzzled, …"That is actually his project, you know? This client of his bought that small island, and he wants to develop it into a resort".

-Mr. Schofield, all I want to ask you now is: how much do you think I should charge him per hour? I really have no comparison to this sort of work with that of routine surveying and computational work. For that I would charge anywhere between ten to fifteen dollars, but this, …is, … really something else, I must say".

-Oh, sure! We could not even find anyone, who would do it" he said, "I myself could not do it, I must say, it's over my expertise so, to answer your question, I think 25-30 dollars an hour is not out of line, by any means, but let me take you back, you must be getting back to your class".

We drove to the office and parted at the parking lot. I was a few minutes late to the afternoon lab but I simply could not hide my happiness. I was radiant. The students noticed it. They were smiling and whispering at my back among themselves, smiling right in my face, as if they knew the secret of my exuberance. But I was sure they were thinking about my whereabouts at lunchtime being something altogether different from where I actually was.

* --- * --- *

Frank Hancock was a typical "successful" surveyor in Essex County, Massachusetts. His office was an 18-th century home, listed on the National Register of Historic Buildings, once belonging to a Capt. John Felt and located right across the street from the County Courthouse with the Registry of Deeds in it. A truly strategic location for a surveyor's office. He bought the building together with the previous surveying business, with his partner, a younger fellow, after he became registered. I never found out about the circumstances of his separation from the Schofield firm, he never mentioned it, and I never asked. But it was evident, that he was in good terms with them, and that they both respected each other.

After he showed me some enlarged photographs taken on the island, as well as the British Overseas Survey Directorat's (BOSD) maps, I asked him to show me a graphical representation of the triangle network itself. I told him that this is necessary mostly for myself enabling me to assess the magnitude of the work. There was such a plot mounted on the wall, which was a copy of what he submitted to the people at the BOSD. Also, he gave me the Manuals of Instruction how to tie surveys of any single Island into that system, so I began, very gingerly, to ask my questions.

-Mr. Hancock, would you please show me your computing facilities! You know, I am sure, that this sort of triangulation adjustment does require IBM 730 or larger capabilities. There is a way to solve simultaneous equations on smaller computers, but the preparatory work involved, the error screenings, the formatting the input data of the observation equations is, ..."

-Professor, please stop, you have lost me already," he said with some mild degree of frustration in his voice, "this here is our computer, it does handle COGO, ... and is capable of storing coordinates for up to two thousand points, ... I thought ...this certainly could handle what we have here" ...and, as I asked before: please call me Frank".

-Well, let's see, how many new points do you have in the network", I asked, "you see, this gives us some idea about the size of the array to be solved.

-What do you mean by: 'new points' Professor? These are **all new points**, there were none here before we set foot on this island" he said, "this is an uninhabited island, we established 16 high accuracy new triangulation stations".

-Well, Frank, that means already a minimum of 32 unknowns in our system of equations to be solved, ... I don't think you can set up such an array in this, ... er, ... and also, ...for instance, how did you tie your network to their coordinate system"?

-Oh, I see what you mean, they showed us two navigational beacons on adjacent islands with fixed positions and we took directions from our main stations. I am going to give you all the observations, these are in two full field books" he said and started to get all the material together.

-Frank, I was going to talk about the scheduling; right now is final exam time, after that come the Christmas holidays, but following that we can start working, ...if that's okay with you; As I can see I have to make arrangements through a friend of mine, who has access to an IBM 730 machine where he is working, and if we here prepare all the punch cards with the equations, he might run it for us", I said, "Oh, one more thing: I will count on your cooperation as far as the assembling the observations goes"...

-Professor, what sort of hourly rate are we talking about here and... if you can...to come up with an estimate ... you know, I have to alert my client about this unexpected extra work and expense, ... due to the British Government requirements."

-Frank, at this point, …all I can say, that my hourly rate will be $ 30.00 and I will have to add something for traveling, because it takes 35 miles driving, one way. But …for the driving I will not charge professional time, okay"?

-Professor, I really appreciate it, and thank you for helping us out with this, I think you are very generous with your time and knowledge … and, I think, we all learn by this experience.

-Frank, you know, I think, for a professional, that should be the most important consideration".

He seemed genuinely worried about the cost of this work added to the overall project cost. It was merely not envisioned beforehand and not calculated in the total cost. A painful business error, not a professional oversight. The truth being that none of these sort of tasks are surfacing in an everyday land surveyor's practice; maybe never.

Chapter Six
(The great American melting pot)

My first semester at Lowell Tech went by in a frighteningly short time. In my classes were mostly good kids. The rebels were well treated, as I had done with the ones in my class at Cornell, in the late 60-s, so I knew how to disarm them by now. At the end of the semester they had a real sense of accomplishment, and I am sure most of them felt that they have learned something worth while. They felt outsmarted by the professor by everyone gotten a different, personalized, taylor-made assignment. I appealed to their pride they must feel, when they hand-in their design, which is entirely their very own work.

I always made it a point to order the latest of the educational movies from the ASCE (American Society of Civil Engineers) film library and have shown them in the screening room, in the basement of Lydon Library. The few movies the class saw towards the end of the semester were dealing with road layout and construction. There was a definite atmosphere of obsolescence in these movies, (mostly done in the 50-s) but that effected only the movie production, the vintage of the heavy equipment employed, but the narration was as up to date as it could be expected.

After each movie we have discussed how the scenes related to the image the members of the class developed during the laboratory assignments and with the design project. I was always trying to find out how they would poise themselves in any given phases of the construction in the field; would they be lost if a supervisor has sent them out to do a particular task? Would they know exactly what to do? Would they get an overall idea what it was all about? This latest question being perhaps the most important.

I realized that a large percentage of the class was not really 'college material' in the sense of the elitist educational philosophy. Some two third of each class was struggling along to keep up with the brighter students, that is, if they really had the ambition, the drive, the professional curiosity that should sustain them for the latter part of their life. But those who lacked it, … they hardly ever rose to the level of performing truly engineering tasks and became technicians for the rest of their professional career.

But we needed technicians! was the mantra of the administration, and we, the faculty, had to comply and deliver. The luckier students were satisfied with their position on the professional ladder, usually had a decent job offer upon graduation, so they fitted in the overall mechanism, to take their job as: 'a job' that had to be done, the way the boss wanted it done. If, later, they became more interested in their profession, wanted to know more, (even more than the boss,) the answer was: 'back to school'.

Thus, by natural selection emerged the new '**elite**': the graduate student. At the civil engineering department there was no such a thing. First of all: 'the undergraduate faculty' was overloaded as it was. Ardent fights were put up at the college (division) level for a more copious budget to hire additional faculty to handle the impact of undergraduate enrollment. Any plans for graduate offering had to be looked upon as something in the more distant future. Second: potential programs had to be identified, planned and assembled, so if a graduate planned to become a M. Sc. in civil engineering, it had to be ensured that he/she would be able to absorb all the additional material from course offerings, that will put him/her up to par with the graduates from the programs offered at the well established larger, and private schools. MIT was a mere 30 miles away, WPI (Worcester Polytechnic Institute) about 40. As I saw it at that time, in the turning decade of the 70-s, it was the impossible dream, the unreachable star.

Giff came into my office one day during semester break when he found out, somehow, through the grapevines, that I was in. I had to study and come up with some best format on punch cards, to put the data on cards for an observation equation for this job on the Turks and Caicos

Islands. I had made excellent progress with that job, after I explained to Frank the steps involved in this process. He assigned one of his man to convert the angles to a station (horizon) closure and plot the resulting directions on a work-plan sheet of the entire triangle network.

-Gabe, how is it going?" he asked nodding his head towards the format plan I was working on. "I heard you got yourself into some 'real' work, some real challenge…I am so glad for you … and … I know what it must mean to you", he said and sat down on the chair next to my desk.

-Giff, I am slowly getting used to the fact that everyone seems to know about everything around here, but … this …I must say, does come as sort of a surprise", and it was no use for me trying to hide it. "How did you …"

-That's okay, I think I owe you the courtesy to tell you that Herm told me about it. He is convinced that your registration and licensing in the Commonwealth is imminent. So, my first order of business is to extend my congratulation", he said smiling. I really liked when he was smiling, liked it from the very first time.

-Thank you Giff, you must know, I am sure, what it means to me, as you put it, and … not just this", … I was fumbling with the words, "how did he…

-Oh, you know that Herm is well known in the surveying profession. Actually I came to see you to let you know that I put you up for a raise, sort of … you know! … to remedy what I could not achieve in the summer at the time of your hiring. Now to take advantage of your good work with the Transportation course, I had some leverage in my hand and I used it. So, you will find an adjustment in your pay the next month", and he was smiling again.

-Giff, I really don't know what to say, … except … perhaps, that I relish your attention to our, … our … trying…"

-That's all right Gabe, …by the way how is your family? …the new house? …and, oh my God I almost forgot: …how is Maria doing with your little one?" I hope everything is okay…please say hello to her for me, will you? Okay, I shall let you work", he said and slowly left my office.

Down in the department office I found a sheet of paper in my mail slot with an invitation typed on it. It also had a small map on its lower half showing how to get to the place. Evidently the Gifford's were having a party for the civil engineering faculty at the next Saturday. Joan was alerting everyone of us about it.

-Professor Szikszay-Farkas, I do hope you will make it, and, ... of course you will bring your wife, I didn't even have a chance to meet her yet"...

-Mrs. Fallon. I wouldn't dream of going without her" I said and noticed her Mona Lisaesque smile again.

*--- *--- *

-Oh, hi Maria, I am so glad you could make it, with the baby and all"...said Harriett. "How do you manage ... did you get a baby sitter? ... Oh, I forgot about your two older kids ... they can take care of everything I am sure", she greeted us right in the foyer.

We met the Giffords in the summer in the Hannah Dustin Motel days, when they came to visit us. We had a nice time on Sunday afternoon that we spent mostly at the poolside. They did not feel like taking a dip there, but I wouldn't be surprised if Giff would have come in the pool, had he have a swimming trunk with him. He was such a good sport.

Maria took an instant liking of Harriett. She seemed like a very good mother: talked about their two daughters quite a lot. Giff was giving the 'grand tour' to Dario and the Sinclairs who did bring along their daughter: Pat. As I suspected in the back of my mind, that was an opportunity for her to meet Dario. She was college age, perhaps a freshman or sophomore, at the American University in Washington D. C. as we found out later.

I was quite intrigued with Giff"s power tools in the basement, he had quite a setup, mostly very sophisticated woodworking tools, even a planer on its own stand. Naturally, very proud of them, and of the fact that he finished the basement himself, and ... still had all his fingers.

Upstairs, as usual, the ladies had already formed their little circle. I found Patricia in light conversation with Dario in the kitchen, where the bar was set up near the sink, complete with an opulent ice bucket. It was a self serve bar. While I fixed my overture drink: the 'Rumhatten', I asked her if she, by any chance came across a ravishingly beautiful coed from New Jersey by the name of Cindy Aldridge. Both she and Dario raised eyebrows and gave me a suspicious, startled, disapproving look. "I think I heard about that name" she said, "is she a sophomore'?"... "how did you get to know her'?" she asked.

-Never mind", I said, "it's kind of a long story, but if my memory serves me well, I recall her being a very beautiful girl with genuine southern Italian features, black hair, dark complexion", I said adding: "you can check it out next time you are back at the school".

-Don't you worry, Professor Szikszay-Farkas, I will do that", she said with a dose of admonition in her voice. She was a pretty good looking girl herself. Of course neither of us could envision then, that in a few years hence she will end up being enrolled in my sophomore surveying class at Lowell Tech.

That was the time when I first found out details about the Sinclairs; that they spent a lot of time in Saudi Arabia. Jack Sinclair was with Aramco, in soil mechanics and foundations. His wife, also Patricia, was a nurse in the Aramco Hospital. This was how they met. We heard about all the beautiful Mideastern artifacts, carpets, etc. they accumulated while in the kingdom. I mentioned again, with some nostalgia my ill fated faculty position at the University of Riyadh. Jack seemed to know the place quite well and was talking about it at length. (This was the first time in New England that I ever committed one of the ugliest cardinal sin: I envied him.) It was obvious to me, and most likely to others as well by then, that I was totally obsessed with Arabia.

The guests were pretty well saturated with the hors d'oeuvres and cocktails, so we were all invited to the buffet. It was a sumptuous assortment of delicacies. We were speculating with Maria that it must have been 'catered'. Not that we underestimated Harriett's culinary capabilities, but this much could not have reasonably been expected to be prepared by the division chairman's wife.

Tom Cilento was actually a mechanical engineer by training. The classical engineering curriculum 'course spectrum' had a number of overlaps between the disciplines. The civil engineers took numerous courses identical with that of the mechanicals. The electricals had very little in common with the civils, but more so with the mechanicals. The architects also had some common grounds with the civils. But architecture was nonexistent at Lowell Tech.

Tom fitted in quite well with our course offerings. He was coordinating an engineering graphics course of which I had to be teaching one section. These were the times when computer aided graphics was still in its baby shoes. Computer imagery was in a more distant future. Graphics was still only 'line drawings'. But this was exactly what the engineering profession badly needed. We have discussed these things with Tom, and I offered that I will make arrangements with Itek and Kongsberg Systems for a half-day demonstration for each of the classes. Tom was taken by the unusualness of this arrangement and gave it a lukewarm reception; but when I convinced him that a demonstration of this sort would be a significant eye opener to these students, and that the whole thing can be easily arranged, because I have one of my former colleague from Ohio State working at Itek, right here in Burlington, he agreed and at the end of the semester the students saw all the state of the art equipment working in real time.

He was a good decade older than our contemporaries. His wife was also a nurse. We learned, that their acquaintance and ultimate liaison was second world war vintage. At the time, their children were already past college age. Tom had been working on a 'patent' which was somewhat too nebulous for me to fully grasp, for that reason I never showed a deep(er) interest in it, that would go beyond professional courtesy. His wife, her name escapes my memory now, however, was a 'sweet lady' in every meaning of the word, the kind that men usually refer to as: her man being a 'lucky' guy. And that definitely applied to Tom. It was devastating for me to learn years later, that he came down with Parkinson's disease.

Herm was the kind of guy who dominated a party, and notoriously, everyone of his classes. He was the very soul of it. Not only supplying the jokes and anecdotes, but even amusing short stories and quite often, piquant ones too. Always, however, strictly within sharp boundaries of impeccably good taste: he was a surveyor, ... so he knew his boundaries. And his vocabulary ... for me, who was not grown up with and in the (English) language, it was simply: awesome, the ultimate. Writers, probably poets too, and politicians for sure, could have envied him for that. He usually had an expression for everything, quite often a quote, which I, of course, could not tell its origin.

I have introduced Herm earlier in another chapter: at the picnic. He was about Giff's age, and contemporary to Tom Cilento as well. Jack Sinclair was somewhat younger. Now, Herm took some time out from the party and devoted it to my consulting project. He seemed to know the broad parameters of it; As it turned out: from Lou Schofield, whom he knew well. The Schofields have gotten a fair share of contracts yearly of State Projects, so Herm informed me. He started asking questions about the adjustment of the triangle net, which, right away told me the vintage of his knowledge about it. The mere fact that he was thinking in terms of 'condition equations' (this is what he asked: "Gabe, how many conditions'? that will give me the idea of the net") startled me. I told him about these all being interlocking triangles, and many, many of them, its not feasible even to start recognizing 'independent' conditions, unlike in a chain. Therefore, we apply the method of 'observation equations' ."Well, then you must have a whole bunch of those" he began to realize.

-Yah, certainly, I said, "we are assembling them just now and there are already close to a hundred".

-But how many unknowns do you have eventually to solve for'"? He asked.

-So far we have 32 variations to the coordinates for the 16 new points, as the unknowns" I said, "and that's about it, because the navigation beacons they tied to, are considered fixed". (No variation to those!)

-Oh, yah, I see", he said, "Lou told me something about it, but even he did not know much more. I assured him that you will take care of it"..."By the way", he also told me, "you will be getting your registration soon so I heard" and he winked at me.

Herm did not bring along his wife, Eileen, evidently she had taken a fall and her shoulder and collar bone was in a cast, which immobilized her for all practical purposes, such as this occasion. Most everyone, who new her, expressed their sorrow.

The structures program was the strongest program with the civil engineers. In fact the only 'major' available at the time. Bill Hapkins was the lead man. He came over from Merrimack College; Giff was successful in luring him over with an increase in salary, and, which was not exactly unheard of, **with tenure**, right at the hiring. But this was definitely very rare. He, of course had tenure at Merrimack already, so it was sort of ... justified. He also started working towards his doctorate at the University of Massachusetts, at Amherst.

He also had ample teaching experience, many years, in fact, not to mention his practical experience. He was also registered as a PE. (Professional Engineer) in the Commonwealth. He kept his diploma certificate in his office at the school. To my knowledge he was the only registered PE. in the Department at the time. Later years, I suspected that Jack Sinclair was too, but I never knew for sure.

Bill Hapkins was a tall, handsome, athletic man, very much the embodiment of a classical 'WASP'. Approaching middle age, or already at the threshold, with a poise to accompany all the above. The students seemed to revere him, and the faculty members fallowed suit. He was altogether an impressive man; radiating success, without being condescending towards his colleagues. Little wonder that he was eyed as a successor to Gifford, when ever the time will come for his retirement. A very suitable replacement indeed. Everyone knew that the double position that Gifford presently held will not survive his retirement.

Even his philosophies matched that of Gifford's. He carried on the concept that there is a certain **body of knowledge** any candidate for a degree in civil engineering must show proficiency at. There shall not be shortcuts. Those who do not measure up should find another suitable niche within the profession. At the time, the term: sub-professional was not at all a derogatory or diminuend term, and it should not have been either. (It still is not such in this day and age.)There is a great need for them too. So much so, that, for example, in the medical profession there are several levels of professionals lower than the almighty (MD.) doctor. The technical fields likewise had differentiated between the designer, the technician end the technologist.

For a short while, after the Gifford years we had been sharing an office on the main floor of Ball Hall. He was cheerful most of the time, quite often I overheard him humming tunes which were, of course, familiar to me. Most of them from American (Broadway) Musicals, and some Philip Sousa marches which of course I knew many. In- frequently, he switched to some of the better known tunes from Gilbert and Sullivan operas, which was definitely a side-step off the ordinary musical taste, as far as the average (cultured) American of our age group, was concerned. I can't remember, ever that he would have turned to any of the hundreds of beautiful tunes composed by European composers (the [British] 'Savoy' operas, previously mentioned) exempted. This was quite natural, however, since he probably never set foot to Europe. But I had to notice that he was the only member in our rather small community within the faculty, who openly displayed an inclination towards music-loving, to the extent of actually, unashamedly humming the tunes as they were flowing right out of his soul, most often reflecting his present mood. He was a delightful person by any account.

His wife Lillian, was a frail, sort of ultra thin, delicate woman who, when side-by-side with him, seemed to be the daughter rather than the wife of gigantic Bill. But when it came to temperament, the two of them seemed to match perfectly, like two well tuned musical instruments. They had a son who was assuming his father's bodily attributes, both in size and shape. He was playing football on the varsity team in his school. He was a high school senior. Lillian liked to describe to us, how he effortlessly, can devour 2 or 3 hamburgers with all the trimmings: for breakfast.

Dan Lepine was one of the junior members of the structures team since the Fall, the other one being Dario Campanelli, since he joined them, the same time I was hired. I actually never really went as far as finding out exactly how they have broken down, or rather distributed, among themselves the great number of structures courses offered in the college bulletin.

Dan was a personable individual. Equally friendly with any and all of the members. If his teaching stile was as no nonsense and straightforward (I never actually attended any of his classes) as his presentation of any administrative topic at faculty meetings, then I must conclude that he was not only a good teacher, but an experienced administrator as well. He seemed to do a lot of extra work in developing a future graduate program offering in the structures area. Giff, needless to say, rewarded him too, the following year: just before he was 'advised' by the high administration to take a retirement. Giff promoted Dan to associate professor.

Back in the fall semester Dan was the only member of the team who had invited the entire ensemble to his house in Tewksbury. His wife, also a nurse (it was getting almost mysterious, how the civil engineers of New England tended to be attracted to the members of this -at the time- predominantly female profession) had all the attributes, manners, etc. of the professional nurse, without being bossy, domineering, as quite often they are. She organized the wine and cheese tasting party to which all of us were invited.

At that time I was rather unassuming, and happy to observe that I was in a sense, readily -**if not actually**- absorbed, but at least 'admitted' to our little community. There was a lingering atmosphere around suggesting all of this being only superficial, that I (or rather we) were still somehow looked upon as an 'exotic animal' freshly admitted to the zoo. There was this (safe!) distance between the 'new creature' and the zookeeper, which was advisable to keep before his full domestication could be accomplished and assured. In my case, on the faculty level, this distance was prevalent even several more years after the initial, cautious contact was made.

The wine-cheese tasting party at the Lepine's was the first, tentative trial to break through this distance. At least this was our impression with Maria. We were keenly looking out for these signs, and any other smallest of signs, or indications to this effect. I wasn't quite sure where Dan's original 'home' had been before he came to New England. There was some mention that he went to grad school in Colorado, but what about before that? One thing was sure, that the couple, as well as their two sons (both the same age as our two oldest kids) seemed to have no problem shooting down roots in this area. For us, it was not so easy.

In contrast, we were rapidly absorbed in the Midwest, in Akron, in spite of our accent, (or maybe because of it,) our frequently inadequate vocabulary, our curious customs, our sharply incomplete Americanization at the time. But we 'felt' much more 'at home' there. That was the real, great American 'melting pot', the Midwest.

At the University of Akron, the faculty wives, within each opening semesters organized the -so called-'circle suppers', a genuinely delectable idea. Every second week those 'raffled' into a 'circle' (some 20 couples, all faculty members and/or spouses) were meeting in 5 different homes for supper, approximately 4 couples each. The host couple knew ahead of time exactly who the 3 guest couples will be, and got together over the phone making all necessary catering arrangements. The host couples also rotated among the circle members. It resulted in an incredible social interaction. The engineers were mixed (blended) with other college faculty members, and soon the entire faculty began to know each other quite well. That is: only those, who voluntarily participated in this ingenious program. There was a goodly percentage who stayed away; some shy foreigners (we were not among them), Westerners, and New Englanders. Unfortunately, there were hardly any from the South. As we have learned to know the South later, it was a pity. But that was the Midwest! A great big family.

------*

Giff was the only one, so far, who saw, and knew where our house was, but has not come inside until he has first invited us during the semester break, to his party. We have never been invited to anyone of my other colleagues. The only exception being that of the above mentioned party at Dan's house. I still recall it as a very pleasant afternoon event.

Speaking of "crossing (or closing) the distance": there was an other occasion that I quite vividly recall. Herm, after the spring semester's last surveying field exercise invited 'everybody' to the newly opened 'Lums" fast food restaurant in the center of the town in Chelmsford, for sort of a rapid, ad hoc faculty meeting, the purpose of which was for everyone to make an input about the success and (if any) failure of the field exercise. Following the almost obligatory pizza and beer, I made a cautious suggestion, first only to Herm, who was the boss of the meeting anyway, for the whole gang to hop over to our house, a mere spit away, and have a tour of our modest 'head-quarters'. A quick glass of my recently acquired Pinot Chardonnay, well chilled, was assured for everyone.

Herm immediately took charge of the 'operation' and within minutes, six cars pulled in to-and- next-to our driveway. Maria was close to being petrified for the first few minutes, observing this invasion, after which the master of ceremonies: Herm, took charge of the 'visiting troops', quickly smoothed all the ruffled feathers, and I was finally able to take over as the host. I never forget Dario's keen interest and observation of Gabor Junior, who at that time (past his first birthday) was having a delicious afternoon nap in his crib. Dario was the only unmarried, bachelor member of our faculty at the time, so he never had the occasion to have his guests looking over his baby son.

I was under the impression that at last, that 'safe distance' from the corral fence was finally crossed, hopefully by all members of our group, and that the 'creature' was considered fully domesticated, thus the gate of the corral may be left open for good.

I was badly mistaken. As it turned out in the years ahead, my position here, was an exile, within our exile.

------*

The Caicos island project was about ready to be punched on the cards. It needed a short utility program to calculate all the coefficients and the misclosures for each 120 equations. My computer programming experience dated back to the early 60-s at Ohio State where the FORTRAN language was king. Every graduate student was expected to be reasonably proficient at it. I too had the basics, but as soon as it came to 'diagnostics', error messages, and other delicacies, my trying to do it, was a total waste of time.

I visited the computer facilities, which consisted of a donated IBM 1620, a desk size threshing machine, fed by a card reader the size of an armoire, which was swallowing -and reading- approximately a card a second. This was considered 'pretty fair' speed, since the processor also set-up the equations in between time.

I consulted the head of the facility, one who looked like the typical 'cyber-man' of the era. I introduced myself and presented the problem to him, which he readily acknowledged. I asked him if there might be a grad-student, or a senior, who could use a few extra bucks, by taking care of the preparation of the cards. He was under the impression that when these equations will be ready for input, then a Gaussian solution would also have to be first programmed, that shall fit this machine, "and that ... you know... Professor Farkas, would be a considerable and time consuming job", he alerted me.

I then explained him that nothing else is necessary, because an old colleague and very good friend of mine from Ohio State will be running these input equations into the ready program on a big IBM machine, that will do the entire job, to the finish. He works for a contractor to the Coast and Geodetic Survey, doing programming and computing. All I needed, here and now, was a whiz-kid who would do this 'detail'. Then I will send the cards to him by mail for processing, on the big machine.

He then mentioned the name: Swanson. He said this kid has more experience than any of his own students would have. He is hanging around the computer facilities and helps out the students, who need it. Thus he makes a few bucks. Like a freelance consultant for the students, in need of his help. He is not a regular student, sort of in between classes, each semester picking up some credits. I asked him if he knew how to get hold of the kid. Then he asked around his own students if anyone knew his number. So, I left word with one of his students, if they see him tell him to see me ASAP. I told them my name and room number in Ball Hall.

Next day Paul Swanson was waiting in front of my room, introducing himself and said that his father knows me. I instantly recalled the meeting in Gaithersburg last fall, where his father actually asked me to …kind of look out (probably did not want to use the word: 'after') his 'rambunctious kid' who has the attitude of an 'I know it all' kind of guy. Judging from his rather sloppy appearance, he definitely needed serious 'looking after'.

Although I was accustomed in my years of teaching, to this, or even much sloppier looking students, so, Paul's attire did not alarm me. However in the 60-s this was a pretty sure sign of being a 'rebel'. I sympathized with them, sometimes even admired them for their 'independence', but had only these conditions: that they were bright, diligent and productive. As it usually turned out, they were all of the above.

Paul had a thoroughly 'I don't give a damn' attitude. I did not know virtually anything about him or his circumstances. He had sky- blue eyes, which seldom met those, to whom he was talking, and they were focused to almost infinity, only sometimes to a closer object at hand. As I concluded they were 'dreamy' eyes, not unlike ones you see on drug addicts.

I decided that I have to find out more about him, before I would get to play the role of surrogate father. So, after I opened the door I told him to sit down across from me at my desk. I asked him to tell me about himself, anything he feels important for me to know. In a few sentences he summarized that he does not live at home; that he has fallen for a coed in his class; that they are in love; and that neither parents approve their liaison; (the typical Romeo and Juliet story!); that she wants to elope with him, does not matter where to; and that he feels like never before in his life; that he is sort of at his wits' end.

-Well, … Mr. Swanson, nothing you have told me so far is strange to me. Sooner or later we, and I mean 'us': men, go through similar predicaments in which you presently find yourself", I told him, and suddenly found myself getting involved in something I was frantically trying to avoid. "So, where do you live, if you don't live at home? I asked.

-I, ...sort of ... hang around in the computer lab, ... that is open usually all night long" he said matter of factly; "I make some money doing programming for students, who need my help", he said, "and that carries me through the day, ...I can get by on a minimum, essential food, I don't need much", he explained.

-Well, Mr. Swanson, ...

-Professor, would you please call me Paul, ... please?" It seemed as if this meant a great deal for him, but again, this would seem to emphasize the situation I was frantically trying to avoid.

-All right, ... Paul" I said, and found myself getting deeper into it, "I must tell you that I am bewildered of your situation, and don't know where to begin, but I will try", so I began. "I think, and correct me if I am wrong, that you expect something from me that your father should give you, and that is: 'advice'. That is the number one duty of fathers. I must ask you: do you think this is an acceptable lifestyle for yourself?"

-No, it is not!" he said and at the first time he looked straight at me.

-I will try not to lecture, okay?" I said, assuming that he was sick of lectures. "Your father seemed like a reasonable, hard working, certainly ambitious man, in a supervisory position ...how do you think he got there where he is? It sounded to me, when I spoke with him, that he cares for you, ... pays your tuition –which I must say is not the present and expected norm! ... and, ... he probably expects you to live alike or a similarly responsible life. Am I right? or am I way out?"

-Yes, that sounds like him, all right" he said subdued. "All I wanted was to take Julie home with me to us, ... where she could live with me", ...and he paused. "She would help out with the household chores, ... we would really be no trouble, ... no trouble at all."

-Paul, is she in trouble? I mean right now...already in trouble? Believe me, I am talking from my own experience now: This is quite an important point," I said and wanted an answer.

-No, ... no! she is not! ... Definitely not!"

-Good, I said, "by the way, this is the first positive input I got from you so far, I think we can pursue the situation further, but first let me ask you a few things", I went on looking at him, which presented a rather deplorable sight. "Did you make any plans at all, how you will live, ... you know, ... when you will break away and will try to make it on your own, ... being independent, ...sort of?"

-Yes. Professor, we both can work, we had been working on summer breaks, I used to be on Highway Department field crews in summers, ... my father ... talked to one of the supervisors, and I got a position, ... I was an instrument man two past summers, ... I can always get a more

103

permanent position with the DPW, ... And then again, Julie is a diligent girl; she has a full time job at an evening shift at a 7-11 store, she has her own car, ... she can also do key-punching, she is clever..."

-I understand, still, it does not seem to have a solid enough foundation, ...I mean ... where do you want to live? The computer lab could not enter into the equation any more, I am sure you agree."

-Yes. This is the main reason for I came here; I would like to find out what sort of a job do you have for me, how much will I be making, ... these sort of things..."

-Paul, I am afraid I have to disappoint you. What I have right now is not a job, ... per se, ... it is one of those quickies... you know, a one time shot, ... an assignment, a certain detail problem that must be solved ..." I said, and watched his reaction, "this is not something you could build on, ... but, it is rather something you could do on the side, if you already have a sustaining job 'to do better', better than the average, do you read me?"

-Yes, Professor, will there be more of them like this? or anything else, ... field work, ...perhaps?"

-Paul, I really feel like giving you a chance, and, ... since this job is a rather urgent one I would like you to start on it immediately. Then, when I see results... I want you to know that I am a goal-oriented guy, ...you know, ...no nonsense! ... results! "

-Professor, I like that, ... really, ... a clear-cut problem, and then I produce the solution, so, ...please explain the task", he said and seemed like being perked-up.

I explained him that he has to set up some 120 observation equations; for each one he has to compute the coefficients, and the misclosures, and punch them out on a set of new cards ready to be input for solution into a much larger machine. When it's all done, and I have the 120+ cards he will be getting $ 120.00, cash.

He couldn't believe his luck. Although I warned him that this is no child's play, and that there will have to be a lot of tedious work getting all the information from the large map of the triangle network, then punch all the cards, compute the stuff and produce a new deck of cards, ... it is quite time consuming, but he did not get deterred, instead I again saw him focusing with his eyes onto that undefined point in infinity that I noticed the first time we met.

Two days later, Friday, Paul was waiting for me in the hallway in front of my door. He had with him a bundle of punch-cards. I invited him in. He put down the deck on my table along with the plan.

-Well, Paul, ... I can not spend much time with you, because I have my morning class, but just tell me now what seems to be the problem, anything holding you up, and then you can go on continue with it. After my class we can spend more time..."
-Professor, there is no problem, ... it's all done", he said nonchalantly, "I come back after your class and then you can look it over to see, ...you know... that... if it is the way you wanted it, Okay'?"

I suddenly didn't know what to say to him, so we agreed to meet after the class. When I came back to the room, we sat down and checked some of the equations and the corresponding cards for a good number of them. They were all there; It was simply awesome. I told him to duplicate the deck, because it has to be mailed to Maryland, and just to be sure, we better have a back-up deck. He came back with it in 20 minutes.

That was the time I recalled my own early experience with the Land- and Soil Survey Bureau in Budapest, after the communist party boss at the Technical University performed his first purge, clearing out the 'clerical elements' from the class of '52. He summarily dismissed some 20 students right from the hydrology lecture, where he burst in and read his first 20 names, adding, that these students are forbidden to come to the lecture halls in the future. The 20 of us compared notes in the hallway; every single one of us had graduated from parochial high schools. (Many years later, -'in my second life'- I finally forgave him; I realized that he was under the communist Party's almighty and constant supervision; he was not doing his own will, but that of the Party.)

Weeks later, while looking for some kind of technical job, another adjunct professor, who was given an additional position in 'Industry', by the Party (also a high echelon party member! to keep an eye on the newly nationalized Bureau's affairs) put me in the Bureau's intern program to start working there. I was out in he field with the crew all over the country, sometimes working 14 hours (of daylight) and found myself in total ignorance of 'difficult situations'. There simply could not be such a thing as: difficulty; those were solved pronto. As we were saying: the 'impossible' things were different: they would take 'somewhat longer', unfortunately. **I was then Paul's present age.**

Paul then got paid. I wrote him a check. He asked if it was all right to cash it right away, which I assured him that it was. He asked if there are some more 'urgent' jobs to perform. I told him that I got to get things organized first, but there actually are a few jobs which require field work first, and that I have to find out how is he doing field work- wise, ... and that we will have to find someone to help him, ... so... hold off, ... cool it, for a while.

Thus came the second avalanche of information from him: he **does** have a helper, namely: Julie, who is very adept in roding and does a better job at taping distances than any sophomore finishing the surveying course here at school. After that I had little ground to doubt anything he said; so I told him to see me after 3 PM at my home in Chelmsford where I will give him particulars about the job and try him at his first field work assignment. I also told him that the job is in Sandwich, Massachusetts, and therefore he would have to stay at a motel overnight for which he will be reimbursed.

He informed me that he could come only around 6 PM because that is when Julie gets out of work, and she has the transportation, so would it be okay after 6 PM. I said it would be.

About 6:30 PM a Volvo station wagon pulled into our driveway. Paul jumped out of it, and came directly towards me. I greeted him, then told him to have Julie meet me. I have not even seen her yet. She looked pale and shy, a frail little creature, obviously overworked and a serious sleeping deficit in her expression. She gave me a shy, tentative smile, not quite sure how to respond to my greeting; just stood there, till finally I realized that she was waiting for me to make the first move. I put my right hand forward, she responded, and we shook it very gently. Both of us seemed to expect something more from the other. Just a little more. I was under the impression that, had I made an encouraging move, even a slightest move, she would have kissed me, like she would have kissed any of her parents.

But this somehow never came. From neither of us. Not that I was objecting anything of the sort. I felt like hugging her, sort of, to encourage her towards trusting me, but the moment passed and it seemed impossible to be retrieved. I had just about became Paul's surrogate father, after all, so it was not entirely out of place if I had adopted both of them under my wings. They picked up the instrument and the instruction sketches of the site to be surveyed, and then drove off.

With that began a beautiful cooperation. He had an assignment almost every week. He did the small topographic surveys for various site plans I was getting more and more of from the Ariel Engineering venture, but found it more and more difficult, time- wise, to do it myself. Paul was traveling to the sites, wherever they were, some as far away as Chicopee or Springfield. I was hard getting paid for some of these jobs. Some of them were falling behind 2 to 3 months. It began to make me nervous, specially when I had to pay Paul. But that story will come later.

The Caicos island project was finished with flying colors. An exemplar in organization, cooperation, and execution. When the computer printouts were returned from Rockville Md. from my good old buddy: Rudy, he sent me his bill, as I asked him to. It was for a mere $ 120.00. I called him up that evening and told him that there will be a bonus for him for good and speedy work. I sent him $ 250. He did not object.

Frank was overwhelmed. Every new point had its error ellipse plotted by the big computer, it was simply super. I then assured him that in case the Brit's want anything else, we will comply, pronto. The entire job was preserved on punch cards, results and all. Evidently BOSD was also satisfied because we never heard from them any more.

There was a last twist to the story though, like in most Alfred Hitchcock movies: the prospective developer overspent himself, he felt the world was at his feet, his newly acquired yacht overturned (it wasn't even paid for! he still quarreled with the insurance company,) his even newer lady-friend was getting fed up with the series of bad luck, they seemed to be having lately, so she left him; thus, he finally declared bankruptcy. Frank had to wait many months before he received his final payment for the job. I haven't heard anything more about the fate of that development. It started out being 'too good to be true'.

Chapter Seven
(Shooting down roots.)

We got really busy in the summer. Geoffry secured a contract with the town of Barnstable to define key spot elevations at a great number of road intersections throughout the Town. The main purpose of these was for preliminary sewer studies in the Town. He did all the negotiations but held back from discussing the specifications of how the job will be executed. The technical part.

There were tentative proposals; the first one, to do the entire job by 'spirit leveling' which would have been a sizable (30-40 day) involvement, practically needing to live in Town for that extended period. After the necessary input-estimates from me this turned out to be prohibitively expensive. I was counting on this because I had, in the back of my mind, a much more speedy way of achieving the same end results: by stereo photogrammetric methods, with a lesser degree of accuracy. I told him to shoot for this, because it can be done within 30 days, without having have to go into the field practically ever. By pricing it right, this has the greatest profit margin.

Geoffry hired a young graduate from the University of New Brunswick, Canada. He did this entirely on his own without even mentioning it to me. All he did was he sent the kid to see me, so that I could interview him about his technical schooling and experience, if any. The kid, Chopra, from India, did go through an equivalent scholarly training of a bachelor's degree in a surveying program here in the States. He did not have experience above that of the lab work in school, but he was bright, and receptive to any explanation I gave him. Geoffry was negotiating his salary, which, when I later asked Chopra how much it was, I became suspicious of why he would be willing to work for such a pittance. None of us knew at the time, that he had been trying to hide here from Canadian authorities. As it turned out later, a Canadian girl was trying to find him to get child support from him.

Nevertheless, he was quick to catch on with the stereo comparator (which Geoffry acquired for the sole purpose of performing the Barnstable job). I suggested to Geoffry, that this desk type instrument, which cost only $ 1,300. would be paying for itself easily with this one, single job. It was part of the deal that the Town will let us have a full set of copies of their aerial photographs. None of the Town officials knew that these would be the main source of our spot elevation information.

None of the competing engineering consultants bidding for the job had the slightest idea how we could do the work for less than half the lowest bid. All they knew that there was no such thing as magic, that there was considerable amount of field work, either way they were proposing to do the work, but none of them had ever thought of doing what we did. This was the first victory I won for the newly established 'Ariel Engineering' firm.

Geoffry, however, was successful in convincing me that the firm was actually struggling financially. He began to show in his books that the firm was still in the red; Ariel Airmap being the financial stronghold behind it, without which the Engineering venture would have gone bankrupt. I kept asking for the billings and payment records, to see why we could not make a decent profit. Why is it that I had to minimize my professional fee on the work I did for the client: the firm, in which I owned a 50% share. The fact was that I could never see these records.

There was another surveying and mapping job in Alston, in connection with an accident site, which I also finished before the end of July. This was done for a Boston law firm. They needed us to show that their client was killed while her vehicle, with its tire-marks shown on the pavement, were within the path of her lane of traffic. The resulting large scale map turned out so beautiful, that they wanted to know the engineer who did it. This was the first time I had the unmistakable feeling that Geoffry was trying to separate me from any and all clients. (Initially I suspected my accent being the culprit.)

Geoffry knew full well, that I was planning to take a European trip to catch up with the rest of my family in August. They left earlier at the end of June, and were staying with various relatives on my and Maria's side. I was supposed to pick up a Volkswagen so called: 'square back sedan' model, in Luxembourg or Germany, essentially to replace the aging Ford Fairlane wagon, and take it with me to Hungary to serve as our basic transportation while in Europe. Then at the end of the summer, import it into the USA.

I told Geoffry to make sure that I would have my $ 2,500. before I was to leave. Two days before that I went to the office in Brookline and took the original Accident Plan, all stamped and signed, with me. He wanted me to leave it there and come back next day for my check. But something told me not to leave it there unless I was getting paid. So I turned and was ready to leave the office, when he told me that he is going to give me a check. I told him:

-Geoffry, there is no need for a check, why don't you come down with me to the bank and let's do it there, when I can cash it in the same time, because I got to get ready for my flight the next day". Hesitantly he came down to the bank, where he had a short conference with the manager. Finally I picked up the cash and I handed him the plan. This gave me the idea that from then on I would simply be an independent subcontractor on these Ariel Engineering jobs. Thus, I could spare myself the humiliating practice of scrutinizing the juggled books, I was, ill prepared to understand. After all, Geoffry had the degree from the Babcock Institute, not I.

------*

Chopra said good by with a heavy heart, when he moved out of our house the day of my flight. He was living there with me all the month of July, working mostly on the Barnstable project. He was quiet and not much trouble. I had agreed him doing some of the cooking, but no real fancy Indian stuff. He was doing most of that when I was out of the house. But had to let me do the cooking European style, when I was preparing it for us. He had only one request: that every day he had to eat rice, at least once. It didn't matter in what form or taste, he just had to eat it everyday. I was convinced that it was some sort of religious conviction, but we never discussed it in depth.

It was inconceivable to me how little social interaction he required. For days at end he did nothing but measure the spot elevations with the parallax bar. It seemed, as if it was his entertainment. Occasionally he was humming some tune totally unfamiliar to me; I never interrupted him, never inquired about its meaning, or its origin. Setting up his stereo model became quite routine after the first week; only at some occasions had he trouble with it, in which case, after a while, reluctantly he asked for some help. He seemed to be perfectly satisfied culturally. In the evenings we were watching TV, whenever there was a good old movie; he also liked Westerns.

I was trying to inquire about his family, without much success. He said he came from a town some 100 miles from Bangalore; applied for a scholarship after high school, and got it. So he came to Canada, to Frederickton, to the UNB, where he enrolled in the Surveying Engineering program. I knew about that program from its director: Gotfried Konecny who did his doctorate at Ohio State. It was he who suggested, (back at the time, when I was looking for an institution to do graduate work,) to go to Ohio State instead of Frederickton, because there were more possibilities there. He was right. And I did.

At one of the weekends, an acquaintance and friend of ours, Teri, a young Hungarian woman called me up from her home in Westford. While talking about my situation, with Chopra sharing my solitude, she suggested that she should invite some of her women colleagues and we should have a picnic and a party after that in their back yard. She made it very clear that Chopra was invited too. I expressed some anxiety about the cultural gap that seemed to exist between him and the rest of us. But Teri thought nothing of it. So we agreed that I will bring him along the coming Saturday.

After the introductions I passed him along to the girls. They had some soft music playing, (Teri was very captivated by melodic tunes, regardless of their era, and quite often sought out my suggestions in this regard) it turned out that Chopra was familiar with a number of Gilbert and Sullivan arias and tunes. It was 'Buttercup' from H.M.S. Pinafore that dominated the evening; evidently Chopra knew a great number of them, from high school plays at home in that Town not far from Bangalore. He was in fact singing them.

He became the hit of the party. One of the girls was dancing with him almost all night long. I was going to leave well before midnight, (I needed sleep!) but I was told to go home, never mind Chopra, he is having a good time…etc. and that he will be given a ride Sunday to our house. Chopra indeed showed up Sunday afternoon, while I had a 'swim' in our little backyard pool. I could hardly recognize him. He was dreamy, still humming some tunes, 'The Wandering Minstrel' from The Mikado.

I was sure he had more to drink last night than I ever saw him having. I was not sure which of the Chopra I was staying with for the last few weeks. I did not give him alcoholic drinks on account of his religion (whatever that was) but the drinks (or whatever else) he had last night seemed to perform magic. He was transformed.

The day of my departure was planned to be his last day of stay at our house. The following day Chopra was to return to the Ariel Airmap office in Brookline. I offered him a ride but he turned it down because he had arranged it already with one of the girls from Teri's party. She came to pick him up in the afternoon. That was the last time I saw him. Upon my return from Europe in September Geoffry informed me that he had to fire Chopra because of his lack of taking the job seriously. It appeared to me that he had the same problem with his entire life: he just couldn't take it seriously.

Geoffry told me the story of his dismissal. One day while Chopra was having his coffee break with the secretary (a fiery, Brazilian girl) and the draftsman, (a Cuban refugee boy) in the office, he was bragging about how wonderful this little Company is, sipping his coffee, "what a good little Company…"etc. while Geoffry was on the phone with the Immigration and Naturalization Service. The officers wanted to know about Chopra working for Ariel Airmap, Inc. Geoffry gave them the bare essentials they were seeking, but when he hung up, he wanted Chopra out of the office. He was ready in less than the time it took Geoffry to write him his pay check.

*--- *--- *

Loftleidir, Icelandic Airline's new jet landed in Luxembourg in mid morning . It took some time before one could leave the terminal with all the luggage; some of the mercenaries on leave from some African country, where they were doing their fighting, were so loaded up with all sorts of exotic stuff, (and their weapons) that they were holding up the customs officials.

I grabbed a taxi and tried to explain the driver the location of the little private hotel close to downtown, as best I could, by remembering where it was, when we stayed there the last time. The owner, a nice lady, who spoke fairly good English was always very helpful to us. She was a member of the 'Friends of America Club' that was formed during the Second World War at the time of the Battle of the Bulge.

I told her that I was looking for a Volkswagen 'Square-back Sedan' model to buy, that it could be a used one at that, it does not matter, so long as I can drive away with it. She was again very helpful, she called some of the local used car dealers she knew, but there was not a single such vehicle available in all of Luxembourg, she was told. But one dealer gave her an idea: namely to tell me to travel to Wolfsburg, Germany, to the factory and one of the factory dealers should be able to come up with one.

So, she told me to have lunch, and then take a nap to get all the jet-lag and fatigue out of my system. Then take the evening train to Köln, where I could catch the Berlin Express all the way to Wolfsburg. She let me sleep on the couch right behind in her private office, where I slumbered till 6 PM, when it was time for me to leave. I never took a train-ride in post-war, rebuilt Germany, so it was a rather unexpected experience. I was only leery of the changing of trains at Köln.

Fortunately the platform master explained to me that all I had to watch for was the train pulling in on track # 3 at 21:58 hr which would depart exactly at 22:00 hr leaving me 2 full minutes to get on it. Plenty of time, no way to miss it. The real mystery materialized when the Berlin Express did exactly as he said it would. I got on, and surely at 22:00 hr it pulled out of the station. I found myself a corner seat at a window, and shortly fell asleep. I woke up several times during the night, every time carefully checking my map for our location. The conductor caught me doing this one time and told me there was nothing to worry about; all I had to do was to set my watch's alarm a few minutes before 4:55, when the train will be pulling into Wolfsburg.

I was no longer surprised when exactly at 4:55 in the morning the train slowed down to stop at Wolsfburg station. It was daybreak already. I walked right to a small cafe next to the station and made myself comfortable. A sleepy waitress inquired what I wanted, and I promptly replied that I needed a Volkswagen, and that's what I came to buy. She was dumbfounded at first, thought I was fooling her, because I had no accent, (or rather an Austrian one, which was definitely unusual in that northern factory town) then because the cafe was indeed the most inappropriate place for trying to by a car. But she began to understand my predicament and explained at length where the dealers were in town, sparing me the trouble of trying to find them later.

Thus, she suggested a breakfast, of a freshly cooked knockwurst, scrambled eggs, cream cheese, mustard, etc. and how I wanted my tea? with rum or cognac? I told her it really didn't matter one way or another, I liked it both ways. I wasn't really surprised when I saw her put two tiny jiggers next to the tee pot each filled with a different amber-colored liquid. She took it literally. The most enjoyable part was still the fresh baked rolls: the 'Kaisersemmeln', which brought back childhood memories. We could not find anything like them in New England. By at 6:00 AM the town was getting busy, people coming and going. The waitress suggested to check my suitcase in the station locker, and just walk up to the factory dealers, two of them less than a kilometer away. I gave her a generous tip. Then I took her suggestions.

It was nearly 7 o'clock, when I approached the first dealership. It was already open, so I entered. A fellow came over from the repair garage part and greeted me. When I told him the purpose of my visit, he seemed confused. He could not understand that without a reservation, without previous arrangements I just 'wanted to buy' a vehicle?

-Just where the "Herrshaften" are coming from?" he asked "we do not have vehicles 'sitting around here' that can be bought on a whim", he informed me. "But if you would wait a little for the boss to come in, which would be shortly, she might have some suggestion …"

-Look 'mein Herr' I told him, "I don't need suggestions, I got more than enough already while in Germany, …all I want is to buy a Volkswagen Square-back sedan, okay?"

-Your best bet is to talk to the boss" he said, making me sit down, read a magazine and wait for the boss, then left me.

Shortly, a very elegantly clad woman arrived, took her dustcoat off, came to me and asked who I was. I introduced myself properly and told her what I wanted. She asked if I was from Europe, because I had a slight Austrian accent. I corrected her that I was actually living in America. Then she was curious of where my German was originating, perhaps I was here during the war with the American troops? I told her that I was actually too young for that in 1944-45. She then sort of concluded that I was an immigrant to America, which I confirmed. She explained that to buy a new car, would be utterly impossible. The factory orders were booked till December. Not a single vehicle would be available before that time, only returned ones, due to defaults, and I certainly didn't want to touch any of those.

The next problem was: what I wanted to do with the car? did I think of exporting it to the US? Take it back with me? They would not let it off the ship if it was not built to American standards, that are somewhat different than the domestic ones. The third problem was, of course, to find a used one, which may turn out to be the most solvable one. Now, what was my decision?

I begged her to find a used one for me, that was in good working order. I told her I was willing to pay her a commission. Then she asked me if I had breakfast. I said I did. She ignored my answer. Then next she ordered espresso-coffee and pastries from the 'Conditorei' which, when delivered, was proof that she knew something about the way to a man's heart was leading through his stomach, and judging from the quantity of the order it was clear that it was meant for the two of us. While she was nibbling on her pastries, she was constantly on the phone. She must have made at least a half a dozen calls. All the while I slowly devoured a goodly amount of the tempting pastry.

Finally, she got up and told me that my patience has paid off. (I didn't want to confess that I had not understood a fraction of what transpired, and that I just hoped that she had not sold me to kidnappers.) Now talking directly to me I understood everything she said. She explained that another dealer's wife from a nearby town was driving the exact same vehicle I wanted to buy. It had some 30,000 kilometers on it and that she was going to bring it down here so I could see it and drive it. With that she got busy doing her own business, and left me with the remnants of the pastries in the reception room.

I could not believe what I saw. The Square-back sedan (which was being referred to as 'the Kombi' by local jargon, was beige, with black and gray interior, it was immaculately clean inside and out (it was owned by the dealer's wife after all) and finally, it was riding like a dream.

-How much?" I asked her. She wanted 5,500. DMark for it. I knew the approximate exchange rate at the time, which was around the 3.00 DM/US dollar. I told her I had US dollars in cash with me, so they called the local bank (evidently the two young women were well acquainted, maybe even friends) where they were told that it was the equivalent of $ 1,800. round figure. I was to give a $ 100. commission that I foolishly promised to the lady-boss at my end of the deal. Even so, I never dreamed of getting a car for this price.

There was, however, quite a lot of paperwork involved with the transaction. Earmarked for export to the US needed more paperwork, and most of all: a temporary license plate, and registration for a person 'in transit'. This could only be issued at certain locations, the closest being in Kassel, if I happened to drive that way. I was. So, after a few pleasantries I said good by.

The official at the registry in Kassel declared to me that it was impossible to issue such a registration at this time. I then, very naively asked why not? He was extremely short with his answer: "because that division is on vacation, 'mein herr', it's August, you know?" I wished them happy vacation. But I asked him, is there, by any chance, another place where this could be achieved.

-If you care to drive down to Würzburg, the provincial capital, they might have someone who could take care of this sort of thing", he said; but I must warn you not to tangle with the police, because you may never get much further than where they stopped you". This was a very helpful hint, for which I thanked him.

Würzburg was indeed one of the most charming city I discovered in all of Germany. I simply loved everything about it. On top of all, the registry office was open for business, and the helpful official took care of everything, not only all the paperwork, but he came out to the vehicle, checked the serial number, and personally affixed the temporary license-plate to the car. It was really getting hot by noon, so he suggested me to take a break and go to the Olympic size swimming pool in the central park where I could have a refreshing dip. There was music, and a kiosk, where I could have lunch too. He was a delightful fellow for a civil servant.

The pool was exactly as he described it. I spent some of the most pleasant time there; taking a good part of a roll of colored film just in the city of Würzburg. I decided that on our way back, we will come through that city again. The 'Burg' (a medieval fort) sitting on a cone shaped hill with an original vineyard cultivated on its slopes, was beautifully restored, and visible from most part of the city.

It was not quite 5 PM by the time I said good by to my favorite city and left. I took numerous pictures of the earlier as well as the rebuilt sections of the Autobahn through Nürnberg and München, to show them to my class in the fall. I picked up a hitchhiker near Nürnberg; as it turned out he was a medical student from the University of Würzburg. We decided to communicate in such a way that both of us would benefit from it: he spoke to me in English (which I was to correct for him) and I spoke to him in German, (the grammar of which he corrected for me). It was a most interesting, intellectual language game, besides being very informative. He left me at the outskirts of München.

It was getting really late and dark by the time I reached the border crossing at Salzburg. An infinitely long line of cars were crawling along the highway, bumper-to-bumper. At the crossing booth the German soldier was waiving through most of the vehicles, (drivers showing papers, passports from the window) only occasionally sending one to the side parking lane, where papers and car were checked by other officials. The Austrian soldiers on the other side acted likewise, they simply could not afford to bog down the traffic to a different, slower speed without risking the entire line coming to a halt.

Thus, I finally got on the Austrian Autobahn to Wien, a 300 Km stretch, which I decided not to tackle through the night. At Himmelreich, a dreamy alpen village (the origin of the Christmas tune 'Stille Nacht') I pulled off and drove right into the first little 'Gasthause', where I spent the night.

The next morning, the beginning of a gorgeous day, I drove off to Wien, where I intended to make a short stop at the Döbliger Verlag's downtown store, to look for turn of the century Viennese composers' works. All I found was a couple of works from Ernst Fisher, Josef Bayer and Alphonz Czibulka, and sheet music scores for a few light ballet music scores which I was familiar with since my youth before the war, while I was studying the piano. It was early afternoon when I managed to leave Wien and took the shortest route to the Hungarian border. The Volkswagen 'Kombi' was probably in its top performing condition, it was simply a dream-car come true. It did not have a lot of power, but sufficient for seemingly any kind of loads. Of course I had very little load to speak of.

The communist government's annoying, idiotic, massive paperwork associated with the formal visa along with a snapshot photo affixed to the pink and white copies of it was well known to us by then. In my case special complication arose from the fact that I was driving a privately owned (I was the registered owner, in 'transit' to boot) vehicle with a 'temporary' West German registration, which was to expire at the end of September. That gave me ample time before expiration, since we had to return for the coming academic year by Labor Day anyways. I felt really sorry for all the people waiting, and waiting with small, cranky children for the border authorities to process their endless paperwork. It was not simple or easy to cross the 'Iron Curtain'.

It was past 5 PM by the time I was speeding eastward on route No.1 which was to take me all the way to my parents' home on the Buda side of Budapest. I hardly reached the next town when I had to come to an abrupt halt on account of a herd of cattle crossing the main highway. I came a little close to the herd, so one of the stray cows was pushed against the right headlight of the car by another cow and caused a dent in its housing. The light was still working, but the cowhand told me that he has to report the 'accident' to the authorities. I gave him all the data he needed, and to his utter luck I spoke Hungarian with him, which simplified the matter considerably.

By the evening I drove into the short street where my parents had a small flat. They were out on the street, in front of the house and were so surprised that they did not recognize me as I was getting out of the car. They never saw the car before, and could hardly guess what was going on. But then everything clicked. Shortly, I was being filled in where my family was at the time. They were at the Lake Balaton at one of Maria's former class-mate, who were running a rooming house for summer vacationers. Next day I was finally catching up with them and commenced our vacation together.

On the return trip we did drive through Würzburg. Visited the brand new Kaufhof and bought our first 12-place-set modern design flatware set. We were really happy with it ever since. Somehow it matches our personality. The next task was to ship the vehicle to the US from a European port. In Luxembourg, they suggested, as the closest being:

the Belgian port of Antwerp. Leaving the family at the Hotel (with 2 AKC registered puli puppies in a rattan basket) I drove the Volkswagen to Antwerpen, (as the Belgians pronounced it) and was desperate to find a shipping company which would take it from me. They wanted to 'containerize it'. Shortly I found out the reason: the price! It cost more than double to ship it occupying a single, entire container.

It was 3 PM and really hot. I was told by a longshoreman who spoke some English that the shipping companies close at around 4 PM. I just had to have a cold beer. Turning into a nearby pub, I began to ask around the place who would speak English?... or German, when one of the bartender girls came slowly to me and with an extremely shy voice began to, or rather tried to, talk to me in English. When I very slowly, with the simplest of words explained what I was trying to do, she took hold of my hand, began to pull me very gently toward the staircase to the building, (all sorts of pictures ran through my imagination: that I could be apprehended, maybe even killed, that she could have an accomplice waiting somewhere and they will rob me (I still had a considerable amount of cash on me) while feeling my hesitation she began to squeeze my hand, all of a sudden the mental images began to go through a drastic change: (I thought that maybe there is a price for her unselfish help she was about to give me, she was a pretty attractive looking girl, but I still didn't know where she was pulling me); I was trying to talk to her all this while trying to elicit her concentration to my problem.

By this time we reached the top of the stairs. She went a few steps down the hall, still hanging on to my hand, and pointed to a door that had a small sign on it; All of a sudden I understood everything: I was ready to hug her, or kiss her, or maybe comfort her; the sign read:

> MOTORSHIPS INCORPORATED
> Shipping Automobiles Worldwide
> Office hours; 7 AM -4 PM

I was totally overjoyed; suddenly couldn't move. The girl was probably beginning to comprehend my situation judging by my utter relief, and began to goad me towards the door, my left hand still in her

119

right one. Then I grabbed hold of hers with both my hands and squeezed it if I wouldn't ever let go, and finally broke the silence:

"Thank you, thanks an awful lot," I said, finally putting an end to this quaint, unusual pantomime. She began to talk in Flemish, gesticulating all the time, trying to explain that I should be coming downstairs and have my beer, when I finished my business with the shipping company. I wanted to let her know that I got all this without the slightest misunderstanding and that I would indeed stop by at the bar.

The clerk spoke fluent English, I could even detect a New York accent. She confirmed that she was from Newark, N.J. and told me how this was usually done. She wanted an ignition key, which opened the doors as well. As I handed it to her I drew her attention that there were certain merchandize in the trunk at front. She said this was something they did not guarantee. She could not give an exact date for the shipment, but wrote down the telephone numbers of the company in the US. and assured me that we will hear from them from Newark. She also made a copy of the car's papers and handed them to me. She then warned me that I will have to travel to Newark when the car can be picked up and that it will have to go through a customs-broker, which I will find plenty of around, when I am to pick up the car. This was all.

It took no longer than about 30 minutes, after which I walked down to the pub (from the street side, because I could not locate the door through which the girl took me to the stairs), and sat down at the bar stool and finally ordered my well deserved beer. Both bartender girls were smiling at me and were talking to each other uninterruptedly in their exotic sounding Flemish.

I took some leisurely time walking quite a distance, trying to find the oceanfront. It was just a waterfront, not pretty, it wasn't even the real ocean, overly commercialized, crowded with warehouses. I wanted to find some of the nicer, more civilized, perhaps landscaped part of the oceanfront, but did not know where to look. So I made my plans: I had to find someone who could give me information about the Town. I began to talk to strangers on the street at random, both in English and German. All of a sudden a man of about my age (40+) began to answer me in good German. He had an excellent vocabulary and a pretty clear pronunciation without any strange dialect. He turned out to be originally from Hamburg, but after the war, when he finished school, settled in Belgium and worked for an international shipping company. His English, that we tried first was poor, much worse than my German.

First he took me to a news kiosk and bought an up to date map, and handed it to me. I wanted to pay him for it but he waved it away with his hand. Then I opened the map. He showed me some of the places he thought I ought to see and I memorized them. Then he asked how long I would be staying in Belgium. When I told him I have to take the train back to Luxembourg tonight, he suggested a taxi to the railway station to make sure I will not miss a good connection at Brussell (Bruxelles). He also called one for me from a pay-phone.

While waiting for the taxi, he told me that he was fighting in Hungary at the end of the war in 1945 while the Wehrmacht was in its final retreat on the eastern front. He said he had fond memories of Hungary. He was just a young kid and was offered civilian clothes and refuge by the locals, but he turned it down because he didn't want to get captured by the Russians or by the Gestapo who would have him shot on the spot for desertion.

When the taxi arrived, we said a warm good by. He had a pretty good (extra) sensory perception, because the train was due within a half an hour after I arrived at the station. By 10:30 I was back at our hotel in Luxembourg. Next day we took our 'Loftleidir' flight back to New York's Kennedy Airport with the puli puppies and all. I had the definite feeling that I had gotten Europe out of my system, at least for a good while.

There waited my next task for me: At 3;00 AM I took the bus to the bus terminal in downtown, where I had to wait till 5:30 for a bus that took me to Fords in N.J. to our friends house where I left the Ford Fairlane when I drove down for my departure to Europe. Our friends drove it back from Kennedy after I left in August and parked it in their yard. Now I had to drive it back to the airport and complete the last leg of the journey, to Chelmsford.

* --- * --- *

We had another addition to our faculty: Lucas Tartagnetti, another 'structures man' He was proud of his Italian heritage, nevertheless did not speak the language, so he was as genuine American as can be. He was sort of between jobs selling real estate, and God only knows what else, to support his family. He was a fairly pleasant fellow, not trying to show more than he had to show for. He had a master's degree from a local school and Giff hired him on the bottom of the scale. As we started the fall semester, he was also recruited as supervisor for the Saturday surveying field work, but he was truly not very enthused about that. There was another drawback of him joining us: he was at the wrong end of the demographics. Instead of strengthening, he was weakening our statistics.

Giff came into my office almost the minute I returned, but actually it was after our first faculty meeting, the first day of school.

-Gabe, how was summer'? I hear that you were back on the old continent. Did you visit your family'?"

-Sure thing, I said; "come to think of it, we had a very good time; I bought a slightly used Volkswagen Kombi too. I think it was a fabulous deal. But it's not here yet, it's on its way, crossing the Atlantic, … someplace, …I hope".

-Now really? where is it? do you have it shipped over?" he asked, "anyway, what is a Kombi? But never mind that, I came to have a talk with you", he said and sat down.

-Ah, oh" was the only response I could think of, "did I goof …

-No, none of that Gabe" he assured me. "This has to do with our faculty. Let me not beat around the bush. We need to hire 'real minorities'. Now the civil engineering department is perhaps the most polarized in the entire Division, as I am sure you know".

-Of course I know! I am the only minority, and even I don't qualify for that".

-Well, here is what I was thinking" he said as he came to the more difficult part of it. "I was interviewing a very nice, colored gentleman, who is currently working on his doctorate, expected to finish in September. He was looking over the list of our faculty qualifications, you know, the same one I showed you last year, this time showing our new additions. He was very uneasy being the only minority, (he did not recognize you as minority) but he said he would consider the position. He would take it if his other application at Brown University would not materialize. What I came to find out from you is, did you come across any real minority students during your graduate works? Do you know of any who would be interested in coming here; you know, whom you could consider as your friend? Real friend".

-Giff, I can think of two, right off the bat; one is an Egyptian Arab, Ph.D. from Ohio State, currently teaching in Manitoba, you know the place with 40 below winters, the other one is a traffic planner, Cornell

Ph. D. and he is colored, from the Caribbean. Now, what sort of expertise you had in mind? because none of them want to have anything to do with structures."

-Can you find out if any of them want to come here?" he asked.

-I can call Afifi (this is how we call Soliman) tonight; the Parker kid, … I have to find his current phone number from the Division of City and Regional Planning at Cornell. I don't even know if he has finished his degree.

-Gabe, you should make the calls right from here, from the Department office, and let me know how you made out …" he said and left my office.

I thought he must really be strapped for finding minority instructors. I could not get either one of my former colleagues. Afifi was out of town on a Photogrammetric and Remote Sensing meeting. I left word with his department secretary to have him call me when he gets back, and that it was important. Parker, on the other hand, finished his Ph.D. in the summer and left for the University of Jamaica. I could imagine how happy he must have been, he practically went home. His home was in the British Virgin Islands.

Afifi Soliman called me the weekend after he got home. He was really curious of my hurried call. He asked me what happened.

-Fifi, nothing happened yet…but let me tell you a few things that may arouse your brain cells. The Division Chairman here asked me to find some friends of mine, who #1. are minorities, #2. are willing to come here to teach, and … now listen to this: who have preferably, terminal degrees; he is willing to go to lengths and I mean lengths, salary-wise, if all three of the above were fulfilled.

-Gabor, (he always called me Gabor, somehow Gabe did not easily emerged from his lips, ever since Ohio State, where no one called me Gabe) you know we have already started the academic year, I can not quit at the beginning of it. That has to wait till June.

You can tell him that I am interested, and in the meantime I will send him a resume, so he can keep it on his file and have ample time to study it. Then, at the end of May, he can contact me with an offer. I will be listening. Now enough of this bull…t, tell me how are you doing! did it work out for you?"

-Fifi, all I can say is that it looks super, …so far. You know the line: 'everything's going my way', …that is how". I have three classes and two labs per week, and, so far every faculty member got his free day for professional development. Now listen: I got this mapping firm, where I am doing occasional trouble shooting and we set up a sister firm, which does the engineering and surveying works, which is supposed to be under my supervision, … and it seems like it is, but somehow in spite of being 50% partner I can not get the full financial picture of it. Nevertheless I am charging my fee for the various jobs done, and so far even got paid for them, but, … you know, …I am being told by the partner that we have not yet made a profit … you know what I mean?"

-Gee, how did you get yourself in the position of letting the financial aspects go out of your hands entirely" he asked puzzled.

-Well, that is not simple, …but I try. Geoffry, the owner of the mapping firm, has all the connections, he had them well before I appeared on the map here. So now, through his connections he gets all kinds of jobs. These jobs have to be completed by the affiliate firm, that is: the Engineering firm, and upon completion of these jobs are being stamped and signed by me"…

-You son of a gun, did you get your registration already" he asked incredulously.

-Yah, sure, that is how I get all these jobs …now I am charging my fee to my firm (you know, halfway my firm) and that is how I am making extra money. But so far I never saw a single penny profit from the firm, do you get this?"

-Gabor! how much do you make on the side? How much last year?

-Last year all together I made over $ 7,000. on the side, but that is not something certain, you must know that …"

-Well, anyway you look at it, that is very, very good, don't you think? Isn't that something you've been dreaming about ever since Akron? I tell you: charge him some more, pad the bill, put in your profit right then, and then the heck with what he does with the books, may be he shows red to balance his taxes, hell with it".

-Okay Fifi, I guess you're right, he is bringing the jobs after all, he must benefit from them too, or he wouldn't do it at all."

-Gabor, I want to warn you; remember what happened with that envious son of a bitch department head in Akron, don't let anyone! and I mean anyone there, know how much you are making on the side, in your time!" he said.

-Fifi, I had this cleared by the division chairman before I even applied for the job, and he was wholeheartedly on my side. I told him all about the Akron case, and he immediately sided with me. He even promised that until he is here, such a thing can not, and will not happen".

-Gabor, I just want you to think about what I said, Okay?"

Then I asked how they are doing, Susu, his wife, the family. And then he asked the same about us. Finally we broke off.

Part Two

The Maverick Professor

Motto:

"How to handle a woman?
Mark me well! I will tell you, Sir:
The way to handle a woman
is to love her ...
simply love her ...
merely love her ...
love her ...
love her...

From Alan Jay Lerner's Musical: 𝕮𝖆𝖒𝖊𝖑𝖔𝖙

Chapter Eight
(New ventures.)

Mid September I received a notice from the Immigration and Naturalization Service about my upcoming 'swearing in'. Prior to that would be the interview, to which I was supposed to bring along two witnesses, who knew me for at least one year. Searching my memory, all I could come up with -on short notice -was Geoffry Dorfman and my former colleague at Ohio State: Forrest Hicks, who was currently working for Itek in Burlington. The two witnesses did not know each other, which was not a requirement. They were officially my 'sponsors', thus, they had to be US Citizens. Both of them were.

The INS official went through his dozen or so questions which were dealing mostly with constitutional and civil rights. I answered them all but he never acknowledged whether or not they were correct. I was left with utter uncertainty. Looking through my documents his final question was whether I knew if there was a legitimate communist party in the United States. The mere mention of that heinous word irritated me and I became rather agitated, and he seemed to pick up on it. Instead of simply answering I mumbled some nasty remarks about the Communist Parties in general. so much so, that Forrest turned to the official and started to explain him my being a, de-facto, fugitive of the communist regime in Hungary, and questioned the wisdom of posing such question to me. I read somewhere, that indeed, this party does exist in the Country, but I was not quite certain about its legitimacy. So I admitted to him that I didn't know. After this was all over, the official announced that I passed the oral test, and that there will be nothing else left than the pledging of allegiance, which will be held at an open ceremony in the State House.

At the ceremony, held on Saturday the following week, a slight complication arose regarding my pronom, (or title of nobility), which I was required to denounce publicly before the ceremony could begin. Somehow I felt stripped and degraded by this practice but I did not make much fuss about it at the time. Instead, I took it in stride since I have never used it anyway, while living in the Country, or even back in Canada. Along with this I was also required to denounce my (hard earned) Canadian citizenship. Thus, I became a naturalized citizen of the United States along with some two hundred other people, heretofore termed: foreigners. I was looking around them trying to assess some as to their national origin and concluded that the ...'E Pluribus'... part was definitely correct, but the 'Unum'... part highly questionable. I was not quite sure of how many of these foreigners remained foreigners for the rest of their lives regardless of what their papers stated about their status. Then the Commissioner congratulated us in a brief speech. It was actually a pretty simple ceremony.

By the middle of October I received a personal congratulatory letter from Senator Ted Kennedy, our senator from Massachusetts, a reproduction of which I am enclosing at the end of this chapter. Without being cynical, I dare say that all of the above new citizens received the same letter.

*--- *--- *

At the end of September we received notice from Motorships Inc. that the Volkswagen Kombi has arrived. I called their Newark office and made arrangements for it to be picked up at the end of the week on Friday. They were really very courteous, even arranged for a customs-broker to clear the car. I called the broker. He said the only problem with clearing the car is that he needs a statement from a recognized Volkswagen dealer, that the few items to convert the car to American standards will be done by him. He alerted me that it will cost some real money to have that done and that the dealer may want a sizeable deposit before he would issue the letter of commitment. He emphasized to bring the commitment letter with me.

This was a real time (and money) saver. If I wouldn't have the letter with me from the dealer I would have wasted a trip to Newark, which would have had to be repeated later on, not even mentioning the storage fee accumulating in the mean time.

Friday morning I flew down to Newark airport. A taxi took me to the wharf where we located Motorships' pier and enormous parking lot. There must have been at least thousand cars stacked bumper to bumper to one another. A giant crane was located near the middle of the lot. The crane could reach to the remotest part of the lot and could pick up any car on a specially built stirrup and lift it out of its stacked position and place it on an exit driveway. The yard-master located the car on a giant map showing every stall of the lot with an identifying number for the car. Once the crane lifted the Volkswagen out and placed it onto the driveway, the crane picked up another car from near the entrance and placed it back onto the stall vacated by our car. The yard-master then amended his huge map. It was an entirely fascinating operation for me. I never dreamed of being able to see anything like it.

After this came the bad news. The balance on the shipping fee was $175.00. The customs-broker's commission was $ 125.00. and he placed a lien on the car for the duration of time it took to do the conversion. The dealer was saving me a bundle of money by getting second hand parts from junkyards, but the catalytic converter had to be new. All together he charged $ 450.00. I ended up with an extra analog car clock (that had to be changed to the type the American imports had been equipped with). In my transportation class was a kid, the son of an auto wrecker, who got me buyers for some of the parts. I still had to conclude that the auto importing business was not meant for me. The dealer really earns his money on imports.

* --- * --- *

Professor McNair wrote me in November and let me know that he found a young professor at the Department of Agricultural Engineering, who was willing to serve on my 3-member special committee if I would consider changing my research topic to something closer to the realm of soils. He realized that it was not my chosen field, nevertheless encouraged me to explore the possibility. We agreed on a meeting at

131

the coming Friday, after the Thanksgiving holiday in Ithaca, at his office on campus.

I drove down Thursday afternoon and evening to Syracuse and stayed in a motel. Next morning I hopped over to Ithaca and met the new man. He was a few years my junior, obviously had a lot of experience with soils. His vantage point on soils was considerably different from that of the civil engineers, who regarded soils almost exclusively from a mechanical point of view. The mechanical aspects dominated the civil engineers' interest: the 'physical properties' of soils.

He was willing to compromise the research topic, if I would come up with a new, possibly an environmental aspect of soils. We discussed the sanitary field of application, such as 'permeability' in connection with leaching fields and trenches for domestic septic systems. We concluded that I would give it some thought and let him know either way.

This did pose some problem with the other (the third) member, who's primary field was transportation, but McNair persuaded me to go along with this set-up and try to come up with some kind of proposal. After the meeting he took me over to the Ratskeller, which was operated by the Hotel Administration Department. Students did most of the actual work of food preparation, cooking, serving the faculty, (since the Ratskeller was exclusively reserved for faculty use) and the patrons were encouraged to cast their remarks into the lockbox. This obviously influenced the grades of the student members of the class. The Hotel Administration, along with the restaurant operation, was heavily endowed by the Hilton Foundation.

During lunch McNair mentioned that he heard about a comparatively young man at the Colorado School of Mines (his own Alma Mater) who was about to leave that school and that he most likely is going to be moving 'back nearer to his roots in Massachusetts'.

-And guess what, he has applied to the Lowell Technological Institute for a faculty position" he said. Then, since I did not show extraordinary interest in the news, he added, "As a matter of fact, he was the Civil Engineering Department head, and has been **forced** to leave that position under less than honorable circumstances", and he was waiting for my reaction.

-Well, I am under the impression that if anyone is forced to leave a position that must have some "less than honorable" circumstances surrounding the event", I said, and this time I did show the keen interest expected by McNair. "Do you happen to know more about those circumstances professor McNair?" I asked him trying to goad him to tell me more. But there was no need for that.

-Oh, sure!" he willingly got into the topic. "You know, he got that position shortly after he received his Ph. D. in Rock Mechanics from MIT. When he arrived there, he began to survey the faculty and prepared a profile of each member, ...

-What sort of profile?" I interrupted, "I thought that was available for each faculty member anyway the minute one is being hired", I said confounded.

-No! not that kind", he said. Then after a short silence, he continued: "his profile constituted about the member's willingness to cooperate with him in every respect, you know, sort of unconditional allegiance, voting with him all the time, a yes-man, you know, and ... and ...another important thing was: that he had no extracurricular activities, but was able... more than able! to bring research grants to the Department".

-I can go along with his research endeavors, there is nothing really wrong with that, I guess... but what about the extracurricular activities? what was that about? why was that becoming part of the 'profile'?" I asked, still sort of naively.

-That is it!" he said, "now you got it professor Szikszay-Farkas, this is what I was going to elaborate on ... So: this is what I got through the grapevines: those faculty members, -and mind you, there were only a few of them -who were recognized in the profession, had 'private' consulting engagements, frequently lucrative assignments, which he was soon learning about. These were generally all in the soil mechanics and foundation area, a few in structures. One individual was having consulting work on a regular basis. Our man Golding, was really after this prof. Robertson, who was not on tenure, so he singled him out, issued complaints about him by memoranda to the dean of the engineering college. The dean was about to conduct an inquiry in the case, but was suggested by other departments to layoff, because consulting is an accepted extracurricular activity. The dean's response to Golding's complaints was: unless other activities are found of prof. Robertson that are detrimental to teaching duties, like: missed scheduled student consultations, incompetent teaching, neglecting to answer student's questions, etc. then disciplinary action can be brought against that individual". Then he continued.

-Golding, in lieu of such findings, decided to write a letter of ultimatum to the provost, in which he demanded the dismissal of prof. Robertson, or in lieu of such, he himself is going to resign as department head. When the provost notified the dean of the college as to the imminent dismissal of professor Robertson, the dean sent a notice of termination to him. Robertson then met with the rest of the civil engineering faculty and disclosed the dean's termination notice, which came as a stab in the back. The civil engineers rose up, and did one thing that was unprecedented in the history of college education: They sent a memorandum to the dean and to the provost of their unilateral resignation, unless their colleague, professor Robertson is going to stay".

-You can imagine the uproar. Both the dean and the provost after a lengthy meeting, decided to cool the situation, they realized that they could ill-afford the loss of a department's entire faculty, and decided the only logical way out would be to accept the department head's resignation. So, this is how Dr. Golding grabbed the job opportunity offered to him by your division chairman at the Lowell Technological Institute; this is what I wanted you to know". McNair waited, and was watching my reaction.

-Well, this is definitely coming as a shock. All I can say is that I am going to talk to Gifford about what you just told me. I know, that until he is our chairman and department head, nothing like this can happen at our place. Is this, by any chance, privileged information?" I asked him, very much concerned.

-No, not really, I don't think so; and definitely not by the time our man Golding gets actually hired and occupies the new position. By then it becomes history at CSM, a bunch of undisputable facts that are nearly impossible to challenge".

-I see, … I see, … Thank you! this was very educational".

-Yes, I thought you ought to know this" he said, "specially in light of what happened to you at Akron. By the way, when will you be eligible for tenure?"

-At the time of my hiring the collective bargaining guidelines nailed down: not before three years of service or not later than seven years. If one does not get indefinite tenure in seven years, he better start to look for another position elsewhere".

-So, when will you complete your three years?"

-June of 1972, still a year and a half …why? aren't we painting the devil on the wall? According to your story, this Golding guy will come to LTI in the fall of 1971. He is not going to be the Department head, and in 1972 June, if all goes well I will be getting my tenure. That is: if Giff is still there, for which I will have to start praying every night", I said. "In that case, by then, I will be immune against Dr. Golding's machinations."

-I wish you luck. How is your consulting practice developing? You do have your P.E. registration and license, yah?" he asked.

-Oh, yes both the engineer and the surveyor; Actually I am doing really well. We had been getting some sizable jobs. The mapping firm just signed the contract for mapping the town of Billerica, and we hope to get it flown late fall after foliage. A 2-man crew just started to paint targets on pavements, at the locations I marked for them, and I am going to mark the existing monuments with the plastic strips. I, (meaning the engineering firm, in which I am a partner) will be doing the aerial triangulation, that is: measuring the plate coordinates. After I have them, I send them to my buddy from Ohio State for computing the entire block of three flight strips. I am now really doing what probably very few, if any of my graduate student colleagues would ever do".

-I knew it, if anyone, you could do it" he said, "I wish you a lot of luck. By the way did you know that Dorothy is ill?

-No! I didn't!"

-Yes, she is gravely ill" he said, "there is not much hope left. She won't be with us for long. Patricia is staying with us now at home, you know, to help out, be at hand, be her companion; she got an indefinite leave of absence from Amtrack".

-Oh I am so sorry, I don't know what to say". I grabbed his hand, squeezed it, then said good by before I broke down myself.

I left the Ratskeller in a hurry. It was a long walk to the visitor's parking lot. While I walked by the old buildings on Campus I was irritated by the newer, more modern buildings, that grew out of the ground and did not fit into, among the classical ones, the ones I was familiar with; like weeds between the flowers. This was one of the most beautiful campus in all the world. I have been at many, many campuses, mostly in the eastern part of the Country, but have not found one that could match the beauty of its setting, the view from almost all of the buildings to the great valley carved by the glaciers eons ago, and Lake Cayuga at the bottom of it with its silvery surface. It was the queen of the Ivy League schools. For me it was.

A mere 4 years ago I started my graduate studies here. It was a happy time. It came as a salvation from facing unemployment some place in Ohio, after I had to leave Akron U. As a 'Deus ex Machina' McNair got the approval on my teaching Fellowship two days later, and we had to get ready to move to this gorgeous part of the country within a couple of weeks. The McNairs were celebrating even our preliminary arrival with a barbecue, when we drove down to find housing using Realtors. Dorothy was charming to our kids; when she learned somewhat later that Andy will be ten years old in October, she presented him a Long Play record at his birthday. She was a musician and a teacher to boot.

The State Department of Agriculture budgeted yearly sums to the Veterinary School and the Agricultural Program. But there had to be convoluted arrangements made with the State, just how the University would accept the yearly grants without any undue influence or intrusion on the autonomy of Cornell. The students had a dairy farm to run, and prepared a long line of international brand-name cheeses (among many other products), which they sold at an outlet store on the outskirts of campus. We simply loved it. It was so, ... so, European.

From the parking lot I drove directly to the dairy store. It was soothing for the senses to see that it did not change at all. I bought a number of the cheeses, mostly the ones we could not find around Lowell. The two most missed ones were the 'Biercäse' and the 'Schärdinger Rauchcäse'. I left the store with a generous supply of these. Then I hit the road home. I had a lot to think about.

* --- * --- *

In the fall semester our department was getting an additional personnel: Tony Francesco. He was promoted from janitor to take the position of 'Laboratory Technician' as a result of a new State program that enabled 'advancement' for potentially deserving state employees previously employed in dead-end positions. Such were the janitors. After completing some minimal schooling and testing, they could apply for such a position. This was truly 'Affirmative Action' at work.

Tony was a nice fellow. Sociable, modest, well behaved, clean, never called any of the professors at their first name; thereby trying to show his respect towards them. Unfortunately, and this was strictly my own observation, the faculty members did not reciprocate this behavior. They had a hidden disdain towards him. On some occasions they gave him mildly degrading chores, sometimes in excess of his job description. He was, nevertheless, diligent, and always eager to please. Probably because of this, some faculty members felt that Tony had a 'built-in' inferiority complex. As a matter of fact that was my feeling too, but I never would have allowed myself to show it.

The promotion, when it came to these employees (many with long service records in their previous positions) meant a substantial increase in their earnings. At one of my visits to the surveying laboratory Tony was telling to a fellow employee that he had just bought 'an almost new car'. After I entered into the lab and interrupted the conversation, he asked me if he could help me. I was about to borrow the Askania theodolite for the weekend, which he promptly fetched for me, along with its tripod. Again he was trying to be helpful beyond his duties nailed down by his job description. He even offered to carry it down to my car. I thanked him for it but told him that I am all set.

Then I glanced over to a work table and saw a partially dismantled dumpy level, along with all sorts of cleaning utensils, tiny screwdrivers, a can of fine machine oil, etc.

-What happened to this level instrument?" I asked him casually.

-Well, professor Szikszay-Farkas, I meant to ask you about this, you know, I am having trouble to catch up with this work".

-What work?" I asked him puzzled, "what are you trying to do?" I noticed that his fellow employee quietly left the laboratory.

-Well, professor, in my job description there is an item stating that the technician ... "is supposed to check each instrument upon its return as to its cleanliness, possible abuse, and being out of adjustment. In case there is any shortcoming, it is the technician's duty to put it back into good working order, or report it to the assigned faculty member and act according with his instructions"... he sounded like quoting straight from the book.

He stopped there and was looking lost, possibly waiting for me to set him straight. I went to the table and looked at the level instrument. It was dismantled way, way beyond what could have reasonably been expected of the technician to perform. I was suddenly at a loss of words. I didn't want to hurt him, with uncalled for words. But I knew that I had a lot of explaining to do. He was instinctively sensing this. I was searching for a way to begin.

-Well, ...well, Mr. Francesco", I began,

-Professor Szikszay-Farkas, you used to call me Tony, please tell me what I have goofed so bad, because I have the definite feeling that I did something really wrong, now that you are calling me Mr. Francesco, ... you never called me that before".

-Okay, …Tony, you want me to be short and to the point, or…

-No, professor, if you have the time please set me straight, explain this situation, because I think I will never be able to live up to this job," he said, and I saw that he needed help.

-Well, can you undo what you did here, that is … can you put it back together?" I asked him.

-Certainly, no problem there; but what about the 'adjustment' that is such a long explanation in the manual, that I probably never could do."

-Tony, let me be brief: that is **not your job!** Show me some other returned instruments", I told him. His self-confidence rapidly began to return. He picked up one from a row of about a half a dozen and brought it to the table. He opened the box.

"Now, look at this one, this was packed up by the students, because it began to rain, …here are the water spots as they dried. All you have to do is rub it lightly with an oiled cloth, examine it if nothing is broken or cracked, put it back into its box, and then this one is done, … Okay'?" Now, the next one … same thing, these guys must have gotten rained out in the field, so, … take the next one, … do the same thing, …you got it? You can take care of them all in less than an hour, …for sure! Okay?"

-Yes, but, … but, … what about the adjustment'?"

-Tony, didn't I just tell you: that is not your job!? That is for the students to perform in the field, that is for them to learn and quite a few of them have a hard time with it, they hate it, believe me", I told him. All the while he was looking at me incredulously.

I felt really sorry for him. What bothered me most was, that he did not dare to ask any of the other professors. Shea, for instance, the coordinator of surveying. Why not'? Was it again that inferiority complex that was getting in his way'? Eventually it was me whom he had the guts to ask. Was it fear of humiliation by any of the others'? I was bothered by these questions, and I found no answers. But I knew one thing for sure, that he knew that he could trust me, and that I would never let him down. He must have heard something about this from my students. The word got around fast here.

------*

One day during the semester break 3 students were waiting for me in front of my office. I recognized them from my surveying class. I invited them in and told them to sit down, but we soon realized that there were only two chairs besides mine. The situation became somewhat awkward, but the boys were very good about it, they instinctively did what came natural to them: all three of them remained standing.

Their spokesman, Robert, explained that they were members of a rather small fraternity, and they, among themselves, elected me as their **'faculty advisor'**. Now they came to see me to ask me if I would be willing to accept this responsibility. I asked them what exactly would be my responsibilities if I accepted, and was becoming their advisor. They assured me that it is not a very demanding task, that there are almost no formalities involved. But, as the most important thing, it would be: 'to represent them vis-a-vis the administration, which is embodied by the dean of students'. There would also be certain other functions, such as, actually giving them advice in situations that they among themselves found unable to handle.

I asked them what made them choose me. Robert formulated their unanimous answer, that for one thing: they thought that I am very fair, and second, that they collectively felt that they could trust me. Then he was mumbling something about some other considerations that would involve their academic achievements, etc. etc.

-Mr. Dunn", I began, "I am very flattered by your first two considerations, however, let me ask you something about what you tried to bagatellize, namely this thing about you guys' academic achievements? Are any of your members in trouble academically? Or am I on the wrong track?

-Professor Szikszay-Farkas, let me answer that with a definite no but we thought that by being our faculty advisor you could also give us advice in case some of our members would get into trouble, that means, academically; in the future, I mean".

-Okay Mr. Dunn. May I ask: do I have any thinking time, and if so, how much?"

-Professor, to be frank, it is kind of urgent, because we have to give the dean the identity of the faculty member chosen by us. But we also realize that you should get familiar with our members, our Frat House, our sometimes unique problems, and …and sometimes with situations we find ourselves in … so, …we would like to invite you one evening to our house, being our guest, of course, and there you will have a better understanding of the operation of a Fraternity".

-Mr. Dunn, I accept your invitation, and must repeat that I am flattered, and ...touched by your trust in me. May I ask: are all of your members civil engineers?"

-Oh no", he said, and all the while I thought that he was getting frustrated with my ignorance about such matters, "we here, the three of us are civil engineers, the rest of us are others, electrical, we also have mechanical engineers and a chemical".

-I see", I said, "so then let's make a date for the evening get together, and have it confirmed by the rest of your members, Okay? Thank you all for your trust in me, I will try to live up to it."

They all left my office. I began to think more about this episode later. They seemed to be 'nice' kids; Then I said to myself, 'why not'? There must be hundreds of faculty advisors for fraternities at colleges in the country. This seemed to be some of the facts of 'faculty life'. There was one area that gave me irky feelings: I wasn't quite sure where the line would be drawn in 'fraternizing' with the students, ...my students.

------*

Paul Swanson came to see me in between semesters. He was doing very little during the fall in terms of working on my projects. He looked a whole lot more 'civilized' than the first time I saw him. He came to invite me to 'their house' for supper one evening. Naturally I wanted to learn more about 'this house' of theirs. It turned out that through his DPW connections he came across an old provincial looking house in a far suburb: Lunenburg. This was rather a town in its own merit, than being the suburb of any larger city. I knew the place by driving through it a couple of times going to some of the locations where I had a job. A quiet, friendly town it seemed, although I had no business in, or with the town.

The invitation did come as a surprise, first. Julie was to cook supper for the three of us, as Paul told me.

-Paul, where were you? I hardly saw you this past semester" I told him trying to scold him, as mildly as possible.

-Professor, I was extremely busy, ...in the summer, you know, I worked for the DPW and then stayed on as a part timer. I was sensing that there were not many jobs with your company, so I had to make a move towards the kind of life you were warning me about the first time we met. We got the use of this house practically for nothing, I mean for the upkeep of the house and the yard.

-Paul, I appreciate your invitation, but the two of you must have enough with your own chores at hand, with working on the maintenance, and, … I assume you have jobs, as you just told me, …"

-But it's no trouble, really, we would really like to have you over, so you can see for yourself, how we are doing, …you know, we feel that you have a lot to do with how our life turned out".

-All right, … all right" I said and began to wonder: am I, sort of getting myself into developing a 'family' in this place'? A second family'? How many families does a college professor have to have'? The thought that every class will eventually become a family, began to frighten me. Was this all part of the deal?

It seemed that my silence lasted too long, because Paul (perhaps sensing my mental sauntering) reminded me of his presence.

-Paul, I am sorry, I got carried away… there is a lot on my mind, you know? I was going to call you, because there is another big job coming in, …a lot bigger than the last big one, so, I am also glad you showed up. But let me ask you: are you interested in doing some computer work?"

Prof, is there field work involved? because I really haven't got much time for that nowadays, but, … of course computing, I could always do. I could do some field work too, but only little ones".

-Okay, give me your number at your house in Lunenburg. I will call you about that supper, Okay'? Please tell Julie not to go out of her way, …you know what I mean? and, surely I will call you once we are getting closer to this new job. Aren't you curious about it'? This is again something you haven't done before: aerial triangulation" I said and waited for his reaction.

-Oh yah! … I saw the photogrammetrists working on it at the DPW" he said very casually, and he was again playing the role he has at the first time we met. But this time he was a lot more focused, (none of those focusing into infinity, that I noticed at the first time.) I did not want to ask whether they have gotten married. I felt it would have been inappropriate. I thought there was plenty of time for that. Then he gave me his number and left.

*--- *--- *

Geoffry asked me how could we handle the Billerica job in-house, when we have no stereo plotter. I told him: not so fast! First let's just see how we will do the ground control work.

-That is a big job for your information, if you wouldn't know already. Let me ask you how much money would you have to set aside just for that?" I asked him sort of testing him.

-Well, I really don't know, because we have never done that before ourselves. I used to contract that out, usually to the same photogrammetric mapping firm, like LKB (Lockwood, Kestler, Bartlett) in New York. That way they had the whole contract, they could not complain if anything was not fitting onto the control, it was their own responsibility, their own big ball of wax." He was his usual self again, never to come up with a figure, with a quotable figure.

-That's okay, I picked-up from there, "then this time you will ask them to quote both ways: how much by doing the whole contract, including the control work, and how much without it, like, us doing the control?" this way I put him on the spot.

-Gabe, I have done that already, you think I am stupid?"

-I would think so, if you can not subtract, certainly you know bloody well then how much is the difference between the two figures right? Am I right? So, ... how much is it?"

-Roughly six grands" he said in a spirit of total surrender.

It was always like this: getting him finally to admit something, or just to quote a figure, was like winning a little victory first.

-Now, ...we are getting somewhere", I said. "Let's then talk about the split, how do you propose to split this?"

-What do you mean: split? We do it the way you used to do the jobs lately: you charge your fee for doing it; and that's the end of it. Isn't that the way you did the St. Elizabeth Hospital project? You must have made a bundle on that one alone; It almost put me in the poorhouse".

-Geez, you really make me feel sorry for you". I said to him, "you know, Geoffry, I am still wondering why you are still dealing with me? Why are you still hiring me for doing all these jobs if that gets you into the poorhouse? Have you ever tried to hire another subcontractor? I mean who would do these for less than I would? But let's not get carried away from the main topic. To answer your question about the 'split': I would do the entire ground control for the sum that you just quoted, which I recall being $ 6,000."

-How would you do that? Not the way you did the Barnstable job... you know that job still haunts me? You come up with these weirdo methods I never saw being done before, ...it gives me the shivers, ... I am still having sleepless nights about the St. Elizabeth Hospital job too, you know, ... about actually meeting their accuracy requirements, ... I am sure you did some shortcuts there too ... But let's get back to the present: how do you propose to do the ground control on the Billerica job?"

-On an entire town the size of Billerica, ... obviously, by the only feasible way: by aerial triangulation; you will prepare for me a set of glass plates of the three high altitude flight strips covering the town, and I take it from there. And I come up with plenty of photo-points on the ground (that I estimated being some twohundred, or more) which will adequately cover every stereo model on the ground. Then give them to LKB, from which they could do the large-scale mapping."

-Gabe, you have to give me more than that; I have to understand the entire procedure in order to negotiate intelligently with LKB. They will be asking me questions that I will not be able to answer right away, ... then I will have to come back to you to find out the answer to them, ...this is too awkward and time consuming".

-Geoffry, that is your problem, actually, let me say: that is every middle-man's problem. Unless, ... unless, you want to let me do the bickering with them, one on one."

-But Gabe, you don't understand, ...that will make me lose control of the whole thing, ... I have to be in control, that's how we had this entire engineering operation set-up, don't you see?"

-But that is the price you have to pay for it, and you knew that too".

-Okay Gabe, I will go ahead with it, ... and I do it only on your word. I can't belive I am doing this, its incredible".

-No Geoffry, I think you are doing it because you know darn well, that my word is good, and you always knew it. By the way, you could actually do one small favor for me, if you want to, you could type up a, sort of, semi-formal agreement on the control job, so that I can read it, and call me when it's done".

It was always like this with him; it became a fact of life I had to learn to face. But, ... but, on the other hand, given all my obligations, how on the earth could I find all these job opportunities, my situation, with my other obligations, for instance: the teaching job at LTI. I had to face the facts, (like I am sure Geoffry did too) that we have grown to, actually needing each other.

Driving home from Brookline, I kept thinking about the St. Elizabeth Hospital job, that I finished later in the fall. I couldn't find Paul Swanson at the time, to do much of the field work, which was a formidable task, given the accuracy requirements set by the architects. They have an abstract concept about accuracy; thinking in absolute terms, 36-feet being exactly: 36.0000 ft, and expect the surveyor to come up with numbers defined like these. It took me a while, when I met with one of their architectural designer in the field, to explain (and convince!) him that any such quantity is merely an abstraction, an idealized quantity. In reality we always find ourselves confronted with a 'tolerance', assigned to each parameter. That, in our example 36.00 ft may well, in reality, be 36.00 plus or minus 0.04 ft. as found in the field between certain parts of two buildings. In order for them to design a corridor or whatever, between the two buildings will, necessarily have this much of an inherent uncertainty. I thought, eventually, I made him understand this, even if it resulted in an apostasy of what he has learned in school.

* --- * --- *

But Geoffry was right in one respect: I did make a bundle on that job. As a matter of fact, I had accumulated quite a handsome capital already, which I was looking around to invest; and decided to invest it in, what my father always believed in: real estate. I mentioned this to Doug Johnson at one occasion when I delivered him a preliminary subdivision design for an old, small farm, he bought exclusively for that purpose: to subdivide.

-Gabe, you know I am not geared to deal with investment properties, but if something like a small apartment house, or similar housing unit would pop up, what I can do is to spread the word around, and if a colleague does have something along these lines, we'll give you a yell.

It so happened that one of his 'Realtor gopher' found an old, large, mansion-like duplex near the top of Christian Hill in Lowell that was already converted into four, one bedroom units, each having a section in the basement. The entire building needed a lot of TLC (tender loving care), especially the basement, which in its existing condition was, for all practical purposes, useless. The old, inefficient furnace needed to be replaced, and one of the upstairs units needed finishing.

The major disadvantage, however, was that it had no off-street parking, not so much because of the diminished lot size, but mostly because of the topography. There was a 6-foot high field-stone retaining wall on the street front, with only a 5-foot wide opening for a comfortable set of stairs leading up to the entrance. My first remark to the Realtor, when we arrived at the house, was: "hey I sure would not like to be moving in here, you get exhausted just by walking up the stairs". But he assured me that a young couple would surly feel otherwise. And he also assured me he had some of those on his waiting list.

The seller wanted 34 thousand dollars; considering the condition of the basement, the furnace and one of the upstairs unit (unoccupied) being worked on but unfinished, I came up with an offer of 30 thousand. When the Realtor called to inform me that the offer was accepted, I instructed him to draw up a purchase and sales agreement. When all four units were rented, the house was producing an income of 320. dollars per week. The mortgage principal and interest was 450.00 per month and the taxes were 120.00 per month, so the house was producing a gross profit of $ 700. per month. But I had to come up with about $ 4,500.00 to have all the needed work done.

The passing took place at Attorney Richard Halloran's office. I had to borrow a mortgage, so, I decided to borrow it from the same bank where our home mortgage was secured from. I called up prior to the passing telling the mortgage clerk that I will be supplying the mortgage plot plan, so don't get it from some other surveyor. Richard called me trying to persuade me that the bank usually wants to use their 'usual' surveyor, but in this case he will bend and will allow my plot plan to be used, since I am also a registered surveyor in the Commonwealth.

And so it was. I brought the plan along for the passing and handed it to him. He kept looking at it. He was speechless for some time, finally he uttered some words, seemingly to himself, something like: 'incredible, a masterpiece' etc. when finally he turned to me and asked: "Professor, are you doing all your work like this" this must take a lot of time to prepare".

-Oh, yes, as a matter of fact this is not only a 'plot plan', it actually is a survey plan" I said, "Attorney Halloran, if I buy a property for myself, I make damn sure that it is all there". So, what you are looking at is really a survey plan, that may be recorded in the Registry of Deeds if it were rendered on 'linen' instead on just vellum".

-Professor, I would like to show this to our bank's mortgage officer, and I would put in some good words, …would you be willing to prepare the plot plans for our bank, I mean in the future?"

145

-Why, I would be delighted" I said, adding: "they will not be all like this, but the quality, the appearance, … you know, the 'looks' will be just like this one. I am sure you noticed that I added a little vicinity plan to it, for the benefit to those unfamiliar with the area".

-Yes, indeed, I noticed it, …Professor, where do you find the time to do all this work? …I was under the impression that you have a full time job with the school," he said and was staring at me.

-Attorney Halloran, I am struggling to ketch-up with lost time in my **'former life'**, so to speak, and now that I am still comparatively young, and found the opportunity, … I am trying to make good use of it. But to answer your real question: I am beginning to train my own personnel: those students, that I find, could do the work to my liking, my style, I employ them part time, similarly to a mini 'Coop Program'; the students seems to like it too, I still recall the times when I myself was doing it too, as I said: in my 'former life'".

-Can I assume that your answer is in the affirmative?" he asked.

-Indeed you can" I said, "I am looking forward to do all your bank's plot plans, and do them quickly, without delay, and for a reasonable fee, the current average fee being 30.00 dollars".

-Okay, sounds good, but let me ask: what about Land Court work, do you do those too?" he asked, "those are more complicated, I understand, surveyors are shying away from those".

-To be totally frank, I have not done any of them, … yet; But I find no task too difficult to tackle, …I may become even more aroused by the challenge, if you know what I mean…"

-All right then, I might be calling you from time to time".

I did not fully realize, at the time, what this conversation really meant. Within a matter of months most everyone at the school and virtually anybody connected with it learned about my surveying 'service' (as I insisted on referring to it). The Bursar, for example, had an old friend, who was, originally, a farmer with sizeable land holdings in the Pepperell area. Some of the pieces he had previously subdivided into building lots. But that is another story, which I will deal with when it became interesting from a legal point of view. As I described in the foreword: this book is really about 'Law and Justice', in the great American Land, anything else is incidental.

* --- * --- *

I announced in the transportation class that if anyone knows a handyman/finish carpenter, etc. please see me after the class. Next day the Sullivan brothers were waiting for me in the hallway. I explained them what needs to be done. They wanted me to drive them up to the house. So I showed it to them. They suggested right off, to have the basement floor poured with concrete. Then a heating contractor could work on the furnace, and the entire basement would be a lot more solid, where we could set-up 4 lockable stalls, one for each of the apartments. They said this sort of things would attract 'better tenants'. They were right.

I inherited the current tenants from the previous owner. The need for better tenants proved itself in a few weeks, when on a Saturday I went to each apartment to collect rents. In one of the main floor units was a tenant who wore a black leather jacket and he was using a vocabulary I was not used to, in fact not even familiar with some of the terms he addressed me with. In one of his sentences the term 'kike' popped-up, which he used in a definitely derogatory manner, attached to me as my attribute. I did not want to overreact on the spot, so decided to let it fly by, pretending I would not have understood it. The truth was that I did not know the meaning of it, and was trying to look it up at home, but had no idea how it was spelled. Later, I learned its true meaning from an attorney.

One tenant was a graduate student, by the name of Pierce, who was married, his wife (Helen) a grade-school teacher. They had one little girl, who was about 8 or 9-years old. It was his choice from early on, to occupy one of the upper units, this way he was alone on the second floor. He kept his place squeaking clean, his wife even vacuumed the rug on the stairs and the hallway, weekly. I praised her for it, and took the occasion to describe the lower tenant with his huge motorcycle and black jacket.

It was from Pierce that I have learned the term: 'Hell's Angels' just showed the utter lack of my exposure to the full cross-section of American society. He asked me where I was all along this time that I know so little about 'real life' in the Country. I explained him that I was busy bringing my education up to date, and, up to the level where I felt comfortably competitive in society. He concluded for me that I must have had an exclusively sheltered life in academe, and if I wanted to catch-up with all I've missed, this would be a fairly good opportunity to do so.

Pierce opened my eyes to what was really wrong with the house. This was how I really learned the burning need for 'better tenants'. I decided to rid the house from the Hells' Angels guy. But before that could be achieved, an incident involving the other tenant on the lower floor, speeded things up.

This man told me that he was his own boss, had his own carpet business. His name was Coppinger. I found that his manners left a lot to be desired, if he was aspiring to succeed. He had a young wife, probably too young, but that was none of my business. She was the one who paid the rent at the previous two weeks. I usually stood in the open doorway while she was getting the money from her pocket book, and left promptly after receiving it.

On this particular occasion, descending from the upstairs flat I knocked on their door. After the second or third knock the young woman opened the door. I was going to stay in the open doorway as I used to, while she would fetch the money but she told me to close the door because of the cold, she also said, that there must be something wrong with the furnace, because they are not getting sufficient heat in their unit. I noticed that she had only a bathrobe on with hardly any underwear visible beneath it. She thought that probably there was a problem with their thermostat, and that I might want to look at it.

As I was going the few steps towards the kitchen, where the thermostat was located, the entrance doorway flew open, Coppinger and the Hells' Angels guy busted in, and Coppinger hit me on my neck, so that I was grasping for air, all the while accusing me to try to rape his wife. To my great relief Pierce came down the stairs and warned the two dudes that he would call the police right away if they didn't stop, and will not leave me alone. In fact, Helen was yelling down from the upstairs landing, that she had just called them and a cruiser was on its way up the hill.

The two dudes spread out as if a grenade had hit them, and vanished. By the time the police arrived they wanted to hear from me what happened. When I got to the part where Coppinger hit me, they interrupted the process and advised me to follow them down to the station. The one who was higher ranked asked me if I think I would need medical attention on account of the bruise on my neck. When I insisted that I don't, they told me that I better press charges against the man who hit me. As it turned out later the police was after the guy with the motorcycle, and wanted whatever they could get on him, to get him.

So they went over the whole routine, asking me what I was doing there, how I knew the Hells' Angels guy. When I began to explain that I was the owner of the house, and attempted to collect the rent, they lost most of their zeal. Nevertheless, they finished the report, summarized it to me, that I was charging both of them with assault and battery. I objected, and wanted to charge only Coppinger, since he was the one who hit me. But the sergeant said that the other guy was his accomplice, so the charges will be leveled against both of them. We quickly found out then and there that the guy from the Hells' Angels was not the real tenant, he was just squatting with or without the knowledge of the actual tenant who was away some place in the Midwest looking for a job.

The real grenade exploded only the next week. I was knocking on the Coppinger's door, this time Pierce came down with me, to forestall any incident similar to the last occasion. The girl, or rather young woman, opened the door and let me right in. She got into a rather odd story: that 'Mr. Coppinger' left her, she can not pay the entire rent by herself, from her waitress' job. Then elaborated on the fact, that she was not married, Mr. Coppinger was not her husband, and now, that the police is after him, he probably can not, and will not return, ... so, ... she would like to stay in the apartment, and would be willing to pay, what used to be her share of the rent: that is $ 35.00 a week if I would accept that, and ... perhaps, ... if I, would consider ... additional services, she would be glad and actually be flattered, if I would accept such a solution, since she's had it with these sort of dudes; and she can assure me that she is a clean and healthy woman ...

Oh my god, ...what did I get myself into? I thought, ...I never had to face a similar situation before, like this, (even when I would have welcomed it) but this was something entirely different. All I could think about was the 'legal aspects' of the situation. I was utterly inexperienced along these lines. The legal ramifications were enormously complex; what if this whole thing is a clever setup? what do I really know about this woman? how do I know if she isn't actually an accomplice of Coppinger? Maybe she was that at the first time, when Coppinger hit me, ...

-You know, Miss, excuse me that I don't know your name, ... you know, ...now that you are not Mrs. Coppinger, as you have just told me, I would like to ask you something to which I would like to have an honest answer: last week when you were asking me to look at the thermostat, and just exactly then, Mr. Coppinger and the other guy busted through the door, was that actually a prearranged situation?" I asked her, and was trying to look straight into her eyes.

She did not answer. But I was still waiting. After an awkward silence she nodded with her head, still did not utter a single word, still did not look straight at me. I made no move towards her, just stood there, and slowly thanked her for being honest. She was struggling with tears, then I told her that I regarded the Coppinger case closed; that I will hold no grudge against her. But under the circumstances I would have to ask her to vacate the apartment, as soon as she can, and that I will not put undue pressure on her or to urge her to move out, but just do it, like, in an honor system.

I could not get easily over this. On my way home I was thinking about, her being, …actually, a victim, that she, … perhaps wasn't really a 'bad' girl in the full meaning of the word. And she was really a pretty good looker … if one tries to analyze … her physical attributes, … in a comprehensive fashion. Perhaps in her waitressing job she got overly exposed to the Coppinger type guys, who clearly took advantage of these young girls, financially and otherwise. Perhaps she'd have deserved better, than what life was dishing out for her, but life is not fair! everyone knew that.

Then I was getting scared… from myself, really; what is this?.. do I actually have feelings toward that girl, or woman?.. whom I don't even **really know**? That would be totally unacceptable…and yet …

* - - -* - - -*

Next weekend the Sullivan brothers brought along two helpers, and one pick-up truck load of 'Sacrete' bagged, premixed concrete. Another truck had a concrete mixer on it, which the four guys carried seemingly effortlessly up the numerous steps, and then down to the basement. I had the definite feeling that they were trying to show off in my presence.

They really seemed to know their business. It was quite clear to any observer that this was not their first time doing it. They sectioned off the basement floor area and poured a section at a time. The strikig/leveling is the real test after which one can un- mistakenly see if it was a pro- job, or a botched one. The floor was as it should be: smooth and level. The Sullivan Brothers'"construction company" past this test. They were enrolled as 'structures majors' in the Department, so, in their senior year I had no contact with them in any of my classes.

One of the brothers (I think it was Philip, but am not sure} had considerable experience in carpentry; he was working several summers in construction as carpenter's helper. He built the storage stalls in the basement, one for each apartment. The brothers then got hold of a heating contractor, who converted the steam-heat to a hot water system. There was only the one, last upstairs unit's remodeling to be finished. By early spring this was also achieved.

The house was ready for those 'better tenants' I really needed. I called Doug's gopher about his list of young couples on his 'waiting list' he was boasting about. Naturally, as this usually is the case, 'momentarily! he did not have any candidates, but… don't worry! We will have some soon', he said.

Pierce suggested me to raise the rents (naturally only on the other renewed units) to at least 90-dollars per week, and if I would be willing to leave his the way it was (at 70 dollars) he would act as my 'resident manager', see to it that the common areas will be kept reasonably clean, collect the rent from the others and will have them ready for me to be picked up every Saturday evening. All he had to do was to remind me of the Coppinger incident, which, in this case, of course, would never happen. When I was hesitant at first and, sort of wanted to see how things will come along … he mobilized his reserves, that is: he mentioned that a teacher colleague of Helen was actually looking for a small but comfortable place, and kind of liked the other upstairs unit when she was visiting with them. The carpet contractor (not Coppinger!) was still working on it, so they could go in and showed her the place.

That was all I needed to stop procrastinating and hired Pierce on the spot; even told him to get hold of their friend, fill out her relevant data, collect a week's rent and two hundred dollars security deposit. At the following weekend I picked up the money and the personals, handed him a set of keys to the other two downstairs units. He did not miss mentioning that two nursing students will be moving in into the left lower units within two weeks, because that's how long of a notice they had to give to their current landlord: Louis Saab. I warned Pierce that the place would soon be resembling the situation to the one he could recall from the movie: "Under the Yum-yum Tree" with Jack Lemmon in the lead role.

He didn't know what I was talking about (which clearly showed the generation-gap). I suggested him to rent out the movie. By the spring the house was fully rented and was putting itself in the covetous 'positive cash-flow' status.

* - - - * - - - *

Among all our friends to whom we used to send Christmas greetings this year I added Forrest Hicks. Since I did not have his home address, I sent it to Itek. Shortly, in the New Year I got his reply. He stated that he has just bought a small single-family house in the bucolic town of Carlisle, and that he was busy working on its remodeling. Unfortunately he can not spend all the time he would like to, because of his full time job, thus he was keeping quite busy over the weekends. He wanted to make good progress by the time of his upcoming marriage.

Forrest Hicks was a USAF Lt. col. (retired). That was how he retired from the Force, shortly after he graduated from Ohio State University with his Master's degree, in Geodetic Science. He was in active service duty on a program enabling deserving personnel with distinguished service records to enroll in an advanced degree program. Geodesy was a very much desired, sought after field of study not only by Army personnel, but perhaps even more so by the Air Force.

The Air Force sponsored several research projects at the Department of Geodesy, one of the most ambitious being the study on the world's gravity field. With high-speed airplanes and rockets aspiring to leave not only the atmosphere but eventually the gravity field as well, it was a vitally important (and classified) area of study. The Air Force began to recruit its own cadre into this academic discipline. It incorporated this under, what it has established earlier as the Terrestrial Sciences Division. It sent mostly its pilots and navigators to the school.

This was how Forrest, along with many of his comrades have enrolled in the program. I had a teaching fellowship at one quarter (Ohio State operated on the quarter, rather than the semester system) in the Department where I had to prepare and conduct the laboratory sessions. This was how I first met the Air Force officers, who were only to be seen in civilian clothes on campus.

They had to, in order to qualify for this extraordinarily generous leave, put in their minimum required flying time, which most of them opted to do in a concentrated fashion, that is on long hauls 8-10 hours duration, something like flying Military Air Transport Service (MATS) flights to European bases, mostly in West Germany. This way they usually fulfilled their obligation in one round trip per month. This, for most of them was possible to complete within one weekend. Members of my class, when they found out that I spoke fairly good German, wanted me to fly with them to Germany. Most of them had in mind for me, to reciprocate their generosity by me serving as their interpreter. I was going to go along with their suggestion, but could really not take advantage of the situation, because I was poor as a church mouse. They knew about this problem too, and were suggesting, as a solution, to take me to nightclubs where I could be their guest. Many of them were divorced, (Forrest among them) for whom this sounded like pure fun, but on top of my problems enumerated, I was married with two kids. To this problem they were not risking any simple solution.

I visited Forrest at Itek. He apologized for not being able to properly entertain me at home, but outlined the prospect of doing so in the near future, most likely when his new wife would come to the house. We'd been catching up on some of the current events. So I mentioned to him that I am looking for a mono-comparator to rent some time on. He asked me what for. I told him about the Billerica aero-triangulation job, and that I had to measure plate coordinates on some 15 plates. He offered, tentatively, pending the approval of his boss to come in the second shift, when there are several comparators left unused from the day-shift.

He called me the next day and said he got the clearance from his boss, provided that he was staying with me while I am doing the job. He also said that they would not charge anything for the use of the instrument since it would be considered as an in-house usage. This part sounded as too good to be true, and as the saying goes: it was. The main problem with the arrangement was that Forrest was unable to go home and work on his remodeling project. Instead he had to sit there, (and occupying himself with something) until I was working on the instrument.

Nevertheless, he encouraged me and said let's give it a try, see how it goes. The first night it took me more than 3 hours to measure a single plate, with more than 34 points imaged on it. To me it was exciting at first, but I fully realized that this is not a workable arrangement. No way could I expect any friend to sit out the time it will take to measure all 15 plates. I told Forrest that I respect our friendship more than I could accept this sacrifice from him.

Then I began to search for other possibilities, wrote numerous letters, to commercial as well as governmental institutions. Shortly I received a reply from Mr. Clohecy from the Mass. D.P.W. He drew my attention to the fact that the Smithsonian Astrophysical Observatory in Cambridge has some of these comparators, equipped with the most modern projection measuring system, (instead of the classical optical viewing/ measuring one, which usually gives the operator a massive headache after 3-4 hours of work) and that I ought to see a countryman of mine, namely: a Mr. Keresztes-Fischer, who was in charge of the measurement team. I picked up the phone and personally thanked him for this most valuable information. The next call was to the Observatory, where I was asking for Mr. Keresztes- Fischer.

When he answered the phone he immediately asked me if I was by any chance related to a Professor Jozsef Szikszay-Farkas. As to my affirmative: he was my father, he said; "then I want to see you here in person; is your father, by any chance, also here with you"? I told him he was not. A long pause followed, then he asked: "is he alive"? he asked, in Hungarian. "Yes he is", I answered, also in Hungarian. From then on the conversation followed in Hungarian. It was mostly testing of my familiarity with 'verbal politeness'. He was asking me how old I was, and whether I knew his name, of how much I actually knew or remembered about the 'political life' in Hungary, before and during the war' etc. Then he asked me: "do you know my name?" and I told him right away: "of course I do, if your first name is: Ferenc", I said. "All right", he said "now I believe that you know of me; but your father and I know each other personally". (I remembered his name having been mentioned by my father repeatedly. He was the Minister of the Interior for a while, during the War). We agreed on a date, when I will come to see him, and bring the plates with me, to show him, so he could assess the magnitude of my job.

So it was, that I got to measure all 15 plates' coordinates in a greatly economical time, because on each plate, the plate number point ID-number and its plate coordinates were automatically punched on cards, activated by a foot pedal switch and printed on a sheet as a check. It was the state of the art set-up. What else could one expect from the Smithsonian?

Then, next, I needed Paul Swanson, so I telephoned him.

EDWARD M. KENNEDY
MASSACHUSETTS

United States Senate

WASHINGTON, D.C. 20510

October 16, 1970

Mr. Gabor S. Szikszay-Farkas
22 Golden Cove Road
Chelmsford, Massachusetts 01824

Dear Mr. Szikszay-Farkas,

Let me express my sincere congratulations to you on the occasion of your naturalization as a United States Citizen.

I am pleased to be a member of the Immigration Subcommittee in the United States Senate and as my great grandparents were immigrants to this country, I have a very great personal interest in people from other parts of the world who choose America.

Our democracy is strong today because America is made up of men and women from many different countries, religions, races and creeds. Its continued strength depends upon each American exercising not only the opportunities of freedom, but also the obligations of citizenship within our society.

I proudly welcome you as a fellow American and extend to you my best wishes for a happy and rewarding life in our great country.

Sincerely,

Edward M. Kennedy

Chapter Nine
(Strengthening my positions.)

I drove out to Lunenburg on a Saturday evening in the Spring. Paul Swanson's house was right on the main highway, Route No. 2 A, set way back from the road. It was indeed an old house, it was crying for TLC. Paul must have done most of the spring cleenup, because the lawn was free of debris and was showing through green everywhere.

It was still not quite dark. As I parked my car at the end of the driveway, Paul came out of the house and greeted me,

-Hi professor, I was worried that you will not find the house, because we still did not put a house number on the mailbox at the road; but I see it would have been in vain," he said. Julie came to the door to greet me. I was surprised when she kissed me. I have not had a friendlier reception for a good while. It almost embarrassed me. I did not have adequate experience dealing with the so much younger generation of women. But I think I handled myself pretty well. Then I pulled out the bottle of 'Bikavér' (a.k.a. bulls' blood, or sangre di toro, depending what part of the world we are at) and put it on the counter.

-Paul, I think you should start fixing the salad" said Julie, and Paul readily obliged. I asked if I could be of any help, but the both of them reassured me in unison, that I am the guest, so I shouldn't be doing anything, just be happy.

-Now, that's not really fair" I replied, "at least let me follow an old Hungarian custom, namely: I will be pouring some wine for all of us; Julie! Where will I find some glasses?" I asked. Julie put out three wineglasses, and I uncorked the bottle. Then I poured a modest amount for each of us. "Now, before we would say: 'Egészségünkre' each one of us will think of a particular thing, or anything else we wish to become true", I said and we will take 10 seconds to do this, okay?" They agreed.

It was really a very simple little ceremony, which served mostly as an icebreaker in a party where people were not all acquainted with each other. In our case, however, this was not needed. So, Paul and Julie, standing next to one another, closed their eyes for ten seconds, then opened them and locked their gazes on each other. I was still very familiar with the feelings that filled both of them. So I wasn't hastening anything, but after another 10-15 seconds I said the magic word, which they recited in English: 'Cheers'!

Julie went to the oven and took out the meat, which was simmering in its sauce. It was actually fully cooked, so she set it on the table. The mashed potatoes were previously done and also kept warm in the oven in a Pyrex dish. She set that on the table too. We were to sit down. During a short silence I said my blessing, in Hungarian, mute, thus no one should hear it, except whom I invited to our table. Although He was invisible somehow I felt his presence. He must have had an extra dose of love for these youngsters.

The conversation revolved around Paul's class standing at the University. I brought up the topic. His explanations somehow ended up somewhat confusing. I had the suspicion that something was not quite straight in his academic work at Lowell Tech . I suggested him to make a clear-cut decision as to what sort of degree he wants. So long as he is 'sort-of affiliated' with the Civil Engineering Department, but in the same time just picks and chooses courses according his own desire, he will never advance his standing. In other words: he will not get any closer to his goal, if that was to receive a degree.

The philosophy of the school was still based very much on a 'core requirement' in any of the engineering disciplines. At the time there was no such 'discipline' offered as: 'Surveying'. For a degree in this field, he must pick another school, which did offer one, and currently, there is no such school in the Commonwealth, not even in New England.

-But Professor, why should I go through a lot of courses, when I don't have the feel for them, don't have the professional curiosity and ambition for them?

-Paul, I fully sympathize with you. I myself went through pretty much the same agony in the undergraduate course work at the Technical University of Budapest. The core courses were a lot more demanding than they are here at Lowell Tech. It was only my dogged determination that made me comply with all of them in order to achieve my goal: to become a civil engineer, and have a degree to prove it. Because, let me tell you: in today's world, paper still rules, and if you don't believe me, you will find out on your own. It is not **what** you know that counts, it's what **credentials** you have to show for it" I told him, "and I know all this sounds like if it were your faculty advisor talking. By the way did you ever talk to your faculty advisor?"

-To be frank, no. I don't even know who 'my faculty advisor' is".

-Paul, that probably is because, you don't have a clear-cut class standing. Now did you try to talk to Professor Shea? As far as I know he is the overall advisor for the entire sophomore class "I told him. He will then send you, or rather will assign you to someone else if he so chooses".

-Professor, I know that, I have talked to him last year", he said.

-And? What happened?

-Well, he gave me pretty much the same speech what you have summarized just now, you know? ... Commitment to the profession, ... whether I have made up my mind? that sort of things. I told him that I want to be a surveyor, and that I think I would qualify for it right now... "

All this time Julie was intently listening to the conversation. She was practically drinking in the words coming from both sides. She was, without verbally, participating in it more than either one of us. I could sense her tension, trying to assess her future place in her union with Paul. I knew quite a bit already about her devotion, her commitment, when it came to her allegiance to Paul. I didn't want to over-dramatize the situation.

-Well, ... well, Paul, I know that you know a lot more than the average surveyor candidate does. But, and here comes another but; in my opinion, since you have mentioned it, I must say that you are not ready, using your own words: 'right now' for even passing the State Board's exam. And don't hold this against me: you have, for example not done much of any 'real land surveying', you have done more than the average candidate's share of 'engineering surveys', and your handling the instrument is super, but, I must tell you right now you will be found inadequate in the land surveying area. You know, I am sure, that's part of the game in the registration process. So if you want my advice, don't try to hang on to the DPW job, ... you know: field-work, instrument-man, instead: try to attach yourself to a "Right of Way" section, the guys who deal with deeds, boundaries, research, eminent domain takings, and the likes. Now use your connections, whatever you have, in this direction! Do you read me? I sure hope that you did not loose your father's love and affection, and, which is even more important in this case: his **connections**! Another thing, while we're at it: do yourself a favor, take your time to learn as much as you can about what I told you, and I am sure you will get there. That will be your mountain to climb. And thank God for having Julie on your side".

There was a long silence. Each of us was digesting the words I have uttered. I was filling up our glasses; we again clicked them, and sipped. Then we talked about the Aero-triangulation job. I described to both of them their task: Paul was expected to come up with the utility programs to set-up the observation equations. This time they were more intensely geometric than the previous ones: each of the rays passing through the optical center of the lens, the ground point and it's image on the plate must fall on a straight line (after some built-in corrections for several optical phenomena) shall yield an observation equation. This is three-dimensional geometry. Julie's task will be to punch them on the cards. Obviously, we will have to discuss the various formats, etc.

The youngsters were visibly perked up from their previous somber mood that I caused by my perhaps overly realistic assessment of Paul's surveyor's registration. Then I suggested to come-up with a payment plan (and a figure) after they had grasped the magnitude of the job. Either way we looked at it, on a one-dollar per card basis, it would be very close to a thousand dollars. Julie asked me when they could start. This was the best news to them in the entire evening. On this note I said good-by to them, wished both of them lots of luck and happiness in their new house.

--*

Geoffry was on my back by the end of March, calling me every second day: how we are doing. I tried real hard to get him off my back. The first strip's data cards package was sent to Rudi, who had a diagnostic run to check for the internal accuracy of the photo coordinates, actually to check, how well I did in measuring the plate coordinates. One of the plates had larger than allowable misclosures. As it later turned out, it was one of those plates, which I measured at night at the Itek comparator. I quickly had to arrange with Ferenc at the Smithsonian Observatory, to have that plate re-measured. So the new coordinates were input on a set of new cards, this time yielding super accuracy on the fit to the ground coordinates. Thus, we could proceed with the rest of the other two flight strips.

Within the following two weeks we finished all the inputs and forwarded the deck to Maryland. The following week we received another diagnostics: this time the size of the errors exceeded the allowable limits in elevation on several points along the overlapping strips. The only way to correct this was by going into the field and level several of the photo points (not marked on the ground) and derive an elevation for all of them along the overlapping two strips. This was a definite setback not only by additional work needed but also time wise, and loss of efficiency. We lost a good two weeks by this mishap. Geoffry was frantic. He threatened to withhold moneys from the contract price. I still had the entire deck and the duplicate was being worked on in Maryland. I told him what his choices were: doing it over, starting from scratch, was obviously out of the ques-tion, so it actually gave me some leverage. I told him that he will get nothing, and then can start some action in court, if he thinks that will get him ahead; or he can pay me the rest of the outstanding balance, and next week the entire control work would be delivered.

I simply had to make absolutely certain that everybody would get paid. There was no doubt about that. Several people were involved. The only way I could settle with the Smithsonian was to make a donation. As simple as that. They were in no position to bill an **outside** party for usage of **their** instrument. That was inconceivable. This way both of us made out good: the Institution got funds, clean funds, and I ended up with a Contributing Membership status. I was already a member since 1969. To the Swansons I made periodic payments as we progressed with the job. I still owed them some insignificant amount. But payments for the computation were still outstanding.

Finally, all three strips were run together and a general simultaneous adjustment took place. This revealed some local, individual point errors that were larger than acceptable. With these nothing could be done economically; either some field measurements would have had to be made, if the points were really needed for a particular stereo model, or, it could be derived (corrected) on the larger scale model, during compilation. Their numbers were so few (less than 3%) that the job could safely be regarded as completed.

Then came the more difficult part of the game: to collect the rest of the fee on the job. Somehow Geoffry was maniacal to withhold a chunk of the fee. His rational to this was that: 'What if something does not check?'

What if something has to be redone? What if the subcontractor is not willing or able to make corrections? What if? What if? This however was not the case with me. I wasn't going anywhere. I was always available, if anything needed to be corrected (for which there was no precedent as yet). So, there was seemingly no weapon in my hand, except not to do any more work for the firm. This was obviously counter- productive, and was working against me.

All I could do was to withhold delivery on a job in progress, or better yet, on one that was completed. This was the real stinger. In such a case things turned in my favor. If he wouldn't pay the remaining part of the fee, he would lose what he paid up-front, (the retainer) and I would loose part of my work, that part for which I wasn't paid. He would have to hire another sub, and pay another retainer for that new sub, and, eventually he would miss the deadline, or embarrassingly, would have to renegotiate for a new deadline. But, as I mentioned, there was no need to resort to such drastic measures. At least not yet.

I had to be concerned that all my people, my affiliates will get paid, and paid on time. That was a matter of principle for me. I could ill-afford such a circumstance: if for instance I had a debt to Paul, and later, when I was hiring students straight out of my class. What would that do to my reputation at the School? It was simply unthinkable.

*_*_*

Early May, on a weekend, while I was working in the front yard and on the stone wall, out front, I was bothered by a nasty itch in my right eye. I kept on trying to remove what I thought was in it, the way I used to, by lifting my eyelid and pulling it down onto the lower eyelashes using them as a natural brush. But there seemed to be nothing in it. The itch persisted, but it did not originate from the outer parts, it came from inside, from deep down. I also tried to gently massaging it to no avail.

I asked Maria to take a look at it, if she can see anything in it. But she couldn't either. By the second day there seemed to appear a film in front of it, that had millions of tiny dots sprinkled on it. Also: this film appeared illuminated. And the itching persisted. Next day I had my usual classes, but I could not see with my right eye other than blurry images. Other times this sort of thing used to heal by itself. But, this time this thing was nothing like the usual. It was totally different. I saw vaiwy lines instead straight ones, and knew full well that they ought to be straight. So I resorted to put a patch on it under my glasses to eliminate the disturbance it caused to the total image. Everyone at the school urged me to see a doctor.

I finally surrendered, made an appointment with an ophthalmologist, and insisted to the secretary that I must see him, at least have her to tell him about my condition. Let him then be the judge if I could wait for a next week appointment. She was going through the routine, asked if this was an emergency, because only in that case could she arrange for the doctor to see me. I did not care one way or other; told her she may call it such if that's what it takes. I just had to have him see me.

Dr. Kelly was having his day in his Nashua office at that Tuesday. He could see me late afternoon, after his scheduled appointments. I described him my observations on the right eye and the chronology of the events. His immediate reaction was: why didn't I come to see him much sooner, he wanted to know. I explained the situation, that, it first began on the weekend, and then, instead of getting better, it got worse. He then proceeded with his examination, which was terribly painful. I never had anything that painful before during an eye exam. During the exam he was preparing some drawings, which seemed also unusual to me. When he finished, he said I had no time to loose, I lost too much already. "Go home, pack your things, and have someone drive you to the Retina Associates in Boston. There you should ask for Dr. McKenzie Freeman. He will make the arrangements for an operation". Then finally, to my nagging questions he announced that "you have a, so called: 'retina detachment'; that needs to be operated on, otherwise complete blindness is guaranteed. But in any case Dr. Freeman will take over from here".

I obeyed every one of his commands. Maria was frantic. She got my things together in a flash, and by 5:30, in the rush hour, we were on our way to Mass. Eye and Ear Infirmary in Boston. Dr. Kelly's messages were waiting for Dr. Freeman. He was not in at this late hour, but one of his assistants urged me into an examination room and made me assume the same position on the exam table, as Dr. Kelly did. I asked him why this very painful examination was necessary to be repeated, since I brought a copy of Dr. Kelly's sketches with me. (FAX was not around those days, also image quality would have been questionable, even if it were.) He said that Dr. Freeman wants his retina mapping done by his own people, and use it as the guide for executing the operation. The young assistant did a very good job, which, of course, I had no other way to evaluate, than by the degree of pain it inflicted upon my eye.

Then came the admitting procedure. I was amazed that an organization, as busy as this, is flexible enough to admit a patient on such short notice. But that's how it happened. Maria was waiting around all this time. At long last Dr. Freeman arrived. He introduced himself, asked if I had my wife with me. I said she was in the waiting room. For the two of us then he announced that this is a very serious and highly risky operation; the success rate is about 50%, which is not very promising. I asked what is the status for the individual who ends up in the unsuccessful 50%. He made no bones about it.

-It is a variable degree of blindness, some end up in total darkness, some not, but their vision is considered to be 'legally blind' in any case", he said.

-Dr. Freeman, I asked him, "I don't suppose there is anyone opting not to have the operation done".

-Very, very seldom some patient chooses not to undergo surgery" he said.

-What is their fate?" I asked.

-As I said before: guaranteed blindness, and I must add that due to complications developing later, they may end up losing the affected Eye, it may have to be removed".

-Well, under these circumstances... I want to have the operation done", I concluded. "If somebody up there wants me to see, the minimum I have to do is meet him half way".

-That is really your only choice", he said, "I shall have you sign the forms, and we will schedule you for first thing tomorrow morning. This is an estimated 8-hr operation. You will go under total anesthesia; the anesthesiologist will see you in the morning and go over the method to be used. You will go through the preparation tonight; you were already admitted. Try to relax and have a good night's sleep", he said all this as it were a sermon.

Maria drove home. Next morning she called the department, Joan Fallon answered. She was all upset. She told Maria to hang on, because she will ring up Gifford's office and will tell the news to him, also, that he can talk directly to Maria, so she should be holding the line on the department's phone. Giff had the call transferred to his line. He told Maria not to plan to go to Boston, because he and Harriett will pick her up in the afternoon and give her a ride to Mass Eye and Ear. He was quite insistent. He did not want Maria to drive.

At about 4:30 Giff and Tony drove in our driveway in two separate cars. Tony took out a large fruit-basket from his back seat and carried it to the entrance with Giff in his toe. Tony carried the basket inside, put it down in the foyer, then Giff told him he may leave. Giff was waiting for Maria to get ready, she told Andy and Susie to take care of Junior and the house, until she will come home. Then she left with the Giffords.

On the way Giff was philosophizing about these strange things that could happen in the life of good, diligent people, on the way toward success. He asserted to Maria that I will, most likely, not return to teaching before the end of the semester; that he will have to find a 'Temporary Replacement' for my classes, who would close the semester, prepare the grades for the class, etc. etc. But first, of course, they were looking forward to meet Dr. Freeman, and hear what he has to say. They had brought along a box of fine chocolate, by now most everyone knew how much I liked chocolate, in fact that I was most likely a chocoholic.

When they met Dr. Freeman in the hallway at the surgery ward, he was rather exhausted, but quickly described the operation as a success, at least as much as it could be assessed at the time, and gave them his permission to see me. Then he warned the visitors, that I had been under heavy anesthesia, and most likely that will take some time to wear off.

The warning was well warranted. I was in such a drugged state, that I failed to recognize any of them. On top of all this, I was vomiting abruptly, without any preliminaries. Also, I tried to talk to them, but whatever I said was utter nonsense. Maria was terribly upset, called the head nurse, and complained about my condition. She explained to her that Dr. Freeman gave them his permission for their visit, but just look at my condition. The head nurse told them that there seemed to be nothing that could be done to change my condition presently. That I was most likely overly sensitive to sodium pentothal, and that drug would have to clear out of my system before my condition would improve. Very disappointed, they all left. Giff tried to apologize, calling the attempted visit premature, and wanted to repeat the whole thing at a later date, definitely when I would be clear of the chemicals.

Several days later I regained my preoperational condition, but was still wearing the patch over my eye. Geoffry visited me. It was nice of him to do that. In retrospect, however, I thought that there was more theatrical quality to his visit, than real concern. His concern was concentrated in one area: my stereovision. He told me that he decided to buy a Kelsh-type stereo plotter. He found an independent supplier of these plotters, which were built by the man who used to be the repairman of these plotters at the U.S. Geological Survey's compilation division. He was still performing this service under contract. Geoffry was planning to get into the plotting. He also thought that I would be interested in doing the small jobs' topography, which could usually be done on a single stereo model.

-Geoffry, you sure picked the worst possible time", I told him. "What if I loose my stereo vision?"

-Gabe, you must develop positive thinking in connection with this thing you came up with. It was not your fault, right? Everything you could have done was done, right? You are in the worlds top institution, with the best people taking care of you, right? So, you have all things working for you. You have all the reason to hope for the best. You must, and I am sure you will, believe in your total recovery" he finished his speech.

-Geoffry, I want you to know that I appreciate what you just said, and I assure you that I will do my best, what ever that is. And ... sometime later, ... I will see about that plotter.

About a week later I was discharged from Mass Eye and Ear. The patch was gone, but I had to wear dark glasses. And of course, I still had a lot of pain. I was living on pain relievers. I had to get to the Institute. The semester was over, and I wanted to partake in formulating the final grades of both classes. Herm gave them assignments, and found my last year's final exams, and simply repeated them this year. Giff came to see me in my office. He asked me about a student named Harrison.

-What about him?" I asked.

-Gabe, this fellow came to see me about his final grade. He said that he thinks he is going to fail the course".

-Harrison... Harrison?" I was searching my memory, ... Oh, yah, he is the only colored guy in the class, now I remember, ... Giff, I hardly remember the guy, he was absent from most all the classes, I remember handing him his lab assignment at the beginning of the semester, ... but I don't remember ever seeing his work".

-Gabe, just tell me: is he failing? Evidently he saw the dean of students and told him that he thinks he is being discriminated against; and that he feels extremely uneasy, you know, being the only colored student in the class. Dean Kirk called me and told me about him, and you know, I have to give him the info he wants, ...

-Well, let me get this straight. The Dean of Students called **you** to find out about his grade, or... did he call you to interfere about his grade?

-Gabe, he did not sound like wanting to interfere in his grade, first he just wanted to know whether he has failed, or not. And the only reason he called me instead of you was that he knew you had an operation and were incapacitated.

-Okay, let's see, … He hardly ever was present at roll calls; He did not do his lab assignment; He did not take any of the quizzes, nor the midterm exam, I was under the impression that he dropped the course, but he never saw me about that either, he should have had some paperwork in order to drop it. As far as I can conclude his current grade is a failing grade. If he will come and see me, I can give him an 'I' (for incomplete) but then I must see some endeavor from him to do the class work just like any of the other students had done in the course. Thereby I am **not discriminating.** You can tell this to the Dean.

-Thank you Gabe, I think you handled this very well, so far! If the Dean calls you, go ahead and see him, afterwards, however, I want to see you, Okay? It looks to me the student is trying to play some games".

Dean Kirk did call me. He was full of well wishes. He also acknowledged of my selection as the faculty advisor for TEF fraternity. Then he came around Harrison's case. I was ready; I asked the dean what exactly is it he wishes to know. He elaborated on the student's claim of being discriminated against. I then asked: is this all? Or is there more to come? "Dean, did you ever asked him to show you his quizzes or his midterm exam?"

-Professor, Harrison tells me that he never got them back from you; he also claims that he vent to see you about them, but that you could not find them, because your office was full of clutter".

-Dean, he is clearly lying," I said. "You know full well that all quizzes, exams, lab assignments, or reports are handed right back to the students before we go through correcting them 'with the class'. But let me propose something else, and this is to avoid a confrontation of "his word against mine". If he is willing to meet me with six of his fellow classmates also present, I will put only a few questions to him in connection with his claims, but then I want you also be present", I said, "if this is this okay with you, … and him?"

-Well, Professor, let me look into this," he said, "I will be in touch with you". With that he hung up. I never heard from him in connection with this case again. I called Giff right after the phone call. I told him all that the Dean said. Then I added my proposal. Giff was overwhelmed.

-Gabe, all I can say, that you were wonderful. This proposal of yours has short-circuited the entire affair, I bet we never hear from the kid again.

-Giff, the kid must be really stupid if he comes around. He definitely showed finesse and smartness in composing a case like this; he is not going to spoil it with loosing his credibility in front of numerous witnesses. I guess he will chalk it down for experience, that he tried. We have a Hungarian proverb: 'The liar is easier caught than a lame dog', and that goes for all who do not adequately cover their tracks.

-All right Gabe. Now, let me ask you, you will be coming to our usual year end barbecue, will you? I am sure you will feel well enough to come".

-Giff, I would not miss it for anything. So much more so, because we were never invited by any of our colleagues in all these two years, excepting that wine and cheese tasting party at the Lepines, and of course your parties at home, I am sure you know this.

-Yes, I know," Giff was nodding his head in silence. Then all he said was: "You know, Gabe, The New Englanders are a quaint breed. The party will be this coming Saturday. My older daughter will be here from Texas, she would like to meet you two, Maria will be driving, I guess, because I hear you still are restricted due to your vision".

-Giff, Maria would not miss it either, and may I add: **even if I were driving.** So please count with us".

--*

The gathering in Giff's back yard began early. We arrived at 3:00 PM. and were not the first ones. Giff introduced his daughter, who was visiting from Texas. She was slightly younger than us. Her husband was a dentist, who had a blooming practice. He did not accompany his wife. I found her extremely lovable, probably more so than I should have. We talked about medical-dental problems at first. She had the inside info first hand. I thought I will show off too, so, I gingerly led the conversation to music, complaining about the current trends, the lack of artistry, and oftentimes the lack of preparedness of today's composers, and mentioned some of the late nineteenth, and turn of the century composer's names. She was right at home there too, although I was definitely not beaten. I was wondering whether there was anything she was at a loss, or at least was her weak side. I was desperately trying to impress her. No such luck; through her upbringing with a father like Giff, she was right at home; even in the engineering realm. But I knew that anything to be discussed along those lines would be unfair and insensitive on my part.

So, then, okay, she was one of those super women; and an extremely good looking one to boot. I could just visualize her in her college years, how tough it must have been for the boys she dated.

Shortly, the whole gang was there. Somehow, one of the fireplaces was hard to start. It was emitting more smoke than fire. As I approached it to see how to remedy the lazy fire, blowing air into its pit, Mrs. Sinclair ran to me and, using her authoritarian attitude assumed during her nursing career, ordered me away from the fire. She started a lecture what the smoke, and the various gasses in it, would cause to the tissues in my eye. Eventually I myself got scared from all the ugly possibilities she described.

In the meantime, as she was returning to her easy chair, she ran out of her Martini.

Dario was nearby having a conversation with her daughter Pat, so, she called over: "Mario, please do me a favor and fill up this glass for me", she said. But Dario was reluctant obeying her request. So Mrs. Sinclair repeated the request sort of insistently, almost making it a point. Then, very slowly and calmly he approached her, and instructed her that his name was 'Dario'. Mrs. Sinclair apprehensively added: "Dario, Mario, what's the difference? I think Mario is better... like in Mario Lanza, don't you think?"

-But Mrs. Sinclair, my name is: Dario" he insisted, and the situation was close to getting out of hand.

-How did you end up with a name like that? They must have made a mistake at your baptism, is that how it happened?" I was sure, she thought she was cute.

Dario took her glass from her, walked to the bar, (Giff always had an open bar for his faculty) prepared a Martini, walked back and handed her the drink. She took one quick sip, turned to Dario again and said: "Mario, you must have forgotten the gin! Would you please fix it up?

This time it definitely began to look like she was needling him. Some of us in her vicinity became aware of the awkwardness of the situation, when finally Jack Sinclair stepped up to her and whispered her something, which seemed to calm the emerging storm. The rest of the barbecue went down quite normal. We had beef patties, and some nice ribs, whichever way anyone liked it.

There was a rumor going around, that Dario was dating a girl, who was related to Bill Hapkins. The rumor may have reached the Sinclair household before the barbecue.

* - * - *

My vision slowly began to improve along with the healing of the tissues around the right eye. I tried to look into telescopes with the right eye, as I have been used to in the past. It was hopeless; that had to improve a long way before even an appropriate glass could have been fitted to it. So, in order to work with any of the surveying instruments, I had to train myself to use my left eye. There appeared to be a slowdown in the incoming projects anyways.

Geoffry managed to get some smaller site surveys along with topography. So I had to look for someone who could run the instrument for me. I called on Robert Dunn from the fraternity house. I asked him if he would be interested in doing some fieldwork. Fortunately, he was very interested. He also suggested using another 'brother' who could be the rod-man. I told him to bring him along. Both of them had taken the two surveying courses already, so they were supposed to be catching up rather quickly. They did.

By the end of the summer they were a pretty good team. They completed some of the small jobs, like a school in Palmer, a commercial site in Denis, on the Cape. Meanwhile I went down to Braintree a few times to observe the assembly, and later the calibration of Geoffry's new 'Kelsh' stereo plotter. George Wagner did a very thorough job. He didn't do this for the USGS for nothing, they knew whom to pick. He kept explaining the calibration steps to me who did not actually do it, only learned about them from books at Ohio State. George had with him a few pairs of specially prepared photo-plates that had several sets of test-points with known elevations on them. These were used to achieve the correct settings for magnification and elevation readings from the stereo model. This was no longer textbook stuff, it was real life.

*

Late August Geoffry gave me a call. He was trying to frighten me; it was about the St. Elizabeth Hospital job.

-Big trouble Gabe, I just knew it, but you will have to redo whatever they are complaining about at your own expense", he said over the phone.

-Okay, what exactly are they complaining about? Am I allowed to know" I asked.

-I will tell you after I have met with them. Evidently you have screwed up. You also were interfering with my client, you have talked with one of their architect in the field, and you managed to confuse him totally", he said.

A day later he called me, he was furious. When I asked what was the matter, he said that "they want to meet you. I tried to handle it myself but I could really not see what their problem was, so, … darn it, …they insist on seeing you. This seems to be one of your ways to get between me and my clients. I will take you there, because I told them that you will correct all the problems, gratis, also that such things will never happen again".

We met their two architects, one of them the young designer I talked to in the field. This one had problems using the coordinate table computer-printout to derive certain distances, also questioned certain elevations at building corners, how they were derived, etc. Geoffry wanted to leave, promising them that everything will be straightened out they can pick up the entire 'corrected' job from his office; he will call them when it's all done, and it will be very soon.

Now I took over from here. I was not ready to leave in such a hurry. I took the coordinate list, put it on the table, asked the fellow to bring my large-scale plan and let's go over the problems right here. He did bring all that with him and he was pointing out a few distances that they had trouble with. I asked him for his pocket calculator, and then repeated essentially what I told him the last time. This time I demonstrated a simple inverse computation between the two points he marked. He said that they had a lot of trouble measuring this distance in the field, because one of the corners was one story higher than the other, but if it was that easy to derive them from the coordinates they should have done that. Also he apologized for dragging us both down here. He actually recalled that I did explain all this to him earlier. And one more thing: could I possibly give him my telephone number, so they could call me directly with any questions in the future.

170

Geoffry took over the tenor, just as I was trying to hand the young fellow my own card, stating that **he** is responsible for anything in connection with this job, that **he** was in charge, and that the Hospital is **his** client with whom **he has** a signed contract. So, **he** will handle everything in the future too.

.

On the way back Geoffry was giving me a hard time, actually accusing me of trying to steal his client. I told him not to be paranoid, that nothing like that happened, so get with it, concentrate on his end of it, which is: getting the jobs, and then let me be the one who **does them**. And that goes for everything else, and in the future as well. After all, I am the registered professional, I am responsible for the quality of the work, therefore, I am the one making statements and decisions, not him.

As to the accusation of 'stealing his client', I told him that I will ask the Secretary of the Board of Registration what exactly constitute 'stealing someone's client', whether I have the right to talk things over with the client, specially when professional matters are concerned. I left Geoffry with these remarks as food for thought. He did not utter a word.

It so happened that the young architect called me about a week later at home. He asked me if I was now free to provide the Hospital with professional service. I told him that I was, but he should ask the same thing of their administration, preferably the man in charge of contracts. I reminded him what Geoffry said about his contract with the Hospital. He told me that was all a humbug, the contract was completed already so, I should just forget about it. They have a perfect right to hire any registered professional, "the only question is: are you available, and, interested?" he asked. Because they have more work for me in connection with a building extension.

"When do you want to meet me" was all I asked.

Chapter Ten
(Getting arrested.)

The fall semester started with a bang. Actually it started with the introduction of the new faculty. We got two additions: Burt(on) Golding, and Noah Greenberg. Both of them recent Ph.D.-s. Burt is already familiar to the reader. We got him introduced (by Mc Nair) in a previous chapter. Here I will show a few more of his attributes. He was tall, over 6-ft. Some might say he was handsome, certainly his wife, Corey would say so who seemed to admire him. Probably I was the only one who knew about his recent past activities at the Colorado School of Mines, aside from Giff, after I told him. Here he was not hired as the Department Head, and therefore he seemed to have a constant chip on his shoulder. To me he seemed to have an aura of restlessness, of someone, who is being held back by evil forces, wherefore he could not possibly perform at his best.

He was sure that he belonged to a 'higher category' of scholars, (if not 'humans') but that was only my impression, who spent an undue amount of time with him: in **'my office'**. This was Giff's order, actually: his **suggested arrangement**, which was close to equivalent to an order, that we share my office. It first came as a surprise to me, but when I was giving it more thought, I had the feeling that Giff knew what he was doing. Probably this was a means to forestall similar underground moves on Burt's part to those at the CSM. In a sense Burt was being put under my control in this respect, rather than the other way around. But pretty soon this situation turned upside down. In a short time he seemed to know more about me (and my affairs) than I would about his.

172

I, on the other hand, was not nosy, I did not want to know everything about his affairs. I was completely satisfied with whatever he had to offer about his 'troubles', his 'problems', which, when I come to think of it, was about money. I was not seriously interested in his money problems. I had some of mines to think about. But mines had the opposite sign. I was searching for places to invest it into. Real soon he knew about some of my lucrative projects too.

This was so, because he was constantly milking me for information of all sorts. After all, he was the *newcomer* to the school, it was quite natural that he did more of the questioning. Added to that, it was my nature to be much more open, outgoing, than he was. He was whining about how his salary was so low; that Giff got him practically for "a song and a dance" (a direct quote!) and sometimes I felt that he was dying to find out how much my salary was. In those days this information was not privileged, perhaps neither is it this day and age, but it was not readily and easily accessible.

He seemed to have a great deal of problems with his nearly two centuries old house. The house was in the Town of Groton, in an old section of it: in West Groton. He said he had to fire two carpenters already because they did not follow his instructions "exactly". The house evidently needed a lot of work in his attempt to remodel it. I was somewhat curious about it, so it naturally led me to have him describe the whereabouts of it. I could place the house on my memory-map of the area without any trouble.

It so happened, that I had a small survey job on Main Street (of West Groton) late that fall. I had Andy with me, he was my rod-man. The job came through a well-known Realtor by the name of Gosselin, who had his main office in Groton. Burt seemed to know him really well, actually he was instrumental in finding him the old house. My job was somewhat problematic in view of the fact that the entire area was not surveyed, even in any parts, in the last eighty, or so years. The Department of Public Works did survey (and mark!) the road layout, thus the property in question had to be referenced to the DPW survey. When we finished the fieldwork we were within earshot of the Goldings' house so, I decided to pay him a visit. It was a Saturday, and a dismal, nasty weather, so when Corey answered the door she did not recognize me (us) then. By the time I introduced ourselves Burt came to the door and invited us in. I told him that we have been in the vicinity, practically in his back yard, and I was intrigued with the latest problem he had with the remodeling.

He said that was under control, but since we were there already (unannounced!) he would show me a particular problem in the basement, that had to do with the 'center chimney', maybe I will have some idea how to fix it. In the meantime Andy can warm himself up, he looked to be half frozen. Their two kids were about ten years younger than Andy, so they could not readily socialize with him. They were just too young. We spent no more than 6-8 minutes in the basement and when we came up we found Corey in conversation with Andy, which was mostly in the form of Andy answering Corey's questions.

Burt told us all to sit down. Andy was given a hot chocolate, Burt and myself had a brandy each. Burt was cutting to the bone fairly quickly. I had to tell him which of the neighbor's property we surveyed. The neighborhood seemed familiar with the Goldings and that showed both ways. They seemed to know them all too. He then wanted to know how we got this job, did we know his neighbors? etc. I simply told him everything: that I got it through Gosselin's office. He was well known to that farmer's friend of the Bursar at LTI, and that the semi-retired farmer (by the name of Locapo, indeed a very, very nice man), with the sizable amount of land, who would have a whole lot of work for me to do.

Burt then wanted to know more about my surveyor's qualifications, and schooling. Obviously I was not hiding anything, all my schooling and work experience was available on my resume, it was not classified material. He also wanted to know where I got the clue that surveying is much needed in New England. My answer surprised him when I explained that: it was sheer luck, and that I was not really hired by Giff for running the surveying discipline. But it was evident shortly after I came here that Herm's time was running out sooner than mine, (statistically speaking, since he was close to 20 years my senior) so, it was really a matter of time before I, as the most qualified faculty member, would take over the coordinator's role. He wanted to see how on the earth was I hired to be the soul transportation engineering faculty member, when my real expertise was in Geodesy, Geophysics and Photogrammetry and Mapping. I excused myself on the ground that we have taken way too much time already from their leisurely Saturday afternoon, and was telling him that we really should be leaving. But, just to answer his question as shortly as possible, I could add: by my extensive work experience in the transportation field. But we now have another transportation specialist, who is really good in *modeling* and all the newest theoretical stuff available. So maybe we shall discuss these matters further in the office at school at mutually convenient times. He was jovial, when we left the house. I was sensing that this discussion will have serious continuation at another time.

The other addition to the faculty was in the Transportation Engineering area. Noah Greenberg was actually the only other minority member of the faculty. However, strictly speaking his predicament was very similar to mine. He too, was an ethnic minority, born in Transylvania in a Jewish religious minority. He finally, after many Jews were able to emigrate to Israel, enrolled in the Institute of Technology in Haifa, Israel. He also received advanced degrees from that institution. No one questioned anything about their equivalency with the degrees offered by United States Universities. Somehow this never became a question, or if it did, it was quickly swept under the rug. The State of Israel always enjoyed a privileged political and economic status in the USA. And that also extended to its schools and institutions. So, as far as schooling was concerned he was untouchable.

As far as his minority status was concerned, the situation was different. For one thing: he was white, by racial standards. He was not from poverty family. But probably none of these things mattered a heck of a lot. The way he got ahead was through the Jewish international connections. After teaching just a couple of semesters at our Institute, he got himself a research fellowship at the DOT in Washington, D.C. Needless to say this enabled him to keep his faculty position while he was in Washington. To put it all together: he benefited from this arrangement enormously. The Institute was supposed to keep his faculty position open (for him), but had actually no one else to fill it with, who would take some of the teaching load from those who, had to carry it in his absence.

Any ways, his idea about teaching Transportation Engineering was to teach the undergraduate students, de facto, graduate material. This was his 'expertise'. The various modelings, the impact statements, and the feasibility as well as network studies. To an undergraduate junior, this was nebulous stuff. Something totally abstract. They didn't so far, got themselves familiarized with the technology of roads, design of 'links' (referred to in the higher terminology as a section of roadway from point A to B) but were expected to understand roadway capacity, (and how to achieve increasing it) in order to evaluate a certain 'link's adequacy or inadequacy in a network. All this was great, had it been for a course in graduate studies. But there was no such thing in the catalogue of course offerings. So it was something for the 'future'; for the 'long haul'.

Something I became aware of was, that Burt was taking notes when ever I was mentioning my thoughts in connection with these peculiarities. He was also keenly recording my answers whenever he was acquiring about a particular surveying or subdivision job that I had to tackle in an area he was familiar with.

*_*_*

Mr. Locapo, hired me to survey and subdivide a 60-acre hillside, which extended all the way to the top of the hill. The view was simply breathtaking, from the top. This was the first real large job I had in the area. The surveying and the engineering cost was in the vicinity of 10-12 thousand dollars. By any measure this was a 'big' job. I realized that I needed extra help over and above the ones I had for fieldwork, so far. So, I turned to the one inexhaustible human resource: The Fraternities. For one thing: I learned to know them as trustworthy, reliable kids, who were raised by more conservative standards, than many of their contemporaries.

He came to me after his friend, the Bursar, recommended me as the new 'super surveyor' around. He was cautious at the beginning. He first just wanted to clarify one of his farms boundary lines with his abutting owner, I guessed, just to test me out. I had done this to the satisfaction of both owner's by going as far back as 50-years in property records. So, Mr. Locapo told me that 'my boss' recommended him to hire me for the survey. I was getting hung up on this detail, and first tried to explain him that the Bursar is not really 'my boss' as he put it, but it was really not worth the try. He had his mind all made up; the Bursar is an administrative position reporting directly to the Vice President of Financial Affairs, whereas I was only a professor, a lower echelon, of whom there are hundreds of them around.

We started the job with the perimeter survey. Some friends of the few fraternity brothers were also recruited mostly for clearing survey lines in the woods. I was pleased with the progress the boys made. As I came down from the hill to the clearing near the road in the valley, a tow truck's arrival caught my attention, which was readying itself to remove one of the parked cars, which belonged to one of our boys. I tried to persuade the driver to leave the car alone because that is parking there temporarily, but he stated that he was summoned by the owner of the property to have the vehicle towed, so he will follow the order. All I was trying to do was to gain time for our boy to come down from the woods and move the vehicle. In the meantime the kid did come down like a deer charging out of the woods, key in hand opened the door got in, started the car and drove away. The tow truck driver wanted to get paid for the service call. I instructed him to get it from who ever ordered the service. He said he got the license plate of the vehicle, which just left and he will go after it. I wished him luck. (The kid borrowed that car from a friend for that Saturday, who lived on the South Shore.)

It was Saturday evening and I had some of the boys waiting for my arrival at the Chelmsford house. They waited to get paid. While I was making out the checks for them a police cruiser stopped in front of our house. The officers came to the door, rung the bell. Maria opened it and asked what they wanted. They showed her an arrest warrant made out for my arrest. There was nothing else to do than to follow them voluntarily. They explained that in this case they would not handcuff me, which will be a lot more civilized. I followed them. Upon arrival, I was booked at the police station. A vacant cell was being prepared, meaning: cleaned, because evidently the few cells they had at the station were used a few hours earlier by a number of delinquents who were 'stoned' and had been sick.

I sat in the front 'reception room' waiting for my good fortune. Everyone at the station was overly courteous, I thought, but did not know why. The sergeant in charge had in the mean time contacted the court clerk to arrange bail for me as soon as possible. Being a local property owner and taxpayer I was entitled to bail, as I found out from him soon, thus he said he is not going to put me in the cell. We have to wait for bail to be set. He also told me that on account of being Saturday it might take a longer time to have all this accomplished. Some half an hour later the bailiff showed up with a form for bail bond, asked me if I had ten dollars on me. I told him that the big brown envelope in the sergeant's desk has the money in it, they took from me at the time of my booking. The money was then given to him; he gave one copy to the sergeant, one to me, and then announced that I am free to leave. I pleaded with the sergeant to get me transportation from the station back to our home. He went on the radio, summoned the nearest cruiser and in a few minutes I was on my way home by the same officers who took me in.

The paper that the bailiff served on me had, as a condition for my freedom, that Monday morning, at 9:00 AM I will report at the Ayer District Court criminal division. By then of course I had a chance to read over the criminal charges, which were utterly ludicrous: cutting and removing 25 pine trees from plaintiff's property. Sunday morning I called Dom Locapo telling him my troubles with his neighbor. He assured me that he will send his young attorney by the name of Jack Lorden, to be there for my 9:00 AM trial. He said he felt sorry for my troubles, and I should not worry about anything because Jack Lorden will take care of the entire matter.

At 9:00 AM I stepped up to the clerk of the court's counter at the Ayer District Court. I told the assistant that I had a summons. She asked me if I had an attorney, I said I don't, but there should be one here soon. Because if I don't have one the court will appoint one for me. She told me to sit down and wait. After a good while a tall, well dressed, self assured gentleman came directly to me from the clerk's counter and asked me if I was, by any chance, Mr. Szikszay-Farkas, and if so he is an attorney who was arranged for me … I interrupted him stating that I don't need the court appointed attorney because I will have one who was hired for me by my client. But thank you anyways. He then introduced himself as Attorney Jack Lorden, and assured me that he is the one who was hired by Dom Locapo to provide me with my defense. So let's go into a vacant conference room where he could ask me some questions.

After we went through my personal data, he turned to me and asked where my accent originated from. I told him that it is not really a 'clear accent' because we kids had to speak two languages at home: German with our mother, and Hungarian with our father. Therefore these two come across as a blend. I learned English much later in life, as a matter of fact you may consider my still learning it, most likely till the rest of my life.

He wanted me to go through what exactly happened up on Nissitissit Hill. I summarized our attempt to clear survey control lines in the woods, which consists, usually to remove overhanging branches from larger trees that blocked the line of sight. We also cut smaller young twigs and shrubs, which represent a hindrance in measuring distances.

-How many of those small trees and/or shrubs did you cut?" he asked.

-I really have no idea, there were actually, maybe hundreds of them, I never counted them", I said.

-In your estimation, Mr. Szikszay-Farkas, what was the average thickness of those young trees, and shrubs that you cut?" he asked. "You know, you will have to answer these kind of question when you are on the stand, regardless of me asking them, or if and when the district attorney will".

So, it appeared to me, as this may actually be a 'dress rehearsal' of the real thing. I was about to ask him if my feeling about this being a rehearsal is correct.

-Yes, that's right, these are the questions I am planning to ask you; only, be careful, and take your time and think, before you answer similar questions put to you by the district attorney. The more accurately you answer, the more you are coming out as the winner; because, remember, he does not know the facts! Also, I was going to ask you, why was it necessary to cut these trees, and/or branches on the Houvanesian's property? You know that is what their name is". -Well, Attorney Lorden, no one knows as of now, whether those were on their land or on who's land. Since the boundaries are not marked by any means, no one can tell who's they are or, … actually, were. That's what the survey was all about. We would later on compute the position of the true boundaries, which will be referenced on the control lines. People usually don't know about these sort of things", I tried to explain him.

-Ah, … ah, now I think we are getting closer to our goal" he said. "Are you sure that the Houvanesian's did not know where their boundaries were?" he asked.

-Okay, let's use some logic" I began. "Assuming that they knew where their boundaries were, why did they not mark them, so they could keep out trespassers?" I asked him. "On the other hand, if the reason they did not mark them was, because they did not know where they were, was it not to their advantage to let them surveyed by their neighbor's surveyor? And again, if they did not know where their boundaries were, how could they accuse me of cutting these branches on THEIR land?" I asked him. "Does this make any sense?" I asked.

-Mr. Szikszay-Farkas, I tell you right now, don't you worry about a thing". This case is as good as over, … finie, … done! Okay? Too bad they had to waste all our time".

We were called in the courtroom. There was a short conference at the judge's bench, Attorney Lorden, and the assistant DA. were arguing and the judge was listening to them. Finally the procedure began. Attorney Lorden called me to the witness stand. The line of questions was very closely following those of the already rehearsed ones. They all went smoothly. Finally, Lorden had no more questions. Then the young assistant D.A. took over. He soon realized that he better stick to legal technicalities, which were his domain. He first asked me if I was a registered surveyor in the Commonwealth. I said I was. He wanted me to prove it. I recited my registration number from memory, but he was objecting to it. He wanted me to produce a 'valet size' certificate that should be carried 'on me'. I stated that I should be carrying it, only if I am performing my duties in the field.

Attorney Lorden cutting in, wanted the judge to determine whether the issue was my being registered or not. So the judge instructed the D.A. to stay with prevalent issues. He new right then that he was beaten, so he shortly let me off the stand. Attorney Lorden called the Houvanesians (actually: Mrs. H.) to the stand. After a few questions she was totally cornered. The D.A. came to her rescue, objected Lorden's questions about their property boundary. But this did not help, because she already admitted that she did not know where their boundaries were, 'exactly'.

The judge finally ordered Lorden to produce a Xerox copy of my registration certificate within 48-hours, and the Houvanesians to produce a list of the trees cut 'on their' land, along with an inventory of the size of each tree. That, he said, was necessary to determine any amount of damages caused them by my survey operation. In lieu of any of these documents the case will be considered dismissed 'as is'.

It appeared to me that some of the judges in this country still have some common sense justice concept left in them to come up with a Solomonian judgement. This judge threw this vicious, frivolous, 'I get you what ever it takes' case back at the Houvanesians:

now it was up to them to prove all their damages and suffering, on their own cost, because the case is no longer being handled gratis by the state; (since it is no longer a criminal case) they had to hire their own attorney to get to the neighbor, (and his surveyor). Next day I delivered Attorney Lorden a copy of my surveyor's registration certificate. With this the case was closed.

* _ * _ *

On a Saturday late in October I took Robert Dunn with me to Braintree to introduce him to Geoffry's parents. This was only an unavoidable necessity. The real purpose of me taking him along was that I wanted to introduce him to the Kelsh plotter. He was eager to meet the plotter face to face, which he knew only from the surveying textbook, where there was a photographic rendering of it in the prevalent chapter. The plotter was set up in the basement of Geoffry's parents' house. It was, without a doubt, an ideal environment for the plotter. The basement room was large, it was dry, it had forced air heating (which also filtered the dust out of the air), it had a concrete floor, virtually guaranteeing the stability of the plotter, and the electrician had the lighting arranged with a dimmer switch. This served the plotter operator's convenience; he could control the exact brightness needed for the particular model he was working on.

Prior to this occasion I had used the plotter already for a couple of small topographic compilations, just to get the feel of it. My stereo vision was never really fully restored after the retina operation, but I still had sufficient depth perception to set the floating mark on a well defined point on the ground surface. The model was sharp, the photographs were of superior quality, and I could easily recognize a football on the playground in the Palmer Public School. But the compilation of the details was tedious, and a strain on my vision and eyes. I realized that I needed someone from the younger generation to perform this type of work.

Robert was a bright student, the type that makes a teacher soar. He was not really on the cutting edge, but definitely well within the top 10% of his class. For one thing, he was eager to learn, which was, unfortunately not true to a large proportion of the student population of the early 1970-s. He was disciplined! No doubt credited to his parents. More particularly to his mother. He was an only child and his mother, who played an important part later in our life, was doing anything she could to bring his son up to the most he could become. She was one of those second generation immigrants, already born and schooled in this country, who were brainwashed on the principle that his or her kind must outperform the natives in order to be put on a level playing field with them. Robert was well liked by his peers as well as by his superiors. He was a far cry from the rebels of his contemporaries. (His parents would have him destroyed, had he be one of them, which might not be the best word describing the possibilities, but picturesque enough to convey the idea.) I for one, who was grilled pretty much on the same principles during my own upbringing, had a certain affinity with his kind.

Robert came into the photogrammetry game primarily because of his ambition to learn more, as much as possible under his given predicament. This discipline was not part of the surveying course, as described in the catalogue. But the subject occupied only a few chapters in the textbook, and Robert would not have skipped through those chapters when there was a professor from whom he could absorb, at least the basics of this orphan subject.

Getting back to the plotter, Robert had first of all good eyes, with sharp stereovision, a good manual dexterity, he was a well above average draftsman and had a fair feel for the artistic side of engineering. He had, after all, completed the first (freshman) year in a New York State Architectural College by the time he transferred to Lowell Tech.'s Civil Engineering Department. In short, he had everything going for him. Soon enough he learned the basics about 'setting-up a stereo-model', all he needed was to gain experience. The compilation part was the easiest, this was mostly 'drafting the map'; pretty well routine stuff, where the only individual touch came to 'dressing it up'. To make the long story short, in a couple of weeks, he was capable of doing the compilation part without my supervision.

To finish up one of the maps, on which we had already spent two weekends, Robert was going down to Braintree on the Sunday after I have checked his progress on the previous Saturday. He was working for about an hour, when Geoffry himself showed up. (Most likely his parents alerted him that 'the kid' was there in the plotter room 'by himself'.) He introduced himself to Geoffry, who assured him that he knew about him already. He was jovial, as ever; he looked at the map that needed the finishing touches and then praised Robert's 'good work'. After such preliminaries he got right down what he was coming in there for. He asked Robert if he would like to do this directly working for him. Naturally he asked him how much I am paying him an hour doing the compilation. Right off the bat he offered Robert five bucks an hour, let him pick his own hours. Robert was put on the spot; he did not know what to answer. He was stumbling with the words, …that he would have to talk to me first, because … he does not feel confident enough to set-up the model all by himself, … and finally: that he is quite busy with school-work for being able to do this on a regular basis, etc.

Geoffry felt let down. Now even more prone to being exposed with his clandestine approach to hire Robert 'away from me', he tried to take away the edge of the entire approach by sweet-talking him into 'it was just an innocent offer' kind of a thing, which he should better just to forget about. But forgetting about it was the last thing on Robert's mind. Next Monday as he brought the 'manuscript' (as the raw map is being referred to by the jargon) with him to show it to me, he told me all about Geoffry's 'offer'. He also elaborated on his answer to the offer. I alerted Robert to be ready for the possibility of no more plotting work in the future. But he did not seem to be hurt by that possibility, he said in that case he will still be able to put it down as a good experience, which not too many of his fellow students had access to. A very healthy attitude indeed. It did remind me, however, about Geoffry accusing me of 'steeling' his client. I was wondering how he would label what he just did.

*

Around the Thanksgiving holiday Geoffry called me to discuss an extremely urgent job that had just come in. A 'paper' developer came to see him who needed to have preliminary subdivision plans drawn up for a large acreage in Townsend, Massachusetts. He insisted that it be done by the end of the year; otherwise he will lose the zoning status of the land. After January of 1972 the size of the lots will increase to a full acre, thereby he would lose close to half of its value, because he could have only half as many lots on the front, along Tyler Road. If we cannot finish the drawings before the last week of the year we have to tell him right now, so he can find another outfit that would do it.

I went down to the Brookline office where he showed me the area, already outlined on the USGS map. So, I suggested Geoffry to let's do some logistics and tentative scheduling. If we were to do any ground control work, we could start with the compilation sometime in the middle of December, way too late for subdivision design even if it is only a preliminary design. Thus, planning it the orthodox way would never have gotten us there in time. Geoffry said now is the time Gabe, to come up with a real shortcut. Show me what you have up in your sleeves.

-Okay Geoffry, let's talk", I told him.

-Gabe, what do you want to talk about, the ball is in your court. Come up with your magic; let's see what can be done. You have to give me a solution one way or another, or else …

-Or else what? Geoffry, don't you see the guy has to be 'desperado'? Where in the world could he find any outfit in the area that would do it in less than a month?

-So, do you want me to tell him we won't do it? Anyway, I have to leave, I promised Ariel I'll be home."

-Well, I can see, you just don't want to talk about it, is that it? Just now I proposed to let's talk about it and you are already running away from it! First of all, the ball is not in mine, it is in your court. So hit it", I said to him.

-All right, if you want to talk about it, you have to come with me, because if I don't be home in 20 minutes there will domestic trouble the scale of World War III. Let's move! You follow me, I'll show you where to park at my place, it's not easy", he said, and we started out the office.

As we arrived at his condo project, on Jamaica Plains, he asked the attendant at the gatehouse to show me where to park my buggy. I will only be less that an hour. The attendant pointed to a vacant spot that was next to his parked car, and said to me you better be out at 6:30 from this place or you will have to look for your car. "Thank you very kindly" I told him and followed Geoffry up to his unit.

Ariel was waiting for us at the door. She presented her cheek for me, which I understood quite well, so, I did not hesitate to plant a kiss on it. But as I was about to supplement it she pulled away and began to scold Geoffry for failing to let her know that he was not alone. Geoffry told her that he was going to please her by being home according to his promise. That's why he did not throw me out of his office, because we had something to discuss, that we could not finish there in the office.

Ariel turned to me and asked what time do I have to be home. I said whenever I finished my business for the day. Well, she said, then go to the phone, call home and tell Maria that you will be late, because you will have supper with us. Geoffry and I sat down on the bar stools in the kitchen and he began by bringing the gin and the rum bottles from the cabinet.

-Are you still in your Rumhatten streek Gabe? I am asking because we are out of sweet wermouth".

-Never mind, Geoffry, just fix me the same what you will have" I told him.

-Since Ariel is fixing us some cheese and crackers, I'll have a Martini myself, is that Okay with you too?

-Oh, sure! Fine", I said, "let me make my call home so my butt will be covered". Then I went to the phone at the kitchen wall, called home and told Maria that I was invited to the Geoffrys for supper, so I will be late, don't wait up for me".

-Okay Gabe, shoot!" he said, "here we can talk. You wanted to talk, right?"

-Sure, let me ask first: did you give him any idea about the cost and the time involved doing it, or: did you quote him a figure?" I asked him somewhat suspiciously.

-Hell no! how could I have? I still don't know how we will do it?" Ariel came with a small tray of crackers; each one topped off with a lump of cheddar cheese out of a spray can kind of a dispenser. I discovered next to the plate a note, hand scribbled with a felt pen: 'NO BUSINESS WILL BE SPOKEN HERE TONIGHT'. I picked it up, held it for a few seconds, and then I handed it to Geoffry. He started laughing his head off. I myself thought it was kind of original, and certainly very cute.

-Geoffry, since we have some higher orders, that is: from your wife, we better finish the shoptalk", I told him; "We'll never get away with it; I call you tomorrow first thing, so that you can quote him the figure he is waiting for. Let's see if he will like it. If he doesn't, he may still have a chance to look for another outfit. You know that every day going by will work against him. Now, Okay, let's obey your boss' order."

There was never a word uttered about the Townsend job at supper. Ariel was pleased with our behavior. Besides, I learned a lot more details about both of their families, just as they had of ours.

When I called Geoffry the following morning he was all in high gear.

-Gabe, just give me a clue on how are we going to do it, never mind the figure to quote him. I'll take care of that", he almost shouted in the receiver.

-Not so fast, Geoffry, let me put it very simple: we will do it the only possible way that it can be done within the given time frame, that's what you were waiting for, right?"

-Nooooo, nooooo, give me the details, how? that's what I want to know! How?" he shouted again.

-Very simply: from existing maps and plans. The entire job: nothing but graphics, do you read me? At this point there is nothing else to be done. That is where we got capacity; You've got Basiliero, your draftsman, I am even counting on yourself to roll up your sleeves; getting hold of certain items, like: we have to come up with a blow-up of that portion of the USGS map, and I mean blow-up, big, big ... up to a scale of 1"=40'. That will have to be done in sections, so we'll be ending up with some eight map sheets. All of them with the contours, and the road, Tyler Road as the planimetry. This being the most urgent. We have to have this within two days after the client has made a deposit. By the way I don't even know the client's name, not that it matters at this point. Now, if he gives us the job, with a substantial deposit, ... say... something like two grands, then he can be called 'our client'.

-Gabe, you are going too fast" he was pleading. "I can hardly follow you," he said.

-Geoffry, don't play dumb, I know you by now, so just listen. You and I both know that as long as I am making the decisions, I am stamping the plans, then I am responsible. If not, then I am not stamping them, and I am out of the entire deal. Kapish?"

-Gabe, I didn't know you can be as cruel as this, you are torturing me, more: you are ... terrorizing me.

-Is that your conception of the whole thing? I assumed a little more imagination on your part. This time listen to me. Call *Mr. Mystery Client* right now, tell him that the job can be done; set a tentative deadline at the Tuesday after Christmas, and, I almost forgot: tell him that the estimate for completing the job will be $ 5,000. Then call me back.

-Gabe, personally: I don't think you will get away with it, but, ... under the circumstances, ... may be I should say: under the gun, ... I 'll do it. Marry Christmas!" and he hung up.

*_*_*

Burt Golding and I, sharing my office, (a temporary arrangement as we were assured by Giff) turned out to be our real socializing center. In between classes we were 'shooting the breeze', covering topics of all sorts. During these sessions he inquired from me what would it take to add a 'surveying major' (or option!) to our present curriculum. At this time I was not suspicious of hardly anything he said or asked from me. I took it as curiosity since I knew well that he lacked experience in the 'real world'. All his prior involvements were in academia. In one simple expression: he was 'on my back' endlessly asking questions about surveying. It was almost like he was going back to make-up for what he missed in his undergraduate studies. He became fascinated by 'surveying'.

One day he put some questions to me regarding my 'services'. He wanted to know if I considered bidding for municipal jobs. He said he knew people in town, (meaning Groton) who are serving on various boards. He could put in words on my behalf to get some of these jobs. I had no idea why he wanted to do this. Was it merely coming from the goodness of his heart? If so, how come? What was his motivation? This is what really aroused my curiosity.

First I did not show a very keen interest in these 'munies'. Then I was thinking: what if he wants to earn a commission? I knew by now that he was very money oriented (using this milder term instead of 'money obsessed') so maybe this is his motivation. I had nothing against this either. It is an honest way to earn money; certainly the American way. There are innumerable professions based on earning commission. Take real estate for instance. But he never ever mentioned anything about his motivation.

One day, before the holiday break he told me to submit a proposal to the Groton Conservation Commission for a wetland-mapping job that the Commission needed in connection with a development project they were studying. He gave me the description of the particulars, the deadline, the format, scale, etc. and the cost. I took it from him without showing much enthusiasm, but told him: "thanks, I will consider it". During the Holidays I met with Locapo and Marriner, (partners in the Condo project) who told me about the Groton Commission putting through the ringer one of their friends by having an outside surveyor do a wetlands mapping, 'at his expense'. This would not only add direct cost to his project, but may severely limit his project to a scale at which it would not be feasible any more. It clicked in me; this might be the same job the Commission was soliciting bids for (from me, but using Golding's efforts.)

So, I decided to grab that job. Thereby I may be of some help to Locapo's friend doing it for less than any other surveyor, also, sort of not letting his project fall through the cracks of bureaucracy. I put in a super low bid. I knew it couldn't be done for that amount; never mind making any profit on it. Then handed it to Golding. He was staring at it for a while, then asked me "Gabor, how can you do that for this much?" Or, are you really badly after this job? I thought you have enough work as it is".

-Burt, you're right, I do have enough work, but let me ask: do you expect to make a commission on this job?" I asked him almost unconcerned. "Is that why you are belittling my bid? I was under the impression that you wanted me to get this job. Or am I in the wrong street?"

-No, ... no", he said, "I don't make anything on this, I was just curious, ... you know, I am not in the business end of these things, therefore, ... I was wondering about the magnitude of the professional charges on a job like this".

-Burt, you could have asked me beforehand, I would have given you estimates".

*

I thought I ought to tell this to Locapo. When he heard that I did submit a super low bid he was rushing this information to their friend, who then told Locapo that if I get the contract he would reimburse me for the difference that I would loose on this job. I met all three of them at Locapo's farm, where the man brought along the wetland plans that his own surveyor prepared, the ones he submitted along with his subdivision. I reassured him that if I get the job from the Town, it would look essentially the same as the ones his surveyor prepared. I then posed a 'remote' possibility: "What if the Town won't give me the contract, but will give it to some other guy, who will charge maybe a lot more, and comes-up with an exaggerated wetland area?" I asked him.

-Professor Farkas, that means World War Three! I am going to sue the Town for squandering the applicant's money, for conniving with their hired professionals, then withdraw my entire application before they would have a chance to hire any other guy for more than the minimum bid." he said, and in his expression I could see that he meant business. "I would fight it to the end until heads are rolling" he said. I thought I certainly would not like to fight him to that end.

A few days later Golding told me that the Town officials were dismayed of my bid; that really threw a monkey wrench into the works, and that, perhaps they will not award the contract to anyone, after all. I was not going to tell him under no circumstances, that he grasped the matter at the wrong end. But, what he did not understand was not why I wanted to get that job for whatever it takes, because I myself wanted it, but **because I did not want anyone else to get it.** But we never had a chance to discuss the matter any further, and didn't really want to.

Another angle occurred to me somewhat later. Perhaps he only really wanted to find out how much I am making on the side by all this 'Professional Service'. In other words perhaps he was doing mental calculations about the 'size' of my business, to calculate the size of the pie he could be shooting for. But this story will come later.

--*

Geoffry called frantically for me to get down to his Brookline office because we got the Townsend job. Fortunately I was very diligent and had both classes' final grades delivered to the central data processing office. Thus my vacation was fully earned. This was one of the features of my job I would not have traded for any other job in the world.

Geoffry showed me the signed contract and the deposit check of $ 2,000.00 which was made out by an Elbthal Realty Trust, signed by two signatures. So I instructed him to deposit it and write me one for $ 1,000.00 from Ariel Engineering, Inc. marked as a retainer. This time he was acting in his true position, that of a middleman. Then I told him his task: get the blow-ups done to 20-times the size of the USGS map as soon as possible, because winter is on our front yard. I wanted to pick up the 100-scale sheet, which was still fitting on a full size sheet. Over the weekend I would be doing the site enhancement visit with map in hand, sketching the missing features on it, in pencil. I was going to put the lot lines on top of this new enhanced topographic map. Then turn this over to his draftsmen. Let him blow it up 2.5 times to get 40-scale sectional sheets, which then will be the basis of the subdivision base plans. These were all frontage lots, no new road design and layout was needed, which greatly simplified the whole thing. I told him to call me when it's ready.

The week before Christmas I picked up the 100-scale plan. The weather was still cooperating. We had a balmy pre-winter. I finished the site visit and the enhancement over the weekend and delivered it to the draftsman in Brookline. I warned them that there would be no goofing off, that there would also be a Christmas bonus if the plans will all be finished before Christmas. There was no computer graphics in those days to speed up the letterings, all the letterings were to be done by hand; actually by the Leroy lettering guides. The line work was done by the less experienced draftsman: Geoffry himself. (Sometimes.)

We had an informal Christmas party right in the office. I was handed three small coupons as I entered; Two of them (both red) said: VIG= very important guest, good for a double Manhatten. The third one was blue and read: MIG= middling important guest: good for a mixed drink. When I asked Geoffry why am I in two different categories? And how come the third coupon is only good for 'a mixed drink'? He patted me on the back and said: "Gabe, by the time you finished the two double Manhattans you won't care any more what is in your glass". Actually, he was right. Then I picked up my own Christmas bonus, said a great Merry Christmas for all and drove home.

--*

During the school break one of the Sullivan brothers came to our joint office. He said he got a message to see me about our house in Chelmsford. "What has to be done there?" he asked. I suggested him to drive with me to our home. There I could show him what the addition was, that I had in mind.

It was the rear deck we had problems with. It was small. It did not serve as a deck very well; the corrugated fiberglass roof was sagging under nearly two feet of snow. So, we wanted to eliminate the entire deck. We wanted to add a short wing to the house. In this wing was supposed to be a sizable dining room, or 'great room'. Under the dining room, on the basement level I needed a good size office, with a self contained small bathroom, and a shower. It also had a separate entrance from the outside, to satisfy safety requirements. I had to be thinking of the students' comfort too, who were working there most of the time in my present small study. I never anticipated such an explosion of business to take place in such a short time.

The Sullivan kid looked at the existing building. We made sketches, took dimensions. I could just tell he got the idea exactly. He was half way in his own construction business anyway. He was expected to graduate at the end of the school year in May. He was taking it all home and supposedly return it to me shortly with an estimate. He did.

It was a rather semi-professional job, meaning that it did not show every item separately. It was not an itemized estimate. When I pointed this out to him, he became somewhat confused. Then he asked what the reason for this was. I told him that we might want to do some of the items ourselves; therefore we needed a guide to determine if it would be worth our while. He then asked if perhaps, I was dissatisfied with the estimate. I assured him that this was not the case. But he was so conscientious, that he wanted to give me a list of those items on which I may save some money if I get hold of it, or doing it myself. Now this was more than anyone could expect from a contractor.

Then we discussed the timeframe for completion. He had to finish only the outside work phases anyway, thus, during the winter we could do the interior finishing. I had already envisioned some unique finishing ideas. I had collected left over construction material in a section in the basement of the apartment house on Christian Hill. I had a few bundles of tong and groove nutty pine, which I was going to use on the ceiling of the dining room. Some grooved sheets of leftover exterior panels were also there which I was going to use as wainscoting in the office downstairs.

By the end of March the frame and the exterior shell was completed, so we could start with the interior finishing. I could not spare much time myself to participate because I was extremely busy with my large surveying projects, not to mention the class work, which was pretty much routine by now. There were two students working on road profiles and cross sections, which in those days had to be done by hand. These things had to be taught in the transportation lab to the juniors. There were always a few talented students, who were also interested to participate in my 'mini-coop program'. They were already working in the new basement office, while one of the fraternity fellows did work on the interior finishing. These were really busy times. For all of us. I became intoxicated with progress.

191

Chapter Eleven
(End of an era.)

Menacing winds began to blow from the administration building down to the Colleges. The wind brought persisting rumors that Allan Gifford, our 'Founding Father' is going to retire at the end of the school year. The rumors did not stop here; they extended into rumors of a widespread reorganization. There would be colleges with a dean at their head. Giff's position would be phased out. Instead, there will be a VP.for Academic Affairs. Rumors turned into speculations: who would that be?

If implemented, this move of the administration would definitely mean the end of an era. We, the civil engineers were doubly affected by the change: we would also loose our department head, although, till the end of June, Giff would still be it. Words got around: who will be promoted, who will be recommended for reappointment, who with tenure.

On the home front, Giff himself made all the decisions, naturally, by being our department head. At the other colleges the department heads submitted their department's list to Giff, who, in turn submitted it upwards with his own additions. The lists were theoretically confidential, but by the time they get into the bloodstream (meaning to flow through the typists, secretaries, etc.) a lot of the information became rumors, (instead of facts) that leaked out of the system.

I for one learned my status at the incident that took place in our common office, from Golding. He charged into the office one late morning and put a curious question directly to me. He asked: "Gabor, if you had a choice, what would you choose: promotion to associate professor, with the automatic raise in salary, ... or, ...

-Or what?" I asked, since he was dragging out the time for the other choice.

-Or tenure?" he called it out as if it were the ace of trump.

-Burt, what a hell of a question this is", I said looking straight at him. "I thought much more highly about your analyzing capability. You must have known all along that a raise that a promotion would bring along means very little to me in my position. I have been turned down of promotion last year, because there were others ahead of me, ... I was told; again, what would the promotion add to my job security, compared with the indefinite tenure. I thought my answer would be totally obvious to you, ... that is: **tenure**! Tenure means the only thing in my life now, that allows me to plan ahead, ... to feel reasonably secure to reach retirement in some 17 years, so that I do not have to dread the same predicament that of Professor Robertson, ... at the Colorado School of Mines, you know". I called my trump with this one name. (Golding had no idea where I could have picked-up this piece of information, which I had in my possession all this time, but that has never surfaced until now.) He was utterly bewildered.

There was a long pause.

-Burt, did I answer your question? ... I am sorry if I got a little carried away. But I wanted to give you the whole picture. By the way, was this a purely academic question? Or did you pick-up some new rumor, ... you know, there is a lot of that stuff circling around".

-Gabor, this was not an academic question. I myself read it in the faculty newsletter. You will be getting your copy in your mail-slot, I am sure. But the real thing is when you get your notice in the mail from the secretary of the Board of Regents. Giff has reappointed you with tenure"; he said looking at me enviously and incredulously.

-God bless him", was all I said.

-If it really meant so much for you, Gabor, you did show a whole lot of moderation. You did not seem overly enthused about the whole thing".

-Burt, that's only because I am too skeptical lately. I think I developed that "seeing is believing" attitude; you know, it is an inner defense mechanism", I told him while I got my class material together for the upcoming lecture. With that I left. On my way to the lecture hall, I stopped by the department office, went directly to the mail slots, and, sure enough, there was the newsletter. I picked it up and put it into my folder with the lecture notes. Before I could leave the office Mrs. Fallon, and Herm Shea shouted in unison: "Congratulations Gabe!" That sort of woke me up from my daydreaming.

-Gee, hi there you guys, thanks a lot, … I really needed this! You don't even guess how much. Herm, do you really appreciate what this means to me?" I threw the question into their court.

-Gabor, I think I really know, I mean, … what it means to you", Joan said, using the first time my first name, which was sort of an ice breaker. "You can really plan your settling in New England, for good, … you still have your house in Cleveland?" she asked.

I didn't even know where she got hold of this information, but surmised that it must have been at one of those socializing occasions, where she was milking Maria for info, and she must have told her that we kept that house until my tenure is confirmed. It hardly produced the expected income, due to several expense items that went into the pockets of the local caretakers, rent collectors, etc.

-Joan, I am so overwhelmed, that I can't adequately express it," I told her, also using her first name the first time. "I feel like celebrating, … I feel like, … I don't even know what I feel like" I said, probably too awkwardly.

-Gabe, listen!" Herm said, "This is all natural, you put away that embarrassed feeling and let's really feel like celebrating. You know, … Giff is a very fair man, I talked to him about this; he told me: he owed this to you. I am sure he will be talking to you about it too".

-I am thinking ahead already," I said to them, "what if we, I mean the Szikszay-Farkas' would be putting up a retirement party for Gifford?" I mostly looked at Joan but noticed that Herm was also keen about the topic; "Do you guys think that the rest of the gang will be receptive to this sort of thing, … coming from us?" Joan looked at Herm, and then suddenly turned to me.

-Gabor, I think this is an excellent idea. Do you want me to help organizing it? I should be talking to Maria about it, right? You must have just improvised the whole thing. I bet Maria doesn't even know about it", she said. She was all perked up.

-Of course not, I haven't got a chance to tell her yet. I was going to get the feelers first, and it was obvious that I should start right here at the home base". I also noticed that Joan did use my first name, but not the nickname version.

-We should buy him a gift, naturally, the whole department," she said. "Gabor, do you think you will have enough room for all the people at your house? We now have ten faculty members, counting the wives, that's twenty, ... oh, no! Dario is still not married", she corrected herself.

-Joan, I think we also should invite Tony, and, of course his wife" and I looked at Herm, "he always talks so tenderly about her. I don't think it would be fair not to invite them. Frankly, I would go further, I think it would be snobbish", and I was waiting for their reaction. "And Joan, to answer your question, we do have the new great room just about finished, that can serve as the room where the buffet could be set up. And, don't forget about the new bar I built in the basement room and the granite bench in front of the fireplace ... you saw it last time you visited, ... that is a kind of cozy set-up. But these are all detail questions" I said, ready to leave.

-But Gabe, don't forget it, the devil is in the details, you know that, right?" Herm added to it.

As I left, I recalled that Giff never really accepted the administration's appointing Tony to our department. To avoid friction along these lines we have to do some more serious thinking. The party, after all, is planned for celebrating Giff's retirement. Thus, the question is: would it not be insensitive to also invite the department's lab technician, who, for whatever reason, is at odds with the celebrant? or, ... actually, it's the other way around. Ultimately, I counted on Joan. She was a native American, a woman to boot, she was in the position to judge this delicate situation and come up with a practical solution. A good old American compromise. You need women to resolve these.

Another problem has preoccupied the rest of the department. We had to elect, according to the new guide lines, a department head from among the members. The most burning problem was that of eligibility. There were no clear-cut instructions in the guidelines, concerning eligibility. If a democratic process was to prevail, any member who was willing to run as a candidate should be eligible. But that was not the case.

There were criteria set up and thrown at the colleges. Some of them, like: only the Ph. D-s could run, were thrown back in short order. Then: full professors –naturally– on tenure, were added. Again, rejected by some departments, also were unacceptable to us. It was getting near chaos. This was the 'no man's land' between the fully democratic election/selection process, where no one but the faculty made decisions what and how things, affecting them, would be governed only by them, versus the autocratic system, in which the administration only, made

195

all the decisions, and forced it onto the faculty, whether they liked it, or not.

The administration threw in the towel, leaving the process pretty well flexible, but made it mandatory to secure a final approval of all the department heads by the dean of the college. We, at the civil engineers, had a simple case: the old department head (Giff) left it open for anyone to run, except the fact that the candidate had to be 'in good standing' with the rest of the department members.

Since it is distant from the civil engineers to meddle in the administration's affairs, we could hardly come up with any more than two candidates. It just so happened, that both of them were Ph. D-s; but, while Bill Hapkins was a full professor, his opponent was a junior faculty, only an assistant professor by rank: Burt Golding. But Burt was an MIT-man, the significance of which was surfacing soon.

The rules of the election process allowed for a short campaign. Each candidate was allowed to print pamphlets and distribute them among the rest of the members. In the pamphlets they –usually- listed their personal and family backgrounds, their academic credentials, but most importantly: their short term as well as long-term goals of the department. This was similar to a 'program statement' in political terminology. But this was the area where Golding seemed to surpass Bill Hapkins, who by any other attributes, such as human attributes, was superior to Golding.

With me, Golding had a foot in the door. During our 'shooting the breeze' office sessions he started to do his own, private campaigning. He kept talking about his plans of the 'surveying status' at Lowell Tech. He visited those lectures that I held to my group of students, the sophomores, and just sat-in on them, sometimes even taking notes. I was in no position to oust him from the class; I realized that. Nevertheless his presence often annoyed me. Sometime, after class, he gave me very positive evaluations of how I handled the subject. How I was building on the class' previously, established knowledge, the poise I displayed in connection with the know-how of the subject matter, and answering or explaining it to the students. Sometimes this seemed nothing but cheep, buttering-up technique, fitting real well into his campaign, but some other times it reflected a deeper, philosophical evaluation, which, naturally, was extremely flattering to my ego. And somehow, he counted on the positive effect of rubbing this ego. He must have taken important courses in psychology.

To put it somewhat more simply: he new, (or at least strongly felt) that to secure his department chairmanship (as it was supposed to be called in the future) he needed a key vote, a decisive vote. By doing diligent, discovery, one-on-one surveys, he could pretty well count on four out of the available ten possible votes, he new full well that there was a fifth vote he desperately needed in order to secure at least a tie. That was the one he was working on: mine, for 24-hours a day.

To make a long story short, I must say: he succeeded. I held a somewhat rosier outlook for the future of my (real) discipline: Surveying, than I had with casting my vote for a ... sort of **'status quo'**. Because that's what it would have been if I voted for Bill. Such a status quo would eventually put me into a quagmire professionally speaking. It was perhaps more dead-end than that of the janitors, who had their only way up by qualifying for a department technician's job. But what would I have to be qualifying for? 20-something years later I should conclude that I should have opted for that, ...and let evolution take care of the rest.

For one thing: there was a glamour area for the faculty: 'research'. This definitely brought along prestige. Money? Not really. Status? If the principal 'investigator' (as it was most of the times referred to) found a place on his research contract for the department head, (or chairman) he could easily end-up with a recommended promotion in due course. If on the other hand, he found no such place for the 'boss' on his research project, he was soon segregated from the other members, perhaps even exiled, within.

So, I decided to give a chance to 'Progress', and see what happens. I did cast my vote for Golding. Not miraculously, at vote count a tie occurred: five votes each for Bill and Burt. Now where do we go from here? The answer to this question came from the above-mentioned *'significance'* of being an 'MIT man'. In the meantime the college deans also were selected. The faculty did not vote for them. The administration big wigs appointed them. The former mechanical engineering department head was appointed dean of the college of engineering, Dr. Winton Holbrook. He was an MIT man!.

According to the new rules, in any case when a tie occurred within department elections the deans would cast the 'decisive vote'. This turned out to be a powerful tool in the hands of the administration. In our case Dean Holbrook summarily voted for Golding (also an MIT man!). This settled the matter, moved Golding into the department chairman's room. Also, ironically, moved Bill Hapkins into my office, to take up Golding's former place. Although the whole thing seemed, from the outside, as a simple exchange of my office mates, it turned out to be a world of difference. However, no one realized this until much later, in the following year, in the fall semester. For now, our summer vacation thus could begin.

*

The next few days the only leftover business was our year-end barbeque at Giff's place. Then the crowning experience, as far as we were concerned, was the retirement party for Giff. The two events had not been coupled in any sense of the word. Giff's barbeque went very smoothly, one could almost say 'uneventfully'. Announcements were made, like: Dario's wedding, which was planned somewhat later on in June, along with his departure from our faculty. He has taken a position at Case Western Reserve University in Cleveland, Ohio. He had filed the finished copy of his dissertation. Usually the 'defense' of such work was grossly an informal event. He was 'on his way' in every meaning of the word.

Giff's retirement party was a different matter. For us it represented the grand brake in our 'exile'; The first time the entire faculty came to our house in connection with a formal event. (The previous, ad hoc, visit of only a few members two years ago, was totally spontaneous, an event that followed a business meeting at our town). The organizers selected a fairly elaborate gift: a ship's chronometer set in a stylish brass miniature rudder-wheel. When he opened it, he was just staring at it for a long time without a word. There were some pictures taken of this act by some of the wives. The presentation took place in the newly finished 'great room' where the buffet was set up. The selection of the item was based on Herm's suggestion. He knew that it would hit the spot with Giff. They had a boat at their East Machias summer place in Maine. The atmosphere of the party was quite nostalgic, without being somber or depressed.

Giff had a serious discourse with Maria, during which he offered an elaborate explanation that this was the only thing he was able to do for me, before he had to leave, to 'save my neck' from the wolfs. He knew fairly well that I was well on my way to become segregated within, and from, our faculty, if not being so already. Now, with Golding becoming the chairman, the future of my position looked even grimmer. He was well aware of the information I relayed to him after I learned from McNair Golding's fate at the Colorado School of Mines. Giff, with the granting of my tenure meant to forestall any temptation of Golding to repeat his performance here. I fully understood that Giff, (who, the reader might have guessed, became my second role model in the profession) made a tremendous effort, this time, to clear his conscience once and for all.

We could be reasonably sure that the department members had a good time. They had freely roamed the house. Andy, Susie and Jr. were in the great basement room socializing with the wives of Tom Cilento and Bill Hapkins. Somewhat later Dr. Golding himself stopped by, (he must have been tipped off by some of the female company) and began to compliment Suzie of being so 'ladylike'. As it actually turned out, he was teasing Suzie, without her realizing it. She (at the age of 13) was by no means a match to a sophisticated guy like Golding. I still hoped that they were generally delighted with our kids; it certainly seemed so.

--*

I anticipated the summer to zip-by uneventfully as it used to be the previous years. Not so now; This one had some surprises popping up. It really proved itself to become the beginning of a 'new era'. I made it a habit to stop by at least twice a week in the office, if for nothing else, to catch-up with "gossip" (from our secretary, Joan, who seemed to be more communicative ever since Giff's party was held in our house) and of course some official business, which was supposed to be placed in the faculty mail slots. This kind of communication was strictly 'semi-urgent'. The real urgent and 'emergent' news was communicated through phone messages left at the member's home.

At the end of June I found a memorandum in my mail-slot, from Golding. It was dealing with "instrument usage" by prof. Szikszay-Farkas. In a few sentences it stated that the Askania theodolite was checked out a total of 18-days during the last academic year, by: "yours truly". It also stated that I have to make arrangements with the Bursar to reimburse the University for the usage of this instrument. The memo was signed by Dr. Golding, Department Chairman. I went down to Cumnock Hall, (the Administration Building,) where the Bursar's office was located. The bursar greeted me and asked: what's up? I handed him Golding's memo. He looked at it, studied it for a while, then turned to me and asked: "Prof. is this some kind of a practical joke?"

I assessed the situation rapidly, so I told him: "I think you must understand that this fellow is a new member of our department, and he was just appointed by Dean Holbrook as our Department Chairman. I think you know the proverb about 'a new broom sweeps well'".

-I can't believe this" he said, "is this guy some kind of a nut?"

-I don't know," I said, "but I think he is trying to show who is boss, considering that … **he is the boss**, as of now", and I waited for him to say or do something.

-Well, it looks like the best thing for me to do is to write him my memo" don't you think so Professor Szikszay-Farkas?" and he looked at me.

-If you asked me, I don't know the answer," I said. "You must understand that I've never been in a situation like this before. I think it is fair to charge me something for the usage, right? And then I pay it, isn't this the simplest solution?" I asked him.

-I am afraid you don't look at this from the same perspective. If I were to assess the fee for using this instrument by an **outside party**, I would have to go through an economic analysis, … you know, the value of the instrument, … the depreciation, … the longevity of the instrument's life, … then, assuming I have the right figures up to here… I would have to assess the daily charges, … it is not only unrealistic, but here comes the real stinker: how do I justify the income from 'rental fees'? The University is not in the 'rental business'. Do I have to create a new category like this one for the revenue column? Does this new Professor, or chairman, or whatever he is, realize that it needs the Vice President's approval to create a category for a new source of revenue? Come now", he summarized his analysis. "You know what? Professor, I think I would enjoy writing all this in form of a memo to him. I think I would have some fun; You want me to send you a copy of it too? Might as well double the fun, as the saying goes, right?"

-I think I am at a loss, frankly, I must confess, I don't know much about these things" I said, "all I really want is the simplest solution with a minimum of trouble".

-You got it! That's what I will do" he said, and then looked at me. "By the way how is your surveying business getting along? I read the article in the *Public Spirit* about your Condominium project in Pepperell".

-It's all right. Actually I should say: very well, if I could discount all these annoying side disturbances" I told him. "Anyway, it seems to be clear that I have to buy my own instrument; so, we can summarize the lesson from this incident. I am going to play his game! And try to avoid falling into his trap".

-Maybe that's right, but … I have to answer him anyway, just to put an end to this nonsense, … good luck!"

The next thing I did was to drive down to Allston and visit Mr. Musto at B. L. Makepeace, Inc. the chief of instruments at this well established old surveying supply company. I brought him Herm Shea's greetings, which he acknowledged whole-heartedly. I told him about my need for an instrument, "a good one" I added.

-Professor, we have a factory reconditioned WILD T-2 theodolite … a beauty!

-That's it! Don't even go any further, … let me see it" I said, excited like a schoolboy on his first date. Somewhat ceremoniously, he had the familiarly shaped carrying case brought to the counter, then opened it up and pulled out the unique bomb-shaped steel case housing, into which the instrument was fastened. We opened it up. I asked if it was one of those inverted image optics. He said: "no way! this is the latest model. It was leased to a surveying company and got it just returned by them. They opted not to purchase it, so it is up for grabs for the same price as if the former lessee could have purchased it for the remaining sum of the lease.

-And how much is that?" I asked Mr. Musto.

He looked at me at length. Then he asked if this would be my first theodoliote. I said it would be, because all I had was a small mining transit that I acquired in Akron on a government surplus auction, on which I was the only bidder. He went to the back room where he had a lengthy discussion with Marge, who was the 'know-all' around the sales room. I began to (mentally) say my farewell to the coveted instrument, which I knew from my early days in Hungary as a novice 'triangulator' at my first job. The instrument was not only the norm for surveyors doing any precise work, but for me it also represented a great, additional, sentimental value. So, if they have to consult at such length about its price, I will surely not be able to afford it.

Mr. Musto came back, looked very seriously at me and quoted an 'even two thousand dollars'. All I could do was to grab his hand and tell him: "it's a deal, and God bless you all, so that He may overlook and forgive this 'steal'". Then Mr. Musto said to leave it there, because he wants the mechanics to go through a thorough cleaning, oiling, and check all the adjustments. I could not believe my luck. He also stated that it should be ready and could be picked up at the end of the week.

*

So it was, that I became independent from the school's instruments of which I was now the designated custodian. Burt got the wind of my self-sufficiency on the instrument front and abandoned the idea of pursuing for me paying for my previous usage after he received the Bursar's reply memorandum on the subject. Nevertheless, I could tell that something was still bugging him. He came into 'my office' one day and wanted to talk about the school's surveying 'instrument-park'. He recalled my referring to them as 'a museum' several times in the past. Now it was his move.

He asked: "Gabor, if you had money galore, what sort of surveying instruments would you buy for yourself?"

-Burt, even if I had all the money in the world I would still wait till next year, when a number of competing European companies would release their new 'automatic digital readout electronic distance meters' on the market", I told him. "But, is this again one of your academic question, or does it have something to do with reality", I turned around the questioning.

-Well, it does have to do with reality; it so happens that we have left some unspent money on our laboratory instruments budget. I heard that you just bought yourself a modern theodolite. (?) That must have cost an arm and a leg", he said, and I had a definite feeling that he is prying again into private affairs territory, which I used to ignore, but lately I was a little more cautious and alert to supply him with actual data.

-As a matter of fact it is an expensive piece of engineering that is cutting edge technology; it incorporates all of the newest improvements on it that was needed and wanted by the surveying profession. However, with my limited means I had to observe due economy, and lucked out by getting a real good buy on a used one".

-So, you would not buy the same type of instrument for our surveying lab, now? The reason I am asking is, because if we don't spend this leftover money, the administration would cut down our next year's budget on the ground that perhaps we don't need that much as we used to be getting", he said in a spirit of frustration. Probably he was expecting more help from me, than I offered. Then he turned around the questioning. "What about one of those electronic distance meters? may be a used one?", he asked.

-Burt, there are some problems here. First: how much money is there to spend?"

-Around eight thousand dollars" he said. "Could we not get a used one for that much?"

-Burt, here comes problem number two: with this much money you certainly could buy a used 'Geodimeter', but if I were you I wouldn't dream of buying 'obsolescence'. As soon as the new digital readout 'magic black boxes' appear on the market you can't give these away. You could, perhaps donate it to the Smithsonian, to their museum, because no one would use them in the field anymore. Their life is over. You were not here in 1970 when I called upon Lou Schofield and asked him if he could arrange a demonstration of measuring a **long distance'**, electronically, using their field crew at one of our Saturday field exercise. They came out with their station wagon carrying 'the equipment'. Notice, I deliberately didn't use the word: instrument. It was an assembly of gears, gadgets, generators, converters, what have you, some of which the crew members unpacked from the 'wagon', some of it left in it to connect to the 'power source'. Then parked the car within the distance it took to reach the field station with a cable. Then finally, the chief crew member brought out the instrument to be placed on its tripod, and set it up so ceremoniously, much like a priest would perform on a Sunday Mass. Finally, the measurement would begin; they went on the two-way radio and alerted the crew on the other end of the line, over half a mile away, for the commencement of the measurements. To make the long-long story shorter, in about a half an hour they managed to derive an 'uncorrected' (meaning: raw!) distance. No Burt, this gear, or 'equipment' will die the minute the digital readout 'magic black boxes' appear on the market. The guys at Makepeace have them already on order for next year by the very firms that are still using the old gear now.

-Gabor, your answer was an earful. Thanks, but it still does not solve our problem".

-If you wanted my suggestion, ... I would say this: why not use the money as a deposit on a next year's order, now! I am not sure how

Gábor Szikszay-Farkas

this would work, but at least it becomes the administration's problem, instead of yours". After all this, I have not heard from him all summer.

* _ * _ *

Towards the end of June I received a formal invitation card (with RSVP.) for our entire family, to attend the wedding ceremony and following reception for Klari Zakarias and Mr. Leslie Holzman, in Perth Amboy, N.J. The wedding was scheduled to take place in the middle of August after which the young couple was to leave for their honeymoon.

The reader might recall meeting Mr. Holzman in my transportation class in an earlier chapter.(4). Right after that incident in the class, it was evident for me that Mr. Holzman had Hungarian roots. Very gingerly I tested him a few times as of his Hungarian language skills. Following a few well known (and widly used) greetings and courtesies. I was watching him with keen interest to perform the concocting of sentences in Hungarian. I wanted to draw a comparison between him – a second generation immigrant - and our own two older kids' (also second generations) stumbling through this incredible process. I concluded shortly after, what effect the environment (he grew up in New Jersey) had on the preservation and spontaneity in usage of a language that is native to one's parents. New Jersey with its many, many Hungarian organizations, beginning with its private schools, churches, lists of civic organizations, credit and savings unions, and innumerable businesses, etc. - was an incomparable environment in preserving language and culture. He had a slight foreign accent in pronouncing certain words only, but the average man's vocabulary's words came out as any one of the native Hungarian's would have here, discounting perhaps the various dialects.

Our kids, growing up in an exclusively American environment, lost not only their capability of pronouncing Hungarian words correctly but even their inclination of using their parents' native tongue. Their 'construction' of sentences, as a result, became grotesque in Hungarian standards. On the other hand, both Leslie and Klari could converse fluently in Hungarian among themselves. (They grew-up together in European DP-camps). Our kids would not even think of attempting such an endeavor.

204

During the two years Leslie spent at Lowell Tech, while I was on the Faculty there, he came to me numerous times at Friday afternoons to ask if he could bring us any good Hungarian stuff, such as sausages, preserves, various butcher's items, as well as cheeses from those business establishments, which had the stuff in abundance all over New Jersey. He made the trip home every two weeks on a regular basis and before he did, he usually stopped by my office and asked if he could be useful in this respect. It was something only relatives, or very, very close friend would do to each other. Occasionally his mother, who did the actual shopping anyways, would throw-in some extra goodie that she discovered at one of the stores where she did her shopping.

Their parents quite sometimes sent us messages that contained invitations to some Hungarian parties, like Christmas, New Year's and other celebrations of national historical events, organized and held by one of their clubs. It was becoming very, very 'homey', certainly for immigrants and exiles, it was something irreplaceable, touchy, warm and an expression of belonging to an undefined 'family'.

At various occasions Leslie brought along Klari for a week or so, to familiarize herself with his environment at school, the University in the City of Lowell, where he studied, with some of his professors, such as myself, and some of his classmates. We were delighted to have them as our guests. As it turned out, at various discourses, Klari's father attended and graduated from the same parochial High School as myself and my brothers (at the Cistercian Monks in Buda,) attended and graduated from. He was some 9 or 10-years older than myself, thus, at the outbreak of World War II. he was recalled from the reserves into active duty and been sent to the Eastern (Soviet) front as a first lieutenant in 1941. Many times we were reminiscing about the good old days, as they knew it from their parents and we experienced as kids. They were not around at the time.

Both Klari and Leslie were born in Western European refugee camps in the 1948-s and early 1950-s where their parents were dispatched after the war as DP-s (Displaced Persons) by the authorities and they lived in these camps until the end of 1951 when they were finally accepted to immigrate to the USA. These were trying times as it turned out, for both of those Hungarians on the western as well as the eastern side of the 'Iron Curtain'. With their parents coming to the United States their existential problems came to an end as much as it could be said about those people in their middle age, who went through a cataclysm, some with, and some without family and were desperately searching for a meaningful life that's worth living.

Klari's father was descending from a well-to-do, land-owning, gentry family, which managed to hang-on to the middle, upper-middle class life style after the disastrous Trianon Peace Treaty (closing the end of World War I) that tore asunder the thousand year old Hungarian Kingdom, as a punishment to Austria, for starting that war. (A typical French mentality solving socio-political problems in Europe.) Their land was confiscated along with all the others (of their kind) in 1945 by the communist government's order, which came to power based on the presence of soviet troops occupying the country at the end of the Second War. The Zakarias's were not even at home in their country when it happened. This did not, of course, make much difference any ways. It meant little consolation to know that there is nothing left to return 'home' to, after the war. They opted to become 'DP'-s and live in the camps until they could start a new life. Many, many did not; they returned home instead, and ended up in the soviet gulags.

A new life, indeed. They started working on it with unprecedented energy, optimism and faith in the system they could not and would not dare to criticize any time later. They started working on it right after setting foot on the New Jersey shore. Laszlo Zakarias, the intellect, the trained soldier, communicating in four languages was deemed to have no **marketable skills**, ended up working for the Engelhardt Precious Metal Works as a foundry-hand. He was well liked there, was well treated and after some fifteen years was even respected. He attended Rutgers University, evenings, to earn, if nothing more, at least a liberal arts degree. Eventually he assumed the position of production supervisor. (Although the predominantly Jewish high management was reluctant to promote any cadre from the ranks of Europeans, unless they had Jewish roots.)

He made sure however, that every single one of his three children will have a college education. Eva, his oldest, became a high school teacher majoring in languages. Laszlo, (Junior) was finishing Law School at the time of Klari's wedding. That was how we met the entire family in Perth Amboy. Their mother, Lenke, was hardest hit by the social upheaval; she came from a nobility a step higher than the gentry, but this never came to polarize while they were youngsters in that society which they were forced to leave at the end of the war. This put her into a periodic clinical depression as she began fully grasping the doom of her 'class' in the homeland. Nevertheless, she was proud, from time to time when any one of her kids were on the receiving end of academic achievements, or merit awards of any kind.

Klari herself, studied up to pre-med school and at the time we became acquainted she was a medical secretary. A well respected and sought after profession, a cut above the average secretarial positions. She was extremely good looking, with a queenly poise, but without a shred of disdain that usually accompanies such 'winners' of her gender.

Leslie Holzman, (curiously a namesake of his father-in-law to be) came from a patrician family, a sizable one of that. His father was a beaurocrat in the Horthy-regime between the two wars. He was older than the other father-in-law in this union, the Zakarias-s. They were well acquainted with each other, in fact more than that: they became honest to goodness friends by the time the cataclysm hit all of them. They also tend to pull together as aspiring survivors of their doomed class. Their parallel, the contemporaries, those who stayed (or returned to) the home land were pretty well annihilated by 1949 the year of the total communist takeover.

*

The wedding was arranged along the rules of the old customs of this exceptionally unfortunate nation. I could hardly follow what exactly was going on from time to time. But one of Leslie's brothers, I forgot his name by now, (there were three girls and three boys in the Holzman family) kept at my side a reading from a 19-th century wedding ceremony book. This way we always kept abreast of the current part of the ceremony.

Since we were guest principally belonging to the Holzman's, we were put in **their** ensemble. There were innumerable of us. At one point Dario Campanelli also showed up, Leslie invited only the two of us from the entire faculty of Lowell Tech. Dario brought along his fiancée and from the looks it seemed that they did not give much credit to the Hungarian 'folks-wedding', which after all, lasted a mere 2 to 2 1/2 days. According to them an Italian wedding of any merit had to last at least 4 to 5 days; and that is guests and all, so that they can all get acquainted. I told him to stop bragging about this, we'll see the actual duration of their own wedding, provided we will be invited to it. The Hungarian folks in Cleveland will have a few surprises for them, I warned them. But let's get away from all this ethnic stuff.

Klari's father, László, was prepared for the church event in a grand way. I could not believe when I heard him recite –in Latin– an entire Psalm from the Book of Psalms, specially picked by him for this occasion. It was just too much, totally overwhelming. Then he offered his own prayer, very elaborately written and read for the occasion, this one in Hungarian. Almost everyone in the family was crying, it was simply too much to bear. Well, after all, he was about to give away his last daughter in matrimony to the son of his best and most trusted friend. The rest of the church ceremony was left to the priest, to tackle, who was also an old family acquaintance. Evidently he was the teacher of religion to the class of both Klari and Leslie and an old trusted canon of the monsignor in Woodbridge.

After the church ceremony the folks drove over to the reception hall in caravans of vehicles. They filled up almost the entire parking lot; there must have been hundred to hundred and twenty cars in the lot. Fortunately the hall had a capacity of at least 300 people. There was a live band as well as a DJ who came on later in the evening producing the fashionable rock and roll numbers (for the young folks!) The live band produced the music for the ballroom dancing and the easy listening music during the meals.

The dancing started with the bride's-dance. Anyone could buy a short turn of dances for a predetermined schedule of fees. The bride's brother,László, (the lawyer!) collected the fees and kept track of the waiting list and the number of minutes the eligible hopefuls may dance with the bride. I really have no idea how much was the total sum the bride accumulated, but must have been very substantial, since according to László, it was easily covering the entire cost of the honeymoon. After about 20 minutes the general public also began to dance. László Sr. was our self appointed host. He was lingering around us more-less constantly, in fact he managed to arrange us (meaning the entire family) to be seated at the same long table which they occupied. The bride and groom occupied the head table with their immediate families, mostly their brothers and sisters.

Finally the supper began. This was an incredible rank of dishes arranged in an order of increasing concentration (as far as caloric and cholesterol content is concerned). Naturally everybody was fed. Well fed. There was a pause in the music enabling the musicians too to turn themselves over to gastronomic pleasures. The bar was open, and I mean open. When I stepped over to survey the offerings I could not believe what I saw. There were cases of the best vintage Hungarian wines under the bar counter. László told us that he made arrangements with the local (Perth Amboy) wine merchant to set aside some of these world class (Hungarian) wines, which he was to be paying for on a monthly budget. The merchant kept them in his basement storage all this time.

László, Sr. (Klari's father) having been brought up to become an army officer was an excellent dancer. Compared to him I had two left feet. There was hardly any dance that he did not know. He went as far as taking his older daughter, Eva and demonstrated the 'Charlston' for the rest of us all. They were applauded by us. Maria was also a very good dancer, I could never keep up with her, but very soon they discovered each other and became inseparable for a goodly part of the entire night. Folks began to take notice of this and did not leave it without comments.

After Klari finished her obligatory dances (as well as the ones of pecuniary interest) she was free to dance with any one of the guests. She was the one coming to my rescue and we danced some 'csardas' and of course, waltzes. Moreover she was such a queen of her celebration that she, later on, came to our table and asked our Andy to dance with her. Andy was in the awkward age of between childhood and manhood and tried to get out of the embarrassing predicament by trying to convince Klari that he doesn't know these dances. But Klari didn't take a 'no' for an answer from such a young man and led him by his hands to the floor. The musicians knew their business and began to play a moderately fast rhythmic csardas, such as:

> "Sárga csizmát visel a babám,
> Szeret is az engem igazán;
> Sárga csizma hadd szakadjon el
> Csak a babám sohse hagyjon el,
> Sárga csizmát visel a babám,
> Szeret is az engem igazán."

Klari was leading Andy all along, and soon enough, they made out pretty well together. Klari was trying not to be really dominant, but I had the unmistakable feeling that Andy did begin to see the embodiment of 'the older woman' in her.

This reminded me of the times when I was 15-years old at the end of the war and our family was put up in a room of our tobacconist's house in the town of Szirak, a regional center closest to our estate, while the communist commissars were roaming the country carrying out their duties of confiscating all (sometimes hidden) private properties from the Bourgeoisie.

The owner of the tobacco distributorship was a good friend of my father from the 'good old days' before the war. After the front moved through the Country, their daughter-in-law, Gizella, was about 25-years old, trapped in that part of the Country without her husband, who was in the army and was ordered to move to the west with the rest of the troops. She was hospitalized as a result of having just lost her little baby boy during the retreat of the troops and was ordered to be left behind with her close relatives in Szirak. We all tried to have as good a time as was possible in those days; for one thing everyone was much closer to each other than ever since, (save perhaps the 1956- uprising).

She was then the absolute model of *'the older woman'* for me, who never ever before had such an experience. I always loved to help out in the kitchen. It was a natural inclination. On my 16-th birthday I discovered that she was preparing a birthday cake. I guessed (and secretly hoped) that it will be for my birthday but couldn't be sure of that. Ever since she moved in to her in-laws I had a giant crush on her. Even though her health was still fragile, this did not diminish my infatuation.

On my birthday as she presented the cake at the table, following the evening meal, she anointed me with her *'birthday kiss'*. I don't think she had any idea what that caused in me, who from then on had one super ambition: how (and when) could I have that kiss repeated, perhaps even perpetuated, which seemed totally hopeless. The beauty in such a hopeless crush is that it does not require a follow-up action without losing the intensity of the emotion. I wouldn't know how to follow-up properly anyways with her under the given circumstances.

Years later, after the war, when we all moved away from that house I lost touch with Gizella, and finally overcame the crush I had on her. The emotions eventually subsided with both the distance and the time. But the anointing kiss had a lasting effect. I became *'kiss crazy'* and it no longer mattered just who the kiss would be coming from or would be returned to so long as it involved an attractive female. There were several other candidates later, who were no longer 'that much older' either. But that is another story, which will be told in another book, at some other time in the future if this one will have sufficient recognition. (This is a promise!)

Chapter Twelve
(The New Chairman.)

Golding has launched his great offensive shortly after the new school year began. I thought I was ready and prepared. He came on strong right from the outset. He was questioning Herm about the surveying textbook; why are we using such an outdated book? Herm gave him simple and abrupt answers, such as: that the book worked well now for a good 7-8 years and covers the entire content of the course description.

"What other textbook are you suggesting?" Herm asked him.

"Well, certainly some more up-to-date one" he answered, not having with him any specific book to quote. I mentioned him a few titles though.

Golding decided to corner him by mentioning some of my remarks I made about that 'pocket book' earlier during the year. He was using me now against Herm. So he said that "then it is high time that we start reworking that obsolete course content and description".

"Burt, there is really only one serious practical problem here, and that is: timing. You can't change a textbook now when the students already have bought the one that the course description called for, unless you are prepared to start an unrest".

"That's not what I had in mind, but I think we should have some philosophical discussions along these lines. We now have time for those".

"Okay Burt, will you write me a memo on the subject?" Herm asked him.

"I think we should talk about it first" he said and left him. I was dragged into this somewhat later.

* --- * --- *

Golding came into my office and told me that he has something for me. He came directly forward that I should submit a proposal to the Chelmsford Cemetery Commission. I told him that I don't know anything about the details, and asked him where can an interested party get them in order to submit a bid. He then told me that this is somewhat confidential stuff at the present time. But, when he learned about it he put in a word for me, why shouldn't I also be given an opportunity to submit a bid.

"Burt, you don't live in Chelmsford, so, ... how come you know about this sort of information? Are you a member of the Commission? That would be strange, I think", I told him and was waiting for an explanation.

"Gabor, listen, I overheard this discourse while some people were talking about the Chelmsford cemetery, ... that it needs to be extended, and ... that the Town owns more land around the existing part, but a development plan is needed, so that the Commission can have it approved by the Planning Board. Now that is a project I would not mind partaking in, you know?" he was watching me for my reaction.

"Burt, I am really interested in this. Tell me what exactly did you have in mind to work on this project?"

"Well, I don't know yet. Something along the overall design, you know, the extension of the existing plots. Like, ... I was thinking about my participation being in the 'conceptual' part of the project".

"That is interesting. Have you done any such work before?" I asked him.

"No, but I told you before, that I know people; that I talk to people; and the people I am referring to are not just any people, do I make myself clear?" he asked.

"Very! How do I, ... we! get hold of the description of the proposal, the scope?"

"Gabor, I can get this, and, ... of course, I will submit the proposal, ... into the right hands. This is something, ... as I mentioned before, that has to be done, ... well, confidentially".

"Burt, I think I am beginning to see, … I mean your involvement, … your participation in it, as you put it. So, if I … rather, we! get this job, … how did you envision a breakdown, … you know, … a split?

"I was thinking of, … say … how does 50% sound to you?"

"Fifty percent, … of what? If there is fieldwork involved?, … like surveying some or all of the surrounding land, maybe even some topo, … or perhaps soil info, … you know, the Board of Health may want to have some soil profiles? … so you see, there is more to it than meets the eye, for instance, will you be sharing the involvement in these expenditures too? … like, on a 50% basis?" I asked him.

"Gabor, I wasn't ready to answer all your questions in details, not at this time. I guess we can work them out later," he said. "Right now I shall get you the scope description".

"You got it", I said, … "you should! really."

In a couple of days he brought a few sheets with the description of the 'scope' from the Cemetery Commission and left it on my desk. I looked on the bottom line and saw the signature of Dr. Everett Olsen on it. I was hit by this revelation. Naturally I had no idea that the executive vice president of the Institute was a member and officer, -as it turned out to be the case- of the Cemetery Commission of the Town of Chelmsford, our home town. I tried to recognize the names of some other members from the Commission's letterhead but did not know any of those listed.

So, I put together an itemized cost estimate for those work phases that were identified on the scope, produced the total, which came to a modest sum of 1500 dollars. Then doubled the figures, because it was clear to me by now that the other fifty percent would be Golding's share. (He was securing the job for 'us' after all.) Then took it to his room. He was at his desk. I apologized for interrupting him and handed him the proposal He said it looked real neat. There might be only a slight problem later on because he was almost certain that the totals on the bottom seemed way too small, perhaps even miniscule compared to what the 'other surveying outfit' was presenting (mind you only verbally) to the commissioners at the last meeting.

I then looked inside myself; I new I could do the technical part in 6-7 days, or rather evenings, since there were no field surveys involved in this phase. My monthly salary, at the time, was around 1,300.00 dollars. I didn't think this was a 'miniscule' amount by any standards. But then again, maybe I have to start revising, or updating the standards I set to myself. So, for now, I told him to let it fly as is, we can later renegotiate some of the items. First is always to get hold of the job, and the rules of the game calls for a lowest bid to achieve this.

Golding then asked me about a new surveying textbook and course description. How long would it take me to put together a document –for now only in a simple memorandum format- for him-, to form the basis of discussion with our curriculum committee. I told him this is not something one does overnight, and estimated that it needs a lot of thoughts, so, give me a month, I told him. At about midterm I should have something that we could discuss. Then he admonished: "Gabor, this is your future. You should start working on it right now. You know that you will have to take over from Herm the coordinator's functions, and when that happens, ... then we can expand the surveying option to anything you visualize, ... may be even a graduate offering, at least to the M.Sc. degree level".

"Burt, I still think this will be a very tough nut to crack", I said, but, if we don't give it a try we never get it off the ground. I must warn you that many, and I mean many, big name Universities gave up totally on surveying as an option 'within their civil engineering departments. I have one eloquent example: Princeton. I suggest you do some reading about that one example", I said and left his office.

The following Saturday I got a call from vice president Everett Olsen. I was in my new downstairs office. He began by mentioning that he looked at my proposal about the planned Cemetery Expansion. He began at Adam and Eve, first describing how he became involved in this project. That he was elected to the Commission years ago, when it was dealing only with routine matters. This seems to be the first real project that needs the hiring of external 'expertise'. When they looked at the cost of my proposal the Commission didn't know whether to take it seriously or don't even look at it any further.

So far I had hardly a chance to speak at all. Now I expressed that my quote is always based on a careful estimate of time that needs to be spent on a particular phase of the job. And then, -as it's being done in the practice – I translate this into monetary terms.

-Oh yes, professor, I am with you, but in this particular case, don't you feel that you have stuck your neck out a bit too far?" he asked, and he sounded somewhat paternalistic, sort of looking out for my best interest, who's sole endeavor is to protect me from getting hurt – financially.

-Dr. Olsen, am I correct in assuming that you would like to see a larger figure on the bottom line of the proposal? Would that make it look like a more honorable, or more serious proposal deserving a more serious consideration? Er, …am I close, or am I way out?"

-Professor Farkas, (again one of those skipping the first half of my hyphenated name) I don't want to influence your methods of doing your business, but I guess you were correct in one respect, namely, that a higher figure on the bottom line would bring this proposal into the ballpark. Actually we only have one other proposal, which is from an old, well established surveying-engineering firm next door, so to speak, which is well known to the members of the commission. In this respect your proposal would be on a level playing field with theirs".

-I understand fully what you were trying to say Dr. Olsen and let me assure you that a correction will be made. Also, I am going to hand this over to Dr. Golding tomorrow to take it from there".

So, this is how it works. I hated this ball game. In my standards it was 'rotten'. I got sick of it to the point that I didn't want anything more to do with it. Later in the semester Golding came to me and mentioned that we were unsuccessful with 'our bid', because the commission felt that the engineering firm in Billerica should get the contract. Probably, … you know how it is, … these are old, well established firms, town's people know them, etc. Then I told him: "Burt, I did not ask you about the job; I had bad vibes about it ever since the beginning; This was the second job that turned sour due to some pricing problems. I really don't know what was wrong, and, frankly, at this point, I don't care. So, please save all this aggravation and don't bring me any more of these 'munies', unless they are honest, not manipulated and we can be reasonably sure that the effort put into the preparation of a proposal will not be lost, Okay?".

--*

An urgent message reached me from Attorney Halloran. It said that he would like to meet me in his office. There is something I would perhaps be interested in. If I could make it at the end of the day around 4-PM that would be excellent. Naturally, I got to their downtown office around 4-o clock. I made it a point to be very punctual in those days. Kathy (not his secretary) instructed me to please wait in the reception room at front. His own secretary, Mrs. Galloway, already left for the day. There was another man, at least a decade younger than myself, sitting in the room as well, reading a paper.

Shortly, Attorney Halloran emerged from his room and came to me at the waiting room, while the other man rose from his chair too.

-Professor, I'd like you to meet Mr. Lussier", then turned to the other man and introduced me to him. Then he was talking to the both of us: "I think both of you will benefit from this association; Mr. Lussier is a developer and has some ambitious projects coming up, right here in the Town of Dracut. I thought the two of you should get acquainted for mutual benefit. For your information, Professor, I might add that our bank finances Mr. Lussier's projects and it would add to our peace of mind to know that you did the surveys and the subdivision work. So I will leave you two alone to talk things over, all right?". With that he left us in the front room.

Gerry Lussier was an energetic, ambitious men in his very early 30-s. He was on the short side, but muscular, without qualifying for the term: athletic. The many hours he spent outdoors on his projects gave him a robust appearance along with an inimitable, durable tan, bordering on 'creole'. His manners suggested a very much goal-oriented character as well as a no-nonsense attitude. Shrewdness was radiating from him.

I addressed him Mr. Lussier and in turn was expecting him to call me Professor. But this arrangement somehow never really got off the ground. Very early on he told me in no uncertain terms that his name was Gerry, and he is expecting everyone to call him thus. He made no bones about it that he is not intending to call me professor, he thinks that would be inappropriate, almost to the point of being stupid, since we are not in a school here and never will be. But he is willing to address me any short format of my name, even preferred a nickname, something like: Gabe, which he readily borrowed from the TV-series 'Welcome Back Kutter'.

After this no nonsense introduction Gerry asked me where I would prefer to sit down with him to discuss business: in his office, which is added next to his house in Dracut, or at the 1486 Club, also in Dracut. The difference being in the fact that in one place there will be no alcoholic beverage available, while in the other place there will be plenty. "Now, where do you want to go?" he asked.

-Gerry, I don't know either one of these places so why don't we try your place. What do you keep at home in terms of drinks?

-You must be kidding! Water! You may get some soda, or Pepsi. Jackie (his wife) would not tolerate anything else in the house" he said and looked squarely at me.

-Gerry, … I had kind of a long day, … so, … why don't we try that club you mentioned. I take it that there is no prohibition there, am I right?".

-Gabe, don't you know the place?" he asked. "Let's go, you follow me. You'll like it, I am sure", with that he charged out of the law office. I followed him up Lakeview Avenue to Collinsville. There we took a right turn on Mammoth Road. Close to the New Hampshire border he pulled into a parking lot, which was in front of the club. We went inside. I was not used to an ovation upon entering any joint, but this was what we got here: a thunderous ovation. I had no illusion about whom it was for. I've never been in the place before, so: I was unknown.

Gerry picked a table towards the rear of the room and started to pack a number of plans on the table right out from his armpit. That was where he brought them in: under his arms. The next thing he did was he chased away the curious crowd. Somehow everywhere he went, people wanted to know what is Gerry Lussier up to. Quite often I heard someone asking his companions: 'what would Gerry Lussier do in a case like this?

Then he began. He described that they are in the process of closing their first real, good-sized project on the top of Marsh Hill. There will be some finishing touches needed, a few certified plot plans, etc. But, he wants me, (us) to start on his new project on Parker Avenue. No, it has not been surveyed, he answered my question, it has to be done. We will also need to have a detailed topographic plan. This is for start. How much? he asked.

-Gerry, do they have a waiter here, or is this place 'self served'?" I asked him.

-Bob," he was yelling to the bartender. "Do we get anything to drink in this place?" Bob rushed down to our table. He turned to Gerry and said:"Sorry Gerry, I didn't know you wanted to drink, I thought you were conducting business", then he turned to me and asked what I will have.

-Well, I feel like, … say, … can you do a Manhattan, but instead of the Bourbon pour a generous amount of rum into it, you think you can do that", I asked him.

-Oh, sure, I can do that, nothing to it" he said, "what do you call that concoction, does it have a name"?

-I call it 'Rumhatten', but don't quote me on it, okay?"

-Sure thing, coming right up, but how do you want it? on the rocks? or, ...

-Okay, ... now, since you asked, for a starter, pour it on the rocks, but put it in a larger glass, ... you know, to make room for all that ice, ... it's going to melt as it sits here but it will stay cold much longer", ... I told him.

Bob seemed to be a capable fellow when it came to the drinks. He brought it to our table and was just standing there, waiting for something to break. Gerry was staring at him wondering what else he wanted. He was turning to me and watching me taking the drink. I noticed immediately that he put a couple of maraschino cherries on a small plastic skewer in a floating position in the glass.

-Was this your own idea, ... Bob? is it okay for me to call you Bob?" I asked him.

-Sir, please do, most everyone calls me Bob. "I was thinking to tame that rum flavor a little bit, ... you know, I myself am not a rum drinker, but, ... we used to put the cherries into the Manhattan, so, ... I thought, ...what the heck, they can't hurt this drink".

-Very good thinking! Thanks, this way it came really close to the way I make it at home; but let's not get into that here and now. We will do it some other time, okay?"

Gerry was flabbergasted. He was watching the entire routine with some bafflement. He had a simple Scotch on the rocks. Then we returned to the plans. On the tax map he outlined the old pig farm that he recently bought and said that he wants that surveyed and subdivided before and perhaps during the winter. During the winter we can do our wrestle with the planning board, but, ... in the spring he wants to start with construction. Then he wanted me to quote him a figure.

-A figure for what? I asked him. "There are many different things to be done, and the planning board will find some more things to be done, believe me" I said, but he was just looking at me.

-Gabe, I want you to throw a figure at me, how much this will run into, and then stick to that figure. We want no more surprises. We got burned before, on previous jobs".

-Well Gerry, I got news for you! You will find more and more surprises as you go along. These boards keep on changing their own rules, you can really not plan ahead. It seems that you are expecting the engineer to stick his neck out, and work for nothing at the end when the money is gone, exhausted. Think about it! Do you think it's fair?"

-Okay, then do one thing for me: give me a 'ball park figure', which I will not hold you accountable for. How is that?" he asked, smiling.

-I can give you that, but what is it worth? Let me put it this way: The survey and the subdivision design, up to approval, will run into some $ 8,000.00 that is ball park. Construction is something else again. Later, you will need layout work, which we can handle on a per diem basis.

He looked at me at length. Then he asked: "are these drinks giving you these ideas? you seemed to know a lot about these things, ... I mean with the Town Boards and all, but you don't know one thing, that we, ... and when I say we, it means my partner and myself, ... we have some pull in this town".

-Oh, yah, that is very, very smart, I should say: important! Right now I don't want to know about it. As we go along you will fill me in on these little inside, ... now what was I supposed to call them? inside ... secrets?"

-Okay, you let me know what you need and I want you to start with the survey right away" he said. "Now you tell me a few things about yourself, ... your family, ..."

-Well, just exactly where do you want me to start? like, when and how we came to this country,... the usual stuff, that most everybody is sick and tired of being asked?" I asked him.

- You know what?, Tell me about your schooling, tell me how come everybody thinks you're so smart?

Then I began to tell him about my first job on this continent with the Canadian Pacific Railway; being an assistant to the division engineer. That I could not see much of a future in that position in which I was probably destined to stay until retirement, (when ever that would come.) That, when I finally quit my position after more than five years of serving there, the superintendent told me that he admired me for my decision, and, ... that he seriously doubted that any Canadian boy (or young man) in the same position would have opted to make this move, ... (to enroll in graduate school) away from a comfortable position, like this one, from a company that was around for almost a 100-years, and, perhaps,... will be around for another hundred. This was the core of his farewell speech he made at the time the division employees gathered around in his rail car (stationed at a siding track next to the station building) the evening they threw the farewell party for me.

Gerry ordered Bob to refill the glasses, which he willingly complied with. Bob was even hanging around to listen to some of the details in my recitation, which sounded interesting to him. He was a very pleasant chap, not an uncommon trait for bartenders. Actually, I didn't mind the audience, as long as my host did not. Finally I thought that this was enough for the evening. It seemed like that there would be many more occasions similar to this one, perhaps not in the same environment but not altogether different from this.

My host, Gerry Lussier, had graduated from high school, and seemed very well satisfied with that level of education. His partner, Doug Dooley, (whom I have not met as yet) was his buddy. They went into construction together and were employed in several building trades. They came up with sort of an innovation in bathroom tyling. They worked in tandem. One of them applied the adhesive paste to the wall, and let it air, so that it became real tacky after a few hours. Then the other started to put the tiles against the wall with great speed, and inserted thin, solid spacers between every other row. This way the rows stayed, did not move anywhere, and in another hour the walls were ready to be grouted with the grouting cement.

They were soon rich. They subcontracted the bathroom tyling from several large contractors (we mentioned Hicks before in Chelmsford) who built several hundred houses each year. Thus they started to become their own general contractors. Their very first major project was on top of (or very close to the top of) Marsh Hill. There was a breathtaking view from that site far into New Hampshire to the North. They built 34 houses there and were just about finishing up.

Now they could start with their next project: 'the pig farm'. They had a delectable custom: to name the entire subdivision after the previous owner's last name, and register it as such under the registration process in the Registry of Deeds. Thus, this subdivision became known as: 'Bernard Acres'. Also, very appropriately, the main road leading into the interior lots, was named: 'Bernard Road'. The farmhouse itself was totally remodeled. His finish carpenter foreman was given first refusal on that property, which he readily exercised, and did much of the work himself. His wife was in the hamster, guinea pig, and laboratory white mice breeding business. Here she could pursue this at an expanded scale in the barn, which had plenty of room (after the —real— pigs were ousted from it). Before the gutting of the building I mentioned to Gerry that I want the old upright 'baby grand piano' and that I was going to hire movers to move it to our Chelmsford house. In the back of my mind I always maintained an affinity to the good old instrument, and was (perhaps unreasonably) dreaming that someday I will resume the piano lessons that were interrupted by the war many years ago.

221

(Unfortunately this was never realized.) The piano was an antique. It had genuine ivory plated keyboard, ecologically incorrect at the end of the twentieth century.

Gerry and I became an item (that is, in terms of avalanching the Planning Board and the Conservation Commission with newer and newer plans). At some of the meetings the local paper's photo-reporter snapped several pictures of us together as well as separately and inserted them in the local edition of the Lowell Sun.

* _ * _ *

By mid semester Golding was well aware of the great advancement of my 'surveying services', on the local scene. He had several discussions with me. He wanted to know what sort of research areas are available in the surveying field, where we might have a chance to break into. I told him that in the routine surveying realm the instrument manufacturers are dominating the field for their own, mostly advanced, reading, recording and electronically handled (field) data collector and storage devices. No one, but no one gets into these areas except the employees of the research departments of manufacturers, which are kept under heavier security than the CIA can come up with.

Then I mentioned him that there are other areas. Namely: in the software development areas. This is a tremendously open field. The Surveying and Mapping magazine devotes nearly half of its volume just for these trials. (These studies are mostly done in academe.) Several areas are open season for data storage, data manipulation, generating contours from spot elevation data, and last but not least: electronic field reading and storage 'plastic cards'. These latest ones are, again, strictly connected with the instrument manufacturers. Each one wants to be the first to set the standards in 'data recorders'.

Then I asked him if this was again one of his academic questions. He said:"Gabor, these are not detached, but 'attached' to the academic world. Now I let you know that we have approvals from the administration, to employ student "research assistants". These will get paid from a research fund specifically set up for various research areas and the students will work under a faculty member's supervision, who will assign work details for them and monitor their progress".

-Burt, where are we going to get these 'student assistants' from? Do we have some already? I asked him.

-No Gabor, we have to look for them in our classes, identify their specific fields of expertise, then talk to them; find out if they are interested in anything like this. Now, if we found some, then we talk to them about payments, work loads, they can not work more than 20 hours a week on these assignments, and ... they are not supposed to be used for: grading papers, correcting exams, and the likes".

-Burt, I think this is, so far, the greatest idea the administration came up with. I actually seriously think that it wasn't their idea. I think there was some other incentive, ... probably something from the State Education guys...Our boys in admin are lower level, ... if you know what I mean? And, ... I have news for you, couple days ago a kid came to see me; he had some kind of a French name, and he told me that he heard about this thing you just mentioned. He told me that he took three semesters of computers at our Math department. You know I could put him to the contouring problem right away?"

-Gabor, find the kid and send him to me. We can put him to work immediately." Have you any other research ideas?" he asked.

-Burt, I have a number of research ideas, not all in the civil engineering realm. Except one, a biggee! One of global scale. But that's another story. I will tell you about that some other time. That will, perhaps discredit all those short-sighted environmental model's results that predict the rising ocean to flood our shorelines by some insane amount. But that's something for the future. That needs first the perfection of satellite geodesy".

-You may (or may not) know, but I was tinkering with the idea of a **'four-dimensional'** soil permeability coordinate system, This idea came to me after I was toying with soil's applicability to engineering problems, after I talked to that prof. Roemer at Cornell, who is now a member of my special committee. He insisted that I switch to soils in my dissertation topic; he thought that there is a lot more new stuff to discover there than anywhere else in the current engineering materials world. I was not convinced of that, but I thought I give it a shot. So I came up with this four-dimensional soil classification system in which the permeability of a soil can be plotted in the textural classification coordinate system as the fourth dimension being added via contours. But, ... I am not sure you can visualize it, ... it is rather work intensive. Just like my father's projects were, ... always very work-intensive. Now, ...if I had the use of such a student assistant, ... Then, may be it would be worth tackling this thing too. You know I have access to literally hundreds of soil samples with 'field- determined' permeability rates. On these we took perk test in the field. Right now I simply can not find the time to work on these. It so happens that first I have to find some time to sleep, before I get a nervous breakdown ".

-Gabor, I had the same problem. Then I wanted my doctor to give me a prescription sleeping pill, but he did not recommend it to get used –or should we say hooked - on such things. Instead, he said the best sleeping pill is not something you take in (orally) but something you discharge, you know: release ... not orally, ... **from** your body".

-Burt, I always admired, may be even envied, the delicate expressions found by those who's native tong is English, so, ... just to make sure that I understood this correctly, was he, ... by any chance, ... referring to sex?"

-Let me assure you that you did understand it correctly, ... even without having English as your native tongue".

-I see, ... yes, I see. Did he also prescribe the dose? ... you know, of how often ...?

-Yah, I know what you mean," and his smile was beginning to turn to laugh. "I guess that is something every individual must evaluate for himself, taking into consideration his unique, ... er, ... capabilities".

*

To find the kid who asked me about the 'student assistant' program, I called upon the most reliable source: the Fraternities. Sure enough, within days the kid (I recognized him with his classic Latin features) was waiting for me in the hallway at the door of my room. I invited him in, asked him to put his name, address and phone number on a paper. As he did so I noticed (with surprise) that it was the same address and phone number that of Robert Dunn, who moved out of the TEF fraternity at the end of the last school year closer to campus. So, I asked him if he is living with Robert (Dunn). He explained that the three of them are sharing an apartment right here on Riverside Street at the edge of campus. So I asked him who the third of the musketeer's is. He said it's George, George Murray. He is a few years older, now a Junior. He was a lieutenant, and spent quite some time in Vietnam.

Then I asked him about his computer know-how. He described at length his three courses that he took (optionally) in the Math Department. He considered himself an adept programmer up to and including the language called: BASIC. I confessed that these things, including their names, have left me way behind, I am now, where I was at the end of my graduate work, being familiar (but not very proficient) only with FORTRAN, but it seems like I can still do without being an expert at it. He agreed, then added that if everyone would be an expert, there would be no need for so many programmers, and being one would be no big deal. Also, that what he was looking forward to with this 'student assistant' program, (if he manages to get into it) was to hone his skills in programming, while learn things deeper in the civil engineering disciplines. I assured him that this certainly is a laudable objective but don't get discouraged by necessarily doing a lot of 'dog work'. One thing I could promise him, however, and that is, that I will always explain everything he asks, to put things into context for him. Without that, the entire endeavor would be robotic, not worth the travail.

Then I asked him how does he want me to address him, since his name was Richard Bergeron. Would Mr. Bergeron be Okay? He said he would prefer me calling him Rick. Then he asked if all these things mean that he will be hired? I assured him that he will be, nevertheless, he still has to see Dr. Golding, who will take care of the administrative part. I asked him where he was originating from. I assumed that he is from a distance greater than is comfortable commuting distance. He said his father lives in Connecticut, which is where he was living with him last time, since his parents are divorced. He also considered himself lucky that they found a place to live here so close to campus. I also asked him about his relationship (friendship?) with Robert. He assured me that they are great friends and the living arrangements leave nothing more to be desired, save perhaps George's escapades which sometimes prove themselves to be on the noisy side. I asked him if he manages to go home every weekend, (to Connecticut?) sort of, to get away from it all. His answer genuinely surprised me when he stated that he really does not look forward to it one way or another. Instead, he is visiting his current girl friend regularly, every weekend in Lawrence, where she lives with her, rather large, family. She was a senior in high school at the time.

With this our interview, if we can call it that, was concluded. Still, Rick asked me what if he doesn't make it, if he doesn't get the job. I told him I wouldn't worry about that if I were him. Or, on the other hand, does he 'need' that money? All the program pays is minimum wage, which is now $ 2.50 per hour. He said he was counting on it as a regular income already. I told him again not to worry because in case he doesn't get the job I myself will hire him and pay him $ 3.50 an hour like all other kids get who work in my mini coop program. But, … and like in anything else, … there is a but, I can not offer the **prestige** that goes along with a 'University research job'; something he could put down in his resume. With that he went to see Dr. Golding.

* _ * _ *

During the break between semesters Golding called me to his office. He told me in no uncertain terms that I have to make my move. I didn't know what he was talking about. He said that I will have to put Herm 'under'. He is no longer with it anyways. There is nothing he could count with him in terms of research, or meaningful curricular changes, 'improvements' really. That the whole present is nothing than stagnation, being locked into an obsolete status quo.

Therefore, to break out of this, I have to take over from him. That has to start with me discrediting his methods, his questionable expertise, his ridiculous textbook, his lack of challenging new course material, a critical look at the laboratory problems, etc. etc. the list goes on. He wants to give me ample time to accomplish this. In the next semester I should be ready to 'execute the operation'. Then he can recommend me for promotion to associate professor, which, in view of my newest research activities, should have no real obstruction to sail through smoothly. Now what do I say to this? he asked.

I could not help but to remember his **'operation'** at the Colorado School of Mines a couple years back. I was wondering if he himself ever thought about the fact that I knew plenty of details (which I learned from Professor McNair) while he, Golding was still at that school. Did it occur to him that now he is trying to use me to do his dirty work? And, … that: I clearly see all this? If he does believe that I conveniently forgot his 'operation's he must assume that I am either really stupid or am coming down with Alzheimer's.

This came to me like a sneak, night attack. I was utterly unprepared for it. I did not quite know how to handle it. I told him that I will certainly give it a lot of thoughts. And, as it used to be in such cases, I told him that I needed time to formulate a strategy. He said: "Gabor, make sure it does not take too long, okay?"

My main difficulty was a dichotomy: on one hand was Herm's being behind times, (obsolete, for sure) on the other hand, there was this nagging, human aspect (moral, if you wish) to backstab Herm. How will I look into his eyes when we, one day, inevitably, meet over the other side of the Styx River and have to face each other (till eternity), if we will still have faces 'over there'. I decided that I wanted to retain a clear conscious. So I adopted the strategy of procrastination against which Golding did give me a fair warning.

Chapter Thirteen
(Breakup of the Partnership.)

Geoffry was withholding fees not only from the completed Billerica job, but had several other outstanding, unpaid bills, by now, on other, smaller jobs. I had the feeling that such a situation would strain our relationship, perhaps strain it to the breaking point some time soon. I gave him verbal warnings, which he ignored or in his usual business jargon: fended off. At this time he added an accusation, that he thinks the lowest thing is to stab a business partner in the back.

-Geoffry, what on earth are you talking about?" I asked him.

-Gabe, it is the same thing all over again. Why are you after my clients? I heard from Doug that you have a pretty fair size clientele yourself. Why are you after mine? You know, you tried to do this before, and it just makes me absolutely mad".

-Geoffry, you still had not put the St Elizabeth Hospital job behind you? I told you how paranoid you were then. What is your problem now?" I was wondering.

He began to talk about the 'Mystery Client' (as we referred to him) for whom we did the Townsend subdivision job last Christmas. He accused me that I conspired with Mr. Elbthal to the effect that I alone should be doing his future projects. I told him he is out of his mind, that he was drunk already in the morning hours, to talk like this. Then I added that I don't even know anybody by that name, so better get with it, and stop this nonsense.

-Gabe, I really have the good mind of reporting you to the Registration Board, or may be even sue you for damages caused by you stealing my clients", and it seemed like that he meant it.

I told him that he should think about it twice, before making a fool of himself in front of a judge. That he better have witnesses at that time or his case would be simply dismissed. Then he began to unravel what happened. Evidently this Mr. Elbthal came into his office and demanded that he speak with me. When he told Elbthal that I am not in the office – at the moment – but maybe he could help him with whatever the problem was.

-Then Elbthal insisted that he wanted to see you, because he has to talk with you about 'that job' and he wanted your address and phone number, even if he will have to get it from the Registration Board".

-Geoffry, you are not with it. Doesn't that prove that I never saw the guy, never talked with him? Does that mean that I am steeling him from you? Come now" I said, trying to bring him to his senses.

But nothing helped. He was obstinate. We parted under such ill-fated terms. It began to dawn on me that this was indeed the beginning of the end, of our (business) relationship, if not the end itself. So, one evening I put together a summary of the unpaid bills which came to a (then considerable) sum of about two and a half thousand dollars. Next day I prepared a 'demand for payment letter' to him, listing all the balances on the jobs. I still had in my possession the desk type stereo comparator and (although its value was merely about half of what he owed me) I decided to sit tight and just wait for his move. If he never makes the move, I will just keep the comparator. In my own business profile I did not have much use for it, but, if for nothing else, I could keep it for souvenir.

For a regretful souvenir. It was a beautiful piece of an instrument, Swiss made (by WILD) which in itself was a signature of leading technology.

At one point in time I mentioned this affair to Richard Halloran, who told me in no uncertain terms that it would be 'wrong' for me to keep that instrument. But as an alternative, he would be willing to become, sort of a go between, and would write Geoffry a letter, in which he would plead with him to resolve this matter amicably. He was such a grand person, an eternal gentleman, as I have not met the likes of for some time to come. For a great while I have not heard from Geoffry Dorfman. But it seemed like that the embers were live under the ashes, and could cause the gunpowder keg to explode, (buried next to them), any time. For one thing, he did not commission any new jobs.

In the summer I was finally forced to trade my little buggy (the Volkswagen Carman Ghia) for a Volkswagen mini-bus. This was the 'utility vehicle supreme' at the time. It came in a few variety of models, in the USA: the 'pop-top'(or camper) and the mini-bus were the most familiar models. At the end of August we took a camping vacation with the bus to Nova Scotia, where we have never been before and because it was in convenient driving distance. I took my little Beretta pistol with me, which, I was advised at the border, to turn over to authorities for 'safekeeping'. When I expressed my concern as to the return of my property, the official made a solemn promise to return it. He also emptied the magazine of the seven rounds and kept them in the same envelope with the gun. Then handed me a stamped and signed receipt. On our return, another officer handed me the envelope with its contents, which I put promptly in the glove compartment and completely forgot about -at least for the time being.

Upon my return to the business, I found some new developments. A Geophysics professor from the University of Hawaii was about to return to his 'roots' in Groton, Massachusetts, where he inherited 80-some acres from his uncle. I received a letter from the attorneys representing him (one of the most prestigious law firm in Boston) whereas upon the recommendations of Attorney Richard Halloran, they wished to retain my services to survey the land, the subject of the inheritance. The letter also expressed their desire to meet with me at **my** earliest convenience to discuss details. It was almost frightening to me, how I would live up to all these obligations. I was ill equipped to handle them all. But I had to live up to my newfound reputation.

At my meeting in their offices (across from old City Hall) they handed me a set of various vintage deeds (some over 100-years old) and an old sketch of the central part of the property. When I asked Warren, (as he introduced himself) of what are the owner's plans with the property, he informed me that he wants to subdivide the 'Ready Meadows' (a 40 +- acres) part to residential house lots, for a start. So, "there is a lot of work ahead of you, get busy and let us know about progress, or any obstructions, because we want to deal with those immediately. One of the 'Brothers' (the partners!) is a judge, … you know, so, any obstruction will have to be uncovered as soon as possible in order to deal with it immediately". When he asked if I understood the situation I assured him that I did, fully, 100%. Then he handed me a check for two thousand dollars for a retainer, and I left their offices still wondering who and when will be able to start with this unanticipated new project. I knew for a fact that I had to be spending quite some time in the woods of Groton along the 'Unkety Brook'. This was the part of the country referred to as being in 'the sticks'. They genuinely were; in most parts no human set foot in them for the last few decades.

One particular boundary corner was described in the deed as a 'hickory tree'. I knew that I could not find any hickory in the vicinity within a 200-ft radius due to previous logging. But there were about three giant stumps within the area. So I marked and numbered them, then cut samples from each with a chain-saw, packed them and sent them to the University of Massachusetts botany labs in Amherst, to determine which one of them is hickory wood. By October I received the answer that: sample no 2. was a hickory. I notified Warren McLawren that I found evidence for the missing corner and so, the boundary survey can now be completed. But I exhausted the retainer with all this reconnaissance work. He said that's good, go on, and how much more money do I need?

In the meantime, Richard Halloran notified me that a settlement was worked out with Mr. Dorfman whereby upon the return of his instrument in his Brookline office, he will pay the outstanding arrears. I was to make arrangements as to the date. I drove down to Brookline and as I took the instrument in its box under my arm with me, an inner voice told me to grab the pistol from the glove compartment, ... just in case...

This intuition proved very foresighted as hardly anything else did before. When Geoffry 'examined the instrument', to see if it was all there, he told me that: "okay, you can leave now, everything is in order", I asked for my check. He said that there shall be more talk about that. Then I said: that's okay, but at least give me a receipt for the instrument. When he said, very sarcastically, that he was not required to do administrative work by the 'agreement' with Attorney Halloran, I was flushed with anger. I stepped to the desk with the instrument box sitting on it, grabbed it, took it under my arm just as I brought it in, and was about to leave. Geoffry, however, ordered Basiliero, the draftsman, and one of his field-man to block my way. I then made a quick draw, and raised the pistol to point at the two chaps. As I saw that there were no results, I cocked the pistol. They immediately retreated and let me pass. I was on my way to the street, out of the building, to my parked car. As I put the pistol back into the glove compartment I noticed to my utter horror, that the seven rounds were still in there, in the envelope. I had an unloaded gun with me. I jumped in and drove away, to home, to Chelmsford.

I was totally exhausted. First I had to collect myself. Maria told me that the Chelmsford police chief called and wanted me to surrender the gun at the police station. This was actually a message. Then I called Halloran's law offices. Richard appointed his young nephew attorney, Jim Halloran to deal with this unfortunate situation. They found out that there is a hearing scheduled for an arraignment in the Brookline District Court. I was charged with breaking and entering, threatening with a deadly weapon, armed rubbery, as the main charges. Richard advised me to get myself a criminal lawyer because this sort of case is not in their profile of legal services.

So, I called Warren McLawren, the only one I knew having a full service law firm, and told him the entire story. He encouraged me to attend next day's hearing in Brookline. He promised that he will be there. He was.

The first thing he wanted was a retainer for five hundred dollars. I made out a check for him. Then he said to wait because he put me down as a witness in our counter complaint against Geoffry Dorfman for: false imprisonment and bodily threat by accomplices. These were the criminal charges. Then came some others: frauds, dealing in bad faith, and other related charges that could be substantiated by the Halloran law firm, who made the agreement with Dorfman.

Shortly, the accomplices (from Dorfman's office) were summoned, along with them came Geoffry's attorney. (I have met his attorney before and learned that he was specializing in tax and corporate law.) Now that the proceedings began to cost him money, he wanted the whole case over and done with. But not so my attorney Warren McLawren. He had several conferences with the presiding judge, who surly recognized him, and then ruled the criminal part of this case to be closed, provided the pistol will be surrendered to the Chelmsford police. The rest of the case should then be turned over to the civil section. With that, the negotiating began again, regarding the return of the instrument, and payment of the delinquent account. Jim Halloran took it upon himself to take the instrument personally back to Dorfman's office, where the secretary signed him a receipt for it.

The civil case, however, refused to die. Dorfman didn't pay his bill. I had to sue him for the balance. My old acquaintance, Attorney O'Hara took the case. He filed a complaint in the Middlesex Superior Court North District, in Lowell, so that they would have to travel 32 miles to show up here in our City. Ariel Airmap, Inc. as a counter measure, filed a counter suite for an insane amount of 25,000 dollars; damages caused by erroneous, inaccurate survey work, which was not properly specified, demonstrated or witnessed. It was crystal clear to all of us that this was a frivolous suit. Attorney O'Hara drew my attention to the pragmatic side of the entire matter. Since we have filed our complaint for 2,500.00 dollars, we had no basis to go back for that much more. Dorfman, by filing for a tenfold damage has put in a big foot in the door, which put him into a superior bargaining position. He was ready and willing to drop his complaint in exchange for us dropping ours. With this the case was over; as far as the legal system was concerned.

There was no provision in this system for the Solomonian wisdom to prevail. This judge never questioned in his mind: how come one of the parties is willing to forget and walk away from a 25,000 dollar claim, if it is a **bona fide** claim, -or was this another one of the very transparent **frivolous suits** to offset a valid claim? All the other party (us) was seeking justice for is only a tenth of that sum, and made every effort to prove and adjudge what he believes he deserves. Probably, convenience on everyone's side, (but mostly the court system's side) rules in the civil courts of our country. The **settling of cases out of court** became the buzzword. I think we need more latitude for Solomonian judgments in our court system.

I never mentioned this case, or its outcome to Richard, the 'gentleman lawyer' any more, for whom this sort of justice was incomprehensible. He was an idealist; One from the old school. He dealt only with properties, mostly "Real" properties of that, where the rules were pretty strictly laid down for everyone concerned. The first and only time I saw him getting upset by rulings of magistrates, and other 'officials', who made rulings in connection with certain environmental 'regulations' grossly infringing upon the landowner's constitutional rights. In one of such cases on which I was present, he gave up, throwing his hands up in the air, declaring that "he can not practice law under a communist type legal system, being used right in this hearing chamber."

* - * - *

Both of our Puli poppies grew into handsome young guard dogs (actually: they were signature Hungarian sheep dogs). The female: Bogancs, (we picked this name from the hero, a Puli, in one of the highly successful popular novels of the days.) This was how she became Bogancs. Both of them were registered in the Hungarian Kennel Club's genealogical registry. Their ancestor's went as far back as a minimum of seven generations. Bogancs was a classic. It seemed that this was true in every respect. Her (male) companion: Kormos, (we picked him to be her boyfriend, not very successfully, as it became evident later on; their personalities being fundamentally different) was considerably more aggressive, as one might expect from a male to be. His aggressiveness extended itself to almost anyone or anything, which seemingly threatened us or our house and the premises. This trait proved itself to become his doom. We tried many which ways to restrain him from chasing the cars, bicycles or motorcycles on the street, all to no avail.

One brisk morning his barking was cut abruptly short, and by the time Maria and Gabor Jr. went out to the street, the driver, who stopped as instantly as he could, gently pulled him out from under his car. Then told us that he was still alive. Thus, in an emergency situation, an older towel was fetched, Kormos was wrapped into it, and driven to the veterinarian. Although he was still alive even then (the vet gave him a shot that would stabilize him in his shock) but the overall prospects looked hopeless (even after considerable, expectable suffering, loss of limb) so the decision was reached that he shall be put to sleep.

After this fatal incident Bogancs seemed even more careful. She seldom went outside the property, out to the street, as if an instinct would have warned her about the lurking dangers. But inside the stone wall, ... that was a completely different matter. There were various categories of people, whom she did not trust. Any such person arriving in our driveway, could simply not get out of his car. She became vicious, and ready to tear him apart. There were other persons whom she treated with a friendly reception, regardless of what type of vehicle that person arrived in. When Robert (Dunn) arrived in his Volkswagen 'Bug', he was greeted with an exceptional ovation.

As we began to summarize, in a sort of analytical fashion, who are the ones Bogancs likes, it turned out that all of them were friends of our family. So much so, that when for instance Robert brought along another 'brother' from the fraternity, Bogancs seemed to accept him, after some scrutiny.

Later on we also tried to check the reverse situation. We tried to sum up those who Bogancs distrusted, some to the point of such hostility, that needed firm intervention from our part to forestall any bodily harm. (And possible legal ramifications).

One late afternoon two middle aged gentlemen arrived at our house. Bogancs was greeting them with such furor that needed the firm intervention, usually from my part. When the situation was sufficiently calmed and under control, they introduced themselves as Arthur and Larry Elbthal. They were looking for me. Once they were assured that I was the one they came to see, Arthur, the elder, took over the tenor. We invited them inside. Arthur, after recognizing my accent as "German" began to describe the origin of their family's last name: From the Elbe-valley! Assuming that I might not be familiar with the whereabouts of the River Elbe, he added that it was the river, strategically selected by the Allied forces at the end of the second war, becoming the line where the two victorious armies The Western Allies, and the Eastern, Red (Soviet) Armies would meet, leaving no middle ground for any German troupes in between.

After I assured him that he can spare all this historical (and geographical) rhetoric, because I was personally present in that war, and I assumed that he was not. He was very close to my age, as I estimated it. After a more rigorous comparison, Arthur declared that he was one year my senior. Then he asked if he may call me Gabor, I thought such a move was premature considering that our acquaintance was less than 10 minutes old. In Europe, however, it was in accordance with etiquette that the elder person initiated the usage of the second person singular form, which is equivalent with the English usage of first names.

I goaded him to get to the purpose of their visit. Arthur was by far the more eloquent among the two. I noticed his superior vocabulary immediately, also the way he formulated his sentences was music to my ears. I did not fail to note that his English was so much superior to the average man's that I would have enjoyed just to sit and listen to him and converse with him. As fate would have it, this wish of mine was fulfilled later on much more lavishly than I originally imagined. (It turned out that he was a columnist in the regional newspaper: "*The Public Spirit*")

Naturally, I recognized instantly that I had the *'mystery client'* as our guest. Arthur made it a point that he tracked down my address from the Registration Board because that Dorfman-guy wouldn't give it to him.

This was a sure confirmation that I have not 'stolen' him from Dorfman. Then we finally arrived at the purpose of their visit. Arthur described me their delicate situation. Some years ago he ran into serious money down in New York where his folks were living for ages. So the family decided (actually they all agreed with Arthur's decision, as I began to understand the situation) that they should invest the lion's share of this money into real estate. And not just any real estate, but exceptionally low priced real estate. This meant far out locations, large tracts of land in the 'boondocks', which at some strategically right time they would turn into developments and become sellable to builders. All they ever wanted to do to the land was to submit a proposed (tentative) development plan at the right time. When the major parameters of a particular subdivision were firmly established by a 'preliminary approval' of that subdivision, it became marketable; usually at prices multiple fold of the purchase price. Thus came the explanation to the term 'paper developer' as I first heard mentioning the term in connection with Arthur.

As I soon found out they: (the Elbthal Realty Trust) owned more that a half a dozen large tracts of land in Massachusetts and Connecticut. Arthur came up with the idea that I should do the same type of development plans that I did just before Christmas with Ariel Airmap, Inc. I wanted to set the records straight so I emphasized to him that I was at that time a subcontractor to that firm, but due to unforeseen circumstances we terminated that arrangement. So, the only way I would be tackling these jobs would be if I would do them on my own, as an independent contractor. Arthur just loved that. He even asked, if this: 'Dorfman-guy' would be involved in any way at all. I informed him that he would not, and that is the only way I would get involved. He liked that too.

Then he began to produce various plans of lands. I told him that we now should be looking at them in a priority order. One of them was in Western Massachusetts, thus I suggested it to be moved down on the priority list on account of its distant location. But, he wanted this done immediately and be handled as the most urgent one. I told him that the only way I would do it was the way I (we) did their Townsend job. He said that was just fine. After this some three more, smaller pieces, all of them in Townsend got on the list. After this I told him to stop, because now we are booked about three months ahead and under the present circumstances there is no possibility to speed-up the process.

The next order of business was to discuss fees and payment schedules. I made it clear to him that I shall submit periodic bills, which I expect to be paid pronto. Otherwise work will stop. He said that was pretty fair. I noticed that he was ready, maybe even looking forward to, socialize some more, but Maria had enough of them for the evening so we put an end to the unanticipated business meeting. On their way out, Bogancs simply wanted to eat them both, she was that vicious, although she already had her supper. After they both left, Maria told me to watch out for these two guys, and use unprecedented concern and scrutiny, because just look how Bogancs had assessed them. They must have some serious character fault.

Some two weeks later I took the Brookfield tentative subdivision to Arthur's home in Ayer, Ma. The house was something like you find descriptions of in Jane Austen's novels from the Victorian era. I personally like those houses, and think that many of them fit into New England more than anywhere else in the USA, they have a character unmatched by any other architecture, save perhaps the Cape Cod-style which is something altogether different.

The house was not large by the standards of the end of the 20-th century but it had unprecedented charm. Entering through the front door, was a rather spacious foyer from which one could enter either the large central kitchen, or the front living room through a side 'pocket door', or the round staircase leading to the (bed) rooms upstairs. After Arthur's oldest daughter let me in, she told me to wait in the foyer. She excused herself and vanished. Within about 30 seconds I recognized the sounds of Beethoven's Sonatina in F-major rising from the living room on the left side. I am not a great fan of good old Beethoven, but this piece has great charm and delightful melodies. The entire setting had a theatrical character, resembling something totally out of 'Masterpiece Theatre'. While I was still in the foyer and reading *'Better Homes and Gardens'* I was prone to forget about my entire surroundings; I was so submerged in the atmosphere of the last century. A quaint, surreal feeling took hold of me.

Quite unexpectedly a middle aged looking woman appeared in the doorway from the kitchen. She was wearing something one could see in magazines depicting Shaker women in their festive, Sunday outfits. Instantly I got lost in the atmosphere of the moment. She was smiling but her smile was sort of put on to hide something. Her face looked as if it had been made up to hide the remnant features of one had after crying. She announced that Arthur is not at home at the present but will be home sometimes in the morning. Instead of asking me if I wanted to drink something, she brought along a pitcher and two glasses. She let me know in no uncertain terms, that a moderate amount of 'hard cider' is good for anyone, it sort of acts as a tonic. Then she poured some into my glass and handed it to me. Also, she did pour some for herself. Then she sat down across from me.

To start a conversation on a neutral ground I made a comment about her daughter's piano performance. Without trying to sound boastful I mentioned that the reason I know this *"Sonatina"* she is playing, is, that I played the same thing in my fifth year of studying the piano myself. And I added that, that was before the war so long ago that I can hardly believe it ever was. Then she told me that she was always fascinated with Europe, and that it must have been fantastic to study there. She told me that Arthur is convinced that my students are at an advantage that they have a teacher from Europe. She then described that Arthur's family name is actually a German name, meaning: The Valley of Elbe. Naturally I agreed with all this, and did not want to ruin her story-telling mood by letting her know that Arthur has already told me all this.

After a while Mrs. Elbthal told me that her name is Luisa, and asked if I would do her the favor by calling her that. Her age still puzzled me though. I didn't think that she was older than myself or that of Arthur, which put her being our contemporary, since Arthur already calculated the other day that he was a mere one year older than I. In certain situations she did look older than her age, if that was indeed equal to mine. Luisa mentioned that she had an older daughter than the one playing the piano which in my calculation resulted that she had to be at least a few years older than I. Our older kids were in their middle teens therefore, she either did marry very young, or she was older than us. From the exterior she looked perfectly normal. The only time when this did not hold true was when her third child, a son, appeared in the doorway. He was just staring at us, didn't utter a word. First I thought that he had a speech-impairment but on closer assessment I had to conclude that he was a mongoloid. Luisa explained to me that it was inherited from her side of the family.

I noticed that she became uneasy, as if she would had to leave and go someplace. I didn't know how to bring this visit to an end, so I simply asked what I should do with the plans that I brought with me. She assured me that I can leave them with her. So I did and I alerted her that I put my bill within the plans. I was somewhat puzzled when I left that I saw their car parked in the driveway which was to the far left of the property and I recalled that Luisa told me during the conversation that she doesn't drive, she never did and never had a license either. There seemed to be only three explanations to the puzzle: Arthur either has gone away from home on foot, or got a ride from someone, or he was at home in the house all along. This last possibility, seemingly the strangest, was probably the most realistic of them all.

* - * - *

Everyone received a copy of a Memo in his mailbox from Golding. The Memo was actually alerting the department members of an imminent visit paid to us by prospective new faculty whom he invited to Lowell Tech for interview. There were three names mentioned, out of which two were supposed to be highly qualifying as 'minorities'. The minute I read Afifi Soliman's name I had figured out this move of our chairman. He was, in all likelihood, gone over Giff's file on potential new minority faculty. He must have decided to follow-up on some that have never gotten off the ground, but were still just sitting on the tarmac.

The first one scheduled was Wesley Manner. During his entire one-day visit he was supposed to talk to each member 'individually', perhaps to assure some degree of privacy. This also made individual views of both persons possible to discuss in candor. After the general overview of the physical plant (and an introduction of the candidate to Dean Holbrook,) Burt took Manner to lunch, after which the realization struck him that time was running out, so, he suggested to the members, that we should all meet with Manner in the chairman's conference room, which also served as the (growing) faculty's meeting room. By this arrangement the interview naturally lost all aspects of privacy. Only questions or problems of 'common interest' could be discussed.

Wes Manner was a tall man, sporting a goatee almost like his trade mark. He spoke in convoluted sentences that I had considerable difficulty getting the full meaning of. A sentence like this had really no meaningful beginning and by the time it seemed like it was finished, it had not much (if anything) to do with its awkward beginning. His manner of speech had also a lot to be desired. For one thing it was arrogant,

239

sometimes condescending. After we, the members present, ran out of questions posed to him, Burt proposed that now Manner should ask questions, which some of us, who feels most qualified to answer should do so. His first –and most striking- question was: "What's wrong with Lowell Tech?" It was a theatrical performance or so it struck me. A brief silence followed it. Probably none of us felt qualified (or authorized) to formulate an answer. Half sentences, or even single terms emerged from some of us. But this had the aura of incoherence, not unlike that of an orchestra without a conductor, while some orchestras do fine or even better without one. Finally Burt summarized some of the problems he must have had previously pointed out to him beforehand. I then – halfheartedly- threw in the word 'minorities'. Wes Manner directed his gaze straight at me. He never said a word. His gaze did all the talking. I did likewise. Finally he formulated the question: "Faculty-wise, or student-body wise? I noticed that I have seen no color at all here." This concluded his question. I dared to answer him simply by one word: "both". Burt began to explain him that there actually are no 'colored' in neither category and that seems to be a problem by itself only when it comes to 'demographics'. But these were the facts of life in a region where these are the facts of life.

Wes Manner was finishing his dissertation at the Florida State U. in the fall term. His specialty area was water resources. He was to move here in the winter semester break if he gets the appointment. He said something about his objectives both in the course he was to teach to the seniors as an elective, as well as in the research he was supposed to **initiate** in water related topics, what ever might be needed in the Commonwealth. In this respect he was open to suggestions and emphasized that his **real** expertise is in the research field. This is where he would become most useful, just about indispensable. This is what I got out of his usual tortuous sentences. But I think he eventually got there, where he was heading. Nevertheless I was under the impression that it was only I who had that much difficulty following him. Much later I got some consolation out of the fact that a veteran attorney was questioning whether "this guy ever took English in High School". Also, somewhat later, it turned out that this, English, was his only language in which he was expected to be communicating 'perfectly', whereas he proudly put down on every relevant document that he is bilingual, his second language being German, which he spoke at home. At one occasion I was tempted to the point, that I actually spoke to him in German, not much, perhaps one sentence, but he didn't have the faintest idea what I was talking about, so, I had to repeat it in English.

Then he understood, and said: "well, Gabe, it has been a long, long time, … you know?" Yes, I knew.

* _ * _ *

Next week a very distinguished, pleasant, young, colored gentleman visited us for a similar interview. John Thissell was his name. His area was structures, understandably. Since Dario left us at the end of the last school year, so, we needed a replacement. I hardly had a chance even to talk with him but later we met from time to time. Also, as far as I was concerned his being on or off our faculty roster didn't make any difference, whatsoever. I was so wrapped-up in my work.

He was the real break in the **demographics.** The first and only colored person, a *genuine minority.* Giff was the one, who first talked to me about him. Now, as Burt came down with this follow-up idea, John became a serious candidate.

I didn't know anything about him. He also got the appointment, and moved into one of the offices that he was sharing with another structures professor. I always felt that he could have been the 'other' **minority faculty** over and above myself, and that perhaps one day he will be visiting me to have a candid discussion of this issue. But this never happened. He was most likely singing "America" loud enough to mute my own voice in this respect, since he was born in America and I was not. He was a minority **because of his race,** I was one because of my ethnicity. His minority was *conspicuous in a visual sense, mine was audio.*

By the end of February the third candidate, Afifi Soliman was scheduledfortheinterview.Hisdissertationwasdoneinphotogrammetry under the trilingual professor Brandenberger at Ohio State. But Fifi (as I, and members of my family called him) did not have much affinity to the subject. He simply did what had to be done, what Prof. Barndenberger ordered him to do. Fifi even preferred this arrangement. He told me several times that he doesn't give a damn about photogrammetry, he was considering himself a civil engineer at heart, but, … if he will get his Ph. D. in Photogrammetry, so be it, he will stick with it, he will stick with Prof. Brandenberger, he will follow everything and every instruction (or even order,… like in the military: "Sir! yes sir!") to end-up with the degree. He told me in no uncertain terms, that he 'must' be getting his degree, otherwise the Egyptian Government will force his parents to pay back every penny they spent on his studies in the USA. And that alone was such a sum that he never envisioned to save up from whatever his earnings would be in the future to come-up with that money. But he finally made it, he filed his dissertation at the Ohio State University's Graduate School. At the same day he packed up his family and left the country to Canada because his student visa expired and Nasser's government did not renew his foreign student status. They wanted him back home. That, of course, did not much matter to Fifi so long as he got an appointment to the University of Winnipeg, Manitoba. He never taught photogrammetry ever since. Instead he was taking all sorts of refresher courses in transportation engineering, to be proficient and up-to-date in that discipline, which opened the doors for him along with his degree. No one was really interested what he did for his Ph. D. degree and in what discipline. We often talked about this crazy academic world, that was so hooked up on three letters, but didn't care what the wearer of them was really good at.

Fifi was meeting his match in Golding. They both were money obsessed. Fifi 's first question to Golding was "how much this position would pay? "Golding was quoting the Commonwealth's salary schedule as $ 25,000. to $ 30,000. a year. Fifi told him: "Dr. Golding, I don't know how you imagine me to live on 'therty-thosend' dollars with my family?" (This was how it actually sounded like). "I have five kids and a wife to support".

-Well, Dr. Soliman, if you will bring some sponsored research to this institution I guarantee that your earnings will rise substantially."

-Oh, so that's what it boils down to; and when, may I ask, should we be working on the research projects? You're not suggesting at night, are you, Dr. Golding?" he said. "For your information, I let you know that my current salary is $ 40,000.00 that's Canadian. But housing and food and household items cost less north of the 49-th".

It was clear that Burt was not going to get Fifi to accept the position with those salary figures. Fifi came to my (shared) office after the interview and told me the basics. He was doubtful that he was going to be made an offer by Golding. I invited him to our home in Chelmsford. He said that he would not miss it for the world. I asked if he would spend the night, which he gladly accepted, but only after he checked with the airline that he could take the next day flight back to Winnipeg. I offered him a pajama of mine but he could not put it on. He put on too much weight lately, instead. He called Susu at home and alerted her that he would be flying home the next day.

I took him down to the basement office and showed him the various projects I was working on. He confessed that all this is too remote for him now that he switched his career in midstream. He over dramatized the situation, or so I thought first. But then he gave me an example of his fellow Egyptian, Al Mereed, who was a physicist. He, as so many of our kind, did not qualify for security clearance to work in some of the glamorous places like a 'National Laboratory', where he would earn a high enough salary (high enough in his estimation) to have a decent standard of living. Therefore, he was teaching physics in a community college, with Ph.D. The previous year he made the decision to switch his career from physicist to physician. He was granted a lot of credits, mostly in the area of physics and biology and 'all the stupid electives' as he put it. He had another year and a half to finish his coursework. Then with a Ph.D. plus an M.D. he was shooting for the type of employment that would pay him the desired figure. He was still only 36-years young. "There surely are more stories like this one", he told me.

*

Burt called me to his office. He reminded me that my time was up, and I missed to make my move. Next year Herm Shea will be on Sabbatical Leave which is a time when no action can be taken against anyone. So, he was planning on having him removed by the end of the 1974-75 academic year. But now it looks as if Herm will have to stay, he (Golding) can do nothing anymore, for the time being, to remove him. Therefore there is nothing else to do but he must **ask me to resign**. He needs this position to be freed up. He also elaborated on his expectations for me to cooperate with him, even in the 'professional services' area, but that I have proved being uncooperative. So, he has to conclude that I am not a team-player, that I do not fit into our group, or don't want to. And last, but not least, that I am actually using my position here at school to promote my own, selfish endeavors. This is his rational for requesting my resignation. Otherwise, he said, "he will see to it that my stay at this Institute will be as miserable as can possibly be".

I was dumbfounded. I knew that something like this was in the air, but it never came down to earth. There was, however, some indication, to the effect that he already began his offensive. Earlier the year I began to make preparations towards my research project in connection with the permeability 4-dimensional plot. Just to see its magnitude, what am I really up against, in terms of logistics. Tony, our technician, who was my trusted ally by now, was doing some moderate amount of organizing the soil samples that we brought in from the field, and has done 'sieve analysis' on them in his spare time, when he had nothing else to do. It was a slow process, but there was nothing rushing us.

One day Tony told me that Dr. Manner came in to the lab, where some of the 'soil mechanics' equipment was kept and he, Tony was running a sieve analysis test on it. He wanted to know what this was for. So, Tony told him that this was for Professor Szikszay-Farkas. Then all he said was that "he shall look into that". Also, in the mean time he ordered Tony to stop doing this. At least until "he is going to take over this mess".

This was a pretty clear indication to me that the research field was also a frontier on which the upcoming battle will be fought. Earlier, Golding made it a point to stop Rick Belanger from working on my other project: the 'contouring routine' computer program. Rick was hired shortly after he came to see me and was assigned by Golding to work on the routine, and file his monthly progress report. Rick did file some three months' report, but each one was showing frustrations with the task at hand, mostly due to the size of the computer and its capabilities. There seemed to be insufficiency in the massive amount of data that needed instantaneous access, which, evidently the Institute's computer did not have. We were ahead of the times with our ideas but the Institute's computer was behind.

In reality Rick and I were already tackling a massive research area that several large government agencies as well as private companies were (sometimes secretly) working on for 24-hours a day. One was envisioned as the future massive data-bases, storing and handling (retrieving) data on demand instantaneously. On the other hand, the contouring routine idea became the baby-shoe version of which later on materialized as the 'digital terrain model' which, by nowadays, is widely available from the USGS and other, private organizations. Petty jealousy, lack of vision and leadership, and dickering forestalled all this to come to fruition for our department.

Tony was told not to accept any assignments from me. Thus, he could not come to the field and take the soil samples, of those locations (which were percolation tested by the local Board of Health) sieve them, hand the results to me so that I could plot them and catalogue them. Manner visited me and questioned where he could find the results of my 'ongoing research'. I knew what he was after, but I was just staring at him.

-Gabe, you know, I don't like your attitude" he said for an opener.

-Oh, really? that makes then the two of us, because I don't care for yours".

-But I think you don't understand; I was put in charge of all research going on in the department. I am sure you know that. So, what is it going to be? he asked his usual incoherent question.

-Well, I don't know, what's going to happen, I think you asked the wrong person, I am not a prophet, consequently, I don't know, and can't see the future. You should have asked someone more knowledgeable along these lines".

-You know what I am talking about! Your soil samples! You are ordered from now on to submit them to me to do the cataloguing and the entire administration of the project. And, don't forget, these are the department head's orders".

-Well, let me understand this: the department **chairman**, you know, this is what we have, an elected chairman, not a 'department head'! wants 'my soil samples? We are discarding them after the sieve analysis is done. I can't get them."

-Gabe, now you are playing dumb. You know what I am talking about. The ones you bring in from the field for the sieve test. The ones that were already perk tested".

-Wes, -I started as if I were lecturing, "who do you think owns those? I mean the samples: whom do they belong? For your information: they belong to the developer, those are private property. Now, … if you, or the chairman –for that matter- want some samples you might get permission from the owner of the development project to take some. then you can take them and bring them back to the lab for sieve-testing. it's that simple, …really. But surely you can't expect me to do that myself". With that I stopped and was staring at him, waiting for his move.

-And why not, may I ask"?

-For one thing, I was not hired by the Institute to take field samples – on someone else's land, mind you - and haul them back to the laboratory, all to enable someone else to do the research that was originally my idea. For another, ...if he wants to 'steal' the idea from me, so be it, but at least allow me not to assist him in that. Actually it would be too late to steal the idea anyways because it has been already filed with my special committee, and approved as my dissertation topic at Cornell, sorry about that. Kapish?"

-Yes Gabe, I do kapish, as you put it. Let me just tell you that this was not the last word on the subject".

Chapter Fourteen
(A sentimental journey.)

Summer vacation finally arrived and tension was apparently subsiding on all fronts. The new faculty was busy digging into their new position. Golding, as chairman, was ubiquitous. I had no business with him, and liked it that way. For the first time he was getting off my back, leaving me alone. Joan Fallon told me several times that I do look overworked, and that perhaps it would be a good idea to take it easier. Her concern sounded genuine.

At home, Maria, gave me warning signs very similar to those of Joan's. She thought that maybe a relaxed vacation on my own, by myself, to get away from it all would do me a lot of good. I kept fending off the idea using the numerous projects as an excuse. I was now supervising three different crews, even a forth highly mobile one. An entirely new crew had to be assembled just to handle the Lussier project, the 'Bernard Acres', with its Bernard Road to be laid out. The drainage facilities needed almost constant attention for the crew, which, when got some time off this task, began laying out the lots, and started working with one machine doing all the soil tests, soil-loggings and performing the perk-tests. Altogether grossly more than a full summer's business. And this was only for that crew, a very trusted, experienced one.

Gerry Lussier kept telling me to quit everybody else's projects, why bother with them, when he alone could occupy my entire personnel. The Unkety Brook subdivision was going well, approval was anticipated towards the end of summer, and a number of lots were pre-sold already with deposits held by Realtors. I told Gerry that I would not even be considering such a move at this time. What if something goes wrong with one of his projects, he gets mad at me, he drops me out of all his projects? just like he did the previous surveying outfit, that did his Marsh Hill Road subdivision. Where would I be then? I would have to start searching for new clients all over again. Under the present situation we all could be sure that each client gets fairly prompt service, for a reasonable price. And, let's face it, that's what it was all about.

It began to dawn on me that maybe, just maybe, a two-week vacation is something I could risk, to get away from it all. The more I thought about it the more friendly the idea became. I visualized it as a **'sentimental journey'**. So I agreed, and told Maria that I would go to Hungary, visiting both of our parents, go down (actually, geographically it was up) to the loyal folks at our former estate, who constantly kept in touch with us, -ever since the confiscation of the land- even if we no longer owned any part of it; Meaning really my father, whom they adored. He was not only good and fair to these employees and took care of them all, during the war, but was really talking their language. They not only enjoyed being with him but respected him deeply.

So, Maria dropped in to our travel agent in Dracut, who came up with a round trip ticket on short order. It was unusual for him to order only one ticket and he didn't miss saying so. He also arranged for a rental car from Germany, that would pick me up at the Luxembourg airport and drop me off the way back. My flight was to leave in a week, so there was not much time left to buy all the things Maria wanted me to take to the relatives. There were still numerous items on the shortage list, even everyday, ordinary items that the 'communist paradise' did not provide for its citizens, who were overworked and underpaid. For luxury items one had to visit special stores, where the medium of exchange was 'hard currency', which was unlawful to possess by the citizenry. These stores were operated solely to accommodate foreign travelers and tourists. Toiletry, fragrances etc. were on the top of the gift list. These items were duty-free, when taken into the country as personal luggage.

I indulged myself by buying one of those portable SANYO stereo AM-FM radio and cassette recorder/players (nowadays commonly referred to: the Boom-box, which by the way, does not record!) which was top of the line and cost a small fortune in the standards of the behind 'Iron Curtain' countries. I also made it a point to take with me some of my newly recorded favorite ballets (Giselle, by Adam, Voyage to the Moon, by Offenbach, Coppelia and Sylvia by Delibes, and several other lesser known but just as beautiful ballet excerpts by L.Minkus,

D. Auber and R. Drigo which I recently acquired) and recorded over onto several cassettes. These were mostly for my own entertainment, which received low priorities lately in view of the tremendously busy schedule I maintained here. This was the year of my 25-th High School class reunion, which I missed already, it was held in early June, but a select group could always be recruited for the occasion of my being 'back home'.

Maria drove me to the airport and, as we parted at the gate, she made one serious admonition, she said: "Papa, be good! and try to make everybody happy at home. I know you can do that". Somehow, when we were by ourselves, just the two of us, we were referring to that place as: 'HOME'. We always realized the awkwardness of this definition, but only afterwards, always afterwards. Our 'actual home' was here, with the new family we started ourselves, just the two of us in this 'foreign' land. Not yet hostile, but foreign, nevertheless.

I got a window-seat. Made myself comfortable, packing the carry-ons in the overhead compartments, taking the cassette dispenser next to my seat, arranging the blanket and pillow, and all this might have looked similar to a cat when it turns around at his intended lounging place several times to check it out if it's safe and comfty to lie down to. Then I slipped a cassette in the machine, turned the volume down almost to minimum and pressed the play button. The music came on charmingly, so much so, that the lady, seemingly in charge of the group of -several- teenagers traveling together, bent forward to my seat ad said "thank you sir! thank you so much! for not playing some wild rock..."

-So, my dear lady, can I interpret this as an expression of your actually liking this kind of music?" I asked her.

-Oh God, yes, would you please be so good and turn the volume up a bit." Then a little later she added: "would you please tell me where your accent is originating from, I am totally captivated by it".

-It is really not a single foreign accent, it is a blend of Hungarian and German" giving her the info she was seeking. "You see, "... and I went through the routine of having to explain to everyone, how I ever ended up with this accent. She did look sort of fascinated. She was not really 'good looking' by my strict individual standards, although she might have been some time ago. Time, however, did show some wear and tear. But in all honesty she was a rather pleasant person; Definitely the sort that men quickly learn to appreciate. Anyway, I always held that attitude, demeanor and wits are at least 70% of the most important traits in women, and the rest is, by and large, honesty, intelligence, dexterity and, … the love of the arts (music). Looks will follow only after these.

I noticed that the passengers were predominantly Americans, very middle class and sort of educated kind of people. The low price on the fare lured all these people into Loftleidir's fleet of airplanes, and they practically filled them. When years later I started flying other big name carriers like Lufthansa, SwissAir, British Airways and KLM, the coach of those flights seemed like business class compared to Loftleidir's tourist class, there was that much empty space on them. Loftleidir was crowded.

-Sir, may I ask what you do for a living?" the lady bent forward to continue the conversation.

- Well, I really do quite a number of different things" I said, which, I realized that could have been construed as trying to avoid the whole subject, or even the conversation altogether. But in the same time I didn't want to appear impolite so I added: "actually, primarily: teaching, … among other things".

-Teaching? … College?" she asked.

-Yes, as a matter of fact, that is my main profession" I admitted.

-I knew it! I just knew it" she said triumphantly. "My husband, now he is my 'ex', teaches in a junior college, so, … you understand, I can smell a professor from a mile".

-Excuse me, how exactly does a professor smell like? I asked her showing genuine curiosity without coming on as a smart-aleck.

-Well, … you know, … it's in the total picture; the mannerisms, the intellect, some idiosyncrasies, … those are hard to hide. The rest of it is intuition" she said and leaned back on her seat.

-Aha, … yah, … one of women's favorite copout, if all else fails, it's intuition" I said, sort of to myself. We have been airborne for almost 40 minutes by now, flying over Northern Maine and Canada's Maritime Provinces. It was almost total darkness outside, only a few faint lights were visible on the ground. Not bright enough to be identifiable, what they illuminate. We were cruising at 36 thousand feet altitude. The captain gave us all these environmental details, including the ground speed and the air temperature, outside, … "brrrr" 25 degrees below. There was no Global Positioning Systems at work in those days, for the most important ingredients: the satellites, still missing. The details were being worked at Ohio State's Research Foundation's Offices and the Air Force's Hanscome field in Bedford, Mass. I was well familiar with the concept, after all, I was part of the researching team while being a graduate student at Ohio State.

Cocktails were served. The waitresses were extremely busy. Some people were just enjoying giving them a hard time. All drinks were totally free, this was an international flight, after all. When our waitress arrived with her cart at our row of seats, I asked for a Manhattan because I saw that they are serving the 'pre-mixed kind' in miniature-small bottles. Then I asked the stewardess to "please give me a shot of Ronrico rum, just straight by itself". That was no sweat; she handed it right out to me from the cart she was attending. But she asked: "sir, what will you be doing with that"? I informed her that: "I am going to pour it into my Manhattan to ...kind of ...you know: spry it up, and ... if you would be so really sweet and give me a can of raspberry juice I would be ready to make love to you". She gave me a real abominable look, and asked: "sir, you sure you are all right?" ... so, I decided to cool it. But I added: "believe me ma'am, it was a long time ago that I was as happy as I am right now". She gave me now a curious look and handed me a mini-can of raspberry juice. "Would this be all for now" she asked, and I was more than agreeable. I almost felt like being put to shame. I decided right there that I really had to collect myself.

The lady – the professor's ex wife- in the row behind me, leaned forward and asked me: "Sir, do you always give this much trouble to waitresses, ... er... like in this case, to stewardesses?"

-As a matter of fact, I don't" I said turning to her, "I think the devil made me say that, you know? or maybe, ... I guess, ... you don't know! I really don't know myself why I said that? It was not truly me". Then I paused for a moment and told her: "You know, Mrs. ... er... sorry, I don't know how to address you, you never gave me your name, ... anyways, ... we have a real picturesque Hungarian expression, or may be a proverb, that says: 'I felt like kicking out of my harness'; Hungarians were notorious throughout history as being a horse-loving nation".

-But, you do seem like having an exceptional 'know how' when it comes to drinks, don't you think? ... my ex husband, the professor, developed a drinking habit, which, eventually led to our divorce, ... in a situation like this, he would just concentrate on getting drunk, ... he did not have the sophistication you seem like possessing, when it comes to drinks" she said, and kind of waited for my answer. "And, since we are at it, would you mind calling me Phyllis?"

-Oh, I am so sorry, I am forgetting my manners, ... my mother would make me suffer for this behavior, I am sure, but America somehow, ruined me lately. I am doing things I never dared doing in my 'former life', ... "My given name is Gabor, that's what everyone calls me, well, ... with some exceptions, like most of my colleagues at the University call me Gabe, that comes from, I guess, the TV show: "Welcome back Kutter, and is short for Gabriel, the Archangel".

-Oh, that is really cute; So, then, which one would you prefer to be called?"

-You mean by yourself? I think I would really like you to call me: Gàbor, with the accent on the first (long) syllable, and repeated it: Gàbor", and at the first time I turned all the way around, to have a full good look at her.

"Phyllis, I think I am beginning to smell a professor's wife. Of course, I am not as good as you are at smelling the professor, but ... still, you know, ... in our case alcohol does not enter into the equation of 'splitting up', ... I am really sorry to hear what alcohol did to your marital relationship, if ... it was really only that substance to be blamed for the split. I used to be taking sides with the alcohol, but, ... when I hear something like this, ... I am not really sure if, perhaps something else may enter into the equation."

-Well, what if something else does? ... You know, ...enter into the equation, as you put it? Could it be sex? that certainly is a powerful 'separator', as it can be a 'connector' too.. And, you know, ultimately, most everything is connected to sex? Alcohol, for instance, has a devastating effect on the 'performance' of men. By the way, do you have a family, a wife?"

-Yes, I do, but Phyllis, please don't frighten me with these things, I still do not consider myself an 'alcoholic'. And I don't even have to fight it. I could actually do without it; of course, it would take immense convincing my: Brain, as well as my: Gull, ...you know, ...may be even hypnotism, to arrive at a total abstinence, ... for which I am not aspiring just now. But, it has to be controlling convincing... you see, I still derive a lot of sensory pleasure from my, well selected (alcoholic) drinks. For instance I never drink just to get drunk and enjoy the condition (of being drunk) but I do my drinking exclusively for the enjoyment of the palate. If a drink doesn't taste good, ... really good, ... I would consider it a failure, set it aside and don't touch it. You know what I mean?"

-I am not sure what you mean; but, if what you are trying to say is that alcohol does not control you ... "

-Phyllis, my dear, I can assure you that as of now, it does not. Also, that I still can not understand how it does control even some of my best friends. But let's skip this; this is a very sad and depressing topic".

-Well, … Gàbor, … do you realize that this is the first time I pronounced this name the way you instructed me to do?" she asked. "It does have a different melody to it this way".

-Yah, … so, … go on, you just pronounced my name, and absolutely correctly, if I may add; is there more to come?"

-You know? actually there is. Ours is not a highly musical family. We drift along with the tide of contemporary music; the kids never went beyond the popular genre. You probably would not find any classical piece of music in our entire house. My ex was –and I may say still is- a musical illiterate. What I was going to ask you was: what sort of music was that you have played when we boarded the plane? Because we here were all terrified that you are one of those rock-and-roll freaks, and we were already bracing ourselves… when all of a sudden we were in for a most pleasant surprise… that was one piece full of beautiful melodies, …" she missed to finish the sentence.

-Phyllis, you mean to tell me you actually liked it? This is the greatest compliment anyone paid me lately; I think that was one of my recently discovered ballet score, 'Ballet Egyptian,' by Alexander (etc.) Luigini, an Italian. As I was reading up on it, I found out that this was the only single little 15-minute ballet he ever composed, … I mean in terms of ballets, … isn't that a shame? That so many great talents were going to waste? Underutilized? The music 'business' was, unfortunately not as well organized in the last century as it is today. I know this from intimate sources: my grandfather, who was the supreme musician in the family. And, he ended up becoming a casualty of: music, … heavily mixed with politics. Musicians have been known to starve in those days. He did not starve though, he committed suicide that he made look like an accident. It was partly in protest of the Trianon Treaty, which moved the boundaries of countries over the heads of people, of families, … but we better not get into that because we get so entangled that we never untangle ourselves. By the way what was your 'ex's expertise, … I guess, what I mean is: what was he teaching? … History perhaps?"

-Well, … you know, he had no real 'expertise'… he taught English. Actually, he still does. I guess you do have other 'expertise' as you put it, because I remember you said you do other things, teaching being one of them".

-Yes, I am an engineer and a surveyor. I am licensed in both of these disciplines. I may say, as of now I make my living –here I mean most of the money- by these extracurricular endeavors."

Dinner was getting to be served. It took well over a half an hour for the stewardesses just to get through serving everyone. Some people

253

have finished and turned in their dinner plates to the stewardess, when the last group of people were just getting their dinners served. And it was greatly simplified too, choice of fish, chicken, or beef. This was the first item on which the management succeeded to realize a substantial saving. The other one was to fill the planes to nearly 90% capacity. This was a lot easier, by simply lowering the fares to a level that defied competition.

We, the passengers, got a chance to have a limited duration nap before we were all waken up preparing for landing. Also, we lost some three hours by flying Eastward, so it was early dawn, by the time we landed in Keflavik, Iceland. Phyllis was herding her teenage charges, who were all as sleepy as could be. She told me that if I ever happen to travel in the area north of Philadelphia she would really, but, really like to have me as a 'gentleman caller' in the true, innocent meaning of the expression, ... if I happen to know that expression and meaning? (I told her I did!) having been brought up in a (slightly) different culture. Then she handed me her card (she was a teacher) with all relevant information. Then I said:

-Phyllis, my dear, I can't promise you anything, but ... I am enormously flattered, and if ever I promise, ... that is: something, anything, I always, but always keep it. Now, that if I will ever be in the position, ... I shall pay you a visit; and that is a promise." With that I gently took her hand and kissed it, slowly, very slowly. She did not withdraw it or rendered an embarrassing smile as many of her contemporaries would have done, but when I slowly turned her hand around to have access to her palm with my lips, she forcefully, quickly withdrew her hand (as if a viper would have bitten it) and all of a sudden did not know how and where to hide it. Then, while still waiting for the line ahead, she asked me: Gàbor, ... I know it's kind of personal, but may I ask you: have you ever been unfaithful to your wife?"

-Technically, never! but if we count all the lustful thoughts and desires, ... then I must say, I sinned many, many times." Then it was our turn to disembark.

The terminal building was under general overhaul. Certain sections were totally inaccessible for the passengers. We were all herded to the main lobby, from which the tax-free gift shop –as the most important business establishment - and other necessity spaces, like foreign exchange, postal services, rest rooms, travel services, etc. were accessible. Another part of the terminal was reserved for the military, since Iceland was a NATO member state and as such, had to maintain its required standards. The 'cold war' was in full swing. Navy fighters were off for maneuvers and landing every fifteen minutes.

A sizable group of passengers were escorted to two modern Mercedes busses, These were charted to take stopovers into Reykjavik for two-three days and nights in luxury hotel accommodations, along with sightseeing tours in rural and country environs. Phyllis and her kids were in this group. I bought a few informative publications about Iceland, as well as some consumer items to take with me as gifts to our relatives. Then we were readied to board the same aircraft for Luxembourg. We also picked up some passengers for the last leg of the flight. The plane suddenly became more spacious. Some of the luckier passengers could stretch out on the vacated seats. Shortly after breakfast we were getting ready to land in Luxembourg. It was nearly 10 AM local time.

After claiming our baggages and clearing customs and immigration I was to wait in the main lobby of the terminal for the car rental company's representative. There were several of these men lined up, each holding a small tablet with their company's logo showing for their customers to recognize them. I picked out my company's man in a jiffy, who took my suitcase and carried it to the '**Opel Olympia**'. I followed him like a doggy. We drove down to the Town of Trier, in Germany, a medieval town of great historic importance. There we took care of the car's paperwork and: 'Ta da!' I was on my way.

These rental cars were practically new, only a few thousand kilometers showing on the odometer. After each occupant returned it, it was thoroughly cleaned and serviced. Therefore, little wonder that they not only had the appearance, of a new vehicle, but were actually performing as such. The rental company was insisting that the lessee change the oil after each and every five thousand kilometers, for which they conscientiously reimbursed them at the end of the trip.

I was amazed how much I remembered about the various towns from our last trip but probably more surprised about all the **changes** that took place since the summer of 1970. A mere three years ago. In Stuttgart I took a short detour from the Autobahn and drove into town, where one of my old classmate lived, a doctor, specializing in anesthesiology. He owned the eighth (top) floor of the building where his condominium resembled a penthouse suite here in the US. Doctors made good money there too.

Unfortunately he was not home, but placed a message (on a folded sheet of paper) for me to the effect that he had to visit his youngest daughter in Switzerland who was in some sort of summer student exchange program there. And she 'needed her papa'. It was really cute. I was reflecting on how much richer (social) life these European kids have in comparison with ours in America. By the time they finish high school they speak at least two, but quite often three languages, have a lot of exposure to –slightly- different cultures, and are much more at home in the world, -or shall we say the Globe!- than even our own kids, who did get a good dose of diversity from us at home.

I drove on to a suburb before re-entering the Autobahn where I found a small grocery market. I bought some items for the road. The deli-clerk made three sandwiches for me, each one packed with salami, thin sliced beer cheese, green peppers, all packed in fresh 'kaisersemmeln'. It felt like being half way to heaven, and I did not argue with my fate about that, in fact, I enormously enjoyed and felt grateful for it. I looked around in the drink department and found some 'Mosel Muscatels'. I was itching to taste them. I bought three bottles for any case, I hoped they would sustain me beyond the Hungarian border. In fact they did.

It was late afternoon by the time I got to the outskirts of München. There was a lot of construction going on, as I reckoned, it was the circumferential highway around München they were working on. I quickly realized that I better get out of this construction mess. It caused huge delays to the motorists, who were genuinely annoyed by it, using language that I was totally unfamiliar with. I never spent enough time in German language territory to familiarize myself with the 'underground German'; my language skills were insufficient to grasp all of it, although I knew some words.

I decided that perhaps it would be a good idea if I scout out some popular eating places closer to town. I knew just about all the downtown attractions from earlier sojourns, but I did not want to enter the downtown because of the tremendous difficulty finding parking. I wished I could visit the Ratskeller, which was maybe the most popular spot for eating, drinking and 'Omph-ta-ta' live brass-music, still familiar from many years prior to this trip, but, … parking was very difficult to find there either. Therefore I was searching to find a cozy little family style restaurant on the arterial highways leading to the big City.

In the old suburb of Nymphenburg, (which once was the regent's residence, with jewel-like, restored beautiful castles) I came across a small park, with a park-style restaurant sitting in the middle of it. Familiar German brass-band music filtered out into the park. I found a parking place and went inside. A truly nostalgic atmosphere surrounded me as I was wondering around to find a vacant table. There was none within sight but I didn't panic because I knew that Europeans don't even blink an eye to ask some solitary person if they might share the table with them. I did likewise as I found a gentleman sitting by himself, drinking his bier, and enjoying the music. I asked him if he would be kind enough to share his table with me.

-By all means, mein Herr" he responded, "please be my guest, by the way, may I ask where you are from, perhaps, … Österreich? You, kind of, … spoke with an Austrian drawl."

-Oh, nicht, bitt' schön, aber meine Mutter ist eine Österrecherin" I informed him. He was pointing to the chair next to him and said: "machen sie sich gemütlich, … bitte, eine Kellnerin wird shon sicher dabei kommen".

I was unexpecting this sort of warm welcome, nevertheless thoroughly enjoyed it. The conversation came to a halt and we both listened to the band, which now played the familiar "Flieger March" (a highly favorite of all the Second World War marches) with dimmed brass, almost pianissimo, but the leading melody came through even more forcefully, nostalgically this way, as if it were played with 'forte brass'.

A waitress came to our table and put a Stein (a pitcher) of beer in front of me, then handed me a menu, a single sheet, artistically prepared. I really liked it. Somehow it exposed the cultural aptitude the Europeans were always so proud of. While I was looking into it she asked my table-mate if he is ready to have supper. He ordered a dish totally unfamiliar to me, but that did not surprise me. I myself found a "Wildbrett" with potato salad. Then the waitress turned to me, so I had a chance to inquire what sort of wild meat is in the "Wildbrett" listed here. She informed me that this one tonight is the meat of a wild boar, and is roasted, then refrigerated. So the entire meal is a cold plate, served with the potato salad. This sounded so thoroughly exotic to me that it was turning my pallet on. I asked the waitress how long would I have to wait for it. She said only as long as it takes the 'shef' to slice the meat, because everything else is all ready and prepared to be served.

Since it was a warm evening following a real warm day, people were wearing light summer clothes. Our waitress was wearing a Bavarian style black velvet short with white knee-socks and a white, (perhaps silk) blouse. As she left our table her extremely shapely derrière caught my attention, so much so, that my table mate took notice of it too as I did so.

-Mein Herr, I couldn't help but notice the attention our waitress' behind drew from your good self; It seemed like a very natural reaction," he said and was half expecting my remark.

-Sir, I know it is considered impolite to utter a look like I just performed in a public place. But you see, I found her fanny exquisitely shapely, which was even accentuated by the tight short she was wearing. I apologize for causing your upset".

-Oh, but that is not the case at all! I myself am a great fan of the female rear end, especially if it is well rounded, or: stealing your own expression, is: 'shapely'. You may not know, but we have here a 'Callipygian's Club' of which I belong and am an enthusiastic supporter. By the way my name is Siegfried, please call me so" he said. I reciprocated promptly, telling him that my name was Gàbor and that he should call me so.

I was beaten. First of all, because I didn't fully understand what he was talking about. So I followed the golden rule: 'talking is silver, silence is gold' and I went for the gold. Our waitress brought both of our suppers, so we became busy with the food stuff. But I did not want to miss the shapely apparition and rewarded myself with another good look at this exquisite sight. Naturally Siegfried again did not miss my unbridled attention.

Supper was excellent. The wild boar's meat was superbly tasty, in addition, it was lean, thinly sliced and with the potato salad it constituted a well rounded summer meal. Siegfried, on the other hand, had a saucy dish, which had the kind of dumplings with it, that I well remembered from my childhood, the way it was made in our house. The dumplings had roasted pieces of bread, similar to croutons, but smaller, inside of them.

As he was finishing up he asked me if I would enjoy a visit as his guest to his 'Club', since he felt in me a 'fellow rear-end enthusiast'. Now I began to understand what he was talking about before. So I asked him about his club, what are the members really up to, etc. He then went into an elaborate description of the varieties of shows that are featured, also that the membership is free to 'mingle' in a sense that the guests may also participate in the fun and enjoyment. I thanked him for the invitation and told him that he should take the lead and I shall follow him in my car.

When the waitress brought our bills I had to brace myself not to show, -at least to her, -my fascination with her assets. But it got out of control, when Siegfried whispered some intimate notes to her, which I could not hear or understand, as a result of which she turned around and took a bow for both of us but not the usual, regular way: 'facing us'. Siegfried then handed her a bank note, which must have been a sizable tip, judged by a second bow she gracefully performed just for us.

Siegfried drove through Nymphenburg, then into territory entirely unfamiliar to me. Anyway it was already dark, but as long as he found his –or rather- our, way I had nothing to worry about. The place was a vintage pre-war country estate. It was beginning to appear so suspiciously intact, that an unsuspecting visitor may have questioned if there was ever a Second World War as devastating as depicted in many Hollywood movies.

We went inside where the valet clerk checked Siegfried's ID and greeted him very cordially. He then introduced me as 'Herr Gabor', being his guest. The clerk rapidly handed me a 'guest's badge' to pin on my shirt. So we proceeded into the main show room. We found an empty small table with a fairly good view of the podium, which was slightly elevated. We got into the middle of a light-hearted farce (burlesque show) the language of which was way too much advanced for my rusty German. But the plot, even without all the words, was so simplistic, that it did not leave much for the imagination. The act ended with a 'surprise' which was really rather an obvious consequence, than a surprise, as the two rival actresses bared their behinds, even removing their panties, to prove a point of argument to the master of the house, who got a real kick out of it and patted both of them in a sort of 'pacifying manner'. And, needless to say, so did the audience have a kick out of it. The applause was thunderous.

The waitress came to our table with two cocktail glasses filled with a liqueur, that I instantly recognized by its unmistakable color. It was the 'chartreuse'. The real attraction, however, was in the waitress's attire, which looked sort of decent from the front, but the rear end was 'all natural'. Superbly natural. Siegfried reminded me that the rules are: 'all for the eyes, nothing for the hands' you know, ... the way it is in America, with the go-go-girls, who bare their chests rather than the opposite end, but not infrequently both. I assured him that I am a man of manners, that I do not have to be reminded of such obvious rules, and I guarantee that he will have no trouble, whatsoever, that would be caused by me in this regard .

I asked Siegfried: who ordered the drinks, because I did not see him ordering anything for us yet. He explained that these were introductory, complimentary drinks, 'on the house' due to any member (in good standing) who brings a 'novice guest'. And since he has brought me, so these drinks are for the two of us, ... of course, follow-up drinks will be put on the tab.

Shortly, another act was getting to the ready. This was again some sort of social drama spiked with such fervor of sexual flavor that the baring of the rear parts began sort of early on in the act. Evidently the actors were engaged in a card-game of sort, which demanded the removal of a particular piece of attire by the looser; the choice of clothing being that of the winner. (Not much different from the well known strip-poker in the West). This time however there were at least four losers on the scene all of them without anything left covering their rear end. I noticed, however, that none of the female contenders were players in the previous act.

After the next play the curtain opened once more to expose the entire cast that had been players in all the previous acts. There were at least a dozen, or more actresses alone, not counting the actors. After a full frontal view, - and a deep bow- they turned around and repeated the bow in the opposite direction. In this position they remained for quite some time, at the end of which each contender displayed a number, some of which went into double digits. Siegfried explained to me that by my casting a number into a hat with my initials on the slip of paper I could become the winner of one of the owner's of the cheeks I will vote for.

Before midnight I asked Siegfried where would he advise me to go and take a motel room for the night in view of the late hour, and the fact that I would have to continue my journey in the morning. He dismissed my concerns. He explained, that if I should indeed become one of the winners, my worries will become utterly groundless, because along with the 'price' I will also win the room for the night, ... right in-house, upstairs. Then he whispered that it would be up to me to leave a tip for the lady to whom the prizewinning derrière belonged, … provided that we both found the accommodation satisfactory.

I did, in fact, become a winner of the contestant numbered 'four' along with room number 4. The young lady, by the name of Erika, a good decade younger then I, who was sharing with me not only the double bed, but also her prizewinning derrière, bearing the number '4' which she regarded as our lucky number (for some time to come). I was unaware of how many 'sins' this winning (lucky) number resulted for her during the entire night, but for me it certainly meant the 'technical sinning' for the first four times in my married life.

As I was getting ready in the morning Erika informed me that she had a great time she will not forget, perhaps ever, that this lucky chance encounter brought her. Then I recalled Siegfried's reminder about tipping my hostess in accordance with the total enjoyment she afforded me. I hope I was generous enough leaving her a hundred D-Mark banknote on top of the dresser. But considering the scale on which Siegfried based his suggested remuneration to be done, I was afraid that I did not have enough cash with me that was meant for the entire trip. As I was getting ready to leave, Erika came to me, still wearing her nighty, got hold of my right hand, placed it on her rear and gave me a good-by kiss, a fairly long good-by kiss; all the while keeping my hand where she put it.

I was in a daze for some time. On my way down to the main lobby I became disoriented and had to sit down at one of the 19-th century curio tables, which was really not utilitarian for any purpose, but that you had something in front of you as you were sitting on a Chippendale chair, uncomfortable by today's standards. I was like under a spell, wanted to go back to be with Erika. For a good while I was wondering how she was doing. How her day would be progressing today? Was she missing me at all? like I was missing her, or at least half as much?

*

I knew something like this was bound to happen sooner or later. What I was not sure was, how I would be able to handle it. I got way too much emotional about it. But that's the way I was. And I knew it. Last night's elation gave way to today's remorse, and eventually to a catharsis. I was almost devastated. I really didn't know what was happening with me. On the one hand I was happy that I discovered the real "me". But on the other, I had my doubts about the teachings of my faith in which I was raised, which condemned outright what I just did. I could not bring myself to pray for a forgiveness. Forgiveness for what? for what I was feeling last night? for that unconcealed happiness I felt in the arms of Erika? Was that such a 'sin' for which I was to torture myself from now on forward? Something was not quite right. Something didn't add up.

A morning waitress came to me at the little table and asked me if I was all right. I told her that I didn't know. She gave me a curious glance, then, I think she was trying to assess the situation and asked me if I would need some assistance. Medical, perhaps? Do I really feel sick? Should she call for a doctor? I told her no! I don't need a doctor. "Are you sure?" she asked me. I told her that for what I seem to be coming down with, no doctor could render a cure. "Well, what is it then? Should I notify the management? Because I think sir, you really don't look well." When I told her, very slowly, that: what I need most is probably my father, who might suggest a cure, ... Her question of: "Sir how can we call him?" Do you have his number?" sort of sounded the alarm for me, and I thought that perhaps this is the time that I can finally brake away from here, where I was not going to brake away from, unless something drastic happens.

Well, no real drastic thing happened in the lobby of that country castle in Bavaria; The drastic thing that happened was inside me; and I realized that I alone was the one who had to cope with it.

For a long while I was under the spell of this really extraordinary event. For me it was. I didn't know what kind of a fool I would be making of myself if I would go back to the place and ask for how I could be meeting with Erika. And if by some miracle I would, how would I tell her that this was the first time I was ever really! technically! unfaithful to my wife, and that instead of feeling remorse, I was feeling incredible happiness, and that would she be seriously thinking, by any chance, that we could be having a future together? I was actually that crazy.

But I didn't have the answers, and I never, ever went back to that Bavarian country castle to find them. I didn't even know if I could find my way to it. But more than that: I never even tried.

* - - -* - - -*

Returning to the Autobahn was almost automatic by now, although there were a number of new roadway sections built since last time I drove along here. This was the most scenic, the most beautiful and perhaps the most unforgettable section of all the German Autobahns. If anyone would debate this point, I wouldn't know how to argue with him. Probably it wouldn't matter anyway, because I was positively convinced about it. It is slightly longer than a one hour drive to Salzburg, the Austrian border. A mere stone throw away from 'Berchtesgaden' the aerie (or eagle's nest) of the 'Führer' and Chancellor of the Third Reich. I was itching several times to visit the place, but every time I tried, was told that it is not available for visitors.

Leaving the border crossing behind I entered the Austrian Autobahn, which was well familiar to me from the time I bought the Volkswagen Kombi'. It was early morning then and now it was close to noon, and I began to realize that I did not have anything to eat. Not even breakfast; although Erika was mumbling something in my ear about room service, but I was not in a condition to fully comprehend it, or attach any significance to it. Now it invaded me with full force. So, I remembered the little 'Gasthaus' in Himmelreich where I stayed last time and now I drove right in, to have an early lunch.

The Austrian beer did not taste the way I remembered it. The Gösser, which used to be my favorite, did not have the 'zing' of the good old days. But the lunch definitely had an altogether beneficial effect on my mood. I needed that badly. It perked me up to do the entire length of the distance to Wien in some two and a half an hour. I was hoping all along that the high speed and the concentration on the driving will chase away the nagging thoughts about Erika; of what in the world could she be doing right now? And after that? And what about tomorrow? would she be back tonight again in the 'Callipygian's Club' as a contestant? I didn't want to have the answers though. Had they been the wrong ones I think they would have disillusioned, even depressed me beyond measure.

It was already about 3-PM, so I had no time to waste. I zipped through Wien as never before. By a little past 4 PM I was approaching the Hungarian border. Being a weekday the crowd was not too great, so by 5:30 I was on my way on the newly designated Route E-60 to Budapest. By the time I arrived at my parents' place it was past sunset. Then came the surprise: they were not home. I was searching my memory, where could they possibly be this late on a Wednesday evening. I wished my brother had a telephone, so that I could alert him that I arrived, but this was another item on the communist government's list that was not a 'real necessity' to the population. It would have cost a startling amount of money to the government to bring the system up to European (never mind American!) norm.

I had no other choice than to drive to their place on the Lagymanyos flats. Actually a mere 10 minutes drive, on a distance that would have taken nearly an hour on public transportation. I again had a hard time finding parking. Around the block was a vacant building lot, (which was, no doubt, confiscated from its lawful owner, but left to the weeds by the government) so I took the liberty to park there, at least for the night.

My brother found that three-story house a good decade ago and was eyeing it as a potential candidate for building a fourth story on it. After a year's struggle with the housing authorities, (which promptly attached another long-waiting applicant's petition to this endeavor) finally granted the permit to construct the additional story. This was how he finally got a place for himself, where he could take his wife with him. Thus, without an elevator in the building, one had to climb three sets of stairs to arrive on the forth flight. It was a classic 'walk-up'.

When I rung the bell, Klari, my sister-in-law opened the inset window to look out to see who the unexpected guest was, she was knocked over with surprise, then quickly opened the door for me and threw her arms around my neck. We stood in the open doorway for a while, when my brother also came to the foyer, to see what was going on. The instant he recognized me, he did not try to hide his surprise.

Then we moved inside where Klari asked me whether I am thirsty, hungry or have any other bodily desires. She never realized what a chord she struck in me, but assessed from my look that I must be tired, perhaps even exhausted. So I just said: 'all of the above' and as a first priority I need to occupy the bathroom. Returning to them from the first stop of recuperation, Klari was putting cheese, fresh bread, (she buys fresh bread everyday) and some juicy, green paprika and green onions on the table and apologized that this will be all for now, since they didn't know I was coming.

In the meantime Andrew (my brother) needed an explanation why did I not go up 'the hill' to our parents first. "You know, because we will be scolded tomorrow for you not going to their place first". I explained that I did, but they were not home. I couldn't get into their flat. Also, there was no show by any of the tenants from the house, thus I couldn't even ask anyone if they knew where they are.

After some consultation Klari seemed to remember that my parents went on a bus-tour to Krakow and Warsaw and will be back sometime on Friday. So, they asked me what my preference would be: to stay with them, -in sort of crammed quarters- or after supper, drive up the hill to our parent's place and stay there, which, by the way, will be a lot more comfortable as far as sleeping arrangements are concerned. I opted for the hill, but wanted to enjoy their company for a while at least until we all get the distance separating us for the last few years, out of our system. Andrew was going to fetch some super domestic wine, which he always seemed to have around, thanks to his friend, who worked for the 'Ampellological Institute's' Research Center, and as such had access to some of the most extraordinary wines cultured in Hungary. I offered one of the bottles I bought in Stuttgart, the 'Mosel Muscatel' but they waived it down, as an 'inferior liquid' compared to the 'Badacsony-i Trauminer', a bottle of which he found in the pantry.

I was in no mood to argue. Actually I had a fairly long day behind me. I was honestly wondering if, in fact, 'it was all behind me'. I was getting aware of the possibility that some part of this day will **never be entirely** 'behind me'. But, the changed surroundings definitely helped fade away the more difficult parts of it. (Erika was still in my nerve cells.) We were beginning to make plans for my 'two weeks' stay. So many plans were popping up all of a sudden, that it was getting hard to take stock of them. I was emphatic that I will need a minimum of two days to be set aside just to drive down to Pècs, (my favorite City in Hungary,) where my in-laws lived. That was not to be missed, under no circumstances, or my head was definitely rolling when I get home. Andrew took it upon himself to serve as my travel-marshall, who will organize all my itineraries. In fact he was beginning to put it down on paper. Little did we know at the time how such 'definite' plans can turn out to become 'tentative' due to 'unforeseen circumstances'. But let's not get ahead of our story.

Since both of them had to go to work Thursday, I said good by to them and after picking up a set of keys to my parent's apartment, I left them. Andrew promised to call me in the morning from his work place. My father still had his residential telephone, which counted as a luxury. I drove up 'the hill' and in no time made myself at home, and occupied my father's bed. I was not about to fuss with such puny details after 11-PM.

Next morning Andrew did call as he promised he will, from his office telephone. He told me he will be busy during the day, so he can not be with me. Thus, my best bet is to just be traipsing around the City and follow whatever strikes my fancy; A real relaxing 'do nothing' sort of activity. Then he will call me in the evening at our parent's place. If I am not there, so be it. I am a big enough boy by now to take care of myself. I agreed wholeheartedly. Then I too, began to think about the day ahead.

The phone call made me realize that I better get myself ready. So I soaked myself in a long bath, while reading the radio and television programs in the newspaper, marking up some of the numbers and events that promised to be interesting, I began to crystallize my plans for the day. I felt like visiting my former girl-friends, sort of, … just to catch-up how life treated each of them. It was rather obvious that I should start with my one time fiancée, with whom I was engaged to be married, before the Hungarian Army took up its demand on my (free) services for a statutory two years. This engagement broke up sort of uneventfully towards the time of the end of my Army service. Upon my return to Budapest we both found that we gradually drifted apart, meaning essentially, that both of us had developed meaningful (sexual) relationships of our own. I was well aware of this possibility because I knew she could not exist without a man for almost any length of time. I was accepting this fact without much hard feelings, although I had only the **promise** of a new, and beautiful, all consuming relationship, with the girl I learned to know while in the Army service at the relatively far away city of Pècs, who eventually became my wife, and with whom we escaped the communist retaliation together, following the subdued revolution of 1956.

She was living at **her** parent's place, so close to **my** parent's place that I decided to walk the 8-10 minutes over to their place at the bottom of the hill, where the restored Royal Palace of Buda stood. I was somewhat taken aback when I found an unfamiliar name on the brass plate over the door. This aborted my anticipated visit on a short order. But I wasn't the type of chap who frets easily; so, after a short search of my memory I came up with the very pleasant image of a rather petite but extremely well proportioned girl by the name of Ilona, (which was the same as my former fiancé's) whom I first met at the dancing school, which both my younger brother as well as myself attended.

Now this was one extraordinarily smart girl. Neither my younger brother, nor myself held ourselves poorly endowed in the mental department, so we just about took turns in courting her, each of us on our own wit and competence, so much so, that after a while we had to realize that we became rivals ourselves. This situation naturally had to cease. Therefore we decided that we should let **her** be the judge which one of us she will favor with her unique attention.

A curious thing happened. Our youngest brother, Leslie, was the tallest of the three of us, and was generally considered the most handsome, also, unquestionably, the best dancer. (My older brother, Andrew, on the other hand, was widely held being by far the smartest of the three of us;) so that left me sort of being the 'ugly duckling' among us three brothers. I was no winner. But for some inexplicable reason, Ilona found myself to be the the most worthy of her attention.

We went to concerts together, classical concerts, -quite a lot- for which we both felt the same affinity. Her mother, a high school teacher, was chaperoning us in the beginning of our dating, but later she had no longer escorted us, perhaps because she found it totally superfluous. It puzzles me even after all these years, what was 'wrong' with her; wrong in a sense that she seemingly did not need much of any closeness, any warm bodily contact, which was, by the way, considered being the trait of a '**good**' girl. Necking was out of the order. I found that out the hard way with Ilona, (or Ica as she was being called by her mother, and consequently by myself) she somehow developed a contempt towards 'these sort of things', that are, well, ... un-intellectual. She was definitely **not** the cuddly type, which, in comparison, I was (and still am). How she ended up choosing me I could not find the answer for, except, perhaps in the proverb, that 'opposites attract'.

In view of all of these 'opposites' that seemed to attract each other according the proverb, I **did** like her very much, I dare to say: I **loved** her in the full meaning of the word, loved to be with her, talked with her, sometimes for hours! (since verbal communication was the dominant, accepted means between us) and even at my slightest attempt to 'feel' her, (feel her physically) like holding her hand, or putting mine on the small of her back, or just touching her, strictly in a most appropriate way (which was the accepted custom, or the norm between youngsters of opposite gender) she became uneasy, not really 'tightening-up' but just not comfortable until the gesture stopped.

I saw her in her swimsuit too, quite often, when we went to a pool or a beach, and when above I made the remark of her being 'well proportioned', that statement was based on these occasions. Although she was only 5-ft 3-in. tall (previously I used the term petite) she had a full, and fully, and oh, ever so delightfully, developed body that turned me on every time I got up close to her. I suspected that maybe her above described behavior was the result of some trauma. But I never found out.

I could go on, and on praising her. But to summarize this superficial analysis I never really 'cracked the nut', in this case meaning that I never found out what, if anything, turned her on as a result of our really intense, though one-sided, relationship. Later, years later, when I was already attending the University, and did not, could not, find enough time for a lot of dating as I did in my high school upper-class years, I met Ica occasionally on the street, where from she was usually ascending the line of stairs (long line of stairs) leading up to the 'Castle-Hill', (so called,) where her parents lived, during the war. At the time I met her, only her mother and grandmother lived, her father never returned from one of the soviet gulags where he was taken by the (soviet) army engineers, after their intelligence discovered that he was a brilliant mechanical engineer and inventor, held several patents etc. so, they 'forgot' to let him return in 1949, when all POW-s should have been returned according to some of the numerous international agreements.

At these meetings, or rather short encounters, I tried to pry open her box of secrets; very touchingly, lovingly, inquiring about her 'love-life' but never really successfully. She told me once that she had a 'suitor' also a student, at the University's Humanities Division, what she attended, and, of course, received the highest grades attainable, heading towards her becoming the usual 'summa-cum-laude'.

So, I decided to take the extra 8-10 minutes walk, up those long line of stairs and call on her, or on her mother, whomever I could find at home. Fate had it that Ica was away with her mother in Transylvania, visiting one of their relatives, who just had a death in their family and are not due back at least another week, or so the grandmother told me. She was overwhelmingly kind to me, fetched some ice cream with a bit of coffee liqueur, she still remembered this being one of my favorite desserts; asked all sorts of questions about my life and family in America, and expressed her genuine sorrow that I could not meet Ica, who, according to her, was often mentioning or talking about me.

* --- * --- *

Now that I exhausted those two really close girl friends, one with a torridly hot and sensual relationship, and the other, with whom I had but a diagonally opposing different kind (of relationship), nevertheless, with both of whom I could have no trouble imagine living my future life; My further mental search resulted a display in my memory: the girl, for whom I was totally crazy, unreasonably, even sickeningly so, and for a long, long time too, but found no 'real' reciprocation, even when I thought I was making progress.

She was the only child of a middle aged, very jovial couple, with an exceptionally comfortable life style, taking into account the hardest communist governed years, with rations for just about anything and everything. Her father, John, (Janos, in Hungarian) was a civil engineer, with a structural major as background, and was, in the war years and prior to them, an Adjunct Professor at the Technical University's Second Steel Structures Department. After the war he was dismissed from that post due mostly to his bourgeois attitude and lifestyle. But the newly appointed professor in charge of the Department, who received his own appointment from the communist government's minister of cultural affairs, was his former colleague and took care of him by using his (new, communist) connections.

This is how he, János Pataki, the former Adjunct Professor, became the chief of structural steel **manufacturing and testing** at the country's largest steel producing combine, some 100 miles away from Budapest. He did quite a lot of commuting, in the form of leaving Budapest Monday morning on an early train, and returning Thursday late in the evening. This way he was at home for three full days: Friday to Sunday. He also had access to a lot of food and other hard to find items, which they, working for an **elite industry,** were privileged to come by, in abundance. He came home loaded with these items every Thursday evening.

Their daughter, Gabriella, was a real beauty. She was not overly tall (thereby discouraging a number of shorter boys of their possible advances), she was just about exactly my own height, she was bearing the feminine version of my own given name, and was extremely well proportioned, almost sporty, if you wish, also something I considered myself aspiring to, and I was not neglecting this God given athletic sort of attribute, in fact worked on it diligently by participating in every physical activity available to us in those hard, post-war years. Bicycle served me as a means of long distance travel.

Taking into account all these similarities, I became obsessed with the idea that she was actually meant, **by divine will**, to become the partner of my life. She was musically inclined (taking piano lessons from early on); She had a well above average manual dexterity, which I also was recognized for, since early childhood, and well praised in the years after the war in the reconstruction of dwellings (of which there will be ample mention in my next book, that I promised to write, in an earlier chapter).

Perhaps the only aspect we differed was that she was an excellent student, in a scholarly meaning, whereas, I was not. My attention was constantly distracted by far too many practical things in life. Compared with Ica, however, she was well behind in scholarly achievements, but well surpassing her in the sensual department, which attribute we actually both shared. There was no comparison. Gabriella was greatly superior, so much so that her real sensual awakening, along with experimentations engaging me as a partner, and quite often as an accomplice, but leaving me ultimately out of my own accomplishments, only proved her eagerness to learn. I was not really sure about her **own** (accomplishments) though. I often thought that she was getting there, where she was heading at the beginning. Nevertheless, her utter, and endless curiosity in matters of the 'flesh' made me wanting to be with her and assisting her all the time.

She was merely 15-years old at the time of my senior year in high school. We first met at the occasion as participants of a classical play, put on by our graduating class for which we needed four girls in the cast, whom we had to borrow from the Girl's school some 400 yards down the boulevard from **our school** which was owned and run by the Cistercian Brothers, a strictly boy's school. There was no coeducation in those years in Hungary over the sixth grade in the public schools, and none at all in private schools. Gabriella, (or Gabi in the nick name version, which we also shared) became one of the successful contestant for one of the actress' roles. The play had to do with the times of the Roman Emperor: Diocletian and his court, which was heavily infiltrated and corrupted by Christians, and an eventual miracle that turned the Emperor over to the 'New Faith'.

Gabi was playing one of the Empress' lady-in-waiting, and as such had numerous lines, but really a limited amount of 'acting'. It was not a difficult role. I, on the other hand, had quite some acting to do, -or rather just being around the Emperor, - as one of his Chancellors. I only had two sentences in all, to utter, at two different occasions. But we all had been wearing third century Roman costumes: Toga for the men, and various real 'light' garments (Tunics) for the ladies. (Rome has a fairly warm, Mediterranean climate). As a result of being close to the Emperor, the Empress and her lady-in-waiting I had plenty of opportunity to observe the ladies' **costumes,** and sometimes a peek of what they were supposed to cover. These were heavenly times for me. Gabi, naturally took notice of my constant proximity, which was even emphasized by my being around when it was uncalled for.

After all the performances were over and the show was closed for good, all the actors and other participants gathered for an impromptu party. As expected by now, I was at my 'natural' and 'steady' position: the closest possible place to the lady-in-waiting. Gabi, of course, did not miss my steady presence, and at one point turned to me and started a light conversation with me. This was how I finally asserted myself and became one of her numerous admirers. She wished to know if I liked to play cards. I was on top of the world; had my first opportunity to show off my ingenuity. To camouflage my excitement, I tried to be as blasé as I possibly could be, so I asked her: "what kind of card game did you have in mind? and with what type of cards?" She said: "well, we are now assembling a second table of 'Bridge' for kind of, **beginners** at my home on the usual Saturday evenings, and I myself will be a participant on that table, because I am just learning that game. The boys on the current table are mostly all advanced players, and they don't like me as a partner, because I am committing dumb mistakes. Would you like to come?"

My heart was pounding in my throat, so I asked:

-If I am not really a beginner, may I still be on your 'beginners' table?" I asked her sort of pleading for a place at her table. Gabi then made some remarks about my ubiquitous presence at, and around her. It came through as something that was not really annoying, just, ... sort of, ... conspicuous.

-Sure," she said," as long as you are not going to be arrogant, and are not going to know everything better than anybody else, and if you will be just generally a good boy, ... a real good boy, ... then, ... and only then, you may come over this Saturday. But tell me now, are you really a beginner or not?" she asked looking strait in my eyes. I was beat. I sensed that she probably knew more about me than she was showing.

-I can not lie to you", I started, "so I must confess that I had been playing bridge, as well as several other card games, ever since childhood, but I don't care what it takes, even if you don't let me play at all, just watch, … you know, just 'kibitzing', I would promise to be a good boy, which I don't remember promising ever since the war, so long as you let me **be there**". Thus, I finally got it out. Now, I told myself, if she has any degree of sensitivity she would easily figure out my guts. She gave me a long look.

-Why?" was all she was asking. It turned out to be a **one-word question**, which was about the most difficult one to answer.

-Because, … I, … love to be near you, … it means everything to me just being where you are, … I, … guess, I am totally **enchanted** by you", I said to her, and was all of a sudden astounded where all the courage, to say these things, came to me from. I would be curious now, to see how I looked then. There was no mirror anywhere near us at that party, so I could not see myself. Then Gabi simply explained where they lived, and how is the best way to get to their place. She also added, very shortly at the end, that she is expecting me.

So, this started a new chapter in my life. Every Saturday I was anxiously grooming myself to meet Gabi's total approval. I was overly courteous to both Mr. and Mrs. Pataki, which both of them graciously acknowledged. I knew I had to go through this routine just like (probably) any new admirer of their daughter. And, there seemed to be many, and many more. Some young men (not even boys anymore) college students, mostly medical students, the friends of her neighbor boy, (Leslie) with whom they knew each other since early childhood. Even their parents were good old friends. So, this neighbor, (Laci for short), was a 'Sophomore Medicus' (as they were being referred to) had shown all sorts of privileges at the Pataki home. In the same time I could never detect any closer, more intimate terms between Laci, (the med-student) and Gabi. This was a great consolation to me. I finally concluded that they were really, very good childhood friends, and nothing, nothing, nothing more!

My obsession grew out of proportions. Sometimes it frightened me too. I began to ask myself, what if I **will not** succeed in obtaining Gabi as my dearest friend, my confidant, my (sexual) partner, thus, in one word:

my 'everything'. I would have given my life unquestioningly, any time, whenever required, **for her.** All these medieval studies and involvements in history, where men were often required to offer (in accordance with true romance), the ultimate sacrifice for the love of their life, only underlined my infatuation. Soon it crystallized in my mind, that I would naturally do the same, anytime whenever, and wherever required.

I became one of the most dedicated card players, and, I didn't mind if I did not get into any of the tables, instead, was free to **float around** in the great company they invited every Saturday night, simply, as an interesting entertainer. I discovered my capability to entertain other guests with my stories, whom I never even knew before. I began to sense that this whole partying was not only a setup to please the Pataki couple's only daughter, Gabi, but that there was a great deal of their own satisfaction involved, for the parent couple themselves. The 'grand social life', so called, (for which the Hungarian Gentry was (in)famous for) we also were all planning -before the war- ourselves to live, upon entering into it at the proper age, with our family, friends and relatives.

In no time, Gabi's father (also being referred to as Papa Pataki) has kept an observing eye on me and on my involvement at their parties. At a rather special occasion he drew me aside and started asking me questions; personal questions; very, very personal questions. In a curious way he began to paste together relevant information –almost like a profile- about my family, the family's background, including the financial background, which after the confiscation of most of my father's estate and even its remnants, was shrunk considerably, almost to insignificant levels. He must have known some details already from Gabi. In those years we still had our villa on Eagle-Hill, which represented our family's single greatest (remaining) asset along with a certain 'status' in society.

Then, to offset the snoopiness of his inquiry, he finally asked what my plans were after graduation from High School. Am I planning to continue my studies for a college degree? If so, what was my chosen discipline? He never missed to ask about my brothers. Then came the bigee: he wanted me to explain to him what my father was doing for a living 'now that all his capital was lost'. There I had really nothing to hide, in fact I came on pretty proud, telling that he **is a professor** at the Earth Sciences Division of the University, and that I am, sort of, in part- time, doing work as his research assistant in the field of 'Micro-Climatology'. However, I never missed mentioning that I, myself, want to become a civil engineer. Of course, I knew from Gabi all about her father's carrier in that field.

Then came the one that I was mostly, and overwhelmingly afraid of: he wanted to know: "what really are your feelings towards my daughter?" he asked. All I could say under the pressure of the moment was: "Sir, I love her, very dearly, and very, very much". Naturally we both knew that if my plans are to materialize, I will be in no position to think seriously about marrying. Not in the near future, certainly not any time soon. What surprised me the most, was that he took all this information calmly, absolutely 'cool'.

In later years, in my freshman and sophomore years, while I was still a dedicated visitor of their home, (following the Saturday night parties), frequently returning Sunday, in mid morning to their home, so that I could attend the late morning Mass together with them. Both Gabi's parents were walking behind the two of us, as if we were already 'belonging together', as if we were: an 'item'. I liked to think of our liaison being that of 'steady' (boy friend- girl friend).

Little did I know, that I was really a decor, a useful ally, and a trustworthy cooperator in the exploration of the 'dark continent' called sex. The most important area of exploration for Gabi was: the **male's response** to a sexual overture, which she knew nothing much about in terms of first hand experience, only what her friends were feeding her in school (a private girls' school, run by nuns, strictly without any kind of meaningful sex education) and some additional bookish knowledge provided for her by the abundant medical students around. But the exploration, at least which we jointly performed, were always strictly through proper attire, never any piece of garment ever removed from where it belonged. This arrangement served also as a very important safety precaution in case we were interrupted by footsteps outside the door.

* --- * --- *

Often times I was trying to remember what was the underlying reason for our breakup, (if we can talk about a breakup at all) and never was able to put my finger on any concrete fact that was, or could have been the cause. After my dismissal from the University in my junior year, which was described, (or at least mentioned in an earlier chapter) I was looking for a meaningful, definitely technical type employment, in which I was determined to utilize my knowledge gathered during my previous 5 semesters of studies.

In my search for such kind of an employment an acquaintance of my father, actually an architect, came up with the idea that the best place to try (to find a technical kind of job for me) would be at a newly established, state owned, venture: the Geodetic and Soil Survey Bureau to which he had 'meaningful connections', or so he stated. He did take me to the Bureau, but when we got there he seemed to fumble about, walking on the exec's hallway, when all of a sudden I noticed the name of my geodesy lab-instructor at the University on one of the doors. I knocked and walked right in, told my name to the secretary and added that I was a junior in the Civil Engineering Department but got dismissed, by the new Party Boss of the U. Nevertheless, I would like to work in Geodesy.

She returned with my former lab instructor in tow, who indeed recognized me right away and eventually arranged for an 'intern type employment' which paid a lowly starting salary, but left the door open for bonuses, sometimes very, very good bonuses depending on productivity.

Naturally I was very proud of my new position, which, in the same time also lent me a reasonably substantial status in the new "worker's society". At my next visit at the Pataki home I wanted to show off now as a 'man of substance'. Unfortunately Papa Pataki was not sufficiently impressed. He started talking to me about this position of mine being, actually a diversion from my originally set career track, may be an irreversible diversion. We went into philosophical discussions. What if the communist regime prevails? Then of course there will be nothing else possible, than whatever the Party decides. The Party will determine all of sustenance, our future and us. No individual endeavor will survive outside of it. The only way we (meaning Gabi and me) would have a meaningful life was if we would go abroad.

I assured him (which one would do only to someone, whom one could trust 100 %) that my younger brother, Laci and myself, were planning already to flee from this country and live somewhere in the West. Especially so if I could not finish my studies here, 'at home'. At this time Gabi was already a senior in High School. She, somehow found our plans with my brother Laci, outlandish at best, and outrageous in it's reality. She also was well familiar with Laci, since we, (meaning all three of us) frequently attended student parties, all of them included dancing. Without a serious dance program and a high grade Disc Jockey –or even a live band- no party was considered 'classy'. The Agit-Prop division of the Party (always being represented at such occasions) had considerable headaches because of these 'bourgeois extravaganza'.

These were the times actually, when our truly intimate relationship began to loosen up. Papa Pataki was making frequent remarks that he missed me from the (anyway more and more infrequent) Saturday 'gatherings'. The Economy also began to tighten up considerably. He was given a very plausible explanation, (by Gabi or her Mother) such as that I was on 'outside service', meaning out in the country, somewhere. I always made it a practice to tell them, just like I did my parents, where and what part of the country I was dispatched. He knew very well what that meant, he did it for almost ten years by now, under various forms of communist rule. The Party's mentality was the: 'out of sight – out of mind' and, since we, the enemy class, were not around (visible) we were counted not only as being neutralized but almost as non-existent.

Then came the added complication that I met Ica; This was the girl, who was a drafts (wo)man, who quite often was stationed at the same project in the country where the government Planning Department was initiating a new Improvement, or just an Economic Investment. Of course we: the Surveyors, were the Pioneers at such projects. She was permanently stationed in the field office. This Ica was the one to whom I was engaged (who had a total sexual control over me); then later, by 1954, during my second year of (Army) service, I met the girl, (my future wife) with whom we decided to flee the country together, I finally lost contact with all of my former female friends, confidantes, companions, whatever. The revolution against the communist rule and the presence of the Red Army in 1956 put an end to everything in my **'former life'** –as I used to refer to it- and gave us a fresh start, in a true sense, for a second one.

* --- * --- *

So, I took the bus from the Castle Hill back to my parent's apartment, got in my Opel Olympia and drove down to Lagymanyos, where I knew Gabi and her parents were living. (How could I've ever forget?) I parked in the street, where there was no other car. It was 10:30 AM after all, everybody was away. The Opel had a large capital D displayed on its rear along with an 'oval' shaped license plate, which distinguished it from the domestic registered cars.

I walked right in the main floor lobby, from where the three condo unit's doors were opening. Then, learning from my previous fiasco in the morning, I took a close look at the name plate displayed on the door. The brass plate had the six (very) familiar letters engraved on it: 'Pataki'. My skin felt like ants had just invaded it from head to my ankles. I rung the bell, three very short rings, almost like in Morse-code. This was our usual signal (actually an 'S' in Morse-code) in those years, some 20-years ago. From these, Gabi always knew that it was me. I heard rushing foot steps approaching the door, then the usual little 'inset window' opened. Indoors were darker than in the lobby, so I could not readily recognize the woman inside, but quickly placed the question:

-Do the Pataki's live here, by any chance? The name plate still indicates it". I said, and just as I said the words, the woman, without much of any makeup, opened the door, almost screaming;

-Gàbor; ...Oh my dear God, ... I think I am going insane" she said, and I was beginning to get really scared that the neighbors will get alarmed, maybe there is a rapist invading their building, so I quickly, very quickly hopped inside and closed the door to forestall such an unpleasant incident. Then I gathered Gabi into my arms, hugged her, and hugged her, ... until finally she gave me a kiss, upon which I took hold of her face with both of my hands and kept placing kisses on every inch of her skin that I found. For some time we just stood like this, ... kissing, ... there seemed to be no end to this, which I didn't mind, didn't mind at all, I could have just stood there till eternity.

But eventually we both had to come up for air. She asked me: "are you ever going to come in? Where on earth have you been for the last 20 years?" Then she grabbed my hand and began to drag me inside, to the living room. I of course was now on uncharted territory, much like a sea captain who returns to a long forgotten bay, he visited many times before; but not for the last 20-years, and now he wouldn't know what sort of creatures he will encounter. And, I of course told her so. I would have told her always, everything, without withholding an iota. This was the utmost, the fantastic, the super in our relationship ever since it became so intimate. We naturally, always told each other everything. At least I was convinced that we did.

So, she asked me if I want something to drink. I said,

-Gabi, do you also come in potable, liquid form? because then that's what I want", I said, and she gave me a hug and another (long) kiss.

-Gàbor, how come you have not changed a bit? You are still the foolish, exuberant, sweeping and overwhelming boy as you have been before? Where do you find all the energy?"

-Well, Gabi, my dear … dear pal, I am still me, I still am who I was 20-years ago".

-I simply can't believe this … am I dreaming? or is this for real"? She asked.

There came another hugging session. This time we were getting closer and closer, and since we found no disturbance from outside sources, our bodies began to catch fire. I was sure and unmistakable that mine had. Gabi began to feel me as she did as a kid who didn't know then exactly, what was what, but this time she certainly knew everything. She too, did a lot of growing up. She turned to me:

-Gabor, what on earth is going on? I am so sorry, … I won't have to let you touch me if this is what you do in response", she said; "I knew all the things I did to you in those days – 20-years ago, but you dear boy, I had no idea then, what I caused in you …"

-Gabi, my dearest, … Okay, … let's cool down, this way we can never even talk, we have 20-years of catching up to do, do you realize?" and I let her out of my constant embrace. She finally asked:

-Gabor, now really tell me what can I get you to drink? we have some soda, we also have some raspberry syrup, see, … I can make you a raspberry 'spritzer', now how is that?"

-I don't really care, …you know how it was ever since the beginning?, when I told you that all I ever wanted was to be near you… "

-Okay, now really, let's talk sense, this can't go on like that, … so, … sit down and make yourself comfty, you should take your shoes off and put your feet up the sofa, now, how is that? any better? I'll be back in a sec" she said and disappeared in the kitchen. When she returned with the raspberry spritzer I began to ask questions.

We covered immense ground, our dialogue became rapid fire. Very soon each of us had a pretty clear picture of the other's present life. So I have found out that she got married to a doctor friend of Laci, who in the meantime also became a doctor and still has a pretty decent practice in a 'provincial' city. Her husband, shortly after their first baby, a girl, was born, became a brute, a womanizer. Sometimes he even brought to their home one of the drinking (female) companion of the day (or rather night) and wanted Gabi to move out to the living room couch for the night, to make room for them in the bedroom.

Gabi quickly made her move. She gathered their belongings and moved back to her parents along with 'Marchi' her daughter, who was still in her baby shoes. Papa Pataki was outraged. He wanted to take some form of revenge on his son-in-law, but under pressure from Mama and daughter could not achieve more than to have Gabi file for a divorce. They never even sued for child support (the only thing they could have won under the communist rules anyway) because this way they were in the position to deny the doctor's visiting rights. Anyway, he never really attempted to see his daughter before her 10-th birthday. Even after that any effort was halfhearted. Marchi was 13-years old at the time, and was spending the day with a girl friend of hers.

Then Gabi told me about her father's death. One evening, while watching TV, he was going to get up from the easy chair in response of his wife's petition to bring her something to drink. As he took a few steps away from the chair towards the kitchen, he fell as suddenly as if he would have been tripped by a wire. He had no heartbeat, no pulse, no sign of breathing. He was gone in an instant. So ever since then Gabi was living with her mother and daughter, three women, three separate generations each representing her own (generation), but a tight knit unit, nevertheless.

I also learned that Gabi was on vacation of a sort. Thus, she was more less free to make plans for spending our time together. She also asked about my planned schedule for the duration of my stay. I started to elaborate on the things Andrew began to put down on paper with dates. My visit to Pecs was a fully unquestionable item, for which I have put down an anticipated minimum two days. The visit to our former estate was already hanging in the balance, even though it was a mere one hour driving time away but in many respects, half a world away.

Gabi became seriously concerned about over planning my activities. She heard a few cases from friends (which she always seemed to have plenty) where the relatives visiting from abroad became totally exhausted towards the end of their visit. They constantly overtaxed their physical capabilities and instead of having a relaxed vacation they ended up bushed.

Thus I asked her about her plans for the day, before I showed up. She was planning to go to the hospital-resort's swimming pool where she worked as a physical therapist, and spend a good part of the afternoon there. She loved to sunbathe; and of course to take frequent dips in the pool. She was an excellent swimmer and loved to swim. I could tell from the magnificent tan she was wearing that she has done a fair amount of the above activities during the summer. She lifted her short skirt to reveal her tan, even on her thighs, to prove that she indeed had a **'total-body tan'**, which I vehemently doubted, just to give her a chance to prove otherwise. I wanted to have physical proof by attempting to touch her skin but she was rather alert, quickly withdrew her 'physical evidence' she was wearing, and convinced me, with several kisses, that her denying me to examine the evidence, was in **my** best interest, not lack of her love for me.

One word serves as a hundred, we were transformed into our 20-years younger selves. The main difference being that we both had all that much maturity behind us. But deep down we became kids again. She then decided that she is not going to wait for her mother to return, gathered her swimming gear, and we were on our way. By car the distance to the pool shrunk to a mere 6-minutes. It took her one sentence to convince the pool attendant to admit me, simply by introducing me to her as her 'dearest, best friend'. While she (the attendant) measured me with a single glance, asked Gabi "which one is he now? I haven't seen him around yet, is he a new one?" Gabi dismissed her by stating: "No, the oldest, the old-old oldest one, ... from America". Right away she gave me another look, which I didn't mind, so long as my (free) attendance was confirmed. As it turned out: it was, and for my entire two weeks' stay. (Actually this was already the third day. I was anxiously counting the days.)

We swam, we sunbathed, side by side, then swam again to cool down. We hugged right in the pool too, and I felt that we won't last long without putting our fires out by more substantial means. Finally I asked Gabi looking straight into her eyes, while holding her in my arms right in the water: "Are we going to become one? I mean: at all? do you think?" She was always great with 'one word questions' as I recalled. But this was supposed to be an answer to my question. This time her question was simply: "Where?"

-Oh my dear! is this the only real problem?" I rendered as my answer. We have not kept track any more which was the question and which the answer.

-Yes, yes, yes! these are the facts here in the communist paradise" she said, "I have been raking my mind about the possible places, and still have not come up with an answer" she said totally frustrated. Then I told her to get changed as fast as she possibly can and I will wait for her with the car at the entrance.

It took us little more than 10 minutes to drive 'up the hill' to my parents' place. I left the car right out on the street, (everyone's done that anyway) then just like two squirrels sneaked into the apartment in a few seconds. Then we began to shed our clothes like two experienced strippers, and hopped into the bed that I didn't even make up, (when I got out of it in the morning,) we rushed to get the fires quenched.

After the first serious attempt to extinguish the flames, and regained our breath, Gabi asked a few practical questions, like: who slept in this bed? how come it was not made-up? where are my parents now? Is there a chance that they'll be back and find us here? etc. all of which lacked any real significance as far as I was concerned. I could hardly insert my answers in between her rapid-fire questions, but I tried, and sometimes I realized that they did sink in! because Gabi eventually took command of the situation (which I always, but always treasured) meaning that now, after this provisory success of quenching the roaring flames, we now better made absolutely certain that no hidden live embers were left behind under the ashes, that sometimes, accidentally, do turn into another inferno. So, this time we better be really careful in the search for these possible fire pockets, especially that we have all the time to do it, and really should take our time to do a thorough job.

Really soon it became clear that she was the master and I was (as so many times before in those days 20-some years ago) the 'assistant'. But why would I even think of complaining about my status, when I always willingly undertook this assignment and, frankly, always vastly enjoyed it. In a sense, again, history seemed to repeat itself, but in a greatly improved way.

From this time on we found ourselves in need of quenching the flames. They were very stubborn flames. Even the temperature was on the opposite side of us. The end of July was extremely hot. We went out in the evenings too, whereas Gabi stated that they were a homey family, especially in the evenings. They did not go out much in the evenings, except for ice cream for Marchi or to the movies, sometimes, when other than soviet films were shown.

Mama Pataki (or Teri nèni, as we the youngsters used to call her) was asking me whether I have some idea about dinner tonight? She was an excellent cook, and had grown up in a fishing town some 80-miles south of Budapest on the Duna (Danube) River, which was famous for its 'special fish-soup'. She was insistent on preparing my favorite –or sometimes just 'sentimental'- dishes, the ones she remembered I liked. We were no longer 'East of Eden,' we dropped right into the middle of it.

Two days later my parents arrived from their trip of Poland. They were utterly surprised. Since my decision to take the journey was a sudden one, there was insufficient time to alert them by mail for my coming, so at the time I left from J.F.K. they were already gone on the Poland trip. The fact that I slept in my father's bed did not wink an eye, because that was the most logical thing for me to do without parental guidance. Also, Gabi was the one who keenly eliminated any possible evidence that there might have been some other activity in that bed in question, (besides my sleeping in it). This would never have occurred to me, to pay such keen attention to. But, again, this was the woman's touch.

On my way home of the second day of fire extinguishing, I did stop by Andrew's place. It was already kind of late, 9-ish in the evening. They had no idea why they have not heard from me all these two days. I mentioned that I, sort of, was catching-up with my former girlfriend's recent activities, (as I said I would) but the only one I found at home in the country was my dearest 'namesake' by the name of: Gabi, with whom I had a lot of reminiscing to do. Giving them a short background information about her; Andrew seemed to remember quite a few things, but Klari, my sister-in-law did not know about her at all. But as I was describing Gabi for her 'to familiarize herself' where to put her, she was beginning to watch me very intensely. On my way out to the foyer, where every other room was opening from, (including the bathroom) and I was heading to the bathroom, she caught up with me and gazed right into my eyes, and said: "you two then were together all this time! Right?"

I was silent for a short while, all the time trying to avoid her gaze. But she got hold of my face and repeated the previous statement, which in the same time was also a question in a statement form. Finally to put an end to this torture, I admitted that: "yes, yes, yes! ... We were eating, drinking and breathing each other all this time! Now what? What is there to do? What can I do? I am as crazy about her as I was some twenty years ago; but there is a very important difference, this time: She seem to be reciprocating my every feeling, fully, fully, fully!" I concluded for her.

-Oh, my poor darling, my poor, poor darling," she said and still held my face in her two hands. "My heart will be bleeding for you. I am sure you don't know what you got yourself into, what endless pain and suffering", she said and was beginning to struggle with tears. This was the most scary part of our encounter, out there in the foyer with all her predictions.

Next thing I knew I had to do was to turn her on my side. Where do women get all this awesome ESP? I kept asking myself. How come in a few minutes she had just about everything figured out? I knew she loved me in a way like no other relative does, maybe even more, like a relative does one member of her family, who is closest to her fancy. She felt endlessly sorry for me; that much was already clear. She must have foresaw all those enormous problems towering over me after I have to return 'home' (meaning this time our home here, in America) three thousand miles away from that 'home' which exists only as an abstraction. But after this encounter with Gabi, in a very real, renewed way.

Needless to say that soon, very, very soon, the three thousand miles distance will become an insurmountable obstruction. It will put us both into a prison, each one of us into our own separate prison. The prison walls will not be the continents, will not coincide with the boundaries of either of the two countries. Those walls will be the awareness of the fact, that neither of us are 'free'; neither of us will be able to break away from our present predicament, both of our families more less fully depending on us.

In our case, being divorced, did not equal being free. Gabi being divorced, did not mean that she could pack up and move to America, even if she could have her sustenance, her legal status - meaning: residency - adequately solved, without problems. Her mother, (Teri nèni) owned the flat outright they were living in, and received her pension from the Government, as long as she resided in Hungary. In case she would leave the country, her pension would stop for the duration of her absence. Along with that miniscule monetary benefit, her absolutely free health care benefit would also stop, which was the most substantial, by far the greatest benefit in case of an elderly person. Finally, if she decided to emigrate, leaving her condominium behind, that she would lose, since the housing authority would take over ownership of it.

During, (but mostly after) our love making sessions (which necessarily had to be shifted to Andrew's flat, since they were not home during the day) we began to discuss these colossal problems facing us, or rather our future, because that was the only thing we had ahead of us. The past was the beautiful, the idyllic, in a sense: problem-free times in both of our lives, since then we were not charged with the sustenance of our families. Now we were. We never actually fully realized that we have an enormous crisis facing us.

So far we have not even discussed anything along the fiscal aspects of this crisis. In view of the size of my income, I realized that it was quite possible for me to support both my and Gabi's family without much of any strain. I mentioned her once, that I was about to buy a property on the end of a lake, which has two buildings on the premises, one: a full three bedroom house, the other one, a sizable building suitable for my surveying offices. Both needed a fair amount of work to be done on them, but we were fully up to handle that challenge. This 'setup', however, sounded to be derogatory to Gabi and her family (of merely three persons) because of the flavor of the 'arrangement' found in Fannie Hurst's novel: "Back Street", which was also turned into three very successful movies. (I did have the book –in English, but none of the movies were available in those days on VCR).

-If you can not be with me fully, all the time, every day, then you don't really belong to me and I don't to you", Gabi declared.

-Gabi, my dearest, I would …

-Stop it!" she was almost yelling now. "How could I be your dearest? You will be leaving me here in a few more days; you will return to your family, to your wife, who by the way, failed and continues failing to make you happy. Am I right?" she asked like a prosecuting attorney would. "In one certain aspect she did fail you, and I know this for a fact" she said. We both knew what she meant. Thinking back at it, I realize that she was the first one, ever, to verbalize this.

I was crushed, close to being devastated. I was slumped in the armchair where Papa Pataki used to be sitting. I did not, could not say anything. I was simply staring in front of myself and recalled what Klari was foreshadowing in their foyer. So, she was hundred percent correct; except that the pain and suffering she predicted has caught up with me much, much sooner than even she thought it would.

I stretched my arm out towards Gabi, who now was sitting across from me on the sofa. She did not move closer to me, so I could reach her. If any moment like this would be seen on the screen, I would have thought: how over-dramatized a scene this is; There is no such a thing in reality. And yet, …I was the actor, playing that role, but I could still not recognize myself.

Next day in the morning I told my parents that I will be leaving for my in-laws, in Pècs, and return the day after. They both were several years older than my parents, and naturally had plenty of their own (health) problems associated with age. I was in a dreadfully somber mood, which my mother quickly noticed; noticed actually already last night, but made no mention of it then. In the morning she asked me how their health is serving them, but I fended off the question by stating that as far as we know there seem to be nothing special to worry about, and that I will be checking it out.

So, I drove down South, on Route 6, which I knew from my senior year in the University as a textbook example of flamboyant road design, with its ample extravagant structures, even two viaducts, to Pècs. I got to Maria's parents' place well before noon. They were unaware of me coming. Nevertheless, they were very happy to see me, to be with me. My mother-in-law asked me what would I like to have for lunch, because she was about to start preparing lunch for themselves. I tried to be the exuberant, the sweeping, the overwhelming son-in-law, the way I always was, even during the days of the uprising, (which I spent with them in Pècs) when they were depending on everything I said an did, "because I knew everything, because I was so smart". In their eyes I was. Age wise I could have been their grandchild, but my status in society made them respect my know-how, my knowledge (actually, in one word: education) and my life experience gathered in this comparatively short life-span of mine.

So, I suggested to take a ride up to the Mecsek mountain, and I will treat them for lunch in the rotating restaurant on top of the TV tower. They were never up there before. On the serpentine road climbing to the top of the 1900-ft mountain I realized that I was probably driving too fast, because Christi nèni (my mother-in-law) felt almost sick, but did not dare telling me to slow down. We had to wait for a good while, with my father-in-law (a son-of-a-gun veteran from the first world war) for her to recover herself, before we could mount the elevator to take us to the top, another good four hundred feet rise.

As it turned out at the end of this excursion, it was mostly to my benefit, not theirs, because I was never up there, it was a great novelty for me, and I hoped the same to be for them too. But I was no longer very sure about the latter. Although we did have a nice, long leisurely lunch, all the time looking around the surrounding panorama. A superb panorama. My father-in-law (Feri bacsi) began to recognize all the various districts of this city, which he introduced to me one by one. We had a gorgeous view of the Cathedral with its four towers. I was really trying hard to live up to Maria's admonition, and did my best to 'make them happy'. When later, at home, (in their home) we unpacked all the various gift items meant mostly for them, only a few small things to their relatives, they were overwhelmed. I thought I have accomplished my mission.

This ascertainment was, however, based on superficial observation. When later in the evening Feri bacsi settled down to watch TV (he was mostly interested in the news, which he constantly criticized) Mama sat down next to me and began to ask serious questions, which usually only women can ask. It was about our marriage. She wanted to know, first of all how we are getting along. Are we having fights? Disagreements? Generally: are we happy together? more exactly: are we making each other happy? Then she made it perfectly clear that she was not meaning financially. In her concept my earning was incomprehensible, she had no idea how to express that in domestic terms. She knew for sure that we are not having any financial "difficulties". What she was mostly concerned was why am I looking like (and chiefly behave like) someone who is being 'chased'? This was her exact expression. She also tried to conclude –without meaningful input from me- that I must be under severe emotional stress. I was stunned how accurately this woman, with her eight grade education (received before the first world war –in an orphanage, mind you), working hard in her entire life, was instinctively pinpointing exactly the troubles I found myself in lately.

All I could do and admit, was, that we do indeed have troubles. Our sex-life has a lot to be desired, is far from being satisfactory; and that I really do not know who exactly is to be blamed for it. She then asked if I do "have someone -on the side". I flatly denied it, which was actually, 'technically' the truth, because she meant: in our other home, in America. Nevertheless, this answer, which she sensed being the absolute truth, restored her balance considerably.

I was put up on the sofa that Maria bought from her own savings, while working for the Military Academy, where we actually met and after quite a long courtship, fell in love. I was sleeping kind of late in the morning. They did not disturb me when I was found sound asleep, by them, at 8:30 in the morning.. I had to sleep the tensions out of me, both the physical and, perhaps, more importantly: the mental ones.

I loved everything about that city, but one of the most important attraction was its climate, its 'Mediterranean' climate. Spring came early, and the fall was extended late into November. In between we had that long, semi dry summer, which was moderately hot. (I never forget startling Maria at the railway station, with pouring down a full pitcher (half liter) ice-cold beer in one swig. At noon that day the temperature was 39 degrees centigrade and I had my fully buttoned uniform on.) She was about to leave for her end of summer late vacation from the terminal.

I said a long good by to them all (Feri bacsi's younger brother, Mishka also came over to meet with us and shoot the breeze). I drove back to Budapest with one stop at the town of Paks, famous for the fish-soup I mentioned earlier, and had a taste of it the way the fishermen made it in their own restaurant. One could easily live one's entire life on this fish soup, if it's well prepared. I have no doubt that if St. Peter (or Simon Peter) had the recipe in those days, and they –the disciples -would have prepared it for Jesus, the Master, I am sure He would not have complained, but would have approved it every time, especially for its tastiness and nourishing qualities.

I did not dare stopping by Gabi's place that evening, in wake of her mood and attitude, the day before I left for Pècs. We had three more days together; on the forth, Thursday, I had to start my drive back to Trier, and Luxembourg. So, on Monday morning I took off for Szirak (a mere 50 miles) to the folks at our former estate. It was planned as a one day trip. I did stop by at her place though, before I took off, just to let her know that I am still alive, and that I wanted her to know that. Then she drew me in right from the doorway. She embraced me, which I returned with all my might, still trying to avoid crushing her.

-Gàbor, does that mean that you **really** care about me? that you want me; that you understand what it means for me to know about your whereabouts? You know? These things mean more to me than the physical things, because they all express more clearly, that you love me."

287

-Gabi, I don't quite grasp what you are trying to say, I was always convinced that the only real way a man can prove his love is to make love."

-Oh, that is certainly nothing to be overlooked, but you know? ... I guess you don't ever understand all these things, ...you are a man, after all! and I do love this man! Love him! Love him! ... you understand? "

I was at a loss. I felt so 'inadequate' compared to her. Then I told her so. Also, I started to explain something to her that I understood her total frustration the other day. And, 'understanding' is the foundation of every human interaction. That all those things I tried to come up with, in terms of solution, was: me raking my mind of what, if anything I could come up with for our future. Then she asked me if I will be gone all day?

-Yes, ... yes, look, it's already almost 9-o'clock I could be there by 10: AM or somewhat before that."

-Could I go with you?" she asked all of a sudden. "Or would that be too crazy?"

- Are you serious, my love?" I asked in total astonishment. "How long would it take for you to get ready for coming with me?" I asked.

- Is five minutes too much?" she asked, "or you want to leave sooner?" because in that case I just jump right in the car with you, ...I mean right now!" I recall mentioning earlier that Gabi was a good sport. This was just one other proof of that.

We had an unimaginable, totally out of this world, day. All of that on a whim. We drove down on Route 3 to Aszòd, and then turned north into the county of Nògràd. This was the only way I knew the entire district. I showed her the more familiar places along the road, then drove into our main caretaker's daughter's front yard and stopped the car. All too soon, there was a large-scale gathering of the neighbors, (and a bunch of other nosy people, whom I didn't even know) in the yard, from where Ann, the oldest in the Kovacs family emerged, greeted us and directed us into the 'summer house'. It was nice and cool there.

Naturally, I had to introduce Gabi, which, in a certain way presented a problem. They, - meaning the Kovacs family- knew that she was not my 'wife'. So I had to cut way ahead in order to short circuit any further speculations and told them to: "greet my best, very best childhood friend from the unforgettable, good old school days." Evidently this much sufficed. The women folks invaded Gabi with all their questions; they wanted to know everything about her. But she was playing it pretty cool. These rather simple folks could hardly outsmart her. The men did not even wink an eye. They were completely satisfied to observe what a good-looking, sporty, (and why drag on? – sexy) young woman was that with me. We were discussing the outlook of the grape-harvest, which was a paramount concern to them. August's and September's weather was the decisive element from now till harvest.

Then naturally, some cold chicken roast, fresh bread and last year's wine came to the table through Ann's efforts. As always, when some of us (former owners) showed up, and visited them, they kept filling us in of the latest happenings anywhere on the old estate. Almost like if, in a mysterious way, they would still be the caretakers of the entire place. Ann's father, the real caretaker, died a few months earlier the year in an unidentified sickness. I was convinced that it had something to do with, or at least originated in the brain. He never ever gave in, agreed, or accepted the communist's management's ideas and mentality. He was way too much a conservative for that. Something was eating him from the inside, and he slowly wilted away. I hoped he found his peace where he went. And I certainly intend to visit him there if I am allowed to.

We had a pretty good time all afternoon, talking about the war and the times when the three Szikszay-Farkas brothers each found a (temporal) sweetheart among the Kovacs sisters. Ann was the oldest and married already, with one daughter when the war started in 1941 (for Hungary it did) and our father bought the fundamentals of the estate in a greatly neglected state. Then he began to build it up, constantly improving it, reinvesting into it, till the end of the war in 1945. When the new communist regime confiscated it.

Ann brought a large plate filled with freshly baked cookies. They served really two purpose. She was sensing that I had perhaps a little more to drink than allowable for the highway. So she thought the cookies will fix things in our guts. They did so indeed. Also, they served well as a guest detender. John, her husband, in the meantime filled two half gallon jugs with the 'government approved moonshine,' meaning that taxes were duly paid on the 130-proof booze. (One of the bottles was meant for my father and we delivered it.) We finally managed to break away late afternoon.

It was almost dark by the time I dropped off Gabi at their place at Lagymanyos. Her daughter, Marcsi, was waiting for us on the short street. As I drove in front of the house she stood in front of the doorway with her fists on her hips. She recognized us immediately. The Opel Olympia with its oval license plate, gave away the identity of our car from quite a distance. There was a sort of showdown between Mama and daughter.

Marcsi gave us a very disapproving look. Her greatest complaint was that 'we have left no message to them where we went'.

Gabi turned to me:

-Gàbor, do you see now what I mean? Here 'at home' the greatest thing to show your love or even that you care about someone is that you let the person know where you are at; any time, to spare him or her the worry! Tell me this: are you coming tomorrow? that is the day before the last one, you know?" she said and was holding my face between her hands. "Because I want to give you something that I want you to take with you. It has symbolic value in reference to our situation; Okay?"

-Gabi, **my dearest**, … may I now say this word, now, … you know, … the one you forbade me to use the last time?" I asked her and was looking into her face reproachfully. "What made you say those things at our last meeting? Do you realize that these sort of things frighten me. These 'mood swings' I must say, are principally women's attributes. We, men, or rather: I, do not swing them easily. I hold steadfast onto what I have, … and that includes not only my moods but my emotions as well, that trigger them. I want to believe in them, even in desperate circumstances, …until it is utterly hopeless. Then, I guess, I am crushed."

-Gàbor, I want you to know, …you must know! that there is a fixed, very fixed point (you are a surveyor, you know what I am talking about!) and that is here with me, always! always! Whatever happens in our life, I want you never to forget this, Okay? I know it is not a heck of a lot, in this crazy world, but I want you to know and count on this! will you promise me that you will?"

-Gabi, you know I will, … I can promise that much; I shall never, ever forget it".

-And you remember this, … that if anything, anything at all, would go wrong with your affairs, your life, out there, … with your job, with your business, even with, … yes, with your family matters, there is one place on earth, this fix-point, where you can always, always return, it is nothing glamorous, you have been living in this system, you know it, … but I will be here, and you come, … whether you have anything to bring with you or not; … as long as you bring yourself."

With that we parted. But I never, ever forgot her aphorism.

The next day was packing, getting ready for the return trip. In one corner of the living room in my parents' apartment, the items I was supposed to take with me, kept on accumulating. I pleaded with them not to put anything more to what was already there, because all I can pack is one suitcase for the airplane. What am I supposed to pack the overflow into, when the only thing I have with me is a carry-on.

I had to start packing what I could, just as a trial run, to see what must be left behind. Then came the decisions, setting of priorities. A good one fifth of it had to be left at their place. We agreed that I will take those "next time". Immediately the question arose: what next time? when? Then I was trying to get by with the answer: "soon!" But mother would not buy that. So, I tried to be more specific: "maybe at Christmas, yah, let's plan for Christmas", I said, but my mother was already suspicious.

-I wonder where you've been all this time," she asked, "you were supposed to spend some 10 days with us at 'home' and we hardly saw you".

-Well, I have been visiting, … friends, … then I was down in Pècs, … for two days, and, another day I was down in Bèr and Szirak at the Kovacs's. Yah, come to think of it: you were not home, you've been in Poland, … you see," I concluded. But it sounded like hogwash. It was no good. Mother started to ask very similar questions to those my mother-in-law asked in Pècs. It was almost like an interrogation. I could only cut it short by excusing myself, that I still have to pay a farewell visit to Andrew. I could not leave without that. It was still not very late, and the days were still long.

Of course I drove to Gabi's place first. She let me right in, the doorway was not even closed, and they saw me arrive with the car in front of the house.

-I understand that you can not stay long," Gabi said. She fetched some liqueur, which served to reminisce at the old Saturday night bridge-parties, when we used to be treated to various sorts of liqueurs, that Papa Pataki brought home for weekends. I was rather in a somber mood, but Gabi constantly tried to cheer me up. When we began kissing (in the kitchen) both Marcsi and Teri nèni left us alone. There was not much left to talk about. She then reached behind her on the counter and handed me a book. It was wrapped in a festive sort of paper wrapper, there was hardly a choice in the communist run stationary chain stores: 'AFISZ'.

-Promise not to open it till you get home, … your 'other home'" she said, then kissed me, -which I promptly returned- and added: "you will write me", … yes? say yes! … now don't do this" she grabbed me, as she noticed my eyes clouding up. "Look at me, take example from me, just promise to write, that should suffice. I know how busy you are, all day long, but try to find a little time, … once a week." With that she pushed me out the door.

I had very little time left for my visit to Andrew. Klari opened the door, just like at my arrival 11 days ago. But this time sadness filled the air. She was terribly concerned about the future. My future, our future, … with Maria, with my family, … and then again, equally, about this sudden revival of our youth with Gabi. She did become my ally, though, and as it turned out later on, became my messenger and envoy to Gabi. She assured me of her loyalty all along this –sort of illicit- relationship, to which she did not grant a very bright future. Not a long term future. But the present was entirely different. The present was a truly romantic bliss. No such bliss can last very long, she reminded me, but I was not quite ready to accept it. I thought then that she was a pessimist; a 'Pechvogel' who believes in bad luck (only). I, instead, still believed in miracles. I was an idealist, then.

From that point in time the return journey was similar to a fast 'rewind' of the movie, of the journey's beginning part, all without the little detour I took in and around München. The last ten days totally freed me from those nagging memories of Erika, and transformed me into somebody not quite the same as I was before.

Chapter Fifteen
(A Midlife Crisis)

Thursday afternoon our jet landed at JFK airport only two hours after it took off from Luxembourg. We gained back our lost five hours, now flying westward. By the time I cleared customs and immigration it was nearly 6:PM. Robert Dunn was waiting for me at the gate. He greeted me and said that he and his fraternity buddy Bob Conlon wanted to pick me up and drive me home because I will surely arrive sleepy from the jet-lag. He also said that this endeavor was approved by Maria, who even gave him the key to her car, because she didn't want Robert to drive his VW Bug to New York. I couldn't believe this. But then I had no choice, they were there, they appeared like a welcoming committee and spared me the driving, which was really great benefit to me, considering the condition I was in. For some reason Loftleidir did not fly into Boston's Logan International Airport.

I asked Robert if he thinks it to be appropriate for me trying to take a nap on the back seat. He agreed with this wholeheartedly. So we stopped and turned the back seat into a reasonably comfortable bed, using all the blankets and the one pillow Maria always keeps in her car. Then they turned the radio down, and kept their conversation to a low volume. In about three hours, when I woke up, we just left Worcester. I sat up in the back seat and told them to start filling me in about the various projects. They persuaded me not to pursue this topic at this time. I asked sort of suspiciously if there were some problems. But they said I should have plenty of time to find out all about them tomorrow.

Now this was not very comforting news but I agreed with them and didn't bug them about it.

It was close to 9:00 PM. We made excellent time, (I was sure they well exceeded the speed limit wherever it was safe to do so) the traffic was sort of light in the evening on a Thursday, a weekday. When we arrived at our house I thanked them for this extraordinary gesture; That they spared me the hassle at a shuttle in New York; Then the flight with it to Boston, and then from there, finding a limo to a close suburb, like Chelmsford. Even from there I would have needed to call Maria to come and pick me up. Instead, I arrived somewhat rested, even perked up, since I managed to grab a good 2 to 2 ½ hours of sleep.

I wanted to unpack the goodies from the suitcase, but Maria ordered to leave them for now, we'll do all that tomorrow. So, I thought, what is this here? what about all this tomorrow business? No one wants to hear or tell anything about today, about now? So be it. It was late enough to go to bed and I needed to catch up on sleep, so I decided not to argue, be a good boy, and agreed to go to bed.

Next day, a Friday before the weekend, I went out to the various crews on the different projects. They seemed to be in control of things, progress was satisfactory, and the clients, the developers, were evidently satisfied with the progress. The crew members were getting ready to reorganize for a fall schedule. Some of them were planning to quit for the fall semester due to their heavy class work schedule.

One senior student was complaining to me that he had a run-in with this new professor Manner. Evidently Manner was planning to use him in a research project with which the kid wanted nothing to do. I told him that his only remedy would be to see Dr. Golding about that, and that I am not high enough on the ladder to be able to help him.

*

I received a message form the office of Attorney Jack Lorden that he would like to discuss some survey projects with me on various parcels of land that he and his siblings inherited after their father's recent death. He was named as trustee for the heirs including his mother, who was also a survivor. The task was not a tough one, the same story repeating itself, as was that, which we did for the Elbthal's. They needed to present preliminary subdivision plans for a good number of tracts that seemed ripe for a potential subdivision before it became too late for the rezoning into larger size lots was to take effect, and thus, not to loose the coverage by the grandfather's clause.

Since hardly any real surveying work (in the field) was necessary to prepare these subdivision plans, I undertook the work, counting with the help of one of the draftsman kids to put the plans into their final, presentable format after I prepared the conceptual subdivision sketch plans. Lorden was not only friendly, he was more than that. He became very outgoing, maybe this was his basic personal trait anyways, and was actually becoming my confidante. I took it easy; I did not want to bring out my own problems right away, to avoid the appearance of trying to take advantage of our newly formed alliance.

I charged him very moderate, maybe even overly friendly fees for these plans. In retrospect I think this was not quite the right thing to do, but at the time, and with an ESP that told me that I will need substantial legal aid from him in the near future, I thought this will have a beneficial effect on our renewed relationship, (ever since the trespassing case, that he was handling for me) possibly, even the establishment of a long sought friendship. I was really looking for a fellow, an attorney closer to my own age to be befriending, to whom I could be as honest as perhaps, to a doctor, or may be even a priest. I did realize early on that without such a friend (and ally) one does not get far in the business world. The recently closed Dorfman - Ariel Airmap case was a fairly good example to this statement. Fate had it that quite soon I did need such an attorney for which I chose Jack Lorden.

In a few weeks school started and Golding was becoming intolerable. He picked on everything, and seemingly not only with me, but to kind of dampen the appearance of singling me out, he did some other moves against other faculty members as well. But I saw through them although they were meant to camouflage his fury against me. Nevertheless, at the first faculty meeting in the fall semester he announced that he is fully intending to "chew my ass off" if I do not start behaving more like a team member, to pull my own weight, as he expects every member of 'his faculty' to do. After the meeting I sought an eyeball to eyeball exchange with him but he did not comply. I had no idea what, if anything, specifically he had up his sleeves against me. He made that much clear, however, that 'my time is up' and that I either shape up or ship out.

I knew he was pissed because of my previous, de facto, denial of trying to discredit Herm Shea's surveying teaching expertise, with the ultimate goal to get rid of him. I thought, which might not have readily appeared to him, that such a goal was overly unrealistic for him to achieve, but I did not verbalize these thoughts. Our personal relations had deteriorated far beyond that. Herm's credentials in New England were far superior to provide a surface for Golding's attacks. By the time he began to realize this, he switched his furor against me.

When I began to talk about these things at home Maria became withdrawn, introverted to the point of almost being unreachable. I tried to reassure her that I am still the real fighter I used to be, that I am not the quitter type, and that I am not going to take this lying down from Golding (which she all knew real well already) and I declared that: "I am going to fight this (bastard) MIT-man at his own game, whatever it takes". After such outbursts she remained mute. This was very disquieting for me.

Then disaster struck. A few days later around 3:30 in the morning I woke up to complete silence and found Maria hanging halfway out of our bed, her body seemingly lifeless. In a complete panic I called the emergency number. Then went back, to her side of the bed, and tried to lift her back up unto the bed. The ambulance arrived in a few minutes, which seemed hours. But the medics declared her being still alive, and prepared her to be taken to St. Joseph's hospital in Lowell. They wanted me to search for empty medicine bottles. They were on the radio all the time receiving instructions from the ER physician in charge. The most annoying thing in this potential tragedy was the appearance of a police officer, a real gorilla, (I estimated him to be at least 240 lb, whom I never saw on the force before) walking all around inside the house, even looking into the kids' bedrooms, waking them up at this odd hour, who didn't know what on earth was going on. Jr. became terrified of him. I was expected to tell them that their mother was taken to the hospital. (We still didn't know at the time – at least officially – that she has taken an estimated 85 sleeping pills; all the remaining ones in their bottle of 100).

I was late from school in the morning. I had to prepare our two older kids to be ready for the school-bus and had made their breakfast. Junior was only four years old, did not have to go to school (or kindergarten), and suddenly I realized that I didn't know what to do with him. So, I had to put the clothes of his choice on him, while trying to answer his nagging questions about where mama was, all the while knowing that my answers were inadequate. Suddenly I remembered our friend Teri, the young Hungarian woman in Westford (who is known to the reader already from chapter seven, the ominous party where I took Chopra along with me) and took Junior with me to her, explaining her what happened. She expressed her compassion for me, then hugged Junior and took him inside. Her own two kids were already in school.

Golding made great fuss about my tardiness, and my missed first morning class not just pounding about it, but making nasty remarks of my unacceptable 'performance'. I told him in no uncertain terms that he will soon hear from my attorney, in any case, he better just shut-up, and this much should suffice for now. A law suit, that will follow, will set him straight, for sure, at least for a while. He was dumbfounded. He simply didn't know what I was talking about. But it seemed to avert his fury away from me at least temporarily. But I did not feel giving him details about what happened. Not just yet. But I told Herm all about it.

After my second class at 11:00 AM I drove down to Ayer, to the office of Jack Lorden. This time I unloaded my problems on him. He was extremely sympathetic and promised me to write a real threatening letter to Golding as a start. He was still debating it whether he should send a copy of it to the provost to add weight to it. Then he called the hospital from his office to inquire about Maria's condition. The ER charge physician assured him that she is no longer in serious danger; that this was a clear case of attempted suicide, and that after a few days she will have to be turned over to the psychiatric ward in accordance with regulations. She was supposed to be under observation for a while as a matter of policy, until it could reasonably be ascertained that the episode will not be repeated.

Our life at home was turned into a mild chaos. I quickly learned what it takes to be a single parent. Andy and Susie were old and reliable enough to take care of their own immediate needs. For supper we mostly decided to get take-out food from any of the nearby restaurants. I simply could not find myself being sufficiently together to be able to think about cooking. I had plenty to run around, taking Junior in the morning and picking him up in the afternoon, all this over and above my regularly scheduled business involvements. In the late afternoon and sometimes in the evening I finally got the time to get to the St. Joseph Hospital –and after, a few days later - to the Lowell General's Psychiatric clinic to visit Maria, who was still pretty shook up. I also received message from the doctor in charge of the ward that he is planning a consultation with us at my earliest convenience.

My second letter to Gabi was already a week overdue and I could not find the time and energy to put it together. Also, the recent events came to us all as a shock from which I could not yet recover. I was drained. A few days later I wrote her all about this in my office. Joan came in twice that morning, saw me still writing, longhand, even asked me "Gabor, are you writing your memoirs?" I was just mumbling something to the effect that I had to write about this upsetting event to my folks in Hungary, which she noticed and did not miss to remark how sorry she was for me, for us. She knew about the recent episode already, not directly from me, possibly from Herm.

Lorden's letter arrived a couple of days later at the Institute as a missile. He did send a copy of his letter along to the Provost for greater effect. It was certainly a blast. In a couple of days almost everyone closely familiar with the situation and the persons involved, knew the latest events. This was the time when I had to quickly prepare a memorandum to the Provost, in which I described my mental anguish caused by the Department Chairman, as well as pointing out these being the immediate consequences of the deteriorated personal relations with him (and his abuse of power). In a paragraph I summarized my complaints, whereby he chose not to let me teach the subjects of my technical competence, instead assigned me other subjects which could, potentially prove my incompetence, if when adequately proven, could be ground for disciplinary action. Not without a hearing, though, in those days.

Now, that the Provost was no longer totally unfamiliar with the situation at our department, —being the result of Jack Lorden's sending a copy of Golding's letter to him—he also received my memorandum, the main goal of which was to obtain a transfer from the Civil Engineering Department to any of the ubiquitous (mini) departments in the Earth Sciences Division. I offered several expertise in these sciences, substantial enough to teach some of their courses offered in the bulletin. I went as far as suggesting an added 'Mapping Sciences Course' (or two) which I was currently most qualified to teach in the entire Institute. I mentioned my serving on the Governor's Advisory Board to revamp and upgrade the mapping situation in the Commonwealth. A copy of the memo was sent to the dean of our (engineering) college, as well as to the dean of the Pure and Applied Sciences college (the first and only academic dean of minority). I even went to see him but he did not want to get involved one way or another. Not at this point in any case. He was going to sit it out, and see what the administration wanted to decide in this case. I thought then that he was gutless, protecting his position by constantly watching 'over, above his head', towards the administration, from where anything that might jeopardize his position, could arrive.

Our Dean, (Holbrook) who was familiar at this time with the vendetta leashed on me by the chairman (later on my attorney found memoranda of secret faculty meetings forwarded to the dean, on my personal file) was attempting to keep this entire event on a low profile, almost ducking it out, but he could not stop the entire case by calming the waves, that the uproar aggravated, and do it all by himself. First, because there was the dean's answer to the provost. My memorandum compelled both of them (the deans) to answer him. Second, there was the internal news media (by which I mean the secretaries, typists, and other gossip spreading individuals) and finally: my grievance, which I filed with our local representative of the Massachusetts Teacher's Association (The Union!?). He was the only one sympathetic to my cause. The others: the deans and eventually the provost, turned down my request for transfer. I was terribly disappointed by the Provost's competence revealed by his answer to me, in which he described the 'Mapping Sciences' (which I offered to teach) calling them as 'engineering disciplines', which can not be fitted into a basically, science oriented program. These were his exact words.

*

The clinical psychiatrists tried to pinpoint the cause for Maria's suicide attempt. She did have a hysterectomy performed on her earlier that year, but they had not thought of that being substantial a cause for committing this act. They were willing to release her to come home to her family, kids, and husband, on **my signing** to take full responsibility for her future actions. I did not sign this consent because I felt such a thing would have been put on me under duress, in view of the fact that I did not have adequate time to think over the enormity of the responsibility. Maria held this against me for a long, long time. I felt she did unjustly so. I was thinking in terms of a reciprocal situation: whether she would have signed if I had to be released on her signature.

299

We had visitors. Quite a few visitors, mostly our few friends, who became aware of our predicament. Teri came to visit Maria in the hospital and told her all about Junior, for whom she was caring during the daytime. Maria honestly appreciated this show of caring by friends and Teri had conversed with Maria at great length, which was evidently much more beneficial than what any of the psychiatric underlings provided, including the head doctor in charge of the ward, had with his sermons. Kay, for instance, wanted to find answers to basic questions, such as: why would a mother want to chose departure from this life, (in more exact medical terms: exit!) with such force and determination that she could leave everything behind, including her 4-years old son. A mother must be quite desperate to get to this point.

My predicament was not an easy one either. I was on the razor's edge, both at home as well as at my job. (Not even mentioning my newly found potential love life, which, at this point was not much more than a possible escape route; Escape from all the problems here.) Everyone expected some sort of explanation from me about Maria's desperate act. All I could offer both to Kay and the doctor, was, her utter frustration with my job situation, and within that, my relation with the department chairman. It seemed quite a lot like the Akron fiasco repeating itself, which at its real time, created the first havoc in our family life. But we have successfully weathered that one. She directed her fear and anger partially towards me that had an implication such as: "that I can not get along with my fellow employees." But this was not the case. All I wanted was to be left alone, to do my things, do my best for the good of the entire Institute. As a matter of fact I could always get along very well with fellow employees. The same, by the way, could not always be said about my superiors in any of my previous jobs.

It became clear to me, while on the American continent, that I had no respect for a superior, unless he was truly 'superior' to myself in a human way and in every other respect. In the job environment I fully expected my boss (my superior) to surpass me with his knowledge (of the job and any details connected with it) otherwise I had not much respect for him. How could I have? Knowledge meant that much, just about everything, to me. I was used to the fact, exemplified in my formative years, that a superior was truly 'superior' in all these respects. My high school teachers were unsurpassed, each one in his own discipline. I was at an awe, revered not really each individually, as a human being, (because I found out early enough about human weakness, even if it involved priests, -or in this case- brothers) but held each one in awe for his knowledge in his field. My professors at the University were regarded by us students as 'superior beings' based merely on their knowledge.

The Communist Party and its representatives, the cadres, however, who were omnipotent in everyday life, but lacked knowledge or at least experience, were despised. A high Party member with his lowly six-grade education could be given (almost) infinite power by the Party (as it was often the case) but one thing the Party was unable to conway, or even confer, upon some of their highly favored members, and that was: knowledge. This became the buzzword in my vocabulary early on. I evaluated everyone on this basis as I grew up. I daresay: it became my trauma. My mother used to say: (and this was becoming her mantra) "son, what you know is truly yours, nobody can take it away from you". Thus, I became traumatized; those people with knowledge were admired, revered, those without it, were disdained, despised.

I had the definite feeling that Maria was blaming me to a considerable degree of this entire situation. How it had gotten out of hand, how it affected not only myself (the head of the household) but it trickled down onto the entire family as well. The doctor was ready to accept this as an explanation to Maria's possible cause of her action, but Kay was much more reserved. She knew our situation quite well. She visited with us numerous times. She fully appreciated the problems facing a 'first generation immigrant' like those of her own parents (that I myself was too within our family!) finding myself in the midst of all this professional (and lately, monetary) jalousie from all sides. Through her son, Robert, she learned a whole lot of these petty professional jalousies against me, which manifested itself more and more forcefully in our department, ever since Giff was forced to retire.

From Robert she also learned about my business involvements. One of these he himself was a participant in, the Geoffry Dorfman affair. She was well versed by Robert about the pressures these events have put on me. But more importantly, she sensed something, without positive feedback, -mostly by women's intuition- about our own domestic relationship or rather the difficulties involved in it.

In an earlier chapter I made mention that she played an important role in our life, 'later'. This was now the 'later', the occasion. She was a wise woman. Without being formally schooled in psychology she wanted to know the 'why'-s behind everything what happened, so that she could put the whole picture together. She questioned me about very confidential matters. (Our life in the bedroom, for instance.) A priest in a confessional could not have done a more thorough job in this regard. In a comparatively short time she found her answers that the doctors were still searching for. She questioned me about how we are coping with the daily chores at home, in Maria's absence. I tried to give her as clear a picture as I could. The two older kids were really cooperating, they did do a lot of the specific tasks I had assigned them, but most importantly they felt that their best contribution to the cause would be if they gave me a minimum amount of trouble. Junior, of course was much more dependent on adult leadership and guidance, which he was expecting to get from me under the current situation. I was trying to do my best. But I felt it soon enough that I couldn't substitute his Mama.

Then Kay was trying to find out from me if I thought it being a good idea to have Maria at home with us. I confirmed this wholeheartedly but told her the doctors seemed to be dead set against the idea of letting her come home, into the very home where, in a sense, she was trying to get away, to escape from. Then she offered to take on the role of a 'go between' with the doctors. She did exactly so. The head psychologist finally agreed to let Maria come home, at first on a trial basis. If it worked out, she may stay home for good.

*

Jack Lorden advised me not to push harder against Golding. At least not at this time, anyway, the ball is in his court, let's see how he is doing with it. He thought to be better if we let him simmer for a while in his own juice. He will most likely keep a low profile for a while and accept the facts of life; in the present case meaning, that he can not have what he wanted: (just like at the Colorado School of Mines) to have me dismissed. He better learn to live with it and try to make the best of it. Golding did ask me once, whose idea was it to have my attorney write him a threatening letter, also, how would he have been involved in Maria's suicide attempt, or accused of having been responsible for any part of it. I told him that the answer to his first question was: **my attorney**; to the second, he should seek the answer from **his own attorney**. This put the damper on him. He did not give me any trouble for a good while. The armistice seemed to be working satisfactorily.

*___ *___ *

Mr. Sherman from Gosselin Realty in Groton called me and asked me if I am still interested in the lakeshore property in Ayer, which he first showed me just before I took my momentous 'sentimental journey home'. This time he only wanted an answer whether I am still interested in it. The owner seemed to become seriously ill, (on top of that she developed depression and alcoholism) and the family, the relatives, wanted to finalize the deal.

The two relatives, who were running the garden supply store from the shop buildings fronting the road, were now getting ready to close down the entire business for good. They have already arranged to return the entire unsold inventory to the wholesalers. So that part of the shop was all cleared out. The shop buildings were all built onto the garage, to be under the same roof. This way, at the time the expansion took place, there was no need for additional building permits. The property had a 'grandfathered' commercial zoning still in effect, which made it far more valuable (for the right buyer) than what the sellers wanted to realize from the sale. Their asking price of $ 29,500.00 was quite reasonable and I had no difficulty meeting it.

The residence, a 3-bedroom single family home, was sitting on a very large lot fronting on Groton-Harvard Road and having a backyard on Fletcher Pond, with a moderate length of waterfront. Mr. Sherman informed me that I could, actually, acquire the property without any down payment, simply by blanketing the mortgage that covered the apartment house in Lowell, (This reminded me of the hidden fact that these people (meaning the Realtors) had a fairly up-to-date profile on every potential buyer.) He took me out to Ayer and showed me how it was looking like now. The shop buildings were mostly flimsy construction both in materials as well as in workmanship. Almost all of them had to be dismantled and I pointed this out to him. He told me that he knew that, but, he also pointed out in reply, that any discussion along this line is pointless since there is not a remote chance that they would be willing to come down with the price. Actually there were now several buyer candidates lined up who were told that I had priority ahead of them, (I had first refusal), they could only be considered as buyers after I refused to buy it.

The residence part was also in deplorable condition. Everything was dirty, there were a dozen trash bags accumulated in the kitchen, they have never been moved out. At least they were not even put out to the street for the collectors all this year. The wallpaper was peeling both in the living room and in the hall-way to the bedrooms. I opened the pantry, sort of accidentally, and a couple of empty whisky bottles rolled out to the kitchen floor. There were some two dozen more empty vodka and gin bottles piled up inside. That was when I saw the effects of depression at a close range. I myself started feeling depressed. Mr. Sherman told me that the lady (the owner) was not even 60 years old. I was only 45 and began to wonder: what age, had to do with this. I could not have imagined myself in this condition 15 years hence. But this is only proof-positive that we (humans) will never see the future.

All through the drive back to the real estate office I was in a somber mood and was grateful to Mr. Sherman that he did not disturb it. He didn't talk at all which would have been frivolous to my present mood. He must have sensed it, so he just duplicated my own manners, never uttered a word. I began to imagine what would it be like if Gabi maybe even her daughter, Marchi too would come to live here, and I would not be a guest but I would be living here with them. It was much more difficult to assume the responsibility of having Teri neni transplanted here, who was heavily dependant on medical attention, which she

The House, Garage & Office complex after extensive remodeling. The extra lot (with a building already on it) is at the extreme right.

earned in that society, but totally lacked in this one. Buying medical insurance for her would not be without problems either since she had not worked in this country, had been already retired, and had not acquired any kind of coverage. And, I could foresee her proudly refusing to become a burden on this, second, surrogate family of mine, if it would become to materialize. Nevertheless I was toying with the idea of having them here, the lake in the back yard, where I could take Marchi out to the lake for a row-boat ride. It definitely had a lot of romantic possibilities. But here, now we were facing harsh reality.

Back at the office we went through the paperwork with Mr. Sherman, who secured the listing, thus: this was 'his deal'. He asked me what I wanted to do with the 'entire property'. I knew what he was getting at. He was waiting for me saying what he wanted to hear: that let's just **flip it over**, and sell it to the next guy, who was willing to pay at least $ 40, 000.00 for it. Thereby he would quickly sell it again, and make a second commission. In the meantime make me about a $ 10,000.00 speedy profit. The lot was over an acre and a half, very large, considering the half-acre zoning, which prevailed in this section of town. I told him to 'lay off' for a while, I have to sort things out. There is a lot on my mind anyway. I needed more time to think about this whole thing. First I needed to see what is there. I wanted to see if anything could be done in terms of subdividing the lot into two parts. There was at least a 120' of 'no man's land' from the house to the neighbor, which in itself was suitable for a residential lot. All it needed was a subdivision plan that did not required Planning Board approval, a so called 'Form A' Plan. This could even have had a small, back-yard frontage on the Pond. The vacant lot was worth at least twelve thousand dollars.

I was also seriously considering to turn the Office Building, which was situated at the corner of the lot, that cornered on Oak Ridge Drive, into my surveying office. The only thing missing was: me living there in the residence, to be close at hand. But I was, in fact, living with my family in Chelmsford, which was a mere 25 minute drive away, but in a sense it could have been 2000 miles away, because I was not living there and the commuting time was lost time, that I could ill afford.

We had a long, warm, sunny fall that year. Nothing was really rushing me, so I took account of the manpower I had at hand and started to assemble a wrecking crew, to demolish the shop buildings out front on the road. To separate the garage from the office building, we had to cut off a section of the roof and modify it in a sort of awkward, asymmetrical

305

form. But statically this was still stable. It also provided space separating the garage (which really belonged to the residence) from the office building, which became now a new entity in its own merit. This building had an ambitious concept, which I quickly grasped. It had a tile floor. It had a foyer and a small office to the right of the entrance with a modest window looking out to the road. From the foyer opened a large office area, which was supposed to be used for the drafting tables, the computation room, and the map-storage chests. In the rear of the building there were three more rooms, one for a garage from the side (the Oak Ridge Drive side) then a center part for a kitchenette, finally, a room suitable for a full bath. The problem with these was that they were all unfinished. Not a formidable problem when one had connections to builders and their equipments. In no time we had a new concrete floor poured in the entire rear part, the bathroom finished with a sunken, custom built, bath tub (suitable for double occupancy) and a larger office, the walls of which I had covered with USGS Map sheets, instead of wall paper, showing the entire Middlesex County and part of the adjacent areas all the way to Cambridge and the western parts of Boston. Shortly I had George Wagner assemble a Kelsh –stereo plotter in this room, which not only looked very substantial in terms of 'mapping' but was awesome looking in the eyes of the prospective client beholder. A dear friend of mine, who was a professor one time at the University of Maine, was totally overwhelmed by the appearance of the instrument and its setting in this environment. He did not miss making the remark, that I was the only surveyor, whom he ever saw owning (and using) such an instrument. For me, (the real pro), however, it was clear that the days of this instrument were counted, when new computer governed, automatic plotters will be coming on line. Naturally, for some ten times the price of this analogue type instrument. Still, in the meantime, they were the leviathans of the detail mapping industry.

There were some real drawbacks. This building was not connected to the utilities of the residence. In another aspect this was a blessing in disguise, because the year 1975 and the following ones proved to be depression-years in New England. My developer clients were slowing down, cutting back in the speed of moving forward with the developments. I myself was not disaffected by this turn of the economy. But I still had no trouble meeting the mortgage payments on the various properties. They were all more-less still in the positive cash flow status anyway.

I had to write about this new situation to Gabi. I even enclosed some photographs. I did it with a heavy, almost bleeding heart, because I could foretell the impact of my letter on her. More than that: I could predict the answer to it too. Somehow all the fears and negative anticipations, which were overshadowing our relationship, were becoming realized, or more: emphasized. I wrote her that I am now definitely planning to go 'home' for Christmas. Asked her to give me some clues what would she like me to get her. As usual, she did not want anything. I had to resort to enclose another separate little note for Marchi in which I asked her for clues. So what did I get? She told me to get some cassettes from the groups called: 'Middle of the Road' and 'ABBA'. Now, this was real help, typical of coming from a teenager. And truly; while I was there, observing the material things, like utensils in the kitchen, beddings in the bedroom, everyday wear for bathroom and similar occasions, I had to conclude that these were the areas of life where everything was drabby, stereotype, nowhere a touch of elegance, not to mention luxury. This was the typical communist's mentality of caring for the people's needs. And, almost amusingly, their motto was: "Our greatest value is our people". Sure, that's why they all want to flee your cultural, ideological and economic system.

No, they were not denuded, they had 'things' to wear. They had some towels for bathroom use, though bathrobe was a luxury item. They even had some negligees for the bedroom, but the quality of each of these items was like if it came from a western flea-market. Yes, they had kitchen utensils, knives in their drawers, (I peeked in at some occasions) but the knives resembled prehistoric knives. Surly in the middle ages the Arabs had fancier Damascus knives at their disposal. In one word: as far as materialistic needs were concerned, the people were in total neglect. The communist elite, however, didn't give a damn; they had everything they needed, even appliances; from the West.

So, on the last two weekends before Christmas I visited some shopping malls, and gathered a great deal of these everyday items, also looking out for a fancier bathrobe for Gabi, a teenager set of nighties for Marchi, (as well as for her mother who got a real kick out of them) a bunch of kitchen utensils (not exactly designer quality, but still ...) for Teri neni, who I knew loved her kitchen and all the activities in it. Then started packing. I told Maria, starting back in November that I will be leaving "to my parents" for Christmas, that: no one could tell how long I will still be able to see them, etc. Somehow she was not overly suspicious, lacking details of my dalliances, which she did not know about, following my summer trip. She was sort of in a daze yet, trying to sort out what she caused with her suicide attempt in the fall for every member of her family. But when a 'stray, misdelivered letter' finally turned up by the negligence of the Postal Service, Maria opened it up driven by curiosity, (who is this writing me who never did write before) found out, if not everything, but enough to put the puzzle together. This is how my, so far secrete, parallel, second life eventually revealed itself.

On Christmas vigil Maria drove me to the airport. She was unusually calm, probably as a natural consequence of the medication she was still supposed to take. Actually, she was becoming to depend on it. I was very happy that she did not have to go to a job outside the home and that she had all the time to take care of everything the way she wanted to, **inside the home**. This was her real domain, after all. Years later an analyst speculated that perhaps this was not a desirable arrangement for her. That she would have been better off holding on to a job **outside the home**, to distract her from the home activities instead of being locked into them. But psychoanalysis was, and still is far from being an exact science. It will probably never be.

I assured her that I will be fine, also that I shall be back home after the 6-th of January. I was also planning to bring with me one of the automatic level instruments that the Hungarian Optical Works originally designed and produced and still held the international patents on. A former colleague of mine arranged for me to buy one at 'factory prices' which constituted a legalized steal, taking into account the fabulous exchange rate on hard, foreign currency at the time.

But above all, I was anxiously looking forward of holding Gabi in my arms again since last summer. I was half way out of my wits to see a solution for our future relationship, if any existed at all. I learned already that it is very hard to nurture a tight relationship from a long distance, even within the same country; never mind from another continent.

Again, by flying East and loosing six hours, I had to miss Christmas eve, arrived in Zurich's Cloten airport on the morning of Christmas day. Early afternoon on Christmas day I finally arrived at my parents' place. To everyone's surprise I announced that I had an appearance before anything else, which will take only a few hours. After that I shall be back for the evening and I don't want anyone to worry about me. I shall be fine.

Gabi was apprehensive at first. She scolded me for not answering her letter she sent me to the usual mailing address at the University. She did not want to believe me that I did not receive her letter. She told me then what that was all about; that she wanted us to disengage from this ill conceived, overly optimistic, but in fact, un-workable endeavor, because it had just far too many hurdles. Much more than Romeo and Juliet encountered and they at least were living in the same country on two adjacent estates. She had written in that (lost) letter that she had enough of my erotically charged lines. She saw no hope for us in the long run. Why did I still have to come to upset the intermittent, fragile balance, while we are still, sort of, recuperating from since last summer.

While all this lamenting took place I began to unload the gift items from the suitcase. Gabi did refuse to look at them, at first. I would have been a moron if I wouldn't sense her utter bitterness, over her helplessness. But Marchi started to sort things out. By sheer intuition she separated out her own gifts from all the others. I saw on her face an unmistakable disappointment, when she looked at the two albums by the 'Carpenters', then, tong in cheek, she asked what they were, that she did not know them, and finally: could I not have gotten hold of the 'Middle of the Road' albums? Although as bizarre as it sounded in midst of all the other gifts, somehow it came through as cute. These were the most important items as far as she was concerned. She then began sorting out the rest of the items. When she has gotten to her nighties, she ran into the bedroom (there was only one) and tried them right on, modeling them she returned to everyone's amusement and delight. It seemed to chase Gabi's somber mood away. So much so that she was trying on some of her own gift garments. The bathrobe looked magnificently luxurious on her. But somehow all these things were superficial, like a band-aid in trying to heal the real wound, (or vulnerability) deep inside her.

The winter was rigorous in all of Europe. Right in Budapest there were serious traffic difficulties due to unusually deep snow. I could hardly take care of the business part of the trip. Although I met twice with the export official at the MOM factory, the progress in the paperwork was extremely slow. I tried to figure out the reason. My brother explained that this is the regular way business was conducted in the system, mostly because of the tremendous amount of paperwork, which was designed to check and double check each step of any transaction along the way.

But Gabi gave me a hint. At one of our downtown shopping spree she told me to call up the factory's export clerk and told me to hand her the receiver once he was on the line. In a few sentences she asked him to meet us at the "Darling Espresso" (so called, a gourmet coffee-shop, a *'conditorei'*) which was really not far, sort of within walking distance from the factory grounds. When he met us in a quarter of an hour, we first treated him to the finest brandy –an East German blend- that was available in the store, and instructed him to select anything from the fine pastry display that meets his fancy. While he did so, Gabi asked me to hand her a 50-dollar bill.

Then she took over from here and as the clerk returned to our table she started to explain him that this transaction needs to be consummated in a maximum of two-three days, because I will have to leave following that. And, … if he thinks he could … possibly … complete it all by then … and deliver it to her address, … well, in that case … he would receive a 50.00 dollar bill from her as a bonus. With that she showed him the fifty dollar bill, gave him her address, where he should deliver the papers and the instrument the day after tomorrow. Gabi also reminded him that the instrument should be packaged in such a way that the customs inspector should have his stamps on the package, meaning that it was pre-cleared by customs. That way nothing has to be opened at the border crossing. It appeared that the clerk was sufficiently impressed by the bonus (which represented a goodly extra month's salary for him) all he wanted was 'something extra' to be used as a tip for the customs-clerk at the factory. To me it was crystal clear that this was one of those "truly good deals" on which everyone made out good.

At home, with my parents, things did not go as smooth as this. They had no difficulty figuring out the situation with me and Gabi. Actually Gabi came with me one day visiting my parents, which she acknowledged she owed me for the last 20-or so years. At that time (20-years ago) after a movie we watched in the afternoon, I could talk her into jump up to our villa at 'Eagle Hill' and pay an introductory visit at my parents. I wanted this real badly: to introduce her to them as my 'steady', steady, steady girl friend. But somehow, in the last minute she chickened out and the introductory visit never materialized.

This time, however, she was quite willing to come with me and visit them. Their present circumstances were by far more diminished, compared to the earlier years. But she did not mind this, perhaps even welcomed this setup, which made the entire situation look more homey for her, more acceptable. Only my father was home at the time. He was, as I think way back, always smitten with any of my (current) girl friends. To brag about his son's good taste in women he made remarks about them in certain University circles (to which I had connections too) and received feedback of what my old man said about the particular young lady I was dating. My fiancée, Ica, was perhaps the most enchanting to the old man. I would not have been wondering if he began to court her at suitable occasions (which he never missed doing anyways). Ica visited my parents frequently while I was away in the army, I think mostly to assert her claim on (and bond with) me. My old man must have sensed the same pheromones that turned his son on some thirty years after 'his time'.

He was totally charming to Gabi. In the meantime he was not insensitive to the (good) womanly values of Maria he knew about well enough, but those, under the present circumstances were sufficiently dimmed by the enormous distance not to interfere with the subject at hand, which was: Gabi. It was so clear that the old man understood the entire situation in a flash, but what he did not understand were the sheer hurdles, the total emotional background of this complex predicament we were in. In his time, that society had a lassay-fair attitude towards simultaneous relationships, (carried on by both members under the marriage umbrella) and I could tell the old man's delight in seeing this come true in his son's life as well. Almost as if time stood still ever since then, which in this upside-down world had represented a steadiness in society, in social values, that have, in any other respect not survived the cataclysms of the twentieth century.

We had such a great time. The old man fetched some of his cherished liqueurs and offered them to us, to Gabi, when he found out about both of us liking the stuff since practically our adolescence. We had an impromptu, mini party. That is, until my mom arrived home. She never met Gabi before either, but she must have had some mental images assembled as she heard more and more (obviously not from me) about this "affair" I seemed to carry on in my native land. Her moral standards were diagonally opposed to those of my father. Hers were Victorian. Very strictly Victorian. Un-hesitantly she would condemn (and most likely convict) her son for this sort of actions. She was that bigoted. In the summer she had no actual, factual knowledge of what happened with me, with us. But evidently she must have put two and two together by now.

One thing deserves recognition on her part though, that she did behave civilized. Although I felt her aversion towards the entire setting, the presence (and outgoing friendliness) of my father imposed a definite moderation on her actions. There was one thing that always came through with my mother, and that was her unwavering expression of her conviction. I found out, as an adult, that she was, generally, not well liked because of this quality. Evidently she did not care. (She could afford it.) The rest of the visit was sort of uneventful, probably because it was cut short. I want to add to her credit, that she never ever mentioned this affair any more. But I was convinced that she had discussed it at great length with Klari, her daughter-in-law.

*

I felt something simmering in Gabi. We had perhaps four to five days left of my vacation. I had accomplished all the 'officially' scheduled activities, the instrument was packed, ready to go. So I had some real relaxing time left on my hand. I was not really sure about our (more exactly: Gabi's) sexual appetite. She was not overly enticing, has not shown any eagerness that was the order of the day, everyday, in the summer. That imposed a great deal of moderation on my part as a response. I decided not to push the issue. I left all this sort of initiative to her, as always. I found out from experience that this was the only right way to go about it.

One day Gabi took me to an other branch of the hospital, also administered under the physical therapy department, to show me where she was recently transferred to. Not far from the previous place. This was a rheumatological and radiation therapy unit. There was a radium hot spring fed pool and therapy facilities connected to it. She was promoted to this position. She was in charge here. Her salary nearly doubled. She was glad and sort of proud about it.

As we went home in the afternoon no one else was at home. We began to evaluate each other's desires as we were relaxing on the sofa, listening to music. At one point she asked me if I ever had any desire to have her all this time, because if I did, I certainly didn't show it. I tried to describe my awkward feelings, that I felt like an intruder, who had no earned rights of his own, but subordinated my feelings, emotions and desires to coincide with hers. In other words, I was willing to assume my usual role as the **'assistant'**. I told her (as we always have told each other everything) that I no longer will be aggressive, which with her was totally unnecessary anyways; and at my 'other home' was out of place because it did not result in any satisfactory outcome. I was sort of spoiled by her. I always awaited (or expected, and welcomed) the initiative from the female. That brought me the only real, real, satisfaction. I accepted and supported the idea about this behavior as the most fruitful, because it was in coincidence with nature; meaning the animal kingdom. This one powerful human instinct has often been referred to by the adjective as the "animal" (instinct).

So, for the rest of my stay I practically moved in to their place as a 'fixture', a fourth member of their (doubly incomplete) family. I was no longer worried (and hurried) to rush 'home' to my parents, now that the entire circumstance burst out into the open. I have been arranged to take my lodging on the sofa at the alcove next to the (old fashioned) ceramic *'kandallo'*, which supplied the heat practically to the entire flat. I helped Gabi every morning with setting the fire in it. But I soon became the assistant again, when my role was reduced and limited to carry the fire-wood up from the basement storage. During the afternoon and evenings this was the most practical place from which to view the TV-set. There was no program broadcast in the mornings. This was communist paradise after all.

Marchi left sort of early in the morning for school, so all we had to wait for was until Teri neni also took off for the market, to catch the best selections of practically everything she wanted to buy. That too had to be done early. At later hours she would had to be contented with what was left. That was the awaited time, when Gabi took over command. And I was back in heaven, all over again. I had a slight suspicion though that she did it mostly to please me. This puzzled me quite a lot, later.

The day before my scheduled departure Teri nèni sat down with us. She started to comment on how much "they learned to like me" (the word in this place used in Hungarian is much closer to loving than to liking), and how unfortunate this whole predicament is with me having have to 'divide' my presence not only between two different places but more so because of the tremendous distance between them. Somehow I had the feeling that what she was trying to say was, that our problem would not be half as bad, had I been living with my family at home, in Hungary instead of … in the West. But most likely this was only a result of my overheated fantasy and not her unwilling suggestion of accepting that sort of solution.

The winter turned even harsher during this time. Many flights were cancelled, including mine. As a consequence I had no connection from Budapest to the major European hubs. The only way was to take the Orient Express from Budapest to Wien. From here an Austrian Airline plane was supposed to take me to Frankfurt, because there was no direct flight left to Zurich, where I was supposed to depart for Boston. The Alps were under 3+ feet of snow. On top of all this bad weather came the Arab oil embargo, which prompted additional flight cancellations. An unsuspecting passenger was put on a plane, but his itinerary was quite uncertain. Soon the waiting areas at the airports became filled with detoured, tired passengers many of them squatting on the floor, some with family, even small children.

I had to lug the instrument as a personal baggage in addition to my suitcase and carry-on, and check the tripod as a regular luggage with the Railway to Wien, where it had to be claimed, then, gotten a taxi to Schwechat Airport. That fare was so staggeringly high that I thought instantly to buy the taxi from the cabby, then charge him that fare, then turn around, and put the taxi up for sale. I might have made out better that way, financially. Maybe I could have a 'break-even' on the fare. Fortunately the Airline took the tripod and checked it in as a baggage all the way to Boston's Logan, but they did not, could not guarantee the arrival by the same airline or the same flight. It was almost like in Twilight Zone.

All the carryon-s were with me everywhere through Europe. The Austrian Airline plane had to land in Amsterdam, the only one able to receive us, at 10 PM, from where, the passengers were told by the captain, will all get to their destination next day. In the meantime, KLM will issue courtesy vouchers towards our accommodation in the City. Thus was the first time I have seen this City at night and at daylight the following day. A new snow storm kept us there for a second day. Finally two days later a KLM plane took what's left of us original passengers, over to London's Heathrow, from where we finally took off for Boston. I left that 'Old Continent' severely depressed, as probably never before.

Chapter Sixteen
(Winning small victories)

Herm Shea went on his first sabbatical leave at the end of the fall semester. He didn't even think about showing up at the School. His mail, whatever came to the Institute addressed to him, was forwarded once a week to his home in Newton, by Joan. His seclusion was perfected by this arrangement. Ever since his son, a State Representative, died (by possible suicide??) the Shea's were avoiding any publicity (and the public in general).

I had not been invited to his home so far at all, which was sort of quaint, since he was a good friend, even buddy, to Giff, who in turn, was the closest to me of all the civil engineers. But in view of the fact that I was not invited by any of my other colleagues either, this did not register as an exception. As a consequence, I did not know exactly where his home was. Therefore, I called him up and told him that I would like to talk with him. I left it up to him to select the time and the place. When he asked: "Gabe, can't we do this over the phone?" I pleaded with him: "Herm, I would really like to do this face-to-face, if you don't mind". He said he didn't mind, and instructed me how to come to his home.

The winter was really harsh, with quite a lot of snow, which was piled up high on the edges of the roads and the sidewalks. I had a hard time finding the house numbers in the curvilinear streets. Many a house numbers could not be seen from a car on the street. One had to get out of the car and peek over the snow banks to be able to see them. But I eventually did locate his house and managed to park my car in his driveway.

Herm was waiting for me. He opened the door before I could have rung the bell. He figured that I had considerable difficulties finding his place because he asked me: "Gabe, what took you so long?" I told him about the rigors of the winter, which he was well aware of, also adding that I just returned from my European trip at the middle of January adding, that it took three full days, which was only the return leg of the trip, due mostly to dozens of flight cancellations at many airports. My own, original flight was re-routed three times, due to fuel shortages and merged flights. I had to spend two nights in Amsterdam which was not even on my itinerary. KLM put us up in small downtown hotels for these nights. This was really groovy. The Saudi Arabian and Middle Eastern oil embargo made itself felt not only here but also, all over Europe.

Then he told me to sit down and let's go through on what is troubling me. "What is Golding up-to now?" he asked right off. He knew this much already, that the chairman is the main source of my troubles. I started right on telling him that he just hired a young Greek fellow, by the name of 'Nick' from Northwestern University, who has just finished his course work for his Ph.D. degree under prof. H. Carrara. (Herm evidently didn't know much of anything about that program or its director, so I told him I could fill him in anytime later if he wished me to do so. That program was not calling itself simply Advanced Surveying, or Geodesy, or Photogrammetry and Remote Sensing any more. Instead it invented for itself the new (more glamorous?) name: 'Geometronics'. The term implied that this 'new' discipline is not simply dealing with 'geometry'. It was no longer a 'Geodesy program' as Ohio State was still calling it (and was offering it for a long time now), but is something rather mysterious, something that intertwines geometry with electronics. Henceforth its name. Basically, it involved the application of computers and electronically measured distances in solving complex geometric problems in one sweep through. Truly, there were very few software solutions available at the time, meaning: automatic computer solutions, (which call only for data entry, then it proceeds from there) to any, and many, three dimensional, global geometric problems.

The emerging, and rapidly developing satellite positioning systems too demanded computer solutions. So did the automated stereo plotters. Of course, in the meantime, meaning the middle seventies, incredibly powerful and fast "supercomputers" were being developed and built. So, professor Carrara's group (mainly the graduate students) dedicated itself to generate the needed software solutions all along these lines. He had research money flowing to him from sources an insider never even heard of.

Ohio State graduates were popping up programs of similar endeavors elsewhere, at other Institutions, and to stick to the trend, they all called themselves 'Geometronics' programs. Thus the name stuck on them. As I was going to elaborate on this 'new' academic discipline for Herm's benefit I noticed a fatigue, a burnt out, and a totally 'lost interest' in his attitude. So I dropped the subject and instead continued with describing our new member: 'Nick's personality for him.

A short but husky man, well over a decade my junior, with wide, sweeping movements and energetic gestures as well as a very distinct foreign accent, Nick was difficult to be liked. This difficulty was, however, not due to the attributes just described. That originated from his nature, probably best described by the adjective 'feisty'. He managed to come across as knowing everything better than the person whom he happened to converse with. Even if his knowledge about a particular topic was clearly inferior to his opponent's, he tried to sweep him away with forceful arguments, and gestures. One thing, however, about him was absolutely sure, namely: that I did not hear a single four-letter (dirty) word from anyone on our faculty through all these years, until Nick was hired, and joined us.

-Now at least I was no longer alone in the department with a foreign accent" I told Herm. He did not make much fuss about my remark, so he just let it fly by. Although Noah Greenberg also had a slight foreign accent, but since he was not much around here anymore (he moved to Washington, DC. as I have mentioned earlier) he did not count. Both of us – with the accent - happened to share the same basic discipline: Geodesy, that included 'surveying' by American terminology, but actually extended way beyond it. Thus surveying, as taught in civil engineering schools, was merely a part of the wider, more comprehensive and extensive a subject. Nick's major area, however, was photogrammetry. Within that he selected the 'terrestrial' (as opposed to aerial) version of this science for his dissertation. His wife studied architecture, likewise at Northwestern University, where they both enjoyed living on a fairly generous Greek Government scholarship, in which the most generous part came from the NSF (National Science Foundation). Nick selected to study the possible applicability of photogrammetry to the various ancient Greek architectural remains, chiefly for reconstructive purposes and storing them in CADD databanks. Although it was not anything really 'new', since it has been done in the past, it was still, somehow acceptable as a dissertation topic at Northwestern University.

Golding was at once taken by Nick's attitude and style. He very quickly – and arbitrarily – charged Nick to be the surveying coordinator, (in Herm's absence) thereby fully ignoring me, who was on the faculty two years prior to himself being hired. Thus, he charged Nick with organizing the subject, including the selection of who, within the department will be the assistant. Any assistant had to follow the coordinator's instructions including: the selected course curriculum, the textbook, all quizzes and exams in everyone's section. The assistant always had a single section, the coordinator may had to carry two. This was the way we inherited the system from Giff.

Golding was fully intending to assign the assistant's duties to another, new faculty member, who's principal subject was water quality. But just as soon as Nick found out about my (Ohio State) background he quickly, and forcefully – in his true style – swept aside Golding's selection and told him that I! will be assisting him in the course, and that's that. Little did he know, at the time, about Golding's plans to squeeze me out of not only the surveying discipline, but of teaching at the School altogether, thereby proving to the administration that I am, actually, no longer needed at all. But Nick soon learned about it. It was during the spring convention of the ACSM in Washington, DC. which we both attended, on a shoestring budget (I was not approved for any funds to cover expenses of attending seminars or conventions ever since Giff retired) so I was usually driving my VW bus to these events and Nick joined me driving back together from Washington in my bus, when he learned all about these things. He had to cover his own expenses too. Golding somehow, did not dare (actually lacked the guts) to provide funds for Nick's expenses, in the same time deny them for mine. So, for the time being, Golding had to tolerate of me being around.

Herm, as it turned out during our conversation, knew a lot more about Golding's underhanded activities than I ever would have guessed. He told me of his partaking in one of Golding's (select) faculty meetings on which only a few, 'hand picked' members were present. These meetings had one and only one topic: 'how to get rid of me'. When Golding asked for Herm's input, he set it out for him. First, he said, the chairman is well advised not to single any member of the department, ('out of the pack'). This sort of thing may easily backfire. (I knew for certain that Herm knew of Golding's machinations at the Colorado School of Mines – from Giff.) Second: Herm advised the chairman, who also chaired these meetings, not to come up with any sort of accusations until and unless he has proof-positive of any statements he would venture to make. Third, but not least, try not to continue with these sort of meetings because they have a conspiratorial taste. Fourth, he should no longer count on his (Herm's) participation in them. This kind of put the damper on Golding's endeavors because it gave these meetings an illicit taste.

I thanked Herm for his time as well as for his psychological boost he gave me. This was very, very serious stuff. We have not talked about anything else all morning.

* --- * --- *

At the next technical session of MALSCE-s (Massachusetts Association of Land Surveyors and Civil Engineers) Mr. Feldman, the education committee chairman, approached me and wanted to talk with me. I was surprised and curious at the same time. He explained to me that the other day he met Dr. Silva, the Civil Engineering Department Head at Worcester Polytechnic Institute. During their discourse Dr. Silva mentioned that the faculty member who regularly taught an advanced (meaning in this case: Control Surveying) course in the second term of the Spring Semester was on his sabbatical leave and won't return until the fall. Also, he asked Mr. Feldman, if he could help find someone who would qualify to teach that course and would be willing (and more importantly: would have the time available) to teach it. He would consider it a great favor. Then Mr. Feldman told me that he was immediately thinking of me and has mentioned my name to Dr. Silva as being a possible candidate and decided to tell me about it at this upcoming meeting. He also thought that I should at least try to contact and talk with Dr. Silva. May be something worth while would emerge out of it as a result.

Then he gave me Dr. Silva's telephone number at the Polytech and with that he left me. I was all perked up. All of a sudden I felt being ten feet tall. What a distinction, what an honor. My spirit, which was down the dumps lately anyways, because of all the misfortunes (never mentioning the 'midlife crisis') that befell me recently, were quickly restored. I began to make plans already during my drive home from the meeting but cautioned myself not to raise my hopes too high because a lot of things could still go wrong. Just a couple of days prior to this event, I had to file my 'planned outside activities report' with Golding. This also reminded me that I still have not gotten it back from him marked: 'approved'. The plan, as usual, was not calling for anything over and above the one day per week for outside activities, which was the accepted norm for everyone. He would have been asking for trouble if he would deny that. and he knew it.

Next day I called Dr. Siva's office and made a tentative appointment with his secretary. She promised to call me back if the time would not suit Dr. Siva's schedule. By the end of the day she has still not called. On Thursdays I had no classes at Lowell Tech, so I have set the appointment for that morning. I drove down to Worcester. I meant this drive to serve as a 'dry run', to see how long would it take for me to drive down from Lowell, how do I find the best route within the City of Worcester to the Polytechnic Institute, where was parking available for visiting faculty, etc. etc. In short, this was meant to be a logistics trip. But all this would have been wasted if I would not get the appointment.

Dr Silva received me very cordially. I highlighted for him verbally what was down on paper already on my four-page resume; My schooling, my teaching experience, my practice and my published (and unpublished) articles and the one condensed textbook. He seemed very much impressed and did not miss adding, that their professor, who taught this course was probably not as well versed in the realm of control surveys, than myself. This was indeed extremely flattering. He then gave me some homework. He wanted a course outline in their own usual style, that he could readily insert into their bulletin. Otherwise, in every other respect, he expected me to handle everything about the course according to the way I saw it best fit. Evidently, by this token, he put me in 'total control' of the course. He used the term "king". I was expected, according to him, to be the "king of the class". (This was the first time I ever heard this expression during my academic carrier.) All these things were utterly unusual but came as a very welcome surprise to me. It seemed as if, suddenly I dropped into **'academic wonderland'**.

Dr. Silva then mentioned that he should find out, from the administration, about the 'remuneration' I should receive for the 7-week course, which I assured him was totally unimportant, at least, for me it was. He was puzzled by my statement, which he said he could not comprehend. They, at the Institute, were used to paying for all of their services received, not getting anything 'free'. He also reminded me that I will have to bear all sorts of expenditures in connection with teaching this course, so it would be fair for me to expect at least, getting reimbursed for them.

Then he mentioned that I should bear in mind that this is an elective course, the students get full credit for it, thus, the students will have to fill out a course evaluation form for the administration. But, since I was an 'outside faculty' this should not bother me particularly. He then wanted me to plan my three one hour lectures and two 3-hour laboratory sessions per week. The course was to start on the last week in March and end on the last week in May with one week at the end of April as the 'Midterm Break'. He then personally arranged for someone from the buildings and grounds department to show me where I should be parking on the designated days.

Before I left, he mentioned that I shall have a graduate student assisting me in every way, who should also serve as a liaison between the Institute and myself, and also in a way between myself and the students. This graduate student assistant knew practically all the students in this senior class. He was to correct and grade the lab assignments, the quiz (there was only one at midterm) and the final exam, all in accordance with usual and customary grading procedures here at the Polytechnic. This way I was not going to upset anything along this line. For this task I was about to ask Dr. Silva anyways, for some sort of assistance. But he was ahead of me by assigning this overwhelming, extravagant help personified by this very sympathetic, well natured and courteous graduate student. I was unbelievably grateful to him for this and really couldn't imagine what I'd have done without the kid. This school was definitely a cut above ours. It was a privately endowed, old, well established school. I hated my lack of good fortune, that I could not find a place for myself on a permanent faculty of such an Institution. Also not to be overlooked was my attraction I began to develop towards that 'small' city. It was actually not smaller than Lowell, but soon I liked it better.

By now it was unquestionable that I was hired. And how! It was truly unbelievable. Something so fundamentally different from the department Golding was running at Lowell Tech, or was trying to. Then came the **utter secrecy**. I could not afford now Golding, or anyone else, finding out about this extracurricular activity. Therefore, I decided that I am not going to report it as my 'regular outside activity'. I had already filed for one at the outset of the semester (which was approved by now). So now it would have needed an amended report, much more elaborate than the routine one.

Scheduling was rather difficult. The three lectures had to be scheduled on Monday-Wednesday-Friday because of the students' regular schedule. The only way this could be fitted into (and in between) my lectures was the 12 Noon to One PM time slot. My first transportation class was from 10 to 11 AM. That gave me one hour to drive to Worcester which regularly took 45 to 50 minutes. The surveying class ended at 12:50 after which I drove back to Lowell, arriving usually at 1:50, leaving a 10-minute safety gap. Not overly generous. From 2 PM to almost 3 I held my Surveying II. class, which regularly continued with the student consultation hour. It was hectic, to say the least.

On Thursdays I went down to Worcester first thing in the morning for the entire day. Between the morning and the afternoon laboratory sessions I touched base with my graduate assistant, who was absolutely indispensable. He kept me abreast of all important Institute affairs, and away from the really unimportant ones as a time saving measure. This was the time allocated for discussing quiz and exam questions, solutions to the lab problems (which had the emphasis on the coursework). It was to work like clockwork. And it actually did so, for a good while.

*

I had a tentative order on the first edition, Geodimeter model 76 digital readout distance meter marketed in our region by B. L. Makepeace, in Brookline, MA. Mr. Musto (already known to the reader) called and informed me that these instruments are now being released and ready to be shipped for those customers who made a deposit in the fall along with the (tentative) order. Since I had made a $ 1,000. deposit I had a foot in the door. The order and the deposit was made without previous knowledge of the exact sale price. Now the price of $ 6,200.00 was disclosed for the model 76, which was interchangeable with **any theodolite**. An adopter was included in this price. The dealer was to notify each customer and extend them the option either to cancel the order and refund him the deposit, or to go ahead with the purchase and have him pay the balance. In my case that amounted to $ 5,200.00.

I knew I could not afford that price. But then an ingenious idea popped into my head. The surveying class at Lowell was coordinated by Nick, so I went to see him about **renting** a Geodimeter model 76 for a two-week demonstration period to give each lab group (under my supervision) a chance for a hands-on demonstration. He was familiar with the instrument from advertisements, thus he immediately jumped for it, and wanted the demo for all the groups. He knew what a breakthrough this instrument represented in the surveying profession, mostly in field procedures. I told him that I can now arrange a model 76 for a two week period from B. L. Makepeace, Inc. who are going to charge a rental fee of $ 2,000. They will be billing Lowell Tech directly for the rental fee provided that they receive a purchase order for the $ 2,000. Nick said that it was a great idea, so go to Golding and talk to him about it. "Nick, in that case we better forget about it, you should know by now how well I get along with him" I told Nick with a distressed expression. That was all he needed. He charged into Golding's office, in his true style, and within a few minutes returned with a purchase order in his hand. He handed it to me and asked me to take care of the whole thing. I did exactly so, very gladly.

It appeared to me that if I were to repeat this performance with my class at Worcerter Poly, in the two weeks following these laboratory sessions here at Lowell, I could possibly secure a $ 4,000 dollar down payment towards the purchase of 'my instrument' merely from these rental fees. Now that was really some good idea!

My next move was to see Mr. Musto. I explained to him my scheme. Thus: I am buying the instrument for myself, but before I do, I want Makepeace, Inc. to rent it out first to Lowell Tech and after that to Worcester Polytech. The plan might loose its luster, it may even collapsed, if **I had to rent it** to these Institutions. In that case I might have had to face conflict of interest. That would mean me being left out, without getting the instrument, and Makepeace, Inc. losing the sale. But, if Makepeace would arrange the rentals (and collect the fees, on my instrument, actually, on my behalf) then all we had to do at the end, was: me paying the balance and walk away with the instrument. Mr. Musto was listening intently to my scheme. He was considering the situation, asked a few questions about particular concerns, such as insurance, while the instrument is in the students' hands, etc. his main concern was: who exactly owns the instrument while it is being rented out to the two institutions? I told him that I am no attorney, therefore I don't know the answer. But I am willing to go along with it anyway the Makepeace Co. wants me to.

So, he told me to wait there. Then I watched him entering the sacristy of Marge. There the familiar conference took place. After a long while Mr. Musto emerged from the 'Sales Temple' and as he got within earshot, he announced that "we got it, actually… Prof. Szikszay-Farkas, **you** got it". He then warned me that the only way the Company could handle it was if I owned the instrument during the rental period, consequently, I had to arrange for insurance covering it. As far as the technicality of the purchase was concerned, the only requirement was, that I pay the balance of $ 1,200. dollars up front which would make me the owner of the instrument.

But to finalize the deal I actually needed to come up with the other purchase order from the Worcester Polytechnic Institute. I promised him that I will be getting that to him as soon as it is being issued. Thus he initiated the purchase procedure's paperwork. Next day I talked to my graduate assistant. He got all excited over the possibility of having a hands-on demonstration for, and along with, the control surveying class, an opportunity he did not have last year, when he, as a senior took the course. Thus I assigned him the task of taking this up with Dr. Silva, telling him to have a purchase order issued to B. L. Makepeace, Inc. which I could take to Mr. Musto, who will reserve the instrument for us. The clockwork kept on working, precisely, according to my plan.

The following day at the laboratory courses in Worcester my graduate assistant was waiting for me with the purchase order in hand, which he handed over to me as I was getting ready to leave. I could see the excitement on his face. So we really had to start scheduling the instrument for the lab classes at both locations. We started at Lowell. The weather was not fully cooperating, it was typical New England spring, but that problem was quickly overcome by Nick's total cooperation in arranging the laboratory field sessions. This hands-on demonstration turned out to be the big event for the entire spring semester's field lab. In case one of the lab groups missed the demo due to foul weather, Nick simply rescheduled and merged it with another group the following

Tuesday so as not to miss the big event. Looking back at it, the entire demonstration was a grand success.

Golding, of course, was attempting to make the whole thing look like the sweeping success of his new, hand picked surveying instructor, the coordinator of the course. He arranged for a short appearance of his own at Nick's surveying class, praising him what a superb instructor he was, whereas Professor Szikszay-Farkas simply took the wind out of Nick's sail and enjoyed drifting along the successful demonstration of this leading edge technology. Just as he finished, Nick got up (actually jumped up true to his style) and 'corrected' the chairman's presentation of the facts. Nick shortly elaborated on the events preceding these demonstrations. He explained his class that, actually, it was Professor Szikszay-Farkas who found out about the availability of this new instrument, arranged the rental for demo purposes, negotiated the fee and so on, and so forth. Therefore it would be more correct to say that the credit for the success was all due to him. He did not miss mentioning to his class that he was quite sure that Professor Szikszay-Farkas will certainly mention the background story of this demonstration to **his class**, therefore he does not want two distinctly different stories to circulate about this event within the sophomore class which happens to be his responsible charge. By the time he finished his speech Golding quietly disappeared from the classroom. I was wondering what he must have felt like. Embarrassed? May be, probably somewhat more than that. But any dishonest person should not be surprised when he has to lye in the bed that he prepared for himself. But, Golding wasn't great with facts, any facts, and I knew it. I was not sure to what extent he realized it.

*

After we finished the two-week demonstration at Lowell and I was in the middle of packing the instrument, along with my own theodolite into my VW bus ready to take the entire gear to Worcester, Golding noticed me in the parking lot. He came over to me and asked where I am taking the equipment. I told him that the demonstration is over, actually we had a slight 'time overrun', the instrument had to be returned! With that I drove away, to Worcester! (In reality it had to be returned to me, since it belonged to me already.)

To further complicate things, a call came from my graduate assistant to our department office at lunch time, while I was on my way to Worcester. It was actually an attempted message from the kid, to let me know that they have a locker already set up to keep the instruments there for the two week demo period, which is to start the following day, on Thursday. Golding was looking for me. He now was really confused about this entire instrument affair. He was unable to figure out how I got into this and what on earth the instrument, the demo and I had to do with Worcester Polytech.

Returning from my class at Worcester about a quarter of 2 PM. Golding stopped me as I entered my office. I knew there was going to be a match of some sort, because I found out that my assistant called here and Golding answered, with whom he left a message for me. So I knew full well that Golding knows something by now, but what I didn't know was, how much he actually knew. He started out asking where I was because there was a message for me and he could not find me. Also, that he remembered that I told him I was going to "return the instrument". I then confirmed that I did that. He also wanted to know just how the Worcester Polytechnic Institute got involved in this instrument affair. I told him that was a very long story and right now I have a class starting over in Kitson Hall, so perhaps we should do this after that. As he left me he said "go to your class, but I want to see you in my office right after".

All through my lecture my attention was distracted by the upcoming face-to-face combat with Golding. The students were sensing this on me. They seemed to have a collective ESP. (If there was such a thing, psychologists would know better.) When I entered his office I knew if worse comes to worse, the only way to cut through it was, if I told him the whole story. But I immediately decided that I was not going to make it easy for him; let him drag it out of me, word by word. Well, drag it, he did!

He almost entered into a shock when we came to the part that I was actually teaching a regular credit course there. Later his shock turned to anger. He pulled out my 'outside activities report' from his drawer, which was dated at the beginning of the semester. He shoved it in front of me, told me that I will have to see the dean about this, because he will certainly report it to him. I listened to his tirade calmly, quietly. But whence he started accusing me of 'cheating on my request form', which is grossly equivalent with 'lying', I simply walked out of his office. He came after me and in the hallway shouted that he will initiate disciplinary action against me. I never even turned around.

Dean Holbrook left a message with Joan for me, to see him at my earliest availability. Since it was Thursday, the first day of Geodimeter demonstration, I spent the whole day in Worcester. Friday morning, before my first class, I reported at the dean's office, but was told that he was busy. Therefore I told his secretary that I will be at my classes from 10 AM on. Just before noon Dean Holbrook sent for me, but Joan told his secretary that I won't be back probably somewhat before 2 PM when I have a surveying class. He left word with her that he wanted to see me after that.

As I walked into his office I could see on his face how nervous he was. I made a quick mental assessment how to calm him. I tried to keep my cool so I answered his questions very matter of factly, all the time watching out not to raise my voice. He started with Golding's memorandum, requesting the initiation for disciplinary action against me. Then I asked him to "please explain me what the specific charges were, because I had to know exactly what rules I broke". We went through Golding's accusations. Number one was my missing classes. I thought that I succeeded proving the dean that I have not missed a single class or laboratory session here at Lowell, in fact I did more than my share of participation by doing the Geodimeter demonstrations for most of Nick's lab groups too.

The next real tangible, and most serious complaint in his memo was that I have undertaken teaching duties at another institution while being a full time faculty member here. He informed me that this was really serious stuff, if I hadn't known. He then wanted to know how I became a visiting professor at Worcester Polytech without anyone here knowing about it. I told him that it was really a lengthy story, but he assured me that he has the time to listen to it. So I described him how I learned about the need for substituting for a faculty member being on sabbatical leave and of the circumstances about me being asked by the MALSCE's education committee chairman to help out. He assured me that he is aware of my deteriorated personal relations with our department chairman, but still, at least I should have sent him some sort of a memorandum. At least he would have known about it, **that's all**. I told him I wasn't so sure about **that being all** and was afraid that he would disallow the entire endeavor, which would have resulted in the cancellation of the course at WPI. Then, to answer my question, he said he did realize that this activity did not, in fact, interfere with my teaching duties here. Therefore he thinks that a disciplinary action would be unwarranted, perhaps more: it could easily be left without any positive proof of the charges, thus having the appearance of harassment.

Then he softened his tone. He asked me to send him my explanation in a detailed memo as my answer to Golding's so that they could be kept on his file. Then he asked more practical (may be even: more human) questions, like: why have I undertaken this extra, very substantial load. I told him: purely because of my love for the subject matter, love for my profession in general, which was good to me, unlike I was handled here at our Institute. He also wanted to know how much money was I getting for handling this course. I responded that I thought this was a sensitive and definitely a personal question. He then softened a little further by stating that by this question he was attempting to evaluate whether I was doing it for the money, or, for perhaps some other consideration. When I told him that I did not know just yet exactly how much, because it is still being kicked around at their administration, he became flabbergasted. "Would you have done it without getting paid at all?" he asked incredulously. I confirmed that I certainly would have, and more: I would consider to do it in the future as well, merely as a service to the profession. After all, this was how it started, I did not go after this assignment (which I really did not know about) it was the profession asking me to contribute my time, knowledge and effort. And, as the example proved, I responded positively. Finally I mentioned that I also arranged the same demonstration of this new instrument for the class at WPI right after ours here was concluded, just so that those students will not be shortchanged. He mellowed considerably by now.

I then began elaborating about the conditions at Worcester Polytech. I started out telling him how I was treated: I had a designated parking place in the faculty lot; had a graduate assistant exclusively for myself, assigned solely to this course; how everything was geared towards smoothly working together with the students, for the students.

And last, but not least, the student body itself. Their courteous manners, respectful behavior was a far cry from these students here, which were getting worse year after year. I admitted though that there was very little opportunity for faculty interaction due only to my inability to have enough time to spend there with them. At one particular day early May there were no classes at all in the entire Institute, which I was unaware of. Everyone was at leisure, walking about the grand common, where students displayed their artistic talents and endeavors, played music, faculty was fooling with students and vice versa. It resembled a great big carnival; They called it 'Spree Day'. It was an unforgettable experience for me. Holbrook was listening intently for everything I said. Our meeting lasted just over an hour. At the outset, I did not anticipate nearly as much time as it actually took. My memorandum to the dean is enclosed within at the end of this chapter..

There were no follow up events after this. The case seemed to become closed, quietly, all by itself. Closing of the semester was just over, in a couple of weeks away.

* --- * --- *

My field crews really began to appreciate the new digital readout distance meter. In hindsight, by today's standards it was a bulky instrument, after all, it was aptly being called 'The Magic Black Box'. Although from the outside it was clad in the familiar "Geodimeter orange" color (a bright orange-red fluorescent color), only its trim was black. It was a second-generation instrument. That first edition model 76 had a ruby-laser type modulated carrier wave. A small red dot (smaller than a dime) indicated where the beam hit an object, thus it was a stupendous help in aiming to a target. The red dot (actually the reflected laser beam) was well visible from miles, which was to show that it was indeed a powerful laser. Its range well exceeded 6-miles with a double prism, but such lengths seldom appeared in an average surveyor's practice even when he was called for a lot of control surveys to perform.

On top of being much larger than a theodolite, it was also cumbersome to work with. The method of measurement was the culprit. The theodolite, after completing the observation of all the directions, had to be lifted out of its tribrach, then the 'magic box inserted into its place via a special adopter which had to be fitted to the particular type theodolite in conjunction with which it was being used. After this changeover, all distances had to be measured to all the points (targets) to which the directions were previously measured. This required the target prism to be held at every point once more. The helper had to visit every point twice.

Still, in spite of the drawbacks enumerated above the model 76 was considered a breakthrough in the practice, since it eliminated the need (and use) for the steel tape and the tedious taping process, and the reduction computations. Also, the laser beam of this instrument shot through traffic easily any time a survey had to be performed along (or across) roads and highways while traffic was uninterrupted. It easily measured through and above obstructions such as a river or a ravine. All it required was a small opening to be cleared for the beam to shoot through. Thus, it was far superior and a real time saver in wooded environment as well. Very little clearing was needed. All in all it revolutionized the control survey practice. And this was only a second generation instrument. The third generation was already on the drawing board.

------*

In the interim Jack Lorden needed us to come up with a 'potential development plan' for his gravel pit. He entered a lawsuit against the Town of Pepperell, which intended to exercise an 'Eminent Domain' land taking, right in the middle of a large tract of land upon which the gravel removal operation was located. It was quite obvious that the Town wanted to cease the gravel operation, which was operated under a permit valid for another seven years. Because the taking (a mere 6.5 acres) was meant to be used for a well field and pumping station, (clearly a public need) to boost the Town's water supply's output, seemed the perfect means to achieve this goal. At the time the water operation was to begin, a mandatory 1400 feet radius wellhead protection zone was to be enforced, within which no housing development, as well as other restricted use, might take place. The enforcement of this zone ruined the possible developments for some 45-50 new houses.

A comprehensive 'potential' development plan was ordered by the most prestigious (140-years old) Boston law firm, which represented the Lordens. This was a very unusual assignment. It called for a development plan that reflected on what 'could have been done' on the site, before any of the land taking. The designer's frame of mind was constantly burdened by the knowledge that this development will never be realized. It will actually never happen, but still refrain from trying to show unrealistic density of new building lots merely for the sake of increasing their number. Its hole purpose was to substantiate collateral damage caused by the 6.5 acre taking. Perhaps the town elders hoped all along to get away with a mere $12,000. compensation for the 6.5 acre actual taking. Needless to say that the actual total damage, on final count, was more in the vicinity of $ 700,000. We did pretty well on that job. And, of course, so did the Lordens and their attorneys.

Again the case was eventually settled 'out of court' which became the buzzword in the litigation practice in the Commonwealth. Jack's attorney included in the settlement that the gravel excavation would continue until all the gravel, for which the original permit was issued, will get excavated. The limits of the excavation was to be marked on a plan and inspected by the Town, from time to time. Jack then hired me to continue monitoring the amount of gravel excavated from the pit on a monthly basis. This arrangement generated a continuous monthly income for my firm, and obviously, for Lorden too. We made a monthly survey of the excavation area to determine the volume of gravel the operator excavated. Thereby we were keeping an eye on the volume of gravel, making sure that he paid for every cubic yard he took from the pit. To summarize the situation: everyone got his fair deal.

*

Words get around fast in small towns, maybe even faster in New England. Soon I was notified by one of Lorden's acquaintance, perhaps also a client, that he has found a special situation for me in the form of a small, four-unit apartment house that is now available for sale in the rural, bucolic town of Pepperell.. When he called me he added that I would certainly be interested in this 'beauty'. He was a Realtor and very well known all around in the area. He took me to the place without delay. The apartment house was a very handsome, well built building, a mere few years old, sitting on a 1.5-acre nearly level lot fronting on a secondary town road close to the center of town. It had generous parking alongside of the building. The rest of the lot area was covered with luscious grass, perhaps too luscious, because the soil was rich, farmland soil, from which the surrounding lots were cut out by this new subdivision.

The handsome 4-plex House in Pepperell.

It was hard to find anything 'wrong' with the building. I fell in love with the place faster than with a beautiful woman, and that was really saying a lot. It was the typical love at first sight. The realtor was utterly contented almost like a marriage broker had been after a successful introduction. I asked him: "what really is wrong with the building Mr. Shuttack?" He could not find the answer. It was so unbelievable that it was becoming suspicious. I asked why is it for sale then? The saga thus unfolded: The owner was ready to retire, he wanted to move to Florida and just has to unload this project along with his others. So, he soon asked me if I liked the place. "Are you teasing me Mr. Shuttack?" I asked him. "So, … how much?"

The first real problem with the building soon became evident. He quoted the price as fifty thousand dollars. That prompted my remark as "that is then the real problem with this building". That was 12,500 dollars per unit, which was almost outrageous given that it was in a rural town. But he tried to convince me that it is becoming sort of a trend, to move out of the over-crowded city and move into more rural towns, with a more laid-back lifestyle. He assured me that there would be no extensive vacancies, people love this place. I told him that I can not afford that price. He suggested to hold on, because he wants to 'work on the deal'. Well, work on it, he did. The deal went back and forth for a good while until we settled for $ 46,500. dollars, being the net purchase price. Everybody compromised on the monies to be made on the deal; the owner reduced his price a small amount, the Realtor reduced his commission, the 'finder' reduced his finder's fee, until the deal could be consummated.

I came to know one of the tenants, an accountant, who was at home quite often when I visited the place to collect the rents, whereas the others were hardly ever home. He noticed my frustration and at one of these occasions offered to help me with the task. He said he worked out of his home and did freelance accounting for his numerous clients. Evidently he was a bachelor, (I never saw a woman's touch at his place) and lived in the smallest unit, which was the only one smaller than the others, due to the utilities taking up some room from the floor plan. He offered to act as my resident manager in case the need would so dictate. This brought into my mind the situation with the apartment house on Christian Hill in Lowell.

But here very seldom was a need for 'managing' anything, except to collect the rents. He did not want any compensation for this service. All he was looking for, and he was not shy stating so, was, that I should not raise his rent. I thought that he was under the assumption that the rents will be raised automatically following a new ownership. But since I did not intend to raise the rents I happily agreed, which brought the situation even more into resemblance with the Lowell house.

At one occasion in winter, when the snow had to be plowed from the parking area numerous times, he kept paying the contractor for it (with the checks I left with him) he gave me a lecture on how to turn this place into a **positive cash flow** venture. He seemed to, amazingly, have all the relevant figures at his fingertip (he was an accountant, after all), which clearly showed me that the rents were behind times. Since the place was located in a rural area, it did not appear to me that I should raise the rents. I was convinced that they were up to norm. After some long discussions he took over the entire operation and in a sense, I became one of his clients. But it seemed to work out real well.

* --- * --- *

Arthur Elbthal called me and apologized that he still did not pay my fee for his plan. As an excuse he referred to his problem, namely: having serious financial difficulties. He said he would like to meet with me to discuss some possible solutions to this problem. I explained him that I did not consider myself to be the right person for solving his problems. I could only offer him help in this regard if they had to do with engineering. I also reminded him about our verbal agreement, which I was fully intending to keep, meaning that no further work will be done on his projects until the completed work is paid for. This agreement was actually very generous on my part, since I did not collect a retainer fee from him. But, I told him, in view of his paying habits I shall do so in the future.

Next thing I knew was that he sent me a check. I called him to acknowledge it and asked which of his Pepperell land should be the next priority. He named the one on Elliott Street and added that he would still like to meet with me. I told him: "Arthur, you know where I live, right?" Then we agreed to meet on the following Saturday. He did show up in the morning but I received a notice from the bank on the day before, on Friday that his check did not clear. When he arrived, and we went through Boganch's routine rage of welcoming Arthur, I invited him inside the house. Before anything else I asked him if he brought $ 750. cash with him to buy his check back from me, because if he did not, then he must do so before we could discuss any further business. He then assured me that he had the cash with him. So, I told him to sit down. He did. Very elaborately he pulled out his pocketbook, then one by one counted out the 15 fifty dollar bills. While he did so it seemed that he made friends which each bill from whom he now had a tough time parting. Altogether it looked as though he did come prepared. I regarded this as a good sign, which provided the basis for further discussion.

Arthur showed me the next project. He rolled out the plans he brought with him in addition to the one he left with me last time.. This was a 44-acre parcel located well outside the center of town, referred to by Realtors as being in the 'sticks'. He wanted me to do a preliminary subdivision plan for 35 lots, a minimum of one acre each. Then he pulled out the carrot dangling it in my face. He repeated saying that he had cash-flow difficulties and that he heard from "reliable sources" that I am receptive to 'swap deals' if they appear attractive to me. He stopped here, but I told him to go on, I am all ears, which brought a wide smile on his face. He assured me that he has not heard this expression for some time.

So, he began to elaborate on his proposal. If I would come up with a subdivision plan that would maximize the number of lots then he would split the lots that were over and above 35 with me fifty-fifty. He worked out an example: If my subdivision would have 37 lots I would be getting one lot deeded to me, if there were 39 lots, then I would be getting two lots, and so on. All this in lieu of me billing him for the work, sort of in exchange for it.

I told Arthur right off the bat, that this is something I would have to look into further; First, we are looking at paper, not the land, second, we don't even know exactly how many acres are contained in the parcel, which renders his proposal highly speculative, almost a dream, without at least a perimeter survey. The fee for something like that would be about 7,000 dollars. Now, if he would hire me to do that survey first, then both of us would have a much more realistic base to judge just what could be done with the land. Consequently, we could then work out a swap-deal much more realistic, much less risky for either of us, thus more advantageous for the both of us. Without this it would be much like a cat-in-the-bag sort of a deal. This way (without the survey) none of us would be able to guess what either one of us could get out of it. I told him I was sure that none of us wanted to get burned. In any case the perimeter survey was the entry ticket to do a subdivision.

He agreed to this in principle. The only thing bothering him was that he did not have the $ 7,000.00 to come up with, to pay for the survey. He reminded me that he informed me about his cash problems. So I proposed a different approach.

-Arthur, let **me** assume the cost of the survey. Then, since I am taking the gamble, I will take the first 3 lots for the perimeter survey. After that, the next 30 lots are yours. How does that sound?"

-Interesting," he admitted. "That means I pay for the work with land, is that it?" he asked, and I detected a mischievous smile on his face.

-Not really, Arthur!" I told him, "at that point you have not paid anything, because the subdivision is still up in the air at that point, and you have nothing to pay with. You can not pay with lots at that time, because you don't have them; Are you with me?"

-That's true" he said, "but I could deed any lots to you after the approval of the subdivision. Then I guarantee that you will be the first one to get the three lots."

-No Arthur, first, because your guarantee, verbal guarantee, is not an acceptable basis for us doing business; second, because you will not be in the position to deed any lots until the **final subdivision** goes on record, but we both know that will need the preparation of a final subdivision plan, which was not even part of this swap-deal."

This was the final stumbling block. I saw through him that he was shooting for me having to prepare the final plans too, in addition to the preliminary one, as the whole package. This was something totally different from where we started our bargaining. Clearly this was a get something for nothing proposition. Something going a step too far. I told Arthur, that we do not seem to have a meeting of the minds without which there can be no agreement. I suggested him that maybe his best bet would be to approach some other engineering firm. That would be definitely fair to him. With that I raised myself from my seat and waited for a while, but Arthur was still reluctant to get up from his chair. The situation became really awkward. He seemed to believe himself still being in the superior bargaining position, - without any cash input. To put an end to the situation I told him:

-Arthur, please come back when you have a more realistic, and let me add, more fair deal to propose to me. Also make no mistake and note that I am still listening. I can assure you, by the way, that your source of information was indeed reliable. I am interested in the swap-deals". I was still standing.

-Gabor, please sit down, and let us go back to your proposal in which I will be paying for the perimeter survey, … you know, … the one that costs 7,000 dollars."

-Arthur, I was under the impression that you didn't want that because of your having problems … like you said, … you know, lack of funds"…

-I can still, always raise some cash," he said, and was staring at me; … "Gabor, … I am still not quite in the poorhouse" he said mildly apprehensive.

-Arthur, believe me, I am genuinely glad to hear that. The impression you raised in me about your financial circumstances was giving me angst. Also, while we are at it, I want to remind you to the mantra: a deal, any deal, is a good deal only if, it is good for everybody involved in it."

-Gabor, of course I know the mantra, … you are too young to teach an old man that. So, … if I choose that last alternative, … if I pay for the survey, … how much of the 7,000 do you want as down payment?"

-Let's say, … 3,500 dollars would get me going" I said.

-Gabor, don't you think that is a little too much" and was looking at me as a teacher would look at one of his pupils, who did not give him the right answer.

-In that case, Arthur, I suggest you go back to Geoffry Dorfman, ... remember? He was demanding only a two thousand dollar retainer on your Tyler Road job, and even that only because I told him to do so. Also, if this is your idea of carving out a 'good deal' please save this to the Dorfman type guys."

-Gabor, I am shocked of your tough bargaining."

-Well Arthur, it seems to me that you want your cake and eat it too. This never works, not with me. Have you forgotten the mantra already? All I can say is that you should come back when you are ready to do business."

-Gabor, ... are you throwing me out?" he asked, while still sitting.

- No Arthur, I am just trying to remind you that you are taking up a lot of my time, ... productive time, and you are not ready to do business, ... honest business. What do you hope the outcome of such bargaining would bring us?"

-Okay then! If I get you the $ 3,500 retainer will you go ahead with the perimeter survey right away?"

-Sure, I don't have the habit of going back on my word, you must know that by now, right? ... otherwise you were not here dickering with me".

He then pulled out his pocket book again, got out his check book, and made out a check for 3,500 dollars. As he was handing me the check he asked again: will you now go ahead with the perimeter survey? I assured him that I will. With that he left.

I started to do some preliminary work on his project. Made an enlargement of the USGS map of the area, then I prepared an equivalent scale map of the town tax map, superimposed the two and, ... to my astonishment found an approximately 6-7-acre piece of wetland falling right on one side of the parcel. It was sort of a trapped drainage. This came to me as a mild shock. I began to wonder if Arthur knew about this already. If the site can not utilize this wetland, even to fulfill lot-area requirements, we are essentially dealing with a parcel having some 36 acres usable area for lots, roads, cul-de-sacs, drainage and other easements. hardly enough for 30 one-acre lots. Nothing would be left over for us 'to split'. What a scheme? and I almost walked right into its trap.

All this took some four to five hours of office work of my time, but it turned out to be invaluably well spent time. I had a much clearer picture of what I would have gotten myself into. But still, first things first: I was waiting for Arthur's check to clear. In the meantime I set the project aside and put it in a 'dormant projects' drawer. It never emerged from that drawer, never woke up.

* --- * --- *

Summer soon drew close to an end and school started in early September, as it always did. I loved these September school starts. They represented something of a renewal, may be even: renaissance, which may sound rather bombastic, but the expression is not entirely out of place.

Golding handed out the new teaching assignments for the coming semester. I was totally surprised, almost flabbergasted when I noticed that I will be the coordinator for the surveying instruction. All of it. I got more surprised when I learned that I will be such all by myself. This meant that I had no assistant at all in the course. I was to handle all three sessions of classes. The total number of enrollees were 102. The only obvious help assigned was that for the field exercises consisting of three faculty members. For a good while I could not understand what has happened and how this came about. Later it dawned on me that perhaps Dean Holbrook had a talk with Golding after my meeting with him and the memo that followed it.

My first move was to revamp the course, starting with the course description and to assign a new textbook. Time was very tight but I managed to have the Campus Bookstore 'special rush order' 100 copies to have them in by the time classes started. Fortunately the publisher gladly complied. As it turned out a bit later, this started the entire course on the wrong foot. As the students picked up the book, peered into it, they began flooding Golding's office up in arms. They complained that this is not the 'right' book. How come all of a sudden they have to start learning different stuff than their predecessors in the very same course? At the beginning Golding sent them to me, told them they have to talk with me about it. But that didn't work. Their attitude (and goal) became clearer when a small group got organized and '**demanded**' that they are **entitled** to the same education as the previous classes. (No one ever found out who's idea that was.) Finally Golding had enough, put his foot down and told the rebels that times change, science does not stand still either, so get with it and better stop whining. This brought about a temporary armistice.

To my utter surprise I noticed early on, as I read the class lists, that Pat Sinclair, (Jack Sinclair's daughter) whom the reader have met in earlier chapters was enrolled in one class. I was under the firm impression that (based on positive information) that she attended the American University in Washington, DC. and majored in Humanities. Early in the semester, after one class, I stopped her and asked for some clarification in this regard. More specifically, I wished to know if she has, in fact, changed majors. She informed me that she has. I was curious why she did such a switch. Did she really want to be a civil engineer? She told me that her father had enough of her taking all sorts of courses, semester after semester at American University, without the real prospect of receiving a degree for a marketable skill. So she made up her mind, moved back home and enrolled in the program here. Her brother was already a junior in civil engineering. Evidently she knew – or got convinced - that there was a future for women in this profession. It showed that she grew up in an engineering environment. Also, she took advantage of qualifying for quite a lot of freshman and even elective courses such as Mathematics, Physics, English, Biology, etc. Thus, her class standing was that of 'sophomore'.

This was the first surveying course in which three girls were enrolled. They were like swallows announcing an early summer. In any previous civil engineering classes there were no coeds enrolled, except one in the senior class in my first year here at the Institute and she left after graduation in the spring of 1970. I actually met her only once in the winter at a hockey game in the gymnasium, where she was a spectator of the home game played at this occasion, and I was assigned as the faculty advisor in charge of the event. She was the one who greeted me somewhat bashfully and began talking to me, since she knew me being the 'new' professor of our department. During our conversation as it turned out, her family descended from Bergen County, New Jersey and had mixed Hungarian-Polish ancestry, she made quick headway towards my liking her. After her graduation, however, as I recall, there was no continuation of this trend. No coeds were enrolled until the fall of 1974.

Pat seemed to develop a closer friendship with an out of state student (from New Jersey of all places) who was the embodiment of the rebellious, hippy student. They seemed to form the core of a small group of students who used to go over every single lecture and had a series of questions assembled with which they started the consecutive lecture. They 'demanded' explanations. Their questions, and of course, the explanations robbed considerable time away from the lecture at hand and after a couple of weeks this class began to fall behind the normal progression of the scheduled course material. I had no other choice than to announce to the class that they should come with these time consuming questions to the consultation hours, or organize an extra lecture hour, which I will be glad to hold for their benefit. But we must catch up with the other two class sessions.

Soon I began to suspect that assigning this huge class to handle by myself, was ominously fitting into Golding's plan to cause it to result in a failure of some sort. It was unprecedented for a coordinator to become the sole instructor of a class this size. But that may well not have been the case. It could have been meant to be a test of myself making or breaking the upgrading the surveying instruction altogether.

I was determined to pass that test if that's what it was meant to be. The introduction of the chapter on **general error theory** and its application within the surveying discipline as well as a **chapter on adjustment computation** was really my intention to bring the course up to a comparative equivalency with the surveying offered at a number of other universities. Evidently this class was not quite ready to fall into line. The rebels were establishing themselves as constant 'obstructionists'. They also began to boycott the student consultation hours, which deemed to be an unsatisfactory way of handling the difficulties they had with the course.

After a short while, I found out, that the students began to pay increasingly frequent visits to the dean of students as the ultimate remedy to their problem. The dean was more than willing to provide a shoulder for their spokesman to cry on. We were approaching the first midterm exam, thus, his proposition to the students was to wait for the outcome of same. Then it happened. The results were so crucially polarized than perhaps never before. They clearly showed that some of the students understood the basics, were able to answer most of the questions, thus, achieved fairly good results, the rest of them, however, failed miserably. Some boycotted the exam by handing in a blank sheet, with only their name on it. They were the majority. The other two group's results resembled those of the most rebellious one but, by far not to that extent.

The class was grossly overreacting. They organized a massive withdrawal from the class. They approached the department chairman with their petition forms to 'drop the course'. The situation became overheated, Golding felt himself to be put on the spot. The administration was waiting for him to produce a solution. He met with the academic dean: Holbrook, who in turn had several meetings with the dean of students. He soon pointed a finger to the professor (always the professor, never his 'beloved students') and came up with a tentative proposal: have the students continue and finish the course disregarding the grades they are going to earn, just grant them passing grades. I objected, this time, still very mildly, pointing out: that would constitute a gross interference of his in academic matters, which happens to be against the basic principles laid down in the faculty manual. The dean of students also implied that this 'disaster' has a lot to do with the 'professor's incompetence'. (Who was he to evaluate this, anyway?) Once the decision was reached by the deans I had to defend my integrity and I told them that I will do so. They could not guess, at the time, what and how I was planning to do that.

After the second midterm exam the blame was clearly put on me for the fiasco. Thus, I decided to see the elected Chairman of the Faculty: Brendan Flemming, a professor at the Mathematics Department. He at that time was also the elected mayor of the City of Lowell and, as such had considerable political pull. I knew him better (through some of my closer contact with other members of that department) than he knew me. As I explained him some of the backgrounds of this unfortunate event I had the definite feeling that he sympathized with me. He suggested that he will package this into one main issue, which was: 'academic freedom'. He wanted to let this become a crossroad to the recent trend of the gross erosion of this last fortress of the faculty. He described the trend as: "paving the road for the students, catering for any and all requests which began to morph themselves into demands". Then he instructed me to file with him a request for an inquiry into the propriety of my actions, including the possibility of disciplinary action against me, … if warranted. I was seeking a clear break.

Mayor (and professor) Flemming knew his ways – and byways - in politics. He called me into his office a few days later to, officially, announce me his decision. He said he was going to appoint a three-member committee, everyone a full, tenured professor and all three of them from **other than the engineering college.** With this move he was to put a damper on any and all actions that would interfere with both the academic standards, academic work, and disallow administrative overreach until the committee would render its report.

The committee went to work in the early part of November. It decided to do a very thorough job. This was clearly no longer "Mein Kampf" alone anymore. This was the fight of the entire faculty. The committee read all the student's complains and after doing so, they also reserved a full morning to hear me out. They went through on all the points one by one and noted my reaction to each and wanted to hear my remarks and conduct during the course. They allowed my comments in connection with, actually, any course I would care to make not only this one at hand. They also spent considerable time with Dean Kirk's report of the events, which were, in some cases vitriolic. He described in his report an 'incident' in the class, stating that "the Hungarian professor threw out a (particular) student from the class room" claiming that he interrupted the lecture and for physically threatening him at the instructor's desk. I explained them, to their amusement, that this student was on the athletic team, was over 6 foot 4 inches tall, weighed at least 230 lbs, whom I was clearly in no shape to be able to 'throw' out. But I admitted that I sent him to the department chairman for disciplining and have stopped the lecture until he complied with my order. Thus the lecture was interrupted for some 10 to 15 minutes, which seemed like ending in a stalemate. The student was yelling and (finger wagging) that "he has a 'right' to be at the classroom, that he paid for his diploma, (notice, he did not use the word: education) and I better see to it that he gets it because that is my job for which the Institute hired me". Against such attitude I refused to yield. Finally the rest of the students themselves intervened. They, overpowering him, persuaded him to leave the classroom. I never ever found out whether he reported to Golding or not. By then this was a minor issue.

The rest of the time the committee interviewed a great number of students. Some known by their name, some others by random selection, to cross examine their stories. It was early December, close to the end of the term. Everyone was anxiously waiting to learn the committee's findings. Probably most impatient was Dean Holbrook, which I concluded from his unusual actions. He visited every one of my morning classes, did not take notes, his mere presence was sufficient to forestall any disorder. By the time the committee's report was imminent to be released, he took the podium (after ceremoniously asking my permission) and rendered a short speech in which he explained to the class how the Chairman of the Faculty appointed the committee. That I initiated this action, in a sense 'against myself' to, sort of clear the air, and put an end, one way or another to this unfortunate situation. He finished by telling the class that the report should be available soon. In the meantime behave prudently, holding on to their end of the bargain, which is all laid down in the bulletin.

Golding also showed up earlier, before the dean did, at some of my classes following the student's unrest. He concluded then, admitting it to me face to face, that the lectures were clear, understandable, concise, that they were building on previously presented – and explained – material as a foundation to build the consecutive material on and was simply bewildered what could have caused the student's resentment.

A week before final exam Dean Holbrook called me to his office. He presented me, verbally, the committee's findings. On the main issue they found no wrongdoings, whatsoever, on my part. They concluded that I acted well within the guidelines set down in the Faculty Manual concerning 'academic freedom'. On the minor issue they concluded that the students' petition – actually: 'demand' – (concerning reverting to previous textbook, course contents, etc.) was unwarranted, therefore should be dismissed, and that the dean of students' intervention in these academic matters was a gross overreach of his administrative powers, and well advised to be prevented in the future.

The students' spokesman argued (through the Student Trustee on the Board) that under these circumstances those members of the class who attempted to drop the course in midstream were denied this opportunity therefore should be given a passing grade in any event. Les Kirk, the dean of students vehemently supported this view and went further by offering to be present at the final exam, "to prevent any unrest." Dean Holbrook, very reluctantly went along with it, but Golding objected, on the ground that **it could set a dangerous precedent** for any future classes to take advantage of, and copy this case. All they would have to do, in the future was, to organize a similar objection campaign and to pass any course without really studying for it.

The next unsolved problem was the grading the final exams. I insisted that I grade the exams based on evidence that no similar case to this has occurred ever before. I will make the grades and file them with Data Processing as described by the Manual as if nothing would have happened. Then, what the administration intends to do with them was their business. But I announced to the class that those students who want to hand in their exam papers to me, to be graded by me, will receive their fair grade from me. Those who don't, should hand them directly to Dean Kirk, sparing me the time and the effort to be spent on them which would be a total waste. Dean Kirk may initial them if he cares to, if not, the students may just pick them up from his office. This was how it ended.

As an interesting aftermath, it's worth mentioning, that the students who handed their exams to me (slightly over half the class) all received passing grades or better, with the exception of two, who received an 'I' for incomplete because deficiencies in their laboratory assignments. They were told that if they are willing to make them up they will be getting their valid, earned grades. They both did so.

Now, based on moral and academic standards, there existed **two different sets of grades** in this class: one set was legitimately earned, based on their earnest input into and diligent work performance in the course during the semester. The other set was handed out by Dean Kirk so authorized by the administration; all of them a passing grade. This was to remedy the situation with the students who were intending to drop the course, but were denied the opportunity to do so.

There were, however, some ramifications regarding the two different grades. These were the complications these grades had on the second semester (the advanced) surveying course. Those students who did not study for the course but received their passing grade anyways were, most likely, going to fall behind at the outset of the second course, which I refused to coordinate. I was willing to assist in the course, anyone, but was thinking in the first line of Nick. But he already asked for a lighter load in order that he could finish putting together the first draft of his dissertation, which, if accepted would enable him to return to Greece in the summer, where a faculty position was waiting for him in Athens. But I soon found out that Manner had other plans concerning myself.

Another consequence in this story surfaced when Golding announced that he resigned his position from the Institute as of January of 1975, which he described as "unworthy of his services". It was never clarified **why exactly** did he resign. Speculations got off the ground that he felt inadequate as a department chairman based on his botched handling of the surveying class problem of 1974 fall. Only I knew this being his second failure as a department chairman within the last three years, save Herm who knew about his first one at the Colorado School of Mines, not from me, but from Giff. The questions about his motivation to resign, revolved around the possibility of originating from his conscience, that he failed as a chairman. I opposed this opinion. But I offered my view, as I openly stated, which was my firm belief, that the cause being most likely monetary. He let everyone of his colleagues know that he was going to join a Geological Engineering firm as a principal. His earnings could easily have doubled by this move. I knew that he never got the fiscal satisfaction out of academe that he was aspiring for, ever since he joined us. As the saying goes: "Those who can, do; those who can't, teach". It seemed that he arrived to the point where he was serious about trying to join the 'doers' (and see if he really "can do") which he did not try before, but was planning to do now.

Without a doubt Golding's resignation meant a little victory for me. It solidified, strengthened my status. I dare say, without exaggeration, that it almost made me feel invincible. But, by this time, again, another election of a new department chairman hung over our head. Just as before the eligibility posed an inconvenient, nagging problem. Since Bill Manner had his Ph.D. degree, he became a candidate. Several of us tried to convince Bill Hapkins to run for the post, without success. He became disillusioned with the position, or that was, perhaps, only my feeling. He declined to run against Manner. Maybe the failure of his last endeavor bothered him and was troubled that it might repeat itself. I felt deeply guilty about that, and decided to correct that mistake this time. But without Hapkins there was no one else qualified to run against Manner. Dean Holbrook moved in decisively, quasi announcing Manner being the chairman. The democratic process finally broke down.

This new position suited Manner perfectly. He hadn't have to teach any course, he was coordinating the teaching and research activities of the department, and,... generally, administering the affairs of the department. Soon I moved up higher on his agenda. He resorted to unorthodox methods to achieve my 'removal'. He obviously was an active participant of Golding's secret meetings. He seemingly pledged to carry on his crusade. Since this also included an eventual riddance of Herm Shea, he appointed Nick as the coordinator and good old Tom as his assistant. Both of them were dead set against their assignment. But Manner's plans called for this being a partial solution. He put a graduate student TA (Teaching Assistant) in charge of the Transportation course. Then turned to the dean, clearly demonstrating that there was no more need for my services in teaching at the Institute, therefore, asked him to act in the direction of my removal, if not from the Institute, at least from the department. In hindsight I would not be surprised if he attempted to use my "Request for Transfer" (on my file) to corroborate his 'solution'. But Dean Holbrook brusquely dismissed Manner's proposal, informing him that I was a tenured faculty member who can not be dismissed without due process, therefore he must insist that the chairman will assign me a comparative full load of teaching duties.

Nick, burst into his office and reminded him (with a barrage of vulgarities) that he was promised a lighter load in view of this being his last year if his dissertation was accepted. Then: (a direct quote!) "I will leave this f…ing place all behind, where you can do what you want, but not with me! only to these sheep who are misfortunate enough to be under your chairmanship." This too, threw the grit into Manner's gears. He committed a tactical error and, at least had the vision to realize it. He quickly created too many enemies for himself. A mistake. But the problem was partially, and temporarily solved by the return of Herm from his sabbatical leave. So, he assigned Herm to coordinate the surveying (second) course to be assisted by myself and Nick, one-one section for each of us. This way neither of us (all three of us) were overloaded. But the crusade against me had to be postponed. He was furious, decided to swallow it but never gave up.

To fulfill his promise (he has made earlier in the cafeteria) he had to put a sting into my assignment. To assist one section of surveying class was really a cushy assignment so he needed to find the sting to put it in for me. He assigned me one course of sophomore 'statics'(a course which I never taught before in my entire academic career, and there will be more about this to follow in the next chapter) and the lecture plus a 3-hour lab for a new (to be developed) course in Engineering Materials specifically suited for "In-service Personnel" of the Commonwealth. I had the feeling that he gave me this course to collect more ammunition (bad course evaluations) on me for my "dossier". But this turned out (at the end) as becoming the most rewarding of all the courses I have ever taught at the Institute. The class and I practically developed this course together as we went along. An old textbook was adopted for use, mostly in the laboratory, which was originally written for engineering technicians. It was no longer used in the civil engineering curricula anywhere.

The various (engineering) materials were dealt with in separate chapters. Stone, earth, wood and brick were the classic, ancient ones. Then came concrete steel and other metals, finally: modern, manufactured (man-made) materials. The registrants in the class were all practicing in various engineering and sub-professional State jobs. All of them had substantial practical experience but had no engineering degree. They were a great bunch of guys who actually assisted me in the class, had contributed to it with meaningful suggestions. The cooperation was extraordinary. At the end of the course in May I actually sat down with them what grades should each one of them receive. It was at the first time in my academic career that I felt like, actually itching to give everyone an 'A'.

At the end of the course Manner came to the last class to collect the course evaluation forms 'personally'. He encouraged the class to be candid, critical because no one but himself will see them. He got his wish. All 16 of them were praising the course.

------*

A heartbreaking thing happened early in May. Maria's Father was gravely ill, so she had to leave on an emergency basis. Distances still dominated over mankind when it came to physical presence. Communication finally managed to bridge any gap. There was instantaneous communication available on a global scale, but getting there in person, instantly, ... was still in the realm of angels.

It took her over 22 hours to get to Pècs. As the saying goes: all roads lead to Rome" in the case of (what's left of the mutilated country of) Hungary, there was no, or hardly any cross-country transportation available except through Budapest. No domestic air transportation in the entire Eastern Block. It would have been uncontrollable to prevent any plane from being 'high jacked' somewhere, a few minutes from the western border. Within the country there were: railways, busses, automobiles, or boat transport (over the Duna River) but no air transportation.

Maria's father (known as Feri bacsi to the reader) was on life support system for the last few days already. Her brother in law, being a physician, explained practically to the entire family that there is really "nothing specifically wrong" with the old veteran, what it seems like it is, is the "entire system" that quit and refused to put up with more of the earthly struggle. He wasn't doing really that bad, considering,... he was 87 when he past away a few days later. An active participant in the four years of WWI in the common army of the Austro-Hungarian Monarchy, from which he returned with a 50 % disability without any pension because of the country has been dismantled and none of the sides assumed any responsibility of a disabled veteran; A member of the reserve and National Guard in the Second War, the soviet takeover, and the 1956 uprising, finally completed his duties here on this earth.

Maria stayed for his funeral. Her mother, Cristy nèni was begging her to take her to our home to America (and let her pass away there) but she was very closely in the same condition as Feri bacsi, only she did not know all the various ailments eating away her tired body. She passed away within six weeks after her (son-of-a-gun) husband. They are now placed side by side in a Columbarium, built in the open air in the Main Municipal Cemetery of Pècs, and, as the 'Announcement' at the main gate declares: are waiting for their resurrection and eternal life.

Memorandum

To: Dr. W. T. Holbrook, Dean, College of Engineering

From: Gabor Szikszay-Farkas, Assistant Professor,
Department of Civil Engineering

Subject: Teaching at Worcester Polytechnic Institute

Date: May 23. 1974.

As per your request I am submitting this memo to enlighten the circumstances of my teaching a six-week "Control Surveying" course at W.P.I.

At the beginning of the Spring Semester I had anticipated to continue to do my usual private consulting of 8 hours a week and have filed the necessary forms to cover this activity.

At the February meeting of the New England Section of A.C.S.M. I had been nominated to the Educational Committee and had been informed by colleagues that one of the faculty members of W.P.I. Civil Engineering Department, who used to teach "an advanced surveying course" is on sabbatical leave and that I ought to see if they would need any help to teach that course if I possibly could fit it in my schedule.

I saw the Civil Engineering Department Head at W.P.I. who confirmed the above information and was very glad to learn about my qualifications in the surveying field. I was very enthusiastic to prepare an outline for the course which in itself was a challenge in view of the extremely short duration allocated for such a course.

I did have one day without classes at L.T.I. (as most other members of the Department did) so we had to fit my schedule for these classes when I had vacant hours here during the week The course consisted of 3 one-hour lectures and two three-hour lab sessions, a total of 9-hours per week. The course was to start on April 3-rd and end May the 27-th. Compensation was immaterial to me and I emphasized that this was not the consideration for which I would be doing this extra load but mainly because my love of the subject and to help out the Institute in need. I was later informed that the administration of W.P.I. appropriated $ 1,550. to compensate me for the considerable expenses that incurred to me. (I was using my rented equipment in the laboratories.)

Since it was already past the middle of the semester here at LTI. and actually I was not going to overextend my already approved outside activities, I have dropped all consulting work for the duration of this course, as well as because of totally deteriorated personal relations with the department chairman, I did not submit a change of outside activities form to him. I realize, that in spite of my reasons mentioned above, this was incorrect on my part but did it only to prevent a possible disapproval and a last minute cancellation of the course at W.P.I. Also, I needed this opportunity for a sense of accomplishment and to restore my self-confidence to that of an earlier level.

Chapter Seventeen
(Getting busy, busy, busy.)

One of the students' long sought for weapon against a faculty member (or, actually the faculty in general) was the so called: 'Student's Course Evaluation'. Naturally, it was not really the course they were evaluating, or more exactly: not **only** the course but in the questionnaire numerous entries were asking for evaluating the instructor of the course. His preparedness, his organizing ability, his presentation, his willingness to provide additional explanation of the material, his willingness to answer questions, his motivating the students, etc. A laundry list, really. All of a sudden the faculty became open season for the students towards the end of each semester. I knew a few professors who were chumming, rubbing shoulders with the students, quasi bargaining with them, holding out the promise of a good grade in return for a good evaluation. Timing was a crucial element in these bargains, since the evaluation had to be performed **before** the end of the semester (the end of the course) whereas the grades were sent to data processing **after** the final exams, when a final grade was eventually arrived at, by the instructor

There were still a number of details to be ironed out of this system. The student's evaluation forms were not bearing their name or signature in order to protect their individual privacy. The Student Trustee made sure of that, which instantly became implemented by the administration. A student (or two) from the class, was collecting the forms at the time everyone in the class completed them, then took them directly to the department chairman. When Herm learned about this procedure, he made a speech at our next faculty meeting (the reader knows already that he was great with speeches; words) that an anonymous statement from anyone, made anywhere, is not worth the paper it's written on. Not under United States Laws anyways. If and when a (bad) evaluation came to be used, in a particular case, against a faculty member, the only (legal) way to handle it –or use it- was to identify the person making a (detrimental) statement against the course instructor; in accordance with the legal principle that, an accused person must have the right to face his accuser. Thus, the anonymous evaluation form would have lost its power, its 'sting'. But that was the principle. Reality was something else.

Still, the 'sting' made itself felt, when a number of 'bad' evaluations began to accumulate in the department chairman's folder on a faculty member. These were relied upon by him to intimidate the particular instructor. This was live ammunition in his arsenal. So, the students now felt that they had a formidable weapon in their hands, that could be used against a disliked instructor. All they had to do was to organize themselves what to put down on their evaluation forms and: voila! the instructor walked away with a 'bad evaluation' that might well affected his or her entire academic career. Promotion, or any other kind of advancement: a raise, or even more crucial: tenure, became a direct function of these evaluations. In this sense Herm's dismissal of the danger was not completely adequate. The students did, de facto, gain the power (almost) to the extent they were seeking it.

According to the classical, ancient Greek (unorganized) University education (system), the faculty 'was the essence of the University'. This system survived up until the 19-th century. There was no such a thing as 'Administration in charge of the faculty'. As the system began to grow in complexity beyond the point, that it required inordinate time from the faculty's part to organize enrollment, credits, academic standing, tuitions, salaries, etc. a body was needed to take care of these functions, and, in a sense, **serve** as a liaison between students, faculty and society. Thus, the faculty decided to hire an administering body and not the other way around. An administration can not function without a faculty.

The problem started, when the various positions within the system were ranked by the administration, which quickly developed a tendency to elevate their own ranks, in many cases, way above the faculty positions. Thus, the faculty's ambition was to become part of the Administration. Many members switched sides and these were looked upon as renegades. When the State began to enter into the system an even greater power made itself to be felt: Politics! Since the State held the purse, it demanded a **total say** in the University's affairs. This was not the case, though, with the privately endowed Colleges or Universities here in the United States. These were sculpted in the classical fashion: The faculty was the decisive body. So far goes the historical background.

As Manner began to collect enough bad evaluations on me, he invited me to the cafeteria. Using the good old method he inherited from Golding: he said he did not want to beat around the bush, so he unashamedly asked me straight out, to resign. He said he collected **plenty** of material on which he could start a disciplinary action against me. I reminded him what Herm said at our last department's meeting about these evaluations. But he dismissed those as overly scrupulous. Then he asked what is it going to be? What is my answer?

I told him that I do not scare easily and if he would care to look up my past performance he could deduct that I managed to weather previous storms. I could, therefore, give him my 'no' answer right now and reminded him again not to toss aside Herm's admonitions. Then he made his historical statement: "Gabe, I feel terribly sorry for you, because your time here, from now on, will be unbearable; I will personally see to it that you will be so miserable that you will quit on your own, and this is not a threat, it is a promise". All I could do at the moment was to thank him.

But I felt a new storm building up. Dean Holbrook picked on my 'Statics" classes. He knew this was way out of my expertise. Nowhere did anything in this discipline show up on my resumes. Himself being a mechanical engineer, must have had adequate knowledge in statics or most likely the more intensive, demanding know-how: **in kinematics**, which was an extended discipline of the static forces into: the moving forces. The civil engineers too had to deal with this subject (terribly involved in higher mathematics), but this was somewhat limited to those students majoring in structures. Fortunately, I had nothing to do with it, and I am quite sure the structures professors would have vehemently opposed, had Manner been trying to assign such a course for me to teach. But, in view of the recent losses in personnel (Dr. Thissell, the only true minority, had quit recently, which I sensed he would, since he was likewise not socially accepted by the rest of the faculty) the remaining structures professors under the coordination of Prof Lepine agreed that it would be acceptable for them if I were to teach the first, basic statics course. Manner was pestering the dean to do something about 'my case'.

He did. He visited a half a dozen of my Statics 201 lectures sitting in the back of the classroom and sometimes taking notes, some other times he did not. Usually after 20-25 minutes he quietly left the room. While he was sitting in the back row the class was so quiet that a pin drop could be heard. The tension was tangible. It didn't take long for the students to figure out what is the story behind the dean's visits. In this class were those students who, for some reason or other, reached 'junior' status but did not have credit for the first statics course, either because they transferred from another school and lacked this credit, or because they changed majors and needed this to advance further, or quite simply, because they flunked it the year before.

This last group consisted mostly of the smart-alecks, they 'knew everything' from last time, when Prof. Lepine found their dedication to the subject or their effort, or quite simply, their attitude, totally unsatisfactory. These guys kept coming to see me after class (but quite sometimes before it too) and brought along their last years assignments, quizzes etc. to show off with those. They wanted to know the 'right' (correct) solution to these sample problems. I directed them to do those as their home work, using the solution manual which I picked up from Prof. Lepine. (Those were usually not readily available for the students, who knows for what reason). I told them to get together and solve them very conscientiously. They were not very enthusiastic about this suggestion, but when I reminded them that better make very good friends with these problems, and more so with their solutions, because one never can tell if one or the other of them will show up at midterm exams or perhaps even at the final exam, they began to listen. Their attitude changed drastically. They got this hint. Basically, they were not stupid, even though they have flunked the course before.

The other group, of course, also got the wind of the secret, so it did not take long before just about the entire class was circulating this material. In this, second group were a number of foreign students who felt disadvantaged because of their language inferiority in comparison to the American born students. These guys flocked around me as if I were their pastor. Deep down I felt a sad sympathy for them. They came here mostly from Arab countries, like, Lebanon, Egypt and from Iran, (perhaps the only non Arab country) where the Shah, Reza Pahlavi sent the brighter students (as it turned out they were not necessarily the brighter once, but those with the right connections back home) with a generous scholarship to improve their academic status, return home with Western educational credentials (a degree was a must) and become the future social (scientific, business and cultural) **elite.** As we know that history – in hindsight— we also know that this noble goal never really materialized.

It didn't take long for me to recall the times when I was struggling along at The Ohio State University's Graduate School, trying to keep up with the highly sophisticated grad students who recognized me as a foreigner from my accent, (and occasional grammatical mistakes) the instant I opened my mouth. But the accent was not much of a concern within the Geodetic Science Department, because all the professors were foreigners, they sported a variety of accents. The only obvious remedy for me was to put in double or triple effort to grasp the intricacies of the subject at hand. It happened quite often that I had to get by with only a few hours of sleep. But my colleagues were very good about it. Soon we formed our own study groups, sometimes just paired up with one another, and tried to explain to each other what we were not quite sure of. This was exactly what I suggested to these foreign students: try to find a couple of the natives who are willing to form such a study group with them. Especially with those students who took the course before.

*

Before the summer vacation began, Manner invited the faculty for his party not quite the way any of his predecessors had done. The reader is quite familiar by now with Giff's faculty parties, which I may venture to describe as 'traditional'. In comparison Burt had only one, so called, 'gathering', which was so uneventful that it did not aspire becoming an item. Manner lived out 'in the country', in this case meaning the most rural part of the –rural-Town of Dunstable, on a narrow road, possibly an old abandoned cow-path, leading to a point at the New Hampshire border where the borders of the towns of Hollis meet with south-west Nashua. He built this brick house in a totally unconventional fashion: the brick was not only a face, a finish, but the masonry structure itself. It certainly had a number of advantages over the more modern, contemporary building methods. Cost was not one of them.

For one thing, it was fireproof, it was far more solid, a higher degree of insulating qualities, but at a substantially higher cost. It imitated an old, New England farm house –without the farm. Off the road, opposite his house was a vacant area, sort of a meadow. This was the place where the collapsible tables, the barbeque pits, and the trash cans filled with a generous supply of bier cans were to be set up amid mountains of ice cubes. Judging from the quantities of the food-stuff and the bier, it became clear that this was not going to be a faculty event. It had to be a mixed party, meaning mixed with the students. He was not planning a real 'faculty party' in the traditional meaning.

In a sense it was also planned to be a farewell party for those members who left us. One of them was mentioned before Dr. Thissell, from structures. The other was 'Nick the Greek'. In him we lost the boundless energy in the surveying field, which, so far always overwhelmed each department chairman. He never just talked to or told something to the chairman, he 'announced' it to him. He assumed a lot more liberty in that respect than any other member of our faculty. He could easily afford it, though, his position with us was a temporary one right from the beginning. Therefore, knowing he is not in it for the long run, he had nothing to loose. He knew, what we all knew, that he is not aspiring to become a permanent member. He was not aspiring to achieve tenure here. His presence was a tumultuous affair, which came to an end without a fanfare when he moved back to Greece. I am inclined to make the remark that the Department became more quiet, more normal and certainly less vulgar after he left.

* --- * --- *

At the closing week of the school year Tony surprised me by paying me a visit at my office before noon. He told me that he came to invite me to a 'nice place' for lunch. He assured me that I would like it. I asked him what the occasion was. He tried to avoid naming the cause, but said that let's just look at it as "to celebrate the memory of a special, sort of unique professional relationship in this academic environment" which was his greatest reward here on Earth. These were great sounding words, maybe too great, suitable for a funeral sermon. He added, that without me it would have resulted in a definitely negative experience for him.

This sounded to me somewhat enigmatic but also as a recognition of my handling (easing!) the difficult interaction of him with the Department. I conscientiously made this as easy as I could for him at all times.

So, after I accepted his invitation, I asked him "where are you taking me, Tony?" He said that over the weekend his wife's friends took them to this restaurant at the Hickory Hill Golf course and country club, not too far, just over the Methuen line. I told him: "Tony, I know the place real well, it's a cushy place, sure you want to take me there? At least let's go dutch".

-Oh no, Professor, I was planning this as my treat to you", would you please? Who knows how long we could still do this, ... you know, ... together"? He asked, which was even more mystifying and I thought there will soon have to come an explanation. I decided to give it its time.

-Tony, what on Earth are you talking about? This is getting more and more difficult for me to understand; am I getting into something here that I will not find my way out of..."?

-No, it is not like that at all; but, ... I have now a different perspective of life compared to what I was used to, and, ... anyway, may we just say that it is to celebrate our working together at the Department, ... where you were always very helpful to me ... and after that, I would like to go out with you to Dunstable, to Dr. Manner's place, I am sure you know all these places around, ... I would like to learn my way to the place, ... you know, ... sort of making it a dry-run, because Dr. Manner told me that I have to be there to,... kind of... helping out"...

- Tony, I think we should go right now; let's go, because I have the feeling that you have a lot more to say than you just did here! So, ... let's go".

We got into Tony's Buick, (the almost new one). He drove out to Methuen on Rt. 113, and just after our familiar Wheeler Road Development, from where he took numerous soil samples back to the lab, he turned sharp right and drove up to the clubhouse on the hilltop, and parked in front of it, showing off his familiarity with it, just as if he were a regular guest here. I sensed that this would mean quite a lot for him. He was at our place in Chelmsford more than once, although invited, socially, only once at Giff's farewell (retirement) party, but he never invited us back to his place. I never could figure out why. (Could it be still his inferiority complex? He certainly didn't know that I had been in many, many simple folks' place before, and ... was not knocked over.

But, after all, it never really bothered me. I was still thinking in terms of time and space infinitum, ... where time or space really does no longer matter. The space (or more accurately in the astrophysical terminology: the Void) in the Universe is filled with the WIMP-s which I always felt had a close relationship, even similarity, with the human soul. But the astrophysicists needed a lot more research to be put into this field. Time, as we know it, on the other hand, is an entirely man derived dimension.

Then Tony started elaborating for my benefit on his current 'therapy'. That he needed to attend a whole program of chemo-therapy, ... because he was diagnosed with cancer. He was telling me about this whole thing as if he would have told me about his unrevealed, secret affair; that he wanted me to know about in a, ... sort of, ... discreet way, the way he was quite sure that I would not pass it on. It was to rest with me, ... and it did.

The waiter came and greeted us, (actually he greeted Tony, whom he must have met not too long ago), and asked if we would have a cocktail. Tony told him right away that he should ask Professor Szikszay-Farkas first, who is most well known in these establishments as "Gabe" what he wanted, and then duplicate it, because that is also what he wanted. The waiter turned to me and was waiting for me to place my order without a single word, looking straight at me, waiting.

Trying to assess his age was not very difficult for me, I had kids of my own already very close to his age. (Andy, was a freshman in college). I asked him;

-Son, if I would ask you to bring me a "Rumhatten" do you think you, or the bartender would be able to come up with one?" and then I was waiting for him.

The kid was quiet, just as if one of his professors would have posed a seemingly difficult question to him. He did look like a college kid on his part time job. Then he found himself, quickly turned to Tony and asked him if he also wanted a rumhatten. Tony just nodded with his head. Then the kid turned around and headed towards the bar.

It turned out that the bartender too was no rookie, because he sent the kid back to us to ask, if we wanted them on the rocks, and with or without cherries. Tony was speechless but was not in any bind, he simply turned towards me, awaiting for me to issue the instructions. Then I told the kid that it was good thinking because the cherries added a welcome touch to the drinks, and that better double those cherries.

The waiter came to discuss the menu with us. The luncheon menu was sort of simple, we both picked the club sandwich, which was something not too elaborate, for which we didn't have to wait for long. Tony was delighted with my selections and I could tell that he put this whole travail down for experience. I was very touchingly, asking him about his cancer. How was it diagnosed. He didn't want to talk about it much, but asked me not to spread this (bad) news around. I assured him wholeheartedly. Then tried to ask him if it may had anything to do with his years at the nuclear engineering facility, where he was a janitor. He was very reserved about that. He said that his doctor did not elaborate on this subject. But, he assured me, the entire thing is fully covered under the Commonwealth's Insurance Program. A sad kind of consolation indeed.

We had a nice, relaxed time. I wanted Tony to feel being a gracious host, in the meantime to show him something more from this world, which he was not sufficiently familiar with, but was getting ready to leave behind, thus I wanted to turn this into a unique experience, the kind he was anticipating. All the time I was thinking about his whole life. At least to the extent as much as I knew about it. He had no children. He was just missing veteran status, because he was too young to be drafted into WWII and into the Korean War. Then, by the time the Vietnam War came around, he already missed draft status. He married late, after he established himself, meaning, with a steady, state-government job. Both of them were simple folks, both of them (meaning his wife) diligent, decent citizens. I always admired these. There was something very basic, something of a 'corner stone' quality about these people, as far as society was concerned. These were the backbone of it. I was too restless to fit into them. I had to make up for lost time.

Right after we finished we drove out to Dunstable, to the Manner's place. I showed Tony the most important landmarks, by which he could always navigate, find his way there at the end of the week. Then he drove me back to the Institute. We both were very quiet. Tony probably because he just gave away his secret, and I, because I just received one that I was supposed to keep, but found it to be overwhelmingly large.

The third member we lost was Joan Fallon. She retired at the end of the school year. Her departure could not have been more quiet than

Tony's, who died in the middle of August. The cancer rapidly invaded his intestines. He did not make it even till the next semester. I never saw Joan Fallon after she left. She was a striking example of the **'gentle woman',** using this expression in a broader sense, expanding it to the "gentle gender". I always had a great respect for her. We heard somewhat later, though, that her husband also retired from his state job; she was only to stick it out until he could do so.

For a brief part of the summer Manner, thus, was being left temporarily without a secretary. But after Joan left, a new secretary, Nicole was assigned to our Department. I met her shortly after she was fresh on the job and I went to the office to pick up my mail. She was petite, she was pretty, fashionably dressed, thereby tried to look younger than she was, which was a total waste on her part vis-à-vis me, who was definitely much older than her. She was close to a decade younger than myself. It would have been utterly futile trying to do anything about bridging or widening this gap. We introduced ourselves, after which she quickly asserted that she heard a lot about me, and, … "come to think of it," as she put it, saw me more than a few times around.

Then she told me that I was being inquired about, earlier today, over the telephone, by a woman from Cornell University's Contracts Division. Her name was Donna. She asked if I would be available for consultation. All Nicole could tell her was that I was on vacation for the summer. But, that she could put a note in my mailbox asking me to call her back, and that will be usually within two to three days the most. But Donna wanted to get in touch with me sooner, she sounded impatient, therefore she gave her my home telephone. She hoped that it was okay. I asked Nicole what this Donna person wanted from me, about this 'consultation'? Did she say?

-I think, Professor Szikszay-Farkas, that you might be in some kind of a trouble" she said. But I told her not to start teasing me with these sort of things and that I was sure that she could do a lot better using other techniques. "I left Cornell 6 years ago" I said, "and had no trouble with them ever since, except to the fact that so far, already two of my special committee members died on me, so, … maybe somebody up there does not want me to finish my Ph.D. degree from Cornell."

-Nicole, is it all right to call you Nicole? I don't know any other name to call you ".

-Well, I am Mrs. Lynn, you could call me by my married name" she said.

-Oh, so you **are** married, you should have told me so right away, then I would not have called you Nicole. Sorry about that" I said apologetically.

- Actually, I am not married, or … no longer married. I am divorced, but I am still using my married name because I did not remarry.

-That was pretty smart, I think,… if you'd ask me; In that case I shall have to invite you for lunch one of these days…to talk things over" I told her, but she interrupted me;

-Professor, don't you want to call up Donna at Cornell and find out what exactly she wanted?" she asked and was looking at me curiously.

-No, I don't think so, I can call her from my office, but, … it appears to me that you want to know more about it than I do, … you seem more curious about it than I am!"

I called Donna in the early afternoon from my home office. She asked me right off if I would be available for consultation. Meaning if it would involve my time only in the summer, during vacation. I told her of course I would be available, consulting is my secondary occupation; But what sort of consultation are they looking for? What sort of engineering expertise is needed? And, generally, what makes her think that I am the guy with the desired expertise?

-Oh, I know that for certain! because you were recommended by the School of Civil Engineering for the type of geometric problems we are facing with our contractor. I am only the 'Personnel Procurement Coordinator' on this project, so, you will have to make arrangements with Leon, who is the Project Manager of the entire project, …"

-Excuse me, … let me backtrack a bit, I want to understand this clearly, … you know, …you must know by now, from my accent, … I mean, foreign accent, … that …

-Professor Szikszay-Farkas, would you be so kind and skip this sort of talk, we have no problem with your accent, our problem is the shape of a parabolic antenna; So, let's get right down to the point, which is: that we need you for consultation, and I want to find out, …

-All right then, may I first ask you two simple questions: one, who from Hollister Hall (the name of the Civil Engineering school) recommended me for this work? and the second: what sort of geometric problems are we getting involved with? A parabola?"

-Well, the first one I can answer you, it was Professor McNair I talked with, about this project. I asked him to recommend a knowledgeable individual, who is really well versed in geometry; About your second question, … well, all I can tell you that this is about the Arecibo Astrophysical Radio Telescope's Antenna-dish, but, … like I said, Leon will have to explain that to you, he is the project manager, I told you that, right? All I have to ascertain now that, indeed you will be available as Cornell's prime consultant."

-Ah, ... I am at a loss, ...Well, Miss ... or Mrs. ...

-Professor, why don't you just call me Donna, okay? Everybody else does, I am used to it by now, so, would you, please?"

-Well then, Donna, all I can tell you right now, that I will be available during the summer, ... I am kind of busy with my things here, but, ... of course I can make myself available for outside work, if we know ahead of time when we must get involved with these things, I mean ... not really by appointments, -like with a doctor,- but just so that we can plan ahead. Perhaps you will allow me to call professor McNair and have a discussion with him about this Telescope, and its geometry, he used to know all about Cornell's projects, and if this one would, perhaps, involve Dr. Carl Sagan, then,..."

-Professor, you have to talk all about these sort of things with Leon, like I said, he is the boss, the coordinator and manager, I want to give you his number, ... or, better yet, I have him call you, as soon as he can do so, this way you two will not miss each other, would that be all right with you?"

- I guess so, ... yah, why don't you do that? And... it was nice talking with you! I will be waiting for his call then."

-Same here, I am really glad that we, ... actually: I, ... have found you, and, more so, that you will be our man. Good by then, you will be hearing from me, I am sure."

*

The two kids came in from the field, brought with them the soil logs for the exploratory pits and perc-test results. They reported that there were no problems. I raised my right thumb, ...then one of them said: except that is; ... what? I asked him; "That Tony Francesco did not show up to take the soil samples from the percolation results to the lab, so, ... we brought four pale-full of samples from the four pits we tested in the afternoon. Where do you want us to put them?" the kid asked me.

Wait a minute you guys! I thought I told you that Tony is no longer available to do anything on this percolation testing business, you know? Dr. Manner gave him other things to do, ... (But thought of somebody up there was getting ready to give him others).

The telephone rang. I told the boys that I was waiting for this call, so, just leave the samples outside the door, and if they have nothing else to do then it's okay for them to go home. Then I answered the phone.

-Hallo, this is Leon Hastings, from Cornell. May I talk with professor Szikszay-Farkas, please?" he asked.

-This is him speaking" I replied.

-Professor, I trust that you have talked with Donna, and that she explained to you that we need you to evaluate the accuracy of the 'shape' of the completed antenna-dish that Memorex has built for us under a contract at the Arecibo Astro-physical Observatory in Puerto Rico."

-Well, I did talk with her earlier this afternoon, but all she wanted to know was if I would be available for consulting work, that is: with you, on your project. She also indicated that you will outline the actual nature of the task for me. So, perhaps the best thing would be if we start right with that?"

-Okay, so, it's like this: … Memorex, the prime contractor who is going to install all the electronic listening, and, of course, recording devices into the observatory's receiving electronic gear, was selected to build the parabolic dish-antenna, which is some 700-feet in diameter, inside of a 'sink hole', I trust you know what a sink-hole is, just outside the Town of Arecibo. That is in Puerto Rico. Now, … the contractor supplied us with all the measurements and the computations for the positions of the tiny targets fixed on the inside surface of the parabolic shaped, sheet-aluminum dish, all arranged along predetermined sections of the antenna. There are a great number of such sections. In addition they supplied us with each and every one of the resulting parabolic sections. Also tabulated are the magnitudes of the deviations for each target from the true, mathematical parabola. We want to know, how well they fulfilled their contractual obligations. That is exactly the job for which we need you. Tell me please, can you help us with this? Professor McNair said if anyone could do this, that would be yourself ".

-That was a pretty nice, and let me add: flattering introduction of me to you. I myself would not have dared to go as far as this. Not at the first time, for sure. But first, let me tell you that I have not done anything like this before, … and, second: that there are a number of things that come to my mind before I can even ask further questions. Third: do you still want me to go on?"

-Sure, go ahead."

-These may not be as critical than the others, but, for instance: who did the evaluating measurements and how were they done? Here I mean;

what sort of method was selected? Who approved them? Who carried them out? And ...er... please don't interrupt me, and, where and how are these results being presented and in what format are they available? ... you know, ... like, numerically, ... or perhaps graphically plotted, ... so, you see? there are a number of such things that just popped into my mind, ...

-Now, you see what I mean, professor, you are already getting into the technical details of which I am not an expert at. These are the jobs of the technical guys. Actually this is exactly why we need you. The measurements, by the way, ... since you asked, were conceived and carried out by the Ohio State University's Department of Geodesy. I understand from professor McNair that you had some ties to that school, ... So, let me ask: do you think you could come up to us, to Ithaca for a day or two? Here, our contractor liaison could show you all these things, he could give you all the results I just mentioned; They are also familiar with the tolerances fixed in the contract. These are extremely important, these are the things we want you to evaluate for us. You know, of course, the contractor swears, that they have fulfilled all their accuracy requirements, that is, the tolerances mentioned in the contract, and hired the Ohio State guys to prove it. Are you still with me, professor, I realize that I am imposing on your patience. But, let me propose the following; I am just thinking aloud, ... how would this be? Could you, perhaps, fly up to here, to Ithaca on a Friday morning; We would send you an airplane ticket, Donna would wait for you at the airport and drive you up to us here. We all meet here, I show you what we have and discuss what our policy is. This is the most important point in the entire affair. After that we could all go down to the 'Lake Shore Restaurant' for lunch, ... while we, sort of, ... familiarize ourselves with each other. Are you still with me, professor?"

-Oh, yah, sure, I am listening! All this sound really fine. So, go on, ...

-Then, in the afternoon you could meet with the technical guys, they will give you anything you want to see, or know, they can give you anything you might want to take with you and study at home, at your leisure; Then we put you up for the night; There is no good direct flight from here to Boston in the evening, and I am sure you don't want to put up with the hassles through New York's airports. So, then you could catch a morning flight from here directly to Boston. How does that sound?"

- Well, Leon, it sounds super, may I call you Leon? that is, of course, if you promise to call me Gabor, instead of: 'professor'. Also, one more thing, we did not talk about the fees, you know, consulting fees; As I mentioned earlier, I am sort of busy here, … but, if the price is right …"

-Oh, sure, by all means, Gabor! I wasn't trying to avoid the issue, you must believe me. I still owe you that piece of information; We usually pay a $ 300.00 per diem fee for most of our consultants, plus, of course, any expenses, so, if you think that would be sufficient, …"

-Leon, I can't see any problem there, I can certainly live with that. So let's shoot for this, the next Friday, because this Friday we are having the faculty barbeque. If that's okay with you people, just have Donna reserve a ticket for me, that I could pick up at the Allegheny gate the next Friday morning at Logan, and then, as you said: I see you later then, okay?"

-Consider it done, Gabor. This is really super! It definitely exceeds our expectations. So, I'll see you then."

*

Wednesday, late morning Nicole caught me as I was picking up my mail.

-Professor Szikszay-Farkas, Dr. Manner was asking me who was that calling you from Cornell, and what that was all about? I told him I don't really know, but that it sounded as if they wanted you for some sort of consultation, … at least, that's what the lady said. I told him that I don't know anything else, but he was very curious, …" so she told me.

-Mrs. Lynn, let me tell you just this one thing: all that is none of his goddamn business, that is my own private business, and that is off limits for him, is that clear?"

She looked at me perplexed, I looked back at her and we were staring at each other for a while. A short while really, when she raised, then dropped her shoulders in rapid successions, all the while spreading her two hands as wide as the room around her would allow. Then she made a grimace and, sort of an eye-catching pout, which made her look almost girlish. She had a very attractive, 'petite type' figure which (I thought I mentioned before) was a turn-on for me from times immemorial.

I was still staring at her, but she was nonchalant, in fact was getting to busy herself whit whatever there was at hand. At the next moment, when she was again looking at me, while I was still frozen in my poise I said to her:

-Mrs. Lynn, ...I am going to take you out for lunch, right now, and the choice is entirely yours. I also want to apologize, if I did behave badly, ... in your judgment, that is, ... so, what is your answer?"

-Professor Szikszay-Farkas, first of all: I want to accept your apology; Second: you do seem to have a reputation around here, which is, ... now, how should I put it as mildly as I can, ... not to ignite you ... "

-Aha, what makes you think I will ignite?" I asked her in a naïve sort of way. "But anyway, you have still not answered me yet. You did give me a 'first', ... and then: a 'second', none of which was a real answer to my invitation. So, let me ask again: What is your choice?" I asked, and was still waiting for her.

-Professor, today I brought my own lunch, ... is that okay? Also, I intend to consume all that, over there in the faculty lounge, where I will have a nice freshly brewed cup of coffee" she said and was looking at me, sort of waiting for my reaction. I must have looked kind of stupid judging from her expressionless face and then she added:

-Now, ...and then ... you may join me for that, and ... I might even pour you too a cup of coffee, just so that you don't, feel entirely let down" she said and looked at me graciously.

With this she managed to eliminate the tension that Manner's unwelcome curiosity raised between us. After I dropped off, then sorted and weeded out the mail in my office, I walked over to the faculty lounge, which I hardly ever visited because I considered it a 'gossip mill'. But right now there were hardly any people in the place. Nicole just finished brewing her coffee as I walked in the room, so I walked over to her and stood next to her table. She picked up a mug and poured it full with the fresh coffee. I was still standing there, sort of unsure of her stance, and probably more so of mine, when she pointed to the chair next to hers. I was waiting for a sign of encouragement something similar to this and when it finally arrived I no longer hesitated. I sat down right next to her. She slowly pushed the full mug towards me, which was a sure sign of truce between us.

Since I was always overly curious of reasons of breakup between married couples, or actually: divorced couples, I started asking my questions in this direction. She apparently disregarded them, but instead, assertingly and straight-out, asked me what the cause of my antagonism was against Dr. Manner. I realized that this topic assumed priority over mine, so I began to describe the Golding affair to her (as a helpful prerequisite knowledge) of which Manner's quest against me was a natural sequel. She listened to all this very intently and absorbed my words like a sponge.

*--- * --- *

The mixed party that took place at the week end was the last time I saw Tony. He was helping with the food and drink supplies, just like Dr. Manner "was counting with him" he was supposed to do. The students were doing most of the barbequing the burgers for themselves, which required the greatest number to be produced. A couple of the new faculty members (freshly hired by Manner) were also attending, quasi introducing themselves to the diminished old(er) faculty.

These two new members, with their wives were both of Manner's previous acquaintances, apparently more than that, friends would be the accurate term. They were both in the same area of Manner's expertise, that is: 'Water'. Both families were chumming all during the Party. It was causing a nostalgic mood in me seeing the old, 'original' faculty becoming so diluted, gradually replaced, by a new one, which was becoming more and more an appendix of the chairman. Manner was digging in, fortifying his position. He was operating more sneakily than Golding, who opted for a more open type warfare. That was one of the reasons why he has not lasted longer.

The ladies at the party were cheerful, formed their own circles. The new ones flocked together with Mrs. Manner, who was assuming the role of 'The First Lady' among them. At one point, without intentional eavesdropping, I overheard a lecture-like discussion, dominated by the hostess, which had to do with 'ejaculation'. I was suspecting a gross misunderstanding on my part, since I did develop a serious hearing loss lately, but as the word repeatedly reoccurred during the discussion, (or lecture) I began to listen more attentively from a background point to make sure I was not mistaken. I always held at parties, long since, that the most interesting and meaningful conversation took place among the female members of the party, so I was poising myself in their midst, if and when it was appropriate, or somewhere in the vicinity if it was not overly conspicuous. After I assured myself that I was not mistaken, I assumed such a position for the rest of the discussion. It actually turned out to be a more highly anatomical lecture than I could readily fit into my inadequate, theoretical knowledge about the subject matter, in which I had merely an 'on-job' training and experience.

Another interesting observation of mine became more less clarified. It had to do with the younger woman at all times accompanying the Manner 'couple' which soon became registering in me as a 'triple' rather than a couple. The woman could not possibly be their daughter, because she was about a decade younger than members of the couple. I naturally assumed that she was a close relative of either one of them, permanently living with them, but this assumption turned out to be incorrect. At one of these occasions I noticed, with great interest, when the topic of conversation turned towards religion; Someone made the remark that 'The Manner's are Mormons'. This finally clarified this last mysterious situation for me.

The students, in the meantime had busily played their football game, in which the new members also participated. As a matter of fact some members of the 'old faculty' like Bill Hapkins also took part in it for a few touch-downs, or field goals, for which I am not even sure that I am using the correct terms. I had not had any kind of instructions in this, or the other equally confusing American sport: baseball, therefore I was unfamiliar with most of these sport's technical terms. The bier was flowing, hamburgers were consumed in incredible quantities, most everyone seemed to have a great time who ever got himself involved in the student's games. Only a few of us, Tom Cilento, Herm Shea, Jack Sinclair and myself, who were the **'older faculty'** had been shooting the breeze, and reminiscing about the 'real faculty parties' and were observing that in all this time we became not only the 'older faculty' but simply: **older.**

* - - - * - - - *

The upcoming Friday, early morning I drove to Logan Airport and parked in the overnight parking lot next to the one of the domestic terminals. At the Allegheny Airline gate the attendant handed me my tickets and a boarding pass. It was already boarding time. I recalled the same type of music (commonly referred to as 'Muzak') that was playing back in 1969 at the time of my interview. I even recognized some of the tunes, very pleasant melodies. No one considers them classics nowadays (I have no idea why?) but I don't think the melodies will ever die. I would consider it a real tragedy if they would.

After the familiar stop at Providence, R.I. we took off for Ithaca, N.Y. The scenery was gorgeous. Probably more so, looking down at it from the air. Donna was waiting for me at the airport. She had absolutely no trouble identifying me. There were only 4 passengers: a distinguished looking lady, with whom I had a long discussion on the plane and, who was the daughter of one of the founders of a building on campus named after her father. There was also, a young couple, possibly students, and myself.

My first, utter surprise was how gorgeous Donna looked. On top of that she was at least ten years younger than myself, (come to think of it I was only 45 +). I found it really difficult to play the role of a scientist-consultant with the constant temptation of wandering off to lot more romantic topics. But I think I do deserve a medal for some lower level heroism of succeeding not to make a fool of myself. She took me right to Leon Hastings' office. He was very cordial, although, when we began to discuss the contractual part of my assignment, he was becoming much more reserved. He could not afford any kind of slip-up, he said. This was his job, his carrier. His neck was on the chopping block, if anything would have gone wrong he was through. Or so he told me and we both knew that he was grossly exaggerating.

So, therefore, he was concentrating on grooming me how to behave at the confrontation with the contractor, and his consultant, which seemed unavoidable. He told me that he was somewhat uneasy because of my accent. That it might cause us being put in an inferior bargaining position at the confrontation. He was mentioning several times that the contractor's consultants are from Ohio State, and that is the toughest adversary we have to face. Their endeavor will focus on convincing us that the contractor did a fully acceptable job. So, with my accent, he was not quite sure if I could present formidable enough of an opponent to them.

An idea hit me as a lightning. I asked Leon if he would be kind enough to give me the names of the parties from the Ohio State group, who did this evaluation work, and consequently, whom we have to face. He asked me: "you mean names? Do I have their names? Of course I have their names." He then searched in his folder for a short while, pulled out a sheet, held it up and read from it: "Vheerasingh! Their leader is a Dr. Vheerasingh. He also has an assistant with him most of the time by the name of: Subraman, ..." he had some difficulty pronouncing the names.

-Leon, ... let me ask first: are these the gents you called our opponents? I happened to know them, and let me make a remark, ... actually an answer to your 'concern': they both have a different kind of accent, if this is what gives you the irks; But my second question is more important: why is it that I got the feeling, ... that you are anticipating default in the contractor's performance? How do you know he exceeded the tolerances?" I asked him. "If you know he did, why do you need me to evaluate it?"

-Well, ... Okay, I see your point. Actually, ... it was our technical guys, who pointed out some excessive deviations contained in their own report, ..."

-Some? You mean to tell me that out of over two thousand targets, or measured, located points on the dish-surface they have found "**some**" of them deviating in excess? ... in excess of the tolerance? ... How much in excess of the tolerance?" I asked him in a manner of throwing the ball back into his court.

-Yah, ... well, these are really the debatable points, these are the disturbing issues remaining to be ironed out, ... but, Gabor, hold it! On who's side are you anyhow? You sound like taking their side's already and we have just hired you to be on ours!" he said apprehensively.

-Look Leon, I am on your side, alright. I want you to know that before we go any further. But, and here comes the first but: Euclidian geometry is a closed, exact science, based on the postulates. That is why I sympathized with it ever since. There is no double talk, no double truth. I am here, ... sort of, ... playing the devil's advocate; I am looking for absolute truth, ... I can never accept a situation in which I am making statements that are based on inaccuracies, thereby rendering my testimony questionable at best, and valueless at worst. In fact, I am going further: If I can, I want to put the opponent in that exact position; ... you know, let **them** make provably inaccurate, or untrue (geometrically untrue) statements. In such a case any of their arguments will just fall apart."

-Gabor, I think you have just won my total confidence. I was not as sure initially, but, ... I can summarize my feelings by stating that: I would not like you being on the opposite side", he said. Then he picked up the phone, and called Donna. He asked her if she was ready to take us down to the lake for lunch. After that he called the 'technical guys' and alerted them that it is lunch time, and asked them if they knew the place where we supposed to meet.

The weather, as I said, was gorgeous, not only Donna, who I noticed, has changed into a slightly more casual attire, but most certainly into a fresh blouse. This was one of those occasions when I was nostalgically falling back on my memories, when I was actually her present age, right here at this beautiful place, and was obsessed with desire directed towards one of the president's secretaries. She, the secretary, was, as it turned out later, exactly my age, divorced, and refreshingly returned from a Peace Corps assignment in South America. At that occasion I was seriously planning that to be my fling, which under those circumstances were not entirely unrealistic, based on superficial observations, but lacking evaluations of deeper human qualities. I was smitten by her personality, but probably more so by her (what I assumed was) 'availability'. I had such a hard time to overcome that infatuation, that I ended up seeking professional psychiatric help, (which I never ever needed before) and which was (fortunately) rendered free of charge by the psychology department, even to the graduate students. This time however, I just looked at Donna, like an art enthusiast would assess the artistic techniques and aesthetic values of a beautiful painting; … however, …not necessarily, and entirely without the desire of owning the painting.

We all got introduced to each other. Actually, I was the one, who had to be introduced to the others since they all knew each other. Donna picked us a table at the lakeshore terrace of this popular restaurant, a table large enough to accommodate the five of us. The two 'technical guys' were well acquainted with each other, sort of colleagues, they both were members of the astronomy department. The entire project was supposed be conceived for their benefits. No doubt Carl Sagan had something to do with fighting for the grants needed to build the system; It was not cheap.

The telescope was similar to a large television dish antenna built on the ground, in a 'sink hole' (Puerto Rico has an ample number of these, at various sizes) the one that was selected was quite larger than a football stadium. This was oriented (its axis pointed) vertically out into space from which it was supposed to pick up electromagnetic (radio) waves. The antenna surface, which, by correct geometric terminology was to be built in the shape of a 'paraboloid', (a rotational parabola) was rested on, and tied down to cables suspended from concrete pillars, located around its perimeter. The structure in itself was a typical example of a statically indeterminate structure. I had nothing to do with its structure, my only concern was its shape.

Adding to the problem was the fact that a freely hanging cable (or rope, or chain) suspended from both ends does not have the shape of a second order parabola, (or even a third order one) but has a unique geometry (the catenary) that can only be approximated by infinite series. At the size of the Arecibo dish –700 feet in diameter- the shape of the catenary could no longer be approximated by a simple third order parabola if the tolerances were not to exceed ¼ of an inch. Therefore, it needed tie-downs to concrete blocks set underneath in the ground, to enable the introduction of limited motions for adjustments. The designers did provide adequate headroom for maintenance personnel moving about under the dish. By properly computed, and introduced adjustments a true second order parabola could, theoretically be achieved; But only along one main direction. Not in any other direction. Thus, the ideal 'paraboloid' was still not within reach. And I pointed this out to the astronomers, the *'technical guys'* as they were being referred to. They did not fully realize this. Nevertheless, I was curious to see their printed results, I told them so, and all three of us were anticipating vigorous discussions in the afternoon.

Donna was, however, apparently the most interesting topic. I learned during the discourse, that she was not married, by her own admission. The astronomers were teasing her about being overly picky, and since she was already 36, going on 37, it was high time for her to get married, or else she might totally miss the boat, or so they were predicting the grim future for her. I did not participate in this discourse because I felt it being inappropriate to mingle myself into. This resulted of me being sort of left out of their game. But I did not mind, I was satisfied with simply enjoying the beauty of the setting, of the lake, of the scenery and, of course: Donna. By me staying totally out of the teasing game she already sensed an ally in me. She couldn't be more right. In any account the lunch succeeded to achieve its intended purpose. We all knew each other somewhat better.

We had an endless discussion with the astronomers in the afternoon. They were trying to dismiss my concerns about the dish not being the segment of a true paraboloid. They kept side-stepping the issue based on the observation that this surface, whatever it **really** is, could still be focused on the sensor(s) placed in the prime focus, which were suspended from three 150 + feet tall concrete pillars by cables and a cat-walk for access by personnel. Their problem so far was that they did not receive any useful pattern of electromagnetic waves. I kept on telling them that due to the system being so complex, having numerous components, there could be a number of (other) reasons why they were unsuccessful in receiving anything so far. I actually tried to introduce them to the idea of '**accepting the possibility**' that the contractor may not be at fault, 'technically'. It appeared to me that they had been brainwashed. They had a mind-set that the deviations of, and in, the dish surface were the culprits. And nothing else! Nevertheless, towards the end of the day I had the feeling that they were no longer so cocksure about their assumptions.

We were still hard at it well past 5 PM when Donna called in astonishment that we still haven't finished our 'fight'. She told them over the phone that she is going to come over and claim me for dinner and that's that. We better finish it all by then. So the techs packed all the material for me to take with me home. By the time Donna arrived I was resembling a mule fully packed for a long journey. A great number of printouts and charts were under my arms since they did not fit into my briefcase. Donna took pity on me by taking some of the overflow from me. She was heading towards the Faculty Club's restaurant: 'The Ratskeller', which I knew from the good old days. The last time I was there, was with McNair, which I could not forget.

I asked Donna if she would consider taking me to the staff's restaurant instead, which was overlooking Beebe Lake and the waterfall through the solid glass wall facing it. She acted receptive, but didn't miss asking for the reason. She was under the impression that I would opt for the Ratskeller with its more faculty-like atmosphere. I tried to explain her that I wish to reminisce, thus, going reversed in time, rather than the other way. She was asking for some of my memories that prompted this mood of mine. And I told her a few. When I arrived at the story of my fling with the 'President's secretary' and tactfully began that description, she did not ask any more of my reasons.

We also talked about McNair to whom she talked a mere couple of weeks ago who told her about myself. I mentioned her that. perhaps it might be a good idea if I would call upon him while I am at the campus. He was living very close, just at the outskirt of it, actually, at walking distance. Then she alerted me to the possibility that he may not be at home, meaning in Ithaca, because she recalled him telling her that he would be going away to Texas A&M, where some of his old students arranged a visiting lecture series for him, to quasi saving him from the solitude, at least for part of the summer here at home.

This was the time when she reminded me that they (Leon and the tech guys) would be anxiously waiting for my summary report (actually the evaluation) so that they could plan for our trip to Forth Worth, Texas, where the final show-down with the contractor would take place, right at Memorex's headquarters. "And you better be ready to tag along" she said. I told her that I am ready any time, provided she is coming along! She waved dismissively with her hand and said: "Oh, you're impossible".

She was not overly talkative, definitely not chatty, which I found to be adding to her attractiveness. She never inquired anything about myself, she left it entirely up to me what, or how much I would tell about myself. Then she explained how to go about my accommodation. I had a reservation at one of the guest houses right on campus, the location of which I was only vaguely familiar with. Certainly never used any of them.

When we were ready to leave I thanked her for dinner, but added that the same, or more, goes for a memorable evening. She was somewhat surprised of me making the remark. It made me wonder how come she was not used to this. She must have had many guests-consultants, prior to myself, whom she had to entertain. One thing kept puzzling me, though, about her was: she did not smile very readily, or a lot. This gave her an unapproachable aura. It did not render her unfriendly or standoffish, but – I was wondering- perhaps there was something behind that the astronomers were teasing her about at lunch. We said good night and she reminded me to be ready at 6: 45 when she would pick me up in the morning and take me to the airport.

------*

One nice, late summer morning as I drove along State Route 113 (a.k.a. Riverside Street) as I always did, which ran through the central part of the Lowell Tech. Campus, I noticed a small, almost discrete hand painted "For Sale" sign on the old building at the corner of Mount Hope Street. From the faculty parking lot, inside the quadrangle, I walked directly back to the building and was thoroughly looking it over. It was crying for TLC (tender loving care) all over. I was trying to enter the building, so I knocked, and knocked and knocked on all three of the entrance doors. I could hear voices from the inside, young people's voices, so I knew the building was occupied. But nobody answered the door.

My decision was instantaneous. I walked back to the parking lot, got into my car and drove down to City Hall and visited the Assessor's Office. Very quickly I had all the information I needed about the building. It was seventy years old, built before the first war. It was assessed for 26,000 dollars. The owners were listed as the Riverside Street Rooming House Inc. but from the owner's address, where the Tax Bill had to be mailed to, I identified the same phone number that was listed on the hand painted sign, placed on the building. Then I stopped by the Registry of Deeds. Took a copy of the deed which agreed with the assessment data, as far as the owner was concerned. They bought it some eight years ago for 21,000 dollars. Then took a copy of the plan that showed the lot with its dimensions and configuration, and drove back to City Hall, to the building Department. From their records I found out not only the dimensions of the building but the floor plan too with all the previous alterations the owners made eight years ago. There was also the permit to operate the premises as a rooming house. This was the most important piece of information. For me it was.

I called the number several times during the day but did not get an answer. Finally after 5 PM. a man answered the call. His voice sounded familiar, but I did not readily recognize him. After the introductions everything fell into place. He was the bursar of the Institute. We greeted each other cordially then I told him that I saw the sign on the house and that I am calling because I am interested in buying it. So, how much were they asking for it? When does the rooming house permit expire? Are there other owners involved? How many tenants occupy the place? How much is the gross income? etc. etc. He answered each of my questions in rapid succession, then I asked when could I see it inside. We made an appointment for the next day, I was to meet him at his office in the basement of Camnock Hall.

Next day we walked over to the house from his office and he showed it to me throughout. It had a double garage too on the premises, built of concrete blocks. This was not shown on the plan, it had to be built well after the building had been built. It was currently used for storage. The inside of the house was even in poorer shape than the outside. Most of the insufficiencies were in the common areas, such as the bathrooms and the kitchen. The individual rooms were all in satisfactory condition. Then he informed me that an inspection is due shortly and that they (meaning himself and his partner, who was the assistant to the director of maintenance at the Institute) did not plan to do all the necessary work needed to be done to pass the inspection. They decided to sell the house instead.

They were asking 35,000 dollars for the building 'as it was'. I told him that they met their buyer, because I am willing to pay their asking price. He could not believe this. We walked right back to his office from where he called up 'maintenance' and asked his partner to come right over to his office. I did not know the man so we got introduced to one another. I told them that I will be making up a P & S (purchase and sales agreement) and will bring it over to them later in the afternoon. There will be a few 'conditions' to the sale, though. They were somewhat concerned about the conditions, but generally looked quite happy. Before I left the office the bursar asked me how the surveying business is progressing. I acknowledged his courtesy of asking and remarked that I had really no reason to complain. He made a final remark to the effect that I must be doing well to walk in and buy a rooming house just like that.

I did return in the afternoon to the bursar but he was not around. One of the accountants informed me that he will not return before tomorrow. So, I handed him the two copies of the P & S along with a bank draft of 2,000 dollars. He seemed to know about the intended sale and told me I could leave it with him. He would put it in the safe and hand it to him tomorrow. I thanked him and left.

The offer was, as agreed, for 35,000 dollars. This was due and payable if the operating license will be renewed by them for a minimum of a 3-year term, by the time of passing. In lieu of this, an adjustment in the price will be made to reflect the out of pocket expenses that has to be born by the buyer; in this case: the price would drop to 30,000 dollars. I found out through the grapevines that the maintenance director had substantial 'connections' to the Building Inspector at City Hall. I wanted him to use them before the sale closed, not after, by then it was worthless, so much so, that it could kill the deal.

This caused some unexpected complications in the procedure. To fulfill my conditions definitely took some time for them, and I could well utilize that time myself. I needed to search the title of the landlocked parcel of land in the back of the corner lot, which had no street frontage on any one of the streets. It was shown, however, as belonging together with the corner lot on which the old building was sitting and the deed confirmed this. In essence the property had more than double the amount of required land of a single lot. The configuration, however, was difficult. All of a sudden both of us became busy. They were asking for an extension of time to secure the necessary permits, which I granted them willingly. I was also working on the floor plans, on both the first and second floor, to increase the number of rooms from eight to ten. This comparatively small investment could increase the income by twenty percent. The spaces on the main floor were wastefully large. The old living room was nearly 300 square ft, whereas the minimum floor area of a bedroom, according to the Code was set to be a 120 square feet. Kind of tight, but definitely plenty for a student. This room had to be divided into two smaller bedrooms still generous in size. One of them also needed a built-in cabinet to be added and a separate entrance doorway from the hall. Another oversized bedroom on the north side was waiting for the same fate as the former living room.

The actual repair work had to be carried out at the tail end of the summer sessions during which the building was usually not occupied by students. They went away for the 3 weeks until new school-starts, after Labor Day. Some left for good due to changes that effected their life here, like: graduating, start in a new job, moving to another school, etc. The sellers asked for an additional 3,000 dollars to the deposit, helping them out to perform the most needed repairs on the bathrooms and the downstairs kitchen. Somehow they persuaded the building inspector to accept these mostly needed repairs only for the license renewal, who was easygoing towards them, and who actually gave him very little, if any, trouble.

The students evidently loved the place. For one thing there were no 'strict rules' over and above the obvious ones, which were standard requirements by the Code of Occupancy. Compared to life at the dormitories this was a most lenient place, and, let's not forget, for a much lower rent. They loved, above all, the very convenient location, which was at the edge of the 'North Campus', practically a 2-3 minutes walk to the classrooms in either Ball Hall or Southwick Hall. The new 'Lydon Library' was just about across the street from there. They did not need to use, or even to have a car if they lived here. Some students did actually own a vehicle which they parked on the ground next to, and behind the garage, just about permanently, but there were only a few, and seldom used, during the weekdays. They were busy studying, or so it was assumed.

I was going to get ready for the floor plan alterations which we –meaning here my construction crew—were geared up to proceed with, when the maintenance director gave me a confidential advice, namely: not to "rock the boat", right now. Let them finish the required work needed for the license renewal first. When that is accomplished, we will be all set for 3 years during which we could do that conveniently and not under the watchful eyes of the building inspectors. Just do it on a touch-and-go basis, maybe even between semesters, when they (the inspectors) don't come around often, if at all. This turned out to be one of the most helpful hint I ever got during all my residential rental operations.

The North Campus was, by now, officially so named because the administration began to work very diligently, implementing the "merger" with the South Campus, to form the new University of Lowell. The South Campus was the former Lowell Teacher's College, and these two institutions were to merge into the new entity. It had a very valuable 'non-technical' library and a music department, which we at Lowell Tech did not have. Several of the other 'service departments' like mathematics, physics, two very different style of chemistry departments, and, of course, languages were all duplicates. These were looking forward to most of the administrative changes as a result of the merger.

The State's idea was mainly a money saving proposition. One of the very important area was the elimination of two administrations, beginning with two presidents, many vice presidents, as well as financial, academic, record keeping, etc. departments. The target date was set to be in coincidence with the Bicentennial: 1976. One of the ubiquitous rumors circulating within the faculty was the selection of the new President. There was ample speculation along this line. A consensus took shape kind of early in the game though, which was: that the appointment will be a political one. All the theatrical elements were brought into the picture. A search committee was set up. Selections of candidates with their resumes were placed in the new campus newspaper: "The Connector". As far as the faculty was concerned, though, very little input was possible. I can not even recall a general faculty meeting being called at any time in connection with this campaign at which a faculty voice could be heard. The game became purely political.

All this hoopla, however, did not affect the regular course of life at and with the rooming house's everyday life. Before Labor Day, applications for rooms began to pile up at the bursar's office, who called me to attend to them. The passing was set for the beginning of the school year. He informed me that the inspection has passed and the license will be ready for the passing. I had to come up with the 30,000 dollars by then. Interest rates were climbing steadily in the past year. Mortgages were still available for around 10% from banks and mortgage companies. I was toying with the idea of private financing. This way I could beat the rates at least by two percentage points.

I called up Teri, our Hungarian woman friend, (known to the reader from previous chapters) who's husband passed away recently by a terribly devastating lymph-nod cancer. She was still in the process of re-arranging her finances. Her two – orphaned—children were qualifying for social security payments. Her job, in which she recently started working, yielded sufficient income for them to live by. But most importantly, she collected the 160,000 dollars life insurance after her husband died. She put that in the bank, into savings. I told her that there was now an opportunity to make 8 % interest on a first mortgage on the rooming house I just acquired. I offered her to put the outstanding 30 thousand dollars, which was due at the passing, into a first mortgage to secure her loan, and earn roughly 200 dollars a month as interest. She went for it. I took her check to our bank, bought a certified check for the amount to have it ready for the passing: a no frills 30,000 dollars, to cover the balance when we passed papers. No bank, no attorney, no fees of any kind were involved, except the 16 dollars registration fee at the Registry of Deeds to register the two deeds. The most clear-cut deal I ever swung.

We picked the most clean-cut looking ten student applicants from the pile. No profiling, no discrimination, no undue priorities. The only preferred tenants were the ones who were tenants in good standing the previous school year. One of the seniors was asking permission to bring along his 'steady' girl friend who might live (the contemporary term was: shack-up) with him. This presented a problem. For me it did. I didn't quite know how to handle the matter, so I asked the bursar about their past policy regarding gender commingling in the house. Then I described him the situation I was facing. He informed me that there were no such cases during the prior years they owned the house, so he is really not familiar with all occupancy rules set by the code. Therefore, the only advice he could give me was to consult an attorney.

The case turned out to be more complicated than it seemed the first time around. Although the rules have been definitely liberalized in recent years there was no clear-cut answer in the books fitting this situation. Evidently there was, however, no legal ground to deny occupancy of any room based on gender. I like to think that my decision in this case was a revolutionary one: I told the young couple to move in, (to room No.2, one of the large rooms, located right next to the rear entrance) strictly on a trial basis. I don't want them to have any kind of trouble with authorities, I warned them, nor would I tolerate any friction within the tenant community.

I am still not absolutely certain to what degree my resulting decision was based on my recollection of the times when my brother and I had to occupy the hay-loft of a farmer's barn, some 25 miles outside of Budapest, in the winter of 1945 when the Red Army evacuated the entire civilian population from the combat area. People were put out on the streets and roads, and they were quite franticly looking for some form of accommodation. The farmer allowed us to hide there overnight, every night, in the hay, so that the soviet patrols would not find us to take my brother out to the front to dig trenches. I was merely 15-years old and would not qualify by their rules, (which were broken frequently by the occupying forces anyway). Andrew, however, was 17. He could easily be drafted even into the army too, which, at this time was illusional, since that fragmented army was fighting already some 60 miles west of Budapest, under German command. Every night, while sleeping in the hay (with all of our clothes on) we thanked God that we found ourselves this 'accommodation' and felt sorry and sad for all those other people whom we saw desperately trying to find a warm place to stay for the night.

But, as I said several times before in this book, that too, was another story.

Chapter Eighteen
(Tumultuous Times.)

I was supposed to meet Jerry Lussier for the Planning Board meting in Dracut on one of their regular Thursday night meetings. We were scheduled to present the conceptual plan for the huge area, in the eastern part of town, that 'Draco Homes Inc.' amassed, actually, assembled from several larger tracts of land, recently. All these parcels were contiguous and constituted an area in excess of 300 acres. Certainly a large piece of land, by any measure, for an aggressive developer. He called me beforehand to make sure I will be coming to the meeting. He said it is extremely important. There will be photographers to take our picture together. It was meant to be put into the paper, the local, suburban edition of the Lowell Sun. He told me that their attorney Richard Halloran (well known to the reader by now) suggested that they buy some publicity. This is an easy and painless way of doing it. But fate had other plans, at least for the immediate future.

On my way out of Chelmsford, a mere half a mile from our home, a full size car suddenly appeared in front of me, turning out from Clinton street, a small side street with a regular stop sign. The car was 20-feet in front of me in a 35 MPH zone (my speed) when I broad sided it. Both vehicles were totaled, both drivers taken to the hospital. After a set of my X-rays taken, I was released, no broken bones were found. The other driver, a 16-year old kid, just past his driver's test a week prior to the accident. The police charged him with driving to endanger, ignoring a stop sign, etc. He was driving his father's car, who, presumably had no other vehicle to go to work the next day.

Jerry was frantically calling at home, but Maria told him, that I had left in ample time for the meeting and everyone became excited about my whereabouts. A friend of theirs, an officer on the Dracut force, has put in a bulletin on his radio trying to locate the Mercury Comet and myself, its driver. Very shortly they found out about the details of my accident. The Comet was Maria's car. It was toed to a local yard. Our only vehicle now drivable was my VW bus. Maria did not drive that, but I was given a ride by my clients upon my release from the hospital. We missed the publicity stunt, and had to reschedule our presentation. I sensed a sinister omen in the event, which, actually, proved itself to be such, but only much later. But, in the meantime, it was a severe setback.

With all the anticipated development work ahead of us I had to think seriously about expanding the business. This meant adding some permanent full time employees to the organization. This, in turn, would have meant a lot more administrative work, payroll and accounting, Workman's Comp and other Insurance, and would have resulted in substantial increase in overhead. This I always loathed and considered it wasteful, lost time, money and effort. I was not mentally ready for such a change. I loved the co-op type part timers – specially students- who were my own trainees, trained to do the work to my 'taste', which was also agreeable to them . Word got around. The students were lining up for part time employment. There was work for them, quite a lot of work. The only problem was scheduling and organizing them. This was the key to success. I needed someone for performing this task, to design a time sheet, who could also keep track of their input times and compute their wages. A few weeks later, after the rescheduled Planning Board presentation, our picture, with Jerry, appeared in the paper.

*

At one occasion I finally managed to get Nicole to join me for lunch. For a short lunch. She seemed to know quite a lot about myself, the gossip mill seemed to work overtime. She not only knew quite a lot about my 'troubles' with the chairman and his predecessor, but other involvements at and around the school as well. And, naturally, she also found out as much as was possible about our domestic 'difficulties'. This was not really a difficult task, I was discreetly courting some selected

381

(and good looking) members in the secretarial and typing pool within a reasonably acceptable range of my own age. The new dean's secretary (a recent divorcee) was a regular visitor at our department. (We will hear more about her, due to other connections within our families, and our real estate rental business in a sequel to this volume.)

During our lunch I returned to our unexplored topic of the cause for breakups between spouses. This time she was more agreeable to talk about **her causes**. She had three very handsome teenage sons (in her custody) and, as one of the causes surfaced, it revealed that she did not even 'like the man,' never mind loving him, (meaning her husband) because of his obnoxious behavior, which he developed lately. My inquiry was into the depth of, and possible causes for, **his behavior**, but she did not offer a plausible explanation. I asked whether she ever tried to find out about his frustrations, lack of successes in his occupation, etc. But she did not offer any more specifics. There was one phrase she used, though, that aroused my curiosity, namely, that "he could no longer satisfy her 'mentally'". This was very puzzling to me, since I was under the assumption that this culture is very similar to the one I grew up in, where a couple of the same 'class' had similar values, education, similar problems, objectives, similar life-plans, etc. I concluded that she was no longer much interested in his 'troubles', probably did no longer attempt to reconnect with him. So, she finally decided to leave him with the three boys. I was trying, very tenderly, to discover any sexual failures, of either party, if any existed. She was not very loquacious about it. But she leant me a copy of a tape on a cassette, which was recorded at one evening at a classy bar, (where she did part time bar-tending in evenings) and was asked by the 'boss' to render (sing!) a favorite tune of hers for the audience. Someone recorded it on a cassette; It was …"*For the Good Times*". She had a very sexy –alto – voice, (on the tape). I didn't make a copy of it, … darn it!!

This obsession of mine with divorced women originated from a dream way back, well before the time our coming to this country over from Canada. It was a very vivid dream, some of the scenery actually resembled some of the places (real places) we were staying after moving away from two years of graduate study at The Ohio State University, and of course, the married student's housing, where we lived, the 'Buckeye Village' (which was a well designed, altogether super project.) Later, in Akron, I almost recognized a small garden- style apartment project, where one of the (divorced) receptionist lived, who was a participant in my dream. Still later, at Cornell, I already mentioned one of the president's secretaries on whom I had an incredible crush probably because she fitted (almost perfectly) the **'divorced woman'** participant in my dream. I became convinced, somehow, sub-consciously, that this is the fate waiting for me: that I will have a divorcee as a mistress, who will fulfill, in an underground setting, all that I was missing in the above ground one.

I did not tell Nicole about these things though, not yet. I was still sort of uneasy with her in this regard. She did tell me, however, that she thinks she understands my predicament. When I put her to the test and asked outright what she thinks is 'wrong with me' she told me right in my face: "Gabor, I think you are unfulfilled". (These times I already called her Nicole). "You need someone who would put in the missing link. But the solution can not come from the 'one night stands', don't even try; I am convinced that you need something more, much more, what you need … is, … a … relationship". "Oh my God, Nicole, are you sure you don't have a degree in Psychology?" I said, and was just staring at her, incredulously. "I can't believe this" I said and was wagging my head. "You mean you had this all figured out by yourself?"

-Well, Gabor, don't you see? … it's, … so obvious!"

-What is? … I mean obvious? … Tell me something Nicole, … You think you could be, I mean, is it possible, that you could fill that missing link?" Then I was waiting for a while, but she didn't utter anything, not a word. She was still just looking at me. Then I continued: "I had the feeling that we could kill two birds with one stone … what I am really trying to say is: solve two problems with one sweep, … I mean, …"

-Gabor, believe me, I know exactly what you mean! But you are forgetting something: One of the problems, that you are referring to, is, … by far, not as acute as yours". "Did I make myself as clear as you did?"

-Ah-ha. That just confirms my estimation, namely: that you belong to the category of **"good women"**. I am sure you know the mantra: there are two kinds: the good ones … and the bad ones".

-Right on! But I am not sure if your estimation is totally accurate. And I know what **you need** now, … or soon, … is, … a bad one."

-Thanks! I needed that, … actually, I knew that". Then I looked at her for a few seconds; "Nicole, didn't you just convince me that I don't need the **one night stand sort,** for a solution? … Don't you want to see that every finger is pointing to you as being the perfect solution?"

-Gabor, if I wouldn't know you any better by now, I would be outraged, offended, annoyed, insulted, mad, upset, ...but this way, ...I think I am just enormously flattered. Thank you! Let's go."

We drove back to the school. Before she closed the door on the VW bus, I turned to her and asked: "Nicole, do you think you could, ... perhaps, ... just perhaps, ...

-Perhaps what?" she asked perplexed, sort of impatiently, holding the door open.

-Well, ... you know, ... introduce me to ... a bad one? a **'good'** bad one?"

-Gabor, don't be so anxious, we might do that some other time, okay?" Then she closed the door of the VW bus.

------*

The "*Tennis Building*" was completed a few weeks ago, located in the "Dracut Tennis Plaza" which I designed for 'Draco Homes Inc.' one of Jerry Lussier's pride and joy commercial developments. It finally brought to the center of Dracut a large variety of stores, a bank, some professional offices, etc. I did have considerable hassle trying to fulfill the parking requirements. He was a visionary. He saw the residential building glut clearly approaching, so he switched to commercials. There was no sizeable shopping facility in Dracut, no variety of stores, only small 'strip-malls' here and there, usually with a liqueur store or a Cumberland Farms convenient store as an anchor. He bought this 6+ acre site on the main drag, zoned for commercial, threw it in my lap and described me in broad strokes what he wanted.

The '*Tennis Center*' was an upscale entity. The structure was a steel frame, onto which a high thermal-insulated, plastic 'bubble' was attached. It accommodated six tennis courts, three on each side of the centrally located club house with all the desirable facilities: a pro-shop with a merchandizing center and a small bar; actually the local classy 'watering hole' for those customers, who did not need to spend much time with anything else but the essentials: the drinks, which were meant mostly for business-men, contractors etc. who didn't want to spend much time with lunch. Upstairs, the restaurant had a spacious, cozy bar with a great number of small tables within and some four-seater tables for parties of more than two people, at the restaurant section. All the picture windows in the bar-restaurant complex had a full view of the tennis courts. The opening was scheduled for shortly before Christmas time, and D T C (Dracut Tennis Center, Inc.) the owner, was throwing a sumptuous Christmas party for all the employees, clients, their relatives and guests. It was a super successful event. The place got so much publicity that it did not know how to handle all the after effects: the reservations for the New Year's eve parties, New Year's lunches, etc.

Nicole became a frequent luncheon guest of mine. But at one occasion she gave me a warning that she thinks too many people saw us having lunch together at certain well known places, such as the press club, downtown, and the Pizza Palace just down the road from the school and they 'made some remarks'. I told her that they (whoever 'they' are) can go straight to hell if they think this is any of their business. But the attention afforded to the two of us did not seem to subside.

It became quite clear to the both of us, that she became my confidante. She advised me in a number of things, she had some very practical suggestions, which I quite welcomed with open arms (and ears!), actually needed, because my mind was getting so overloaded, that sometimes I could not remember all of the things I should have. In a way she almost became my private secretary. And all this without pay. Who thought about pay anyway, I was thinking in much more generous terms, as always.

Upon my suggestion we started going to the Tennis Center's bar for light lunch. We've only been there a few times when the Lussier-gang began teasing me with Nicole. They wanted to know who she was. I told them that this is off limits, and they better stop bothering me with this sort of things or else... At one point I complained to Jerry himself who promised me to take care of the matter, but... first, would I care to fill him in: who she is, more particularly: who she is to me? etc. Then I told him that this is no joke, and I simply did not want to hear anything about it anymore. Jerry cooperated with me. But nothing seemed to work, or it just seemed a sheer lack of luck. One of my upper-class student, part time employee knew Nicole from the school and the rumor seemed to spread even more widely, like cancer.

I made several propositions to Nicole by this time who, I felt, was getting extremely uneasy about the whole situation, and at one point told me that she has made up her mind: we simply must cease to meet. At least in public places. I thought I made it perfectly clear several times that I would just love to fill in the missing link -in both of our life's- but she thought it would not work. She could not settle for missing all those evenings, that I could not spend with her, due to 'my other obligations'. Although, she said, she did not feel being responsible for my attraction towards her, more yet, it can not be her fault that my wife is, evidently, unable to handle me within her marriage. I kept on arguing that this is really a problem with a **given solution**, except, in that apparent likelihood if she really doesn't fancy me, in which case, of course, I would put an end to it once and for all. Since there was no further comment from her part I took the situation at face value, and … and … gracefully retreated.

Obviously we still saw one another at the department office, almost on a daily basis and all of these encounters seemed cordial. And I welcomed that. It seemed like we were still friends. Good friends too. There was no reason not to be. After all, friendship is the most lasting of human connections. Friendship is something intangible, it originates from the heart and soul. It is a feeling that survives passion, even love. It might becomes more intense after passion or love subsided or ended. Passion always seems to die first.

We had, from time to time, numerous meaningful discourses. Once she filled me in with her ethnic back-ground, (origin really), as we talked about it of which, evidently, I seemed to know more about than she did herself. I explained her about that tiny ethnic group in the northern part of present Slovakia (where she told me her father was born) which was a small, isolated group of people, for many generations, trapped in the mountains of the Northwestern Carpathians, close to the Polish border. She often seemed very much in awe of my colorful demographic descriptions. She always thought of her being of Polish descent. Once I summarized it to her saying: "you are a 'Goral' my dear". She thought I was toying with her, … that I just threw something derogatory at her, until she assessed it; that: I was dead serious, and that I seemed to know what I was talking about. Nevertheless, since she was born in this country, it did not affect her one way or another.

------*

My sabbatical year was one year overdue so I was targeting the next school year. I went to see the chairman a few times, telling him the few possibilities I was offered. One at the University of Maine. Not even very far. The civil engineering department there was toying with the idea of starting, very cautiously, a geodesy program in a small scale. They were needing one faculty member in addition to the two, who were well-versed in the discipline, and currently took care of their needs, which were the surveying courses. The additional member would fill in at the beginning (mostly by developing the additional courses, a time consuming endeavor). So my being on an –anticipated - sabbatical leave, (with half the salary coming from my 'parent' institution) was looked upon as a heaven-sent opportunity, which would not put any real strain on their budget.

Another possibility came along earlier that year. A questionnaire was sent to many faculty members in the country advertising available positions for research fellowships in geodesy, astronomy and electronics at the **Oakridge National Laboratory** in Tennessee. These were focused primarily on faculty members planning to spend their sabbatical year at this very famous and prestigious place. I filled it out and forwarded it to them without even thinking much more about it. I never considered myself competitive enough on a national scale, I was sure there were many ahead of me. But at that time I sent along one of my latest publications on a new, modified second order geographic (Global) position determination method, which demonstrated my practical inclination towards field methodology. I put it on the back burner of my mind, there was still lot of time till then, and chiefly, I was very busy with all my involvements here. If anything would have materialized along on this front, it certainly would have caused stress and headaches. But I was not paying much attention to the whole thing at the time. I somehow had the feeling that these sort of things are really designed for *'free spirits'*, not heads of families, with very deep roots; something for, sort of like 'professional students' preferably without family, free to move around, in one word: Vagabonds.

Shortly after I filed with the chairmen my request for approval of my sabbatical leave he called me and announced that I would not be getting my leave this coming year because there are **others ahead of me**. I knew about Lou ('Tarta' – the name Nick attached to him because he said, he had trouble with these long Italian names, having four, some even five syllables, while his –Greek– name had four) who also filed for his, but he came to the Institute **after** I did, so I told him, that I should be getting mine first, and anyway, I thought he was glad having me out of here; Even if it was only for a year. He said that we will see about that pretty soon anyways, but just take his word, and should not plan on going on sabbatical. Rather I should be concentrating on leaving this place altogether. I reminded him once more that that topic is moot.

Before the end of the summer I took a trip to Orono, Maine and visited the department head. As a well advised precaution I stopped by at my very dear colleague from Cornell University, who was right then the head of the geodesy and surveying program and who already put in a word for me with the head of the civil engineering department. It was close to noon when I got there (and I left at 5:30 in the morning) so we had a leisurely lunch at his home. He did not take me to any restaurant. He wanted me to have lunch with him at his home. His young, teen-age daughter, Kelly, (actually only eleven years old) greeted us and said that lunch is just about ready.

I did not recognize her, of course, because at Cornell she was only about a one-year old baby, and that was ten years ago. I inquired about Doreen, her mother, (the lady of the house). This was how I learned about how times change. She told me that her mother is in Madison, Wisconsin, finishing up her Ph.D. in psychology, and now, ... she is now ... here, visiting her daddy. "What do you mean 'visiting'? I asked her. She looked at her father, then at me, then again at her father. Then I quickly sensed that I am missing here an important link in the info chain. So, without words I also looked at Dave, my former dear colleague, so, now Kelly and I, we both did. Now he realized that it was his time to clear the fog.

Dave then told me that in the fourth year of him being the program chairman here, with one additional faculty member under him, he was beginning to ask the basic questions in our minds, of: **what this life is all about?** Is this all there is to it? Is this the meaning, the purpose and fulfillment of studying over 20-years of one's life; obtaining the highest degree available in the academic world; getting "stuck" in a place in the woods, like Orono, Maine, and teach the kids, coming out of high school, the basics of surveying and mapping. Doreen became utterly restless, frustrated, having a daughter in kindergarten, (and a toddler at home) picking her up at 1:PM in the afternoon, stay home, read, and read, and then read some more, which was really her salvation, because she loved reading. Later, when Kelly was home from school, she began to take courses, advanced courses, towards an advanced degree in psychology. That would qualify her for a social worker's job right away, and bring her some independence.

In the meantime his little darling daughter Kelly, put the finishing touches- some spices- on the grilled cheese sandwiches she made for us for lunch, and put some salsa sauce on the table so we can help ourselves to it. The scene was really moving for me to watch. But I sensed that something, the essence of the story, is still due coming. It did. A couple of years in social work, Doreen began to take courses towards her Ph.D. She was working full time, taking courses mostly in the evenings. She was out of the house, most of the time, hardly at home.

Then, she became friendly with one of her instructors, who was in the process to accept a faculty position at the University of Wisconsin and to move there. Doreen chose to move with him, took the girls with her, and filed for divorce. This is about it, in nutshells.

I told Dave how sorry I was for him. Then asked Kelly: "do you like to be here with your daddy?" She said, very enthusiastically, that she does, "everything is so familiar, as if it were ... at home". Then I corrected myself: "what I was really meaning to ask you, my dear, was: do you like it better here or in Madison?" thereby trying to avoid putting her on the spot by having her to chose between her parents. But she was a clever girl and was sensing the trap. She moved her eyes away from mines, ... looked down to the floor, then to her daddy, kind of expecting some help from him. Then I told Kelly how sorry I was to ask a nice little girl such a difficult question, and promised, right away that I won't do it again.

It was time to visit the department head. He still has not returned but left word with his secretary that he expects to be back later in the afternoon, and then he can talk with me. Dave showed me their 'surveying instrument park'. It was not the usual museum exhibit, as it was elsewhere at many, many schools in the country. This was well equipped with the latest model instruments. He told me they had two 'total stations' on order. These were the third generation instruments, incorporating distance and direction as well as the altitude angle, measured all with the same instrument through one sweep. The relative (total) position of any new point became known in a three dimensional coordinate system in a matter of seconds. Our school still did not have one.

The department head was a very careful, reserved administrator. These professors, once they became heads, seldom taught any classes. That was becoming too cumbersome, may be even boring for them. Administering the departmental affairs actually saved them from a total burnout, a meltdown. I have seen examples to these too. They advance along with the Technology to a certain point, and then, "since they know it all," they stop. They lose interest in anything further. (In other words: they get burned out.) If there is no possible post for them to advance to, they become doomed.

Our prospective Civil Engineering Department head here at Orono, was quite rapidly approaching this point. I could tell from the way he described their plans; to add some of the newest computer program packages to the mainframes, so that department's individual terminals would have access to them. It turned out that he was thinking in terms of the 'STRUDL' (the structural engineering program) he hardly knew about the details of the surveying program packages that were rapidly catching up with the rest. I definitely felt that I could gain something here, if I would be spending my sabbatical year here. We could put our heads together with Dave (again) just as we did at Cornell. We would be up to par with technology, and, as odd as it sounds: we could **become 'technicians'**. Technology made its advances on the expense of the professional. Technicians did not want to know any theories any more. They wanted shortcuts, and, most often they got them. The software industry was catering to them. The University rapidly became a technicians school. A mere decade ago all the students wanted to become 'engineers'. Now they had to become technicians in order to get jobs.

It was already after 5 PM by the time we discussed the various courses to be developed, but it seemed to me that he was mostly speculating, not really planning. Towards the end of our meeting he admitted that actually, in all fairness, he must say that they were not really ready for the move. Maybe next year. On our way out I even told Dave that it is better that way because I am really not sure if I could get my sabbatical leave. He was somewhat disturbed. He asked outright "is it **due to you by the law** (rules really!) or not?" I tried to explain him my situation I am in with my chairman. That he wants- really hard -to get rid of me, but so far the circumstances have prevented him to do it. Also, he had tremendous difficulty fighting the fact that I had my tenure, and he still did not have his. The Golding affair was still looming before his eyes.

Then we talked about some personal stuff. I asked him how it feels to be alone, mostly in the evenings. Scholarly activities can only go so far as occupying one's mind- in the evenings. Correcting and grading papers, lab reports, exams are rapidly becoming tedious, slave work. If one had no help with that by a younger person, (a TA.) one inevitably would have become burned out. He agreed. I told Dave about my stupendous experience at WPI. He listened to it enthusiastically, and said how happy he was for me. Not too many of us get an opportunity like that. Even at the price I had to pay for it.

We could have gone on, shooting the breeze, more and more. But time was flying by as it usually does during such occasions. He asked me if I could stay for the night, but I told him I must put in a good distance between here and home tonight and stay at a motel. This way I could manage to break down the distance and leave only 3-4 hours driving in the morning. Then we parted very, very cordially. I also said good by to Kelly, whom I never saw ever since. She must be a beautiful young lady by now.

*--- *--- *

I did stay at a motel on the outskirts of Augusta, the Capitol of Maine. It was late, by the time I got into bed, I did have a long day behind me. I slept until 8 in the morning and noticed that my left eye (the better one!) has a foggy overcast over it. Just as if I were looking through a dirty, dusty window, upon which someone's spilled some poppy seeds all over it, which got stuck to it. I looked into the mirror, washed my eyes gently with a look-warm water soaked sponge, gently massaged it, but it did not improve. Then I knew it. I recognized the early symptoms of retina detachment. I remembered them from back in 1971 when I had them in my right eye, but then I lost a lot of time getting it diagnosed and operated on. This time I simply knew that I must get there as early as possible to save as much of the retina cells as possible. After shaving, showering and putting my clothes on I called home. I told Maria the sad news. I had a hard time convincing her that these symptoms are definitely identical to the ones they were on the right eye, so, she began to realize the seriousness of my predicament. I had to drive home, which in my condition might take 4-5 more hours. It will be well into mid afternoon by then. In the meantime she ought to get in touch with the Mass. Eye and Ear people and have an appointment set up for me immediately. Then, by the time she can get me there it will be evening. If I can not get admitted, I have to stay for the night somewhere there nearby.

391

I got home by 3 o'clock in the afternoon. Maria was more upset than she was at the first time. But she made a tentative appointment with one of the assistant. Dr. Freeman was not available, she was told. He was in Saudi Arabia invited by King Faisal to discuss the setting up of a complete replica of the system existing at the Retina Associates in Boston. The King donated one million dollars to the Retina Associates following the successful operation of a detached retina on one of his sisters. So, we had to be contented with his number one assistant, Dr. Hirosi, who was in full charge of the operation. We arrived at about six in the evening, and one of the interns was already alerted to make sure that Dr. Hirosi would be returning later and have me diagnosed, or so he said. We did not have to wait long. By a quarter of seven Dr. Hirosi arrived and told us that he will perform the diagnosis right away, gave the orders to the assistant to prepare me in one of the dark-rooms. I begged Dr. Hirosi to save all that, which was a waste of time, I knew for sure that I have a detached retina, and time is of the essence. He gave me a skeptical look and asked: "so, Mr. Szikszay-Farkas are you trying to tell me that you have diagnosed yourself?"

-Yes Dr. Hirosi, I have" then to make him aware that I happened to know what I was talking about I added: "You see, I had a detachment on the right eye 5-years ago that Dr. Freeman operated on. But he told me then that the cause for losing a big part of my vision on that eye was due to the **time loss**. It took way too long before I got to the operating table. This time we can't afford any delays".

-Okay, … all right, … just lie down onto that table" he said and dimmed the lights. The assistant already dilated my pupils, so Dr. Hirosi could begin with the diagnosis right away. It did not take more than a few minutes, when he turned away, put his instruments down, turned the lights up brighter and said: "My God, you were right! It is detached at two joint patches, not very large separations; I have your whole file here. Dr. Cross will do the retina mapping on you, he will assist me with the operation in the morning. I will fill out the orders for your admittance." So, we at least knew that we did not lose any time, that the operation will be done the next morning. Maria could drive home reasonably calmed down, that my prospects this time are far better than they were in 1971, even though Dr. Freeman was not available this time.

Dr. Hirosi took charge of the situation. He informed me that this time it would not take as long as it did last time, because they have now one of the laser equipment already operational, and I shall be surprised what that meant. He was very self confident which rubbed on me as well, and I was looking forward to a successful outcome. Also I observed a lot of other little details, and I told him about them the day after the operation. He was utterly impressed and admitted that: "You are a very keen observer". There were none of the **after-effects** like the last time, because they simply did not use the sodium pentathol for the anesthesia and, with the new laser instrument the operation lasted only 4-hours. Since he ordered me to lie on my stomach, (for at least the first night) I had ample opportunity to observe four tiny bubbles floating on the back of my retina, which, otherwise was in total darkness.

I was out of the hospital after five days. All that time I was just being kept there to forestall, or minimize the possibility of infections to set in. A teenager at the other bed played his cassette with the tune entitled: *"Torn between two lovers…"* about every half an hour all day long. I don't think I could ever forget that tune. At my release I was overly optimistic. I felt like a victorious army commander. I was convinced that we had this 'thing' licked. But, leaving the hospital, Dr. Hirosi warned me that, with my other eye being totally inadequate for driving a vehicle, for a long, long time, I will be still considered 'legally blind'. Needless to say how much this frightened me. But much more importantly: how it frightened Maria. She somehow developed a mindset that I will no longer be able to drive a car, **at all**. I was, naturally, still wearing my patch over my left eye. This was not to be removed for a minimum of three weeks. Even after that it could only be done in semi dark rooms.

*

Maria was convinced that I will no longer be able to drive, legally, that is. I did take long walks, my right eyesight was still adequately serving me for that. My left eye's vision was still hanging in the balance. In the meantime school started. I was still incapacitated for an unpredictably long time. The chairman did not want to make any decisions as to my utilization under these circumstances; Since I was blind in the eyes of the law, thus incapable to perform my duties. So he referred my case to the dean. He was anxiously hoping that I will be removed from my permanent position, since all my accumulated sick leave was becoming exhausted in a little over a couple of weeks. And, unless I regain most of my vision, I will be put on permanent disability until retirement.

The dean, however, realized that there were no provisions for such a case in the collective bargaining guidelines, and agreement. Thus, a tenured faculty could be removed simply by being placed on permanent disability. But what about if the disability was temporary? If a recovery is a medical possibility, in fact a prognosis, then what would happen in the interim? The case, very soon became a 'Landmark Case'. The administration had to come up with a so called long term disability status, during which a faculty member is not losing his tenure, is receiving 75% of his salary in the interim, and is returning to active status upon recovery. This was the way it eventually happened. I was out practically for the entire fall semester in this status.

Manner was relieved from any and all decision makings, and it looked like he got what he wanted all along: I was no longer present. He must have been ecstatic. I am not sufficiently familiar with the Mormon teachings to know, to whom the faithful turn with their prayers, but he must have felt his (prayers) "were answered". Answered in a positive manner, that is. I was often wondering about this English expression: that someone's **"prayers were answered".**

I was always convinced that all prayers got answered all the time, only, some, (actually, quite some) got a "NO" for an answer. I knew this from my own experience; knew it only too well. I got too many of those NO's. But so did my father, which made me question the entire sense of the prayer itself when it came to, or had anything to do with human's concept of justice. Invariably, at least in our case, it seemed that who ever was in charge of the 'Prayer Department' up above (to receive them and 'answer' them,) either had no real concept of human justice **as we know it,** or, disagreed with it in principle, like in my father's case (and later my own). But this, again, is getting us ahead of our story.

*

Fate again played a dirty trick on me. To my utter surprise I received a letter of acceptance for the upcoming academic year from the Oakridge National Laboratory for a one-year term as a Research Associate. The area of the research was supposed to be in the development of the Global Positioning System. It was with the understanding that it is a temporary appointment - meant for the duration of my sabbatical leave

- and may be renewable upon the review of my performance at the Lab, as well as with the consent of my 'parent institution's extension of the sabbatical year in form of a leave of absence without pay. In that event I would have had the extension of my stay at the Lab with full pay, while still retaining my tenured position..

This was a clear case of opportunity knocking. But in view of my current condition I was physically unable to accept the appointment anyways. In addition, this problem was topped off by the fact that my sabbatical leave was not granted (approved) by our chairman. When I did look into it, it turned out that he never even submitted it to the dean. Thus, the approval, had it been granted, would have been due to be announced at the beginning of the summer term to enable the faculty member to plan things ahead. But the acceptance, from Oakridge came later, in this case too late.

I had a difficult task, to compose a letter to the Laboratory's Personal Director in which I had to decline to accept the position offered to me. Of course, I emphasized what an honor and privilege the appointment brought me. I enumerated the current two main problems I was facing: my **medical disability** (although temporary) and my, de facto, **lack of approved sabbatical** term. I also had to, kind of, throw the ball back into their court by mentioning a possible difficulty of my obtaining security clearance, which, to my knowledge would necessarily have surfaced sooner or later while I was at the Lab. Since this *'System'* was sponsored entirely by the defense establishment (and here I am referring to the monetary backing) it had bound to be at some level of secret classification. We knew, through our intelligence sources that the Soviets were also working on such a system which was monitored by our Global Tracking Network. Their satellites were catalogued by the US. Naval Observatory, so their (the satellites') orbital elements were known to our people. Theirs bore the acronym: GLONASS. Only we lacked the needed accuracy, because our tracking was only visual, through (Baker-Nunn, etc.) cameras. We lacked the knowledge of the electronics behind their system. Evidently there were not enough traitors among them for our benefit.

I was wondering for quite some time, not only then, but mostly later, how my future would have been developed if this opportunity would have materialized. My dilemma culminated around getting myself into a (tight) position in which I would have been entirely dependent upon a single position, (meaning a single source of income, from the

Laboratory, however much that was), without anything else to fall back on, in case something would go wrong. In our age of uncertainty one never knew what the future had in store for one. I learned this all the hard way after the War.

------*

By Thanksgiving I was definitely on my way to recovery. In the meantime we had to reach an important decision, namely: we had to find a place to live closer to the school. In view of my imminent driving inability, the new place had to be within walking distance from the school. We set an outer limit as a 10-minute walking distance from the school. The Chelmsford house had to be put up for sale, but obviously only after we found the new, more suitably located one around here. Stevie's real estate lady conveyed the idea that it may not be a good idea to sell the place in Chelmsford because those prices would pretty soon explode in view of all the technologies moving into town just a couple of miles to the South. Why not rent it? it would not only pay for the mortgage and the taxes but there should be a handsome sum left over. Then, in a few years, you may sell the place for twice as much as it would fetch today. Her prediction turned reality next year. But, by then, the place was sold already. We have been playing it too much on the safe side. The house was vacant all winter long.

I officially returned to assume my duties at the end of the semester. At its closing, the new, already 'united' faculty (united with the South Campus faculty) was all jointly invited to a Christmas party, sort of: to a 'warming-up occasion', even the table settings were elaborately arranged in such a way that at each table four-four guests were selected from the South and from the North Campus faculty, respectively. It was meant to be a get acquainted party, although some members already knew each other well from before, and some knew that their position was phased out. Dean Holbrook was to be promoted to VP. of Academic Affairs, and he didn't miss the opportunity to come to our table and brag about his role in solving my 'Landmark Case'. Most likely by coincidence, we were seated at the same table with the assistant VP. of Financial Affairs, (from the South Campus, and his wife, who were Canadians, and had long discussions with Maria, who also was Canadian) so I assumed (afterwards) that Holbrook's visit at our table was not meant entirely to celebrate the successful and happy outcome of my own recovery. Nevertheless, for everyone else it appeared that way.

The new year of 1978 brought with it a number of promises. The real estate industry responded (answered) positively to the slight upturn of the economy and homes were again wanted, needed. I walked around in the vicinity of the Campus a few times just about every week and looked at the houses listed for sale. There was nothing I could visualize as a family home large enough for our family who needed four bedrooms to accommodate us comfortably. We also needed to replace (or have an extra space for) the good size office arrangement we have built out in the basement of the Chelmsford house. The streets all around in the vicinity were tight together, the lot sizes were no more than 5-6 thousand square feet, mostly meant to accommodate a 1,000- 1,200 square footprint house. The prospects for our finding anything near Campus, were bleak.

*

Jerry put the pressure on me to get the surveying services organized. I told him we are holding our own, so lay off with this 'alarm-bird' mentality. But he warned me that it will work only so long as he will remain (finally) our only client. Plus, he kept getting informations, through the grapevines, that other (budding) developers too are seeking my services. This might have a detrimental effect on our performance vis-à-vis his projects. I told him I am unaware of any problems, I could always handle the incoming work, and intended to do so in the future as well. So, don't be an alarmist and try to scare me out of my wits. Then he told me to be his guest the following day at the DTC for lunch, because we have to really get things organized but ... "but make sure you have that good looker lady-friend of yours with you, to ... you know, to liven up the meeting". I told him to get with it, I am in absolutely no mood for fooling, and, that she is not my "lady-friend" any- ways, (at least not the way he thinks about it) so, ... I have more than my share of troubles, ... and I was ready to go on, ... and on, scolding him.

-Oh, so that's what's really troubling you? Did she dump you? Is that it? Well, ... okay, too bad! But to hell with it, that is not the end of the world. We, here, always thought that you could spin them around like nothing, but, ... looks like we all make mistakes, ..."

397

He then emphasized to me that this is going to be serious stuff so let's not get worked up over these 'things'. We did really well so far, and, there is really no need to get worked up over little things, … like 'broads'. (It was always their rough tong that I disliked about these guys. In one sentence Nicole was being referred to as my: 'Lady friend', in the next, she was put into the category of 'broads'.) He said that he is going to bring a future partner of his with him, and they want to talk about reorganizing the surveying service business. Meaning: "my surveying services". I almost blew up. "Since when do you guys think you can boss me around, and decide, what's going to happen with "MY" business?" Then he told me very quietly, to cool down, because there going to be a 'biggee' in the making, so, … don't be your own enemy, haven't you got enough of them? etc. etc.

He then told me to get down to the Tennis Center next day when we will meet his new partner in a brand new venture for which they want to hire me, actually my entire firm, to do the surveys and plans for this new joint venture. And: of course, all the field work, which will be the butter on my bread, …

I told Jerry, that I don't even know if I will ever be the same again, as I used to be. That he must realize what happened to my eyes. Those had to be looked at as my very first priority, … But he very calmly, convincingly, with his simple, matter of fact vocabulary, and his sly smile, finally convinced me that I already assumed the wrong, the defeatist attitude, so, …let's get together and make the best of 'everything'. I was week and vulnerable, so I agreed. We met the next day for lunch. Jerry arranged to have Mona, I daresay the best looking waitress in the entire restaurant, (may be in all the restaurants) with enchanting, Italian features to be our exclusive server, not too conspicuously though, not to arouse my suspicion (and undue interest). She was a real beauty though, and I was weak and vulnerable, as, I think, I already said so. We had eyes for each other. But when later I asked her out for an evening she retreated and I suspected that the whole thing was Jerry's machination and it had very little to do with my macho prowess that I believed in.

The proposal was entirely tailor made to my current predicament. I was supposed to do nothing else than to assign the tasks to the individuals or teems; supervise them, so that everything gets executed to order. This was planned to be an enormous organization, serving three different developer companies: Draco Homes, the original venture,

Winter Hill Development Co. Inc. a Gagnon entity, and the joint venture; Hudco Development Co.

Then came the details of the financial arrangements: They were to underwrite my entire payroll. (Wow! I never dreamed of such a thing!) Then I was supposed to get a 750 dollars a week fee for supervising (or to use their terminology: **orchestrating**) them. (My entire salary at the University was less than 400 dollars, per week, but –to be fair– let's not forget; the tremendous fringe benefits which they, of course were not expected to match. But then, they didn't have to). It just sounded too good to be true. I applied the emergency breaks, not to show my possible over enthusiasm. Then came the rest; to work out the details, (the devil is always in the details! we all knew that). We both knew that. I had other, very small developers, to service. This all had to be handled by an intricate bookkeeping system. We had to show what every part-timer kid was working on, any of **their projects**, and what hours they were spending on 'other' projects, for which I had to pay them.

It was quite obvious, that I was to make considerable monies on the three payrolls as well. I had to pad the hours with the overhead on each one. Then the next thing was to work out the logistics. What I asked was simple; do I have to put up (actually: would Maria have to put up) with the dozen or so kids, coming and going in and out of the office, and the garage, where the field supplies were stored? Janis, Gagnon's wife, came to my rescue. She 'announced' that: a separate office will have to be rented, preferably close to the center of Dracut, where everybody meets anyway, and that's where all the business will have to be conducted. Now I emerged from this meeting with something concrete, that I could show for, actually talk about it, and: present to Maria. At this point, I think, its scale was above anything she could readily comprehend. But I reassured her: just to trust me; I know how to work this. Unfortunately the most important ingredient: **trust**, has diminished recently in our marriage.

*

The next thing was to orchestrate the entire set-up. Nicole took pity on me the next occasion, when she saw me in the department office, and extended an invitation for coffee. I accepted it as a potential drowning victim would have a life saver thrown at his way. She was also a "keen observer" as I surmised. She asked me, why am I so gloomy? Do I feel like coming over to the faculty lounge for a cup of coffee and talk about it?

I said: "thank you! I'd love that! How come you always seem to know my thoughts? Or more yet: my needs?"

Just as we sat down, she asked me: "Gabor, what's wrong? I can see that you are troubled" she said. "This seems to me to be something different, ... nothing to do with the 'good, or the bad ones', ...by the way, I think I have some good news for you about that too, ...and pretty soon too, an acquaintance of mine just got divorced", she said, looking at me trying to perk me up, ... "she has a sumptuous place in Londonderry... with a pool ...etc."

-Oh sure, because you are such a sweetie-pie! You are sensitive and considerate"... and, ...

-Now, skip the nonsense, okay?" she said, looking straight at me; "don't you trust me anymore? I am your friend! do you remember? ... You want to talk about it?"

-Heck, what's the use?" I said. "But I want you to know, that I really appreciate your concern, you sweet thing, ...give me your hand! I want to feel you".

-Gabor! don't! Don't do this! There are all these people around... I know! ... I know, you don't give a damn about them, but, still, they all know us!" she said.

-I don't know, ... I think I just have to give up, ... I can't go on... not like this,..."

-Hey! wait a minute! This is not the man I used to know!" she said; "Are you sure you are talking to the right girl? Hey, wake up" she said, "This is me, ... remember me?"

-Do I ever? So, you want to know about my troubles?" I asked. "Well, my entire survey organization seems like falling apart. It has to be reorganized, in order to survive." She looked at me puzzled, didn't say a word, just looked at me...

-Okay, ... okay, ...first: I need to find a book-keeper/accountant to look out for my interest in this new, 'joint venture' I got myself involved with, and,... whom I can trust, are there still some people around whom you can trust?"

-What?... Does he have to be a certified accountant?" she asked me .

-No, Oh no, ...it doesn't even have to be a 'he'... why, do you know someone, ... someone, who could do this? ...on a part time basis, ... maybe I ought to look around in the business college, for a kid, or a nice girl, who needs some extra money?

-Well, sure, ... You know, my son Michael is a sophomore accountant, ... didn't you know that? Right here at the school" she told me. We were now staring at one another.

-Okay, can I hire him? or make some kind of arrangement with him?" I asked her.

-Gabor, I will make him contact you; You can interview him; But, let me tell you; you can hire him under one condition: only on his own merit! Okay? Is this a deal?" she asked looking straight at me. "Remember! **on - his - own - merit!**" and said each word slowly, "you do know what I mean? Right? Okay then?"

-Yes, my dear, sure! on his own merit! ... He is hired! Is that okay with you?"

-No, Gabor, no, now you screwed it up, ... don't try to make me believe that you don't know what I meant. I want you to treat him just like you would any other kid coming for a job to your office! Deal?" And this time she did stretch her hand towards me like sealing a business deal; not exactly the way I asked her to do, a minute ago.

*

There was a store building in the center of Dracut, called Collinsville; A small business center with a CVS pharmacy and a bank across the street. The store was in a very old building, it had a law firm on the upper floor, and the lower floor was recently vacated and some minimal improvements added, like: new wall-to-wall carpet. The lawyers had a separate entrance with their own stairway right from the street. Next to it, on the same side of the street was a short strip mall, with a greasy spoon fast food restaurant, hair dresser, real estate office, and the fire department had a storage building separated with generous parking places on both of its sides.

Coincidentally, both principals of the developers shared their given name: Gerry, but they were as different in every respect as it could possibly be, including their temperament. 'Our' Jerry, who was our client since the stone age, was short, husky, no nonsense, spelled his name with a 'J', and the new partner, Gerry, was tall, low key, enjoyed being one of the heir-apparent of a large fortune, and dominated by Janis, his wife. Probably the only similarity among them was that they both were shrewd; very shrewd. And both were allegedly oversexed, but none of us (outsiders) had any real proof of that. That was only the appearance, based mostly on their vocabulary.

I got hold of a nice, young kid, Brian, from the Greater Lowell Vocational Tech, who was falling farther behind in his draftsmanship, and it was feared that he might flunk the course. His teacher assigned Brian to this part-time, co-op stile employment, as a remedy, for him. He was not exactly an altar boy, but had a very good upbringing based on solid, middleclass values. At one occasion he got up from the drafting table and started scolding the "new partner Gerry" that he ought to be ashamed of himself **talking like this,** right in the office, where there are "minors" present, by which, he was referring to himself, since he was the only minor. Is this always and only what he has on his mind? he asked him. Gerry was giving the kid a lecture, confirming that: yes, yes, that is exactly – and always - what he has on his mind, and he better get ready for the same fate he will be enduring, for which he is giving him no more than a couple of years to take shape.

Pretty soon this organization got rounded out by an eloquent member addition: a Realtor. An exceedingly mature looking 'giant' (actually he was only in his late twenties) a football hero, recently returning from the army, with the full vocabulary of an army drill-sergeant. He occupied the small, separate room, to which the approach was through the centrally located office. He descended from Greek parents, who were both sizable people. His name was Steven, Stevie for all of us. He very soon turned out to be by far the worst of the entire organization, [regarding (foul) language usage] besides the 'new Gerry' presented above. The only difference that set him apart from the others was that he did not yell, nor raised his voice, in which quality he must have also differed greatly from the hypothetical drill-sergeant in the metaphor above. When he was giving the 'guys' his "sermon" his voice was almost a whisper, but the enormity of the collection of terms would surly have filled a good sized 'special dictionary'. In the 'Underground English' terminology, I learned from him more, than perhaps from anyone else on this continent. My five years, that I worked for the CPR (Canadian Pacific Railways), supervising section foremen and their road-masters, in this regard could only be considered a grammar school.

He had enormous real estate connections, (network really), and knew how to use it; which was obvious, considering that he grew up here, and everyone seemed to know him. He sold all the newly constructed houses; For their appraising, at the bank, (which the joint venture was using), he ordered all the 'Mortgage Plot Plans' from our surveying services, which was in the next room to his own office. But he also found buyers for the smaller developers (who built only half a dozen homes a season) and we did the development engineering and the plans for them too. When he heard that Maria wanted to find a 'suitable' house in the general area (meaning: walking distance) of the University, all he did was pass the word on his network. Very soon, one evening, Maria told me that a 'blond, real estate lady' came to the house, introduced herself, and wished to show a few houses to her, … just to 'get the feel' of what sort of house is she shopping for. Maria was utterly surprised, but recognized, that this was no prank, and went along with her. Then she described me the location, then the house, and then the

price, (which was identical $ 40,000. to the price of our Chelmsford Home), but I simply could not picture the location. The previous year, I had an accident at the location described by her, but I was incapable to recall a "building on the opposite side of the street." It turned out shortly why. The house, a 90+ year old **original farm house** was set way back, over 100-feet, from the street.

It was sitting on a slight hill, overlooking the 'West Meadow', so called, on the old Lowell Atlas, that I got hold of from the Registry of Deeds. The coach-house was its next-door neighbor. Evidently numerous parcels of land were divided up from the estate in the previous decades. A bushy hedge bordered it from the street, which acted as a sound (and visual) barrier. The street was one of the old roads leading to Manchester, New

Hampshire: Mammoth Road. Soon we got very familiar with this name. I loved the house. A love at first sight. I felt that I would rather die than not getting the house. This was actually the only home here in America, that I ever **loved,** as a home. It was like a 'mini castle'. Four levels, including the basement. On the southwest side a large 'sun room' was added by some of the previous owners, with a separate entrance from the parking area. With some TLC, and a lot of work, I could visualize the possibilities this property had. The previous owner was a police man, who just built a new house for his young family, in Chelmsford. But he did not possess a great deal of imagination. Judging by his profession his entire life seemed to be governed by rules.

But he had enough sense to build an enormous, round, above-ground swimming pool in the back yard, so close to the house that one could just about jump into the pool right from the sun room. He had four small children and a wife, who must have given him the orders to build the pool. She was young and stayed with the kids at home, except the oldest girl, who attended first grade. It was the end of May by the time we passed papers on the house. The police man's family was still living in the house until sometime in August when their new house in Chelmsford was ready for occupancy. All they had to surrender right away was the sun room with a small passageway from the house that would be separating the two occupants. We set up my own office in the sun room for the time being. That room had windows all around it, twelve of them, (with shades) plus the door. We also had to have access to the outside part of the basement (which was a greenhouse at one time, but suffered fire damage and was out of use) where we put the copying machine, the computer and its printer. Later when we finally moved over, filing cabinets, one drafting table, the small (office size) refrigerator, book stands etc. were placed in there. During the summer, though, we had access to it from the outside only.

*

Stevie alerted me that there is a block of five contiguous building lots for sale practically right on campus. There is no sign posted on it, not yet. They sit right across from the student parking lots. I drove by Riverside Street but I could not recognize the lots. At the office I told Stevie that I could not find them. I saw no 'vacant' lots. Then he drew me a sketch showing where they were. I told him, "Stevie, what are you talking about? those are not vacant, those are fully packed with parked cars".

-Sure they are! Didn't you tell me some time ago that you want income property? There you got it! Just try to figure out the return from those; no building, nothing to maintain, the taxes are assessed for vacant lots, which means: peanuts. All you need is someone to collect the parking fees from students and even that only for two – three hours in the morning. In fact the guy who lives next door, does the fee collection now. What else do you want, … you, … miserable… (expletive), … greedy (expletives)?

I drove right back, got out of my car, walked to the lot and started counting the cars. When I was more than halfway through counting, a short, shrimpy guy approached me and asked what do I think I was doing here? I told him that I am trying to count the cars. He informed me that these lots are private property and that I was not invited, therefore: not welcome. I counted over thirty cars already, so it did not take much to estimate the capacity of these lots being fifty, or somewhat more. I thanked him for his patience and kindness and walked back to my car. Then I went through the familiar routine: The assessor's office, which yielded the data on the owner and the deed references. Next stop: the Registry of Deeds, from which I emerged with the deed and the plan showing the five lots. Back to the office! I caught Stevie and asked him if he was involved, anyway at all, in this deal. He said no, "but you take me out for dinner one evening if you got the land, okay? I'll supply the broads. One: 'The Bronze Girl' I am thinking about, will be decisively to your liking, I know, for sure. She is a dancer from the Caribbean's. Wow, …woweee,… if you have seen some figure before,". This was Stevie. You could simply not get mad at him even if you diligently practiced beforehand.

I got hold of the owner over the phone, someplace in Newburyport. He asked how I found out about the possible sale of the land, since there is no sign posted. I apologized saying that I was not at liberty to tell. But would he be kind enough to quote me an asking price, … provided that there is one. He assured me that there is one already but he is not at liberty to disclose that. With that he evened the score. "But we shall talk all about these things personally", he said. We then set up an appointment for the weekend. He was to call me upon his arrival in Lowell.

He did. We met at 10:AM on the site. He was alone, introduced himself as Dom. Being a Saturday, the lot was almost vacant, only a few cars were parked on the side of the lot closest to the neighboring house where the 'shrimpy' fellow lived. He was the man who gave me the 'unwelcome' message earlier the week. Dom told me that these cars belong to Arthur and to various of his family members, who live in that house.

A portion of the "Parking Lot"

Then we switched to the topic of money. I asked him to, very briefly, paint me the financial picture of these parking lots. He said he could make that very short; the Trust gets $ 250. weekly and that is really only during the school year. Very little demand is in the summer, because the great student parking lots are practically vacant then, so, anyone can park there free. To summarize it all, the property produces ten Grands per year. Then I asked him: "what about expenses?" He was taken aback: "None! This is all net, ... You see, there is no maintenance, although occasionally they need to remove the snow but that is all done by the older son of Arthur, ... and, the taxes? those are also being paid by Arthur as part of the deal, so, ... actually you may look at this whole thing as a 'net lease'. Huh, ... how's that look?"

-Well, ... Dom, ... I have the irks when it comes to these things that look too good to be true, because, you know the mantra: if they look too good to be true, they usually are; You know? ... I am still looking for the catch, ... there has to be one, ... to me it almost looks like a mafia-operation."

-Professor, actually...

-Dom, I hoped you will reciprocate my friendly approach and call me Gabor, …Right now, … and any other time, we deal, …that is: with each other, … now then, …

-Very well then, Gabor, I think you are getting close to the core of it, but as you see, … it works! … It really does! And, let me tell you, so long as no one throws a monkey-wrench into the present setup, the system perpetuates itself." He finished it by giving me a self-satisfied look.

-Dom, I have the feeling that I must know more about, … the, erh, … monkey-wrench business. Okay, I am not exactly stupid, and not exactly a novice either, … so, I think the best way to approach it is, by asking: is this **'system'** as you called it, … **legit**.?

-Gabor, … you know, the beauty of it is, that: it's more than legit! Let me tell you just one thing, for example, we have not once heard from the IRS. Doesn't that tell you anything? How more legit can it get?"

-Dom, to me, the (system) looks kind of vulnerable, if it is hinged on one person: the lessee, did you say: Arthur? What if anything would happen to Arthur?"

-Well, actually we have no lease agreement with the guy, so, you see, **he is not really** a lessee" he said; "everything is moving along on a very natural path. You know, a kind of self governed, easy does it way."

-What about the 'Zoning'? That seems to be one of the greatest stumbling block in the American free enterprise system. Would **that** be the monkey-wrench? With that hanging over the entrepreneur's head, anything may happen. The Zoning Board may close the entire operation down, … any minute. Then what?"

-Never happened to us, not once! The fellow you have met here the other day, Arthur, watches out for everything and anything that could jeopardize this operation. Their very livelihood depends on it. He is an old and partially disabled man with a very limited income. He has three kids, … big kids, mind you, but still, …his wife is ill,…"

-Dom, you still have not answered my question, what if (for any reason at all) like in an academic question, the City would close it down?"

-Well, look at it this way: those are five **legitimate,** and I mean: are **zoned for** five single family residential lots. You could build five single family homes and sell them, or keep them and rent them out to student groups, just like the rooming house you are operating down the street."

-Now, just a minute, hold it!" I told him. "You must know! that needs another kind of permit, you can't get away with that either, certainly not forever. Also, I don't know the source of your info, but, … you should not have mixed that into this."

I thought I had him trapped. Now the real topic was: money, value! That's what we had to work on. He knew, by now, that I was looking for income, so that was the only appealing element of the deal; for me, it was. So he was working on translating this very substantial income (and even more substantial, since it was tax free) into value, into capital. He was going to pound on that. He sure did. He came forward with the asking price of sixty thousand dollars, or twelve thousand dollars per lot. Which was not unreasonable, taking into account the ten thousand dollars income per year; *after taxes.*

Then I asked him: "Dom, I can see a deal based on the income. But here I can not see the income being a solid, basic value; I just presented to you the numerous possibilities that would render the income go: null, zilch, zero! What is happening to the value in that case? Does that go to zero as well?"

-Well, I told you that those still have substantial value based on the single family residential lots, those are still 'solid value', as you put it."

-Indeed they are; but not at 12 Grands a lot. Why don't you take the figure of $ 45,000 back to your trustees as my offer for the land. That is a whoppy $ 9,000. per lot."

-Gabor, I wouldn't bother with that. Besides, ...you perhaps know about me as well as I do know about you, that we here, ... the two of us, ... make all the decisions in this deal. Correct?"

-Okay, let's not waste more time! Fifty thousand. That is ten Grands per lot. That is my last offer. Period."

-Gabor, do you have a lawyer handling this deal?" he asked, and I knew, just knew then, that I got the "Parking Lot" for fifty Grands. "Or, how do you handle these sort of things, by yourself?" he asked, and looked at me as if he would try to assess the power of a Siberian tiger in a Zoo.

-Dom, I will send you the P & S with my deposit in the mail in a couple of days, and: just so we have an understanding, ... you know? a full meeting of the minds! I am giving you a thousand dollars, as the: 'earnest money' here, right now! as a symbol of acceptance from you, which will be accounted for, in the P & S. In there, I will list a few, very few, conditions; Upon the acceptance of same you will receive the balance of the purchase price. Then if, in the interim, the deal is rejected, what I mean, is; not accepted, then it can be cancelled, by you returning to me the earnest money. Is that okay?"

-I guess so," he said, then looked at me and asked: "Gabor, do you always do business like this?"

-Actually, no; but this was a special deal, don't you think so? ... a very special deal? Those lots are sold, and ... there isn't as much as a 'for sale' sign on them."

With that we parted. Then I began to recall the information given to me by my old friend, and ally, the bursar, who told me that the University was after those lots, in fact, for some time now. But there was one problem: the zoning. The City still had a stranglehold on those lots by the zoning. **Those were zoned residential.** And that, everyone knows, can not be changed, only through a tedious process known as "Rezoning". But, if the breakdown of the present situation ever comes, I had, in the back of my mind, other plans with those lots, **within** their "residential zoning". In any case, if all else fail, I could still sell them to the University, if they really wanted it, ... at my price! If not, ... there would always be someone else who would want it more than I did.

* - - - * - - - *

I received a surprising, and shocking letter from my brother, Andrew. Our mother had passed away while I was in the hospital with my eye operation last fall. I was in no shape to undertake a European trip at that time. It was devastating on all of us survivors. There was not much anyone of us could hope for in terms of spiritual consolation. Perhaps the only consolation we were to hang onto, was that she had found peace, real peace, maybe even with a bit of justice thrown in as a bonus, (not here, but over the other side of the Styx River) for which she was always striving, and expected the same from all of us: her loved ones. I still have my father's letter in which he described the circumstances, and immediate happenings in the hospital, a prelude to her actual passing away.

In my brother's letter, he elaborated on certain details of my younger brother's Leslie's (Laci for us!) recent happenings in his life. This was the main purpose of the letter. I, (actually, we) broke contact with him back at the time we were ready to move from Ohio State's Buckeye Village, just before my graduation with a Master's Degree, where and when he visited us with his family. They were in transit at the time, moving to New York, where he secured a Structural Engineer's position with one of the largest Consulting Engineering firm in the world. (Bechtel!) His wife (an Austrian girl, or, actually woman, a fact that she had a hard time to accept, who –as we later were informed – belonged to the 'other', [the bad] category of women,) gave us a real hard time, denouncing all the phony effort I've put in to my graduate studies, (for nothing! as she assessed it!) using other derogatory terms and remarks going as far as denouncing the entire Hungarian 'race' (as nothing but a bunch of gypsies, as she put it) which is not even capable of putting up an honest fight against their own communists" etc. etc. irritated me to the point of actually ordering her out of our house (apartment really). With this she was ready to comply, but first ordering the other members of 'her family' to accompany her to the Sheraton, downtown, where she is moving, but right now, with or without Laci.

My brother was under her dominance practically ever since they first met, after the ill-fated revolution and freedom fight in 1956. They established themselves a couple of years later in the city of Edmonton, Alberta, Canada, where we lived beforehand with Maria. Our first son, Andy was born there. She was such a termagant, even then, that she managed to drive a wedge between us, the closest of brothers, and perhaps of two human beings, in the world. As I learned real soon, from the letter, -Laci- obtained his final divorce papers in the previous summer, and he felt sort of awkward to contact me and tell me that he is really sorry about all the things his ex wife (that bitch!) caused us, through her machinations, that eventually caused our breakup. Andrew suggested me to get in touch with Laci and iron things out between us, which he now is too remorseful to initiate on his own. And, … after all, …I, being the older brother (to him) it would be very appropriate for me to do this job, which he trusts me, as the one, who could do it best.

I did not call him, but instead, I wrote him a short letter, in which I proposed to sponge the past (not in its entirety, but leaving all the good memories intact,) only the latest decade, or so, off the black board, and start (or rather continue!) everything all over from that point on. I pleaded with him, if he could do this along with me, I would welcome his phone call, I wanted to hear his voice telling me that.

He called us in the evening. He wanted to talk to me, only! He told Maria that he is too ashamed of himself to talk to her, but he would like to talk with me. I came to the phone and over the receiver I heard him saying that he would like me to come to Edmonton, when ever I can spare the time. That he has a summer session to teach, for which reason he is unable to come to us, but if I could come, he would like to, at least, share the cost of the fare with me. He also said that he does not want to talk about anything now, if I will come, we will do it all face to face, as in the old times. I told him I'll let him know as soon as I got my flights confirmed.

Next Friday, late afternoon, I got off the plane at the terminal in Edmonton, which to my surprise, looked like a small provincial city's airport here, south of the 49-th. Laci was waiting for me. Robert, his younger son, was with him, who was behaving extremely shy. He was almost always like that, ever since he was a little kid. We had a long drive to their "new place". As we drove through the main drag on the south side of the city (White Avenue) I told him: "What do you mean new place? you are driving to the old, old, old place, where we used to live back in 1957, after you came to us from Montreal."

-Yeah, ... yeah, you still remember? I can't believe it! You still do?" he said.

-Heck, of course I remember! how on earth can I forget it? Ever? You know I am an elephant when it comes to remembering, I mean old things! You know!... So, how come we are coming here? just so you could show me the old neighborhood?"

-No, not really. I actually bought this house the minute I read about it in the paper. I know, its location is not the very best for driving to the school, (which is on the North side) but, what the heck, I was overwhelmed with memories, you know, memories before Agata came here from Wien. I became nostalgic. I came to see it after I read the ad in the paper, and,...bought it on the spot. The kids don't know anything about these things, they were way too young then. They still don't understand what came over me, to buy a small old house in this neighborhood."

We have been talking in Hungarian all along, so much so, as if we would not even know any other language. When we arrived I turned to Robert and asked him: "Rob, did you understand anything we have been talking about with your father?"

Again, his shyness overpowered him, he looked down, and very quietly answered: "I did grasp a few words, something like, the old times, and the old neighborhood, so, I could get the feeling what it was all about" he said. Then I asked him: "how are you doing with your German in school, I mean, are you still getting along pretty well, your pronunciation must be far better than your teacher's".

-Gabi, don't even mention any of this to him" Laci interrupted ..."he is totally traumatized, any time he has to remember of those times in Wien. I almost had to take him to a shrink, the last time this came about.

411

But since we are just about here, I want you to be very, and, I mean very courteous to Luz, the lady whom you are about to meet inside, okay? You know what I mean?" and he was looking at me with a wink.

-Laci, I don't know what you mean by 'very courteous'; you know that I know how to behave under any circumstances. I mean with ladies, especially with ladies. But I must know, … you know, I have this hang-up, must know the 'relationship' of the person, … sorry! the lady, … is in, with my brother. You know I would never let you down in any … er, … situation, even, … when it is a casual encounter, or,… acquaintance, but, … please! you have to give me a little more than 'being very courteous'.

-Okay, we will talk about it, …very soon, …"

-For goodness sakes, at least tell me this much: would it be appropriate for me to kiss her hand, or would that be out of field? In other words, **will you** kiss her hand? that will set my bearings straight."

We arrived inside the foyer, and put our stuff on the benches running all around the wall. I liked these little oddities, Laci kept coming up with, in his homes to make them homey. Then he arrived at his answer to my question: "actually I will do more than that", he said and he opened the door for me and let me go ahead.

Luz came to greet us both, but she turned to me first, since I was the 'guest' after all, which in itself was the awkward part of the whole thing. We never regarded any of our closest family members as guests. She offered me her hand and I promptly kissed it.

I saw Robert going down into the basement right from the foyer, to his room. Then, of course noticed that Luz and Laci kissed each other. I was wondering somewhat later if they would have done it if Robert were coming in with us into the kitchen.

Luz asked me (in English) if I liked ducks. I could tell from her heavy Hispanic accent that she started learning her English very recently. When I promptly answered: "Oh sure! Roasted!" she started laughing as if it would have been a good joke. That was really the first time I had a chance to give her a good look. She opened the oven door, peeked in, and said it needs more cooking, and immediately corrected herself: "roasting". She was very pretty. That was the first thing I noticed. She must have been some ten years younger than Laci, which was the second thing I noticed. Her dark, olive-tinted skin was the usual complement of a Hispanic complexion dominated by a thick crown of jet black hair for a delicate contrast. She was neither petite nor average height, sort of in between, which was the third thing I noticed. For the time being she was very quiet, which I found no ready explanation for, until she began talking to Laci - in Spanish! Now I was really cut out of the conversation. But that gave me an instant clue about her being so reticent. She knew perfectly well that I do not speak Spanish. And, for me to expect her to start learning Hungarian would have been like a life-sentence were being imposed on her without parole.

She (must have) told Laci, to set the table, because he began to do it. I was on unfamiliar grounds, so I could not offer much help. But I told him I would be glad to assist in fixing the drinks. They both wanted Martinis, which I did not frequent in those days. But to my utter surprise –and pleasure- he had some of the best rum in the house: the Captain Morgan Dark. He did not keep sweet vermouth at home at all, so I told him not to bother, I will have it on the rocks, no complaint, ... none.

The duck was crispy, well done. I did not heed my diet much in those days, I thought myself to be invincible anyways and that extrapolated to feeling almost immortal, ... at least for a good while. I was an outdoorsy man, I was in good shape, my blood pressure was as steady as a 'pressure-stat'. I had not have much trouble with my digestion except that the doctors kept on handing out a diagnosis of "excess stomach acid" every time to my complaints and ordered me to take Tagamet. Many years later this diagnostics turned out to be a colossal mistake but, at that time it seemed to help, at least temporarily. Like any symptomatic remedy would have.

At the table we switched to English. This was an utter necessity. Even this did not prove itself to be a perfect method, because Laci had to constantly do quite a few translations, injected explanations to include Luz into our conversation. I was talking to her in English, since this tong she pretty well had to bring upto adequacy at some point anyways, at least if and when she was to apply for Canadian citizenship. She, instinctively knew, that we soon will have to be left to ourselves with Laci, because we had to bridge an enormous time gap, which just had to be done in Hungarian.

At the end of supper she excused herself and just quietly disappeared. I heard some noises that sounded like making up beds in another room elsewhere in the house. After a while she came back to us to say good night and to wish us "good reminiscing", then really, successfully, and totally disappeared. We kept on talking, ... and talking, ... and talking. At well past midnight Laci showed me to 'my room'. I asked him where 'their' bedroom was, upon which he showed me to a smaller bedroom on the opposite side of the hallway, where the bed has already been made-up, ...for him. It was a single bed. But, to my surprise, Luz was nowhere to be seen. So, the puzzle began to formulate itself in earnest and I came straight out telling him that I was getting more confused than I was before. Then, while I changed into my pajamas he told me that they –officially– don't live together, that Luz has her own address, upstairs, which is a separate unit with an outside stairway leading to it. But he, made a, kind of a, shortcut to the stairs through a small door, opening to the landing on the outside stairway, under an awning. This way he could emerge undetected into the upstairs 'apartment', Luz's apartment.

Naturally I asked, to who's benefit this elaborate secrecy is being enacted? This is the end of the 20-th century, there is really no need to this theater any more, this is last century, Victorian stuff. Or perhaps other, like: Immigration considerations might be involved? I knew already that she was from Colombia, South America on a visitor's visa.

Or, does Luz want to keep her 'liaison' under cover, for some other reason? Laci then told me to my utter surprise that it is because of the two kids. So this was opportune time for him to warn me not to blunder when we are with the kids. For them, ... Luz is a, ... 'household help'. I told him to mark my word: he is not going to get away with it, certainly not for long. They are not stupid to my estimation, and they have eyes, and ears, even if you have made each of them a room down in the basement. He looked at me and with great resignation said: "I know, ... I know, ... and I dread the moment, ... I still haven't quite figured out how to handle that".

We finally - well after 2:AM - went to bed (or so we thought) to grab some sleep for the next busy day, when we had to talk some more. But we had to get up to the present. So, I told him about my midlife crisis, which started a couple years ago, and escalated to the breaking point. I described my "successful" life to him which is over spiced by the incredible trouble the chairman is giving me at the school, and by now, I can sense a cooling down environment within the rest of the faculty members in the department. Although they were not really hating me, at least not yet, certainly not as Manner did, but,... nevertheless, ...they had to establish a clear-cut allegiance: Manner, or me. It does make life kind of miserable. Sometimes I do feel like showing them my long finger complaining how much it hurts,... and, ... take off to Hungary, to

Gabi, (whom he instantly remembered,) and live a terribly regimented, mentally difficult to bear life, from which I, (actually both of us) escaped 20-years ago. If I could just establish some sort of independence, like the one it used to be in the good old days, within the family headed under our 'old man' (our father). Those times will probably never, ever return. Not in our life, and if it would, after all, it would be too late anyways.

Then Laci kept asking me when was the last time we went to Hungary, visiting the folks? I told him just last year, 1976 we drove through central Europe, and the Alps. Took Susie with us, hoping all along that she will meet a nice, shy, bookish Hungarian boy, whom she could seduce at the snap of her fingers and dominate, (after that) who would be overwhelmed to leave the country legitimately, (by marriage). We even engaged my first cousin (once removed) to take Susie with her to places "where the youth are" (based on the Ann Margret movie: "Where the Boys Are") and they went to numerous places, almost every night, but somehow this plan did not materialize.

We discussed Gabi's situation at great length. He asked me if I had any opportunity to meet her, to be with her, ... even for a relatively short time? He was not fully with the whole thing! Obviously he had put two and two together. But I was not sure if he had comprehend the enormity of the problem. He kept asking: "How could she possibly come out to the West? She could easily get a job as a therapist, she possessed a sort of 'basic' English, certainly good enough to hold a job, in her radiation therapy job, where, speech is secondary. Wouldn't it be great to have her here? She is such a good sport! Really! And it was meant to be primarily for her, not for our benefit. But, when I explained to him the unbelievably difficult situation with her mother, (not so much with her daughter, because Marchi could also get into a special-ed high school class for foreigners) he did agree and sympathized with me deeply. He told me that the coming year in the summer, he wants to bring Luz with him to Hungary. We should then visit Gabi, the both of us together, and at least then try to work something out. If we could just try to find some sort of a solution for her to come out. "Gabi, I think that would make a world of difference, once she is out here. She will, shortly, have a different perspective." Finally at the wee hours of the morning we went to bed.

The morning came seemingly in a few minutes. All of a sudden it was full daylight, -evidently it was almost daylight when we went to bed in the small bedroom with the twin beds- and Luz was bringing us fruit juices (as a general remedy for what we went through a few hours ago) and invited us to breakfast, which, as she tempted both of us: "was ready." During all this activity she appeared incredibly desirable. I don't know what exactly brought it on, perhaps the fact that her actions had so much tenderness, were almost 'pussy-cattish'. Obviously she was the embodiment of the 'good woman' so, most of her attention (and affection) was directed to Laci, but quite a good measure had been spilled over onto me (as a keen observer). Suddenly I felt an urge to leave them alone, and jumped out of bed. According to Laci "they were all like this", meaning "these Colombians". He even emphasized it by stating: "just look at her older sister, I show you her picture. They were brought up in a culture where they learned to 'please men'." That was the first time I felt that I made a mistake, that I should have married a Colombian woman. The second time came a good many years later.

We spent the entire morning planning the afternoon; the Saturday afternoon. Luz came up with the idea: "why don't we all go out to the 'ranch'? you two guys could go on reminiscing more about **'Egres-puszta'**, your old estate, where you grew up." Although this is only a **'quarter section',** (160 acres) but still, there are the kind of things to do that would activate your reminiscing mood. It was instantly decided. I asked about the two kids: "are they coming with us? Are they also interested in this sort of life and activity? Do they have enough Szikszay-Farkas genes in them to get enthused about it?" The answer, from Laci, however, hit me like a cold shower, "they have never been there, not once." That was the first time I began to wonder about who their 'real' (biological) father was. Before, the thought – or doubt —has never really, really! crossed my mind as long as it was nothing more, than their (the kids') physical features, but when it came to the behavioral characteristics, ... like this deeply embedded one, the love of, (and for) the land, the love of land, period; now that the land in that far away European country is not likely to ever become our possession any more, ... I did begin to wonder. When Laci informed me that the divorce settlement was based on a "blood test" that revealed, that their last (third) child, a girl, (allegedly being his daughter) was not fathered by Laci, I continued to wonder; Which of his children are 'really' fathered by my brother? There were no tests performed on any of the two (older) boys. Somehow they were taken for grated being his. But, again, this is something, that should really be treated in another book.

All through these (few) years, Laci built a small, really miniaturized, country stile 'Curia' out there on the clearing, as we entered from the highway. When he announced his class that there will be some "hands on experience" work available for students, who thought they needed to "work to improve on their skill", he found quite a few volunteers for every week-end to come out to the 'Ellscott Ranch'. He provided the supervision; and, of course the food and drinks. He was at that time teaching at the NAIT (the Northern Alberta Institute of Technology) structural and general building design courses.

The house had a real 'sexy' loft, just off the main recreation room. The bedroom was too conformist, too traditional, … I slept there for the night, as it happened. But, … they went to the loft. I was, God be my witness! totally free of 'envy'. I was honestly happy for them. Laci also showed me the part of the basement, where, the previous winter a brown bear made himself at home, that is: to hibernate through those very 'unfriendly' winter months in that part of the world. Evidently, their law forbade to kill that creature, unless in the (proven) event when one was forced to defend his/her life, threatened by the bear. But how do you prove of being threatened, … by a bear?

Luz was not to fuss too much with lunch. She revealed that she packed us some pieces of the roast duck from last night, which she had warmed up, wrapped in foil, in the small cast iron stove's limited-sized oven. Thus, we had a genuine 'rustic' lunch, topped off with some Hungarian red wine, supplied by the Liquor Control Board of Alberta. Ever since the sixties the demand for quality Hungarian wines increased multifold, by the published statistics of the Board. The number of ethnic Hungarians in the Province of Alberta had, by then, the population equivalent to that of a small Hungarian city. In the meantime we walked around the 'estate' as Laci insisted in calling it, to show me the progress in clearing the 'corduroy' sized birches, * mostly around the 15-acre pond. to accommodate a perimeter road, a 'corduroy road' (so called) around the pond. (Located at the 55-th degree of latitude the place was very close to the permafrost). The setting was bucolic to say the least, captivating was a more appropriate expression for me to be used in connection with the 'place'. Perfect for a recluse.

I was planning to make it a point to find out more about Luz and her family. The first thing I learned that her older sister: Marina, was working for the Scott (International) Paper Company in their offices in Medellin, Colombia, and (as Luz did not miss telling me that she knew –and loved - most of the music from 'Old World Musicals' meaning: European

Musicals, which Luz knew by now, that I loved so much, that I was close to being obsessed with them. Then to my inquiry she explained that her own name: Luz, was a nick-name for Luzita, or a shortened one. (How exotic sounding a name it was).

Next day, on the way home we finally arrived at the present; brushing all those sort of things that were 'happening' lately at our neck of the woods. I told him about the recent acquisitions in the category of income producing properties. His mind turned into a computer. Immediately he started comparing the possible returns on investments. At the time there was a sizable building boom in Alberta, consequently the duplexes, multiple residences, apartment houses were selling at a premium. The returns were unattractive. These were the beginning times of the 'Carter Economy' with the rapidly rising interest rates and, of course double-digit inflation. The only way he had turned his two projects into attractive producers was to refinance, (twice within the year) take cash out and reinvest into others. He had a flair for the rental properties. He wanted to know all about our 'rooming house'. As I explained him the circumstances with configurations of the land, the lots; That there are these two lots deeded with the corner lot, which had a sizable rear, landlocked parcel behind it with insufficient connecting space between them. But, ... and here came the fantastic possibility: the house next to the rooming house, or rather the lot, the land, which abutted the rear, vacant parcel. He became heady about the whole setup. I told him I will draw him a sketch as soon as we arrived at home. He could not wait. He was all fired up. He began to speed up to 110-115 Km/Hr. Luz admonished him better to slow down or the Mounties will get him.

The neighboring property to the rooming house was the old coach-house for the old farm-house, (the rooming house). It was in a pretty run-down state, a three bedroom two story house. It was owned by an attorney who lived in it with his family. From the degree of neglect it was evident that he was not cut out to be a house owner, certainly not a handyman by any measure. It was not on the market, meaning that it had no "For Sale" sign on it, nor was it listed for sale with any Realtor. But, as the old rule goes, every property in the world is for sale, at the "right" price. With this being our next target, a strategic move for sure, Laci made it clear, that he wants to be part of this "new entity". He will come up with the cash. So we parted the next morning at the airport. We were back in business, together again. He told me we can expect him at the middle of August when he will drive down with his entire family.

*

Upon my return I visited some real estate offices to find out a "fair market value" for the 'lawyer's house'. I was turned away from most of them on account that it was not listed for sale. These were the unimaginative Realtors. They helped me remove themselves from my list of prospective agents. The house was assessed for 26 thousand dollars, so I thought I would shoot for a 30 thousand dollar offer when I am ready to approach the owner.

He used to do volunteer work for the Boy Scouts and was an officer in that organization. Our kids knew his kids from school. (This was probably a drawback instead of an advantage.) At my first tentative inquiry he informed me that they were not thinking of selling it "just now" but they knew that eventually (with four teenage kids) the place will deteriorate to the point that they will have to get themselves a newer –or better - one. I used this point to persuade them to face reality, which was to sell it while it was still sellable, for a reasonable price anyway. He wanted a couple of weeks to think it over. It was the middle of the summer, ample time to find another (better) house, buy it and move into it before the school year started.

The interim time gave him the opportunity to get a feel for the value of the house. The feeling was not to his liking. The appraisers had a number of minuses in their formulae and none of them rose above the 32 thousand mark. I kept a keen eye on the appraising, almost as it would have been already mine. The real difficulty arose by the lawyer's wife not being able to find anything under 36 thousand, for a single family, four bedrooms in decent condition. Thereby their anticipated move was short by at least four thousand dollars. The attorney told me that he would be unable to cover this difference right out of his pocket, and anyways, … the move itself would cost some pretty money, … so what sort of offer can I show him to make the move worth his while, or may be even attractive. I told him not to fret, just hang in there, because we surely will be coming up with a solution to this case. There is a solution for every case no matter how difficult it looks, only it had to be found.

At every one of our discourses he never missed trying to squeeze the information out of me: "what are we going to do with the house", it needed a lot of money to have it fixed up. I did manage to fend off his curiosity by telling him a possible 'second rooming house,' this one for 'girls'. His wife countered that they thought all along that that 'other house' was co-occupational because she saw (at least) one girl entering the house 'regularly'. I dismissed the topic by stating that "that arrangement was perfectly legal, nevertheless, we are thinking about this one being a 'girl exclusive' house. Some parents would prefer that for sure; anyways, look what's going on in the dorms, so let's skip the double standards". With this I set them strait. Thus, the topic never surfaced again.

I was on the phone with Laci on a regular basis in the evenings, telling him all about the progress on the second rooming house. He was ready to yield to the price pressure, cutting ahead of the game and goaded me to give him (the attorney) the 36 grands, let's not waste time about such a pittance, get the deal sealed, let them move out, vacate the house so that we could go ahead with the alterations, in the kitchen, fixing the second bathroom, convert part of the dining room to a fourth bedroom, etc. He told me that he will be coming down to us sometime in August, after his summer course ended and is prepared to give me a hand with the alteration work. But, in the meantime definitely concentrate on closing the deal.

When I met the attorney the next time, I told him that we were willing to 'split the difference' in the price of the two houses: meaning that we would give them an additional two thousand dollars towards his down payment on the new house. But anyway there would be more cash coming their way because the mortgage balance on their old house would be paid off from the cash proceeds.

Laci wired me thirty-six thousand dollars, I went with the attorney to their bank, paid off the mortgage, got a release on the deed, gave the rest of the money to him. Then he was supposed to do the paperwork as his part of the bargain. I could use the little left-over cash to buy the materials for the renovations, prepared the plans and gave them to our own attorney: Jimmy Halloran. He was, by now, the head of the law firm, from which his uncle, my old ally, gradually, (and gracefully began to retire) to file the petition (application really) to convert the house into a 'girl exclusive' rooming house.

The Girls' Rooming House

I was over confident. I took it for granted that the Halloran' pedigree in the City of Lowell was a guarantee to success. I began to work off some of the chicken fat that accumulated on my waist-line over the good life during the summer. I needed a good reliable chain saw and started clearing the woods on the lot behind the rooming house. The lot had some 'sand-dunes', as I called them. They were no real dunes, geologically speaking, possibly some ungraded material left over from the times of the original subdivision work in the 1920-s, which were left there, neglected and eventually overgrown with the woods.

Once the woods were gone, (meaning laid down on the ground) I showed the place to Gerry and asked him to have his machines take all the sand and gravel, which was one of his 'family's business'. When he came and looked at it he asked who will remove the tree-stumps? It sounded as a valid question so I told him:

-Gerry, of course **you** will do it, how else do you want to take the sand? Obviously the stumps have to go first, then you get the gravy, ... the sand is all yours, free."

-You son of ... (expletive) ... of a ... (expletive) bitch. Is this how you think you can operate? ... With me? You had this all figured out? you no

421

good … (expletive)…! getting here a clearin' and gradin' job for free? You know what you are?"

-Gerry, why don't you spare yourself the trouble with all this nonsense? We both know you will need this fine sand for your septic systems on the Winter Hill Project. It's as clean as if it were sifted already, as granulated sugar. So, just tell me when are you going to do it. This has to be cleared up ASAP. We want to park cars here, … kapish?

He looked at me, actually stared at me, without a word; After some time he asked:

-Gabe, … Gabe, don't you have any shame? You have a twenty-grand job with the State University, okay? Then you are making at least twice as much in your surveying business, …and now you are taking away our livelihood, from us struggling developers, … do you realize, at all, that there are homeless people right here in this city, in this County, who don't know where their next meal would be coming from?"

-Gerry, you know what? If you start a soup kitchen, … and I mean gratis for the homeless! … and Janis will come every day to ladle out the soup, I will contribute half the cost of the food stuff, … and I will volunteer to give a hand to Janis for a half an hour every day, … also gratis!"

Then I had to jump away a few steps from him; I just had to defend myself, otherwise he would have hit me while hurdling a barrage of vulgarities at me, thus, I could hardly finish the sentence. Then from a reasonably safe distance I calmly said:

-Gerry, I am sure you remember me telling you about the harsh times I went through in my youth, after the war, and that of my dad, who all of a sudden found himself locked out of his house and property in the country, … and all the land, … none of us could even go near the place, and all we expected was to gather, or grab was: some food?" Did you ever bother to go and see Dr. Zhivago in the movies? Just so that you get some idea in your head how it was there, you know, sort of to aid your poverish imagination?

-Yes Gabe; … I remember, … you know, the other day Jerry and Jacky came to us for a barbeque, and I mentioned to them what you told me last time in the office, … the way your (communist) new regime took away your father's land, … with the stroke of a pen, it was so devastating even to think about it! and it could happen to us here too, if the communists would ever get strong enough, … you know, .. I mean politically! The environmental 'waco-s' are doing it already! There was one thing Jacky put into the conversation, and that was, that she could hardly understand how your old man didn't go cuckoo when this happened."

-Gerry, next time if this topic will ever surface in the conversation at your pool-side barbeque, well protected by the military might of our country, think about all those other countries where similar things to ours took place. Just to mention one, right in our back yard, you know which one I am talking about, the one 90-miles away from our border to the South; where our country's military might did not **dare** intervene to protect democracy and free enterprise as you guys, after World War II did not give a damn to get the Soviets out of Europe, to the contrary of what all the military leaders (Gen. George C. Patton among them) recommended: "now, let's go to Moscow and clean these savages out of Europe." But let me tell you: My old man did not go cuckoo; instead, he was reexamining his past actions, that were in support of the Western powers, even aiding the underground and protecting some Jews against the Nazis, thereby risking his own life. He kept repeating one thing: that maybe he supported the wrong side, thereby referring to the fact that such things could not have happened under Horthy, or the Nazis who were also vicious enemies of the communists and their ideals. We would never had all the trouble if the Soviets were banned from Europe just like Churchill envisioned it. But the US politicians were too short sighted to see this. They were screwed by the French just like after the first war."

* —- * —- *

Early August our new Dean, Krueger called me to see him in his office. He showed me my last year's request for sabbatical leave, which at that time was already one year overdue. He asked me why I have not submitted my renewed request for this year. I told him since our chairman informed me that I am not going to receive my sabbatical leave "because there are others ahead of me, and they should get theirs first". And anyway, he said: "there is a shortage of course coordinators". In the meantime, he keeps telling me that he will have to insist that I should stay for the coming year. Then he wants me to quit after that, because he needs my position to be filled by much more important things (and personnel) and since I refused to quit on my own, therefore he has to look after those, who deserves this privilege, … these were some of the reasons,…

The dean said something to the effect that there are weird things going on within the civil engineers that he can not understand. For instance, to his understanding the sabbatical leave is not a privilege, but something that the bargaining agreement guarantees to every faculty member, and at every seven consecutive years. He also apologized that I did not get my leave so far, and that he shall see to it that I should get mine this coming year. I told him that it was not his fault. In his opinion this was illegal and inexcusable, so he will act accordingly.

I tried to plead with him that this is now almost worthless because I have no gainful research opportunity now, and it is too late trying to arrange for one. I also mentioned that I had an extremely prestigious research position offered to me last year by the Oakridge National Laboratory in Tennessee, but I was in no position to accept it due to more than one reason at that time. And, anyway I was not granted my leave. Then he told me that he could not risk the perpetuation of this quasi illegal situation and will see to it that I shall get my leave. The only remaining question being whether I want it for one semester or for the full academic year. I opted for the full year. I needed to get away from this 'purgatory' for the longest possible and available time. I was really curious for the outcome of this 'power play'.

In a couple of days the chairman had Nicole call me at my home phone to come to his office at my earliest convenience. I asked Nicole what on earth does he want now? She whispered in the mike that this has to do with my sabbatical leave and she thinks that I should come as soon as I can. I told her that I will see him at noon but make sure that I should meet her after the chairman is through with me.

Manner was quite blunt. He also showed signs of being furious, he could hardly control himself. He announced that I will be on my sabbatical leave starting on September 1-st, which will expire at June 12-th 1979, at which time I will be on the regular summer vacation. I was trying to elaborate on this being the dirtiest trick I ever come across, and he should not be surprised at the time I file my end of leave report of the scholarly activities I would have been engaged as my 'professional improvement' in view of handing the leave to me at really, after the last minute.

He turned to sarcasm. After a short description of my 'activities' that do not have much to do with 'being scholarly' what do I care? Perhaps I ought to be glad, that I can now pursue my professional 'business' which is not much 'scholarly' to begin with. So I should spare him this whining about my being deprived of 'equal opportunities' and just 'do my thing'. I remarked that perhaps this will be a time I would cherish, maybe the happiest of time I spent in this Institute under his chairmanship, and am looking forward to it being the most memorable. With that I walked out to the secretary's room.

Needless to say that Nicole overheard the bulk of the conversation. I asked her if she would accompany me for lunch at the Pizza Palace where I will have a Greek salad and she could have anything she wants. She was not exactly in an exuberant mood. She sensed that what has just transpired will have serious consequences on my career, or 'future' as she put it.

-Gabor, I wasn't planning on going out for lunch, but when I saw you coming out from the chairman's office something told me that you are going to need me. Am I on the right track?

-Nicole, … just as usual, …you are right on. I can not, for the life of me, comprehend why couldn't we, … you know, … us, … find a way to get to, … now, help me out, please, … you know this is not my 'real language', … *supplement* each other? But, … you do recall, I am sure, the many offers I extended to you."

-Gabor, let's not go to the Pizza Palace, I made a turkey ragout soup, I would like you to taste. My place is a little further up the road, and you're invited, … that is, … under one condition, … do I have to spell it out … or not?" she asked finger wagging.

Nicole drove us northward into New Hampshire. We turned into that large condominium project that I worked on the preliminary engineering which Dorfman got hold of through the famous TAC (The Architects Collaborative) an upscale Cambridge architectural firm. I did the preliminary road layouts as well as the confirmation of the intended location and elevation for the Water storage tanks serving the project. I recognized the first road she turned onto and the first housing unit on the left with all their garages, mail boxes, etc. She parked the car in her assigned stall. Then we walked to her condo unit only a dozen or so, steps. As she opened the entrance door she gave me another warning:

-Gabor! you have not answered my question, …you know, about my condition…

-Nicole, I think you know me well enough by now, to know, that I am incapable of mixing violence with love. If your condition had anything to do with my not becoming … violent, … I think you better start dismissing the word from my, … er, …our dictionary. The two items:

violence and love, … are so distant, so incompatible, so conflicting to one another that if anything, any violence would enter my, … our, … actions, that would render me, incapable, … you know what I mean! … you always know what I mean, … right? … I-n-c-a-p-a-b-l-e! I do not! … do not want to use that 'other word', …"

-Ok, Gabor, … let's taste that soup! I warm it up in a minute in the microwave, …

hey, … hey, … now! … can you possibly keep your hands away from me? … you must realize, … oh, come on, now! … Gabor! … you promised …

-Yes, I know, … and I am keeping my promise! I am not violent… and I certainly won't get violent; Nicole, do you call this violence? I could only call it tenderness,… I think we are in a confusion of definitions, …

- Oh, … I didn't think your tenderness, oh,… now, really!… is the worst violence, … you, …you, … devil!"

*

- Mmmm, … mmm, …this soup is really delicious! Nicole,… it does have the 'old country' touch. Do you make this often?" … Yah? … Really?

* - - -* - - -*

In a couple of weeks Laci arrived with his family to Lowell and wanted to see the new rooming house, immediately. I took him there, showed him the floor plans, pointed out the materials I bought for the alteration. He said: "Gabi, … you know what? There is nothing more rewarding, mentally – and physically – than to get involved with these things, these projects; actually get things done, and put them to use, put them to good use! and… it is all your accomplishment." I fully sympathized with him and reminded him how our old man always wanted us to be "independent". He himself wanted to be independent, and, …for a short time in his life, … he did achieve it. As I was thinking back into those days I thought that maybe, just maybe, most people, diligent, goal oriented people, would achieve such an aspiration in their lifetime, at least once. The lucky ones; for an entire life time.

Laci asked me if we have enough applicants to fill these four large bedrooms. "We need something like eight girls in here" he said, "the income from them would be close to, say: 800 dollars a month", and I couldn't agree more. I told him that we have applications from about 18 girls, more than 10 came by during the week to look at the place with their parents, while I was clearing the woods in the back, and Gerry came to look at the back lot, to have it cleared and leveled. That will actually be done next week. "We have here almost a full acre of prime, 'multiple-residential' zoned property, which is not readily available anywhere around here", I told him. "What if we would build an apartment house one day on those lots all combined into one large lot." He liked the idea so much he almost got ecstatic about it, which he didn't do much lately.

- Gabi, you know what? I will try to dream up something about what you just said. You should send me a copy of the City's zoning ordinance and all the other building department regulations, so I can study them. I am not very familiar with these here, to determine: how many stories? What floor area percentages, etc. you know what I need!"

By noon he had the studs all erected for the fourth bedroom. In the afternoon I gave him a hand to hang the sheet rock, and by late afternoon all the joints received their first coat of the joint compound. We went home. The kids, all five of them were in the pool, having a hilarious time. Then we were getting ready for the barbeque at the poolside patio.

We were talking about the permits for the new "girl's" rooming house. I asked him to stay with me at the house next day, on Sunday, when the parents will bring along their daughters to make down payments on the accommodation of their choice. He said he would. Next morning we went over to the house, it was only a few blocks away from our new mini castle on Mammoth Road. The parents started arriving from about ten AM and looked over the common-use rooms, such as the large bathroom, (almost a double) which was upstairs, and the kitchen, which was downstairs in the rear part of the house. One anxious mother questioned the adequacy of the food storage in the –anyway oversized- refrigerator, in view of the fact that there will be eight "occupants" as she worriedly put it, in the house. I was quick to offer her a description of the Lawyer's family of four boy-scout kids living in the house, not quite a month ago, using the same fridge and they were not complaining.

Another mom was most anxious to "observe the 'safety regulations and permits' posted in the hallway, which should all be posted on a conspicuous place… should it not?" she asked. I told her that yes, they should be, and will be just as soon as they were issued, … but anyway, she is free to leave and withdraw her daughter's application because there are two others, anxious to fill the vacancy possibly created by her daughter's withdrawal, who was (so far) on the priority list. I suggested her to hurry over to the dormitory tower to secure a place for her daughter while there are still some available. But in the meantime her daughter already began to make friends with two other applicants, who's mom did not seemed to get hung up on such details.

One 'very nice' girl: "Frances" came to see us, by herself, without her parents. She stated that she came from the Southern part of the State, from Bristol County, and her parents didn't agree with her decision to come to this school, so far away from their home in Fall River. She was ash-blond, and her hair was very clean, soft and silky, not overly long, slightly below her shoulders. Her attire was the usual, college coed: a colored T-shirt with some motto printed on it, having to do with love and freedom, clean Levi-s with a pair of just broken-in 'NIKE' sneakers, that would pass almost as regular for a hot August day. Her eyes were like cat-eyes, gray-bluish, with a tint of green and they had a very slight misalignment, which made her look very intriguing.

Then she asked me, in a rather flirtatious manner, if it would be all right to help herself to a soft drink, if there were any in the fridge. When I opened the door she couldn't miss noticing the few cans of Miller's, which we brought for our own consumption with Laci in the afternoon, while working on the partition wall the day before. She instantly went for a can. I stopped her in mock authority and asked her how old she was and, anyway, she had to make a full disclosure on the application form she had to fill out, so there was no use trying to cheat. I still took pity on her and opened up a can for her. As she took it from me she made me a dainty little pout before started to take the first sip. I never forget how grateful she was. It must have hit a spot. She was the best looker of all the girl applicants so far, but that extended to her attitude, her demeanor, and the way she handled herself vis-à-vis male company. All these attributes gave her an aura of "experience", of "having been around". But I suspected that a good part of it was acting, albeit good acting.

This quality sort of put the damper on my responding to her inquiries about the whole setup, with the house, the general rules, etc. I was astounded to find out from her form, that she was only 18-years old.

Frances could easily have passed for a college graduate of 22 or more. She asked about the "owners". When I told her that 'we were the owners' she asked which one of us would she had to 'deal with'. In other words: who was 'in charge?' who was the boss?" I told her I was. Upon her question who 'the other guy' was, I simply stated that he was my brother, a part owner in this venture, but he is from out of state, he will have to leave back home at the end of the summer. Her reaction was: "Oh, he is kind of cute"! I told her, matter of factly, that, for her information: neither of us are really 'available'. She didn't make anything of it. She said casually she sort of guessed that anyways.

Then she wanted to know if it would be all right for her to stay in that bedroom for the night, that we had almost finished, on the main floor. She offered to pay for it in advance. She brought with her a suitcase and other 'important' belongings, (like a small guitar, sort of a kiddy's version of the real thing) because she did not intend to go back home again before school starts next week. It is too far and she doesn't have a car.

Laci was overwhelmed by Frances' forwardness. He had no girl students in his classes so far, (ever) in that school in Northern Alberta. He started dickering with her, asking her to pick another room because this one is not quite finished. We still have to fit a door-lock to the new door so the room could be locked. And the wall needs a finishing touch of compound, along with some sanding as well as a coat of wall-paint. She said that was not necessary right away, we could do that anytime later. "Please, please," she pleaded with him, taking hold of his hand, then his whole arm, and finally ended up just short of hugging him. But in a couple of weeks –or days— later I wouldn't have been surprised if she had done just that. She tried to convince the both of us that she is not afraid staying there by herself, that she is definitely not a timid girl, who grew up on her ant's farm and knows how to defend herself "in case of an emergency." At this point in the conversation I was absolutely convinced that she told us the naked truth.

I don't know exactly how it came about, but I kind of began to like her. She certainly, had some unusual characters in a girl. In the same time I was almost afraid of her. Not in the dictionary's definition of the word! She was, undeniably, overly assertive, for her age. There was something about her, how she came across. I had some experience with these college girls in my previous life as a professor (I had a very special one, almost similar to this one: a boomer, in my surveying class at Cornell) but always strictly in a classroom environment, or at an outdoor exercise, which sort of sterilized everything in such a close encounter. In a classroom, obviously everything was out in the open, whereas here, everything was 'behind the scenes', everything was anticipation. I really didn't think much of the whole thing, or tried not to, since she could easily have been my daughter, as far as age was concerned, but certainly in no other aspects.

I may have shown an undue amount of concern about her 'well being' as she was staying in that house, alone. I have no idea what eventually made me allow her to stay there. My instincts told me that it might actually be a good thing, meaning, for the house too, of not staying there vacant. In a conclusion I must have attributed this 'solution' to the same experience in 'homelessness' that I experienced numerous times in my earlier life. Thinking back now from a good 20-something years' time span, I should conclude that, in a very meaningful sense of the word we (our family) were **still homeless** in this chosen country of ours, which, in the same time, I still could not, or would not trade for any other on this Planet. But, as it happened, our eternal moving around has gradually separated us from most of our even very close friends. They became distant, and in a way we became like shipwrecked, separated into our own, small island here in New England, which we had a growing difficulty to leave, even if we had to. For you could have friends, whom you may see every day, but would not miss them terribly if you were separated from them; On the other hand, you may have friends whom you have not seen for even a long time, but when you meet them, you snap right back where you have left off and reconnect with them as if you were together all the time.

I still very vividly, recall how I was not being able to sleep well that night, and early dawn, putting some T-shirt, shorts and sneakers on, and walked down there to the new rooming house to see if 'everything was all right'. I felt a quaint responsibility for letting Fran stay there by herself. I approached the house from the rear, where I had the woods cleared just the week before. As I came within sight distance to the rear of the house, I saw Fran sitting out on the balcony –of one of the other bedrooms in the rear of the house - with the small guitar in her lap, plucking out very soft notes accompanying her song, which she was ever so tentatively putting together, most likely creating, composing right there, almost like an improvisation.

I was very, very careful not to make a slightest sound, that would have interrupted and distracted her from this unbelievably beautiful scene. It was almost theatrical, surreal under the current circumstances. In the same time I was still cautious not to make any sound that would have frightened her, but in view of her describing herself as a 'brave sort of girl' I was probably more afraid if such had occurred; That it might have frightened me more than it would have frightened her. Although I was quite well seasoned by now, I was still eerie of the ensuing events, had she discovered me there in the back yard, never mind 'demanding' an explanation for my presence at such an early hour, that could have easily been misinterpreted for snoopiness, at best, and something unthinkable at worst. She seemed to have been the only one alive on earth, except for all the birds in the yard, and it would have been a sin to awaken her and make her realize of this being only her illusion.

Some elements of this rather idyllic scene brought back memories of my own, which occurred at the end of summer in 1948, the year of my high school graduation and entry in the engineering college at the University of Budapest. At that time I went on a bicycle trip, by myself, that I took entirely on my own initiative, and decided to hike those mountains just north of Budapest, a State Forest, with tiny little lakes, in the forest. Not a soul around, and; turning on my little battery operated AM radio - just after I took a refreshing dip in one of those clear ponds, drying myself in the early September sun. The announcer telling his audience, that the following number will be the Concert Waltz No. One by Alexander Glazunov. It was the first time I heard this number. It was an incredibly beautiful, romantic piece that Glazunov put together from his haunting and bountiful repertoire of melodies. I was totally lost in it, just like I was lost in this improvisation Fran put on here in the back yard of the rooming house. I always felt him a lot closer to my innermost, than I did his more famous countryman, Tchaikovsky. But if a clear-cut choice had to be made (unavoidably) between the two, it would have been terribly difficult, if not impossible for me, to make.

I was breathless for a good while. Although Fran's melodies were not in par with those of the old master Glazunov, the entire setting was still unforgettable. I was tiptoeing out of my observation point still being very careful not to make the slightest noise. I was not absolutely sure whether she did or didn't notice me, regardless of how careful I was. But neither of us ever mentioned this episode later on. I have met her several times during the following weeks in connection with all the trouble that the Building Department gave us –and to all the girls in the house- giving the entire affair such media attention that ultimately broke down the whole enterprise. Her courageous stand-by at our rights (and theirs, the tenants') in the case, proved her absolute loyalty towards us, (the owners). She was definitely one of those 'rare' girls: the unforgettable ones.

"Diaries of a Maverick Professor"

"After surviving the Communist takeover of his native Hungary and emigrating to the United States Gabor Szikszay-Farkas knew the kind of life he wanted for himself. A talented engineer and surveyor, with ample experience, he was determined to follow in the family tradition and teach at the University level, which would also allow him the time and flexibility to build and maintain an independent professional consulting business on the side.

His first attempts of attaining his goals were thwarted, but when he was, unexpectedly, offered an assistant profess-sorship in the Civil Engineering Department at a Techno-logical Institute in the East, the opportunity to set down roots and realize his dreams presented itself.

Moving from Ohio in a small caravan comprised of two cars, with his family Gabor arrived in the northern Massachusetts city of a Technological Institute just in time to begin the academic year.

In his Diaries, the Maverick Professor recounts how, despite departmental infighting and an array of personal challenges, (including a large dose of discrimination) the author (and narrator) managed to secure a tenured position on the faculty, build a lucrative land surveying business in tandem with developers, raise a family and enjoy a few discrete dalliances with lady friends – all the while fighting to keep his eyesight threatened by disease.

The *"Diaries of a Maverick Professor"* is a vigorous and candid memoir of a unique man with the verve and intel-ligence to live life on his own terms, written in a spontaneously energetic voice that is constantly engaging."

The preceding is a review by an independent, professional editor. The readers are hereby encouraged to write their own.

About the Author

The Hungarian-born author writes under an assumed (pseudo) name. His 'Diaries' are recollections of actual, real events which occurred in his **'Second Life'**, although many of the episodes are 'tinted' (similarly to many a colorized versions of Black & White movies). This, the author felt, was necessary in order to make them more vivid, more enjoyable and more appealing to readers who prefer colored pictures to black and whites.

There are no fictional characters in this book, otherwise it would be a fiction. Most all live characters' names have been altered except those who did not mind their real names being used or are already deceased.

The geographical settings are set in actual, real New England. Thus, the names and descriptions of places are more realistic.

The author lives in the United States, travels to his native land at greatly diminished frequencies. Lately he became increasingly disillusioned in the 'old country', in which ..."New folks stood up to replace the extinct ones" ...(Vörösmarty: Szózat 1836). The media's hoopla about "collapsed communism" sounds and looks fallacious. In Hungary, though, the old system officially vanished, but a new one is alive and vibrant; All the while the old (communist) elite is more powerful than before. Now they **own the whole Country** (illegally, by default), whereas before: they **only ruled it** for 45 years - also illegally: by force.

Justice is still due! One day it shall come for all.

ABOUT THE TYPE

The typeface used in the book is Myrid Pro, an OpenType release of the Adobe Originals typeface Myriad, first issued in 1992. Designed by Robert Slimbach & Carol Twombly with Fred Brady & Christopher Slye, Myriad has a warmth and readability that result from the humanistic treatment of letter proportions and design detail. Myriad Pro's clean open shapes, precise letter fit, and extensive kerning pairs make this unified family of roman and italic an excellent choice for text typography that is comfortable to read, while the wide variety of weights and widths in the family provide a generous creative palette for even the most demanding display typography. Myriad is either a registered trademark or a trademark of Adobe Systems Incorporated in the United States and/or other countries.

Printed in the United States
23877LVS00003B/104